From Benedict's Peace to Francis's War

From Benedict's Peace to Francis's War

Catholics Respond to the Motu Proprio
TRADITIONIS CUSTODES
on the Latin Mass

Edited By
PETER A. KWASNIEWSKI

Angelico Press

First published in the USA
by Angelico Press 2021
Copyright © Angelico Press 2021

Angelico Press thanks all the contributors
and National Catholic Register, The Catholic Thing,
Catholic World Report, National Review, The New York Times,
First Things, The European Conservative, The Spectator (UK),
Inside the Vatican, The Tablet UK, Le Figaro, and The American
Conservative for their kind permission to reprint these pieces.
Dates of original appearance are provided under each title.

For information, address:
Angelico Press, Ltd.
169 Monitor St.
Brooklyn, NY 11222
www.angelicopress.com

ppr 978-1-62138-786-2
cloth 978-1-62138-787-9

Book and cover design
by Michael Schrauzer

In darker moments it seemed to him and his friends as if any wild fancy was tolerated, so long as it did not approximate too closely to the Old Religion, and they grew sick at heart.

Robert Hugh Benson, *By What Authority?*

Eripe me, Domine, ab homine malo;
a viro iniquo eripe me.
Qui cogitaverunt iniquitates in corde,
tota die constituebant praelia.

Psalm CXXXIX. 2 – 3

TABLE OF CONTENTS

PREFACE

HAVING RETIRED EARLY THE EVENING OF JULY 15, expecting mischief on the morrow, I awakened before dawn on the feast of Our Lady of Mount Carmel. After making coffee and praying Prime, I opened my email. The inbox had already exploded with messages, as the motu proprio and its accompanying letter had appeared many hours earlier in Europe. I printed the documents and sat down to read them carefully. The phone rang. Cameron O'Hearn asked if I'd be willing to do a video interview with him in a couple of hours; I agreed, and read and re-read with a growing incredulity and consternation. The interview took place; in the evening I participated in a round-table discussion by video.

Already on July 16 the reactions to *Traditionis Custodes* were like a river in full flood: articles, essays, interviews, podcasts, everywhere and from every point of view. Given my deep love for the traditional Latin liturgy and my keen interest in all that concerns it, I tried to keep up with the response, which multiplied beyond the capacity of any individual to compass. I published a first roundup of articles at *New Liturgical Movement* on July 17, which was then updated four times, to be followed by a second roundup on July 23, a third on July 28, and a fourth on August 6. And still the flood continued. An emotional, spiritual, intellectual dam had broken and the waters of discourse poured forth across the world. The sheer volume of writing occasioned by *Traditionis Custodes* is quite unlike anything seen in the history of papal documents — testimony to a neuralgic subject on which arguments proliferate and passions run high.

The two-month period following the release of the motu proprio gave proof that the traditionalist movement was not a fringe phenomenon but something that had gained significant strength and sympathy during the relatively peaceful years of 2007 to 2021 (the "Pax Benedictina" to which the book's title alludes). No well-informed person could have overlooked the existence of a zealous and articulate minority of Catholics dedicated over the course of the past six decades to the cause of traditional doctrine and worship. But the circle of their friends and allies turned out to be much larger than their enemies suspected. Prominent conservatives who rarely had a kind word for devotees of the Latin Mass were suddenly voluble in their criticism of the pope and effusive in their solidarity with their ostracized brethren.

The purpose of this volume is to gather in one convenient place some of the finest and most appreciated essays and articles published in the period from mid-July through September — not only from America and England (although these predominate), but also from other nations: France, Germany, Switzerland, the Netherlands, Italy, Spain, Argentina, Poland, Kazakhstan, and China. Two articles that appeared prior to July 16, in anticipation of the forthcoming papal act, are given as a prelude; the book concludes with the English text of a "Letter of the Faithful Attached to the Traditional Mass to the Catholics of the Whole World," which has been published in six languages and signed by over one hundred laity exercising intellectual and cultural apostolates. Needless to say, it would have been impossible to include in a single volume all of the excellent writing that appeared in this roughly two-month frame. Hard decisions had to be made. The exclusion of a certain author or article should not to be interpreted as an unspoken editorial rejection of him or it.

The contents are arranged by date of publication. For articles written in a foreign language, this date will be that of the original's appearance, not of its subsequent appearance in English translation (which, in most cases, was only a day or a few days later). When several articles share a given date, they are presented alphabetically by author surname. Although other possible organizing principles might have been chosen for the anthology, the publisher and I believed it would be most interesting and helpful to see how the reactions developed over time, from the pieces published on July 16 itself, all the way to the last piece in the book, dated September 20. This order also recommends itself because later articles make reference to earlier ones. For convenience in cross-references, the items have been numbered and are called "chapters" in the notes.

A few matters of detail. Some articles that were published under merely descriptive titles (e.g., "Thoughts on *Traditionis Custodes*" or "Reactions to the New Papal Document") have received new titles drawn from the author's own words, with the original titles mentioned in the notes. Translators are named in the dagger note attached to the titles of translated items. To avoid the unsightly clutter of hyperlinks in footnotes, most internet sources have been referred to very simply by author, title of piece, title of website, and date. A Google search will turn up any of these in a split second, and if they have "gone missing," the Wayback Machine of the Internet Archive will deliver the goods.

I am grateful to the original publishers who granted permission for republication, and to everyone at Angelico Press for the rapid completion of a complex project.

I am grateful above all to the many writers, from one end of the world to the other, who, like members of a well-trained militia summoned to their posts, confronted the pope's motu proprio promptly, thoughtfully, and fearlessly. It should come as no surprise that the forty-five authors contained herein do not agree on every point; indeed, some fundamental disagreements will be noted over the nature of the traditionalist movement, its constituencies, and its goals. Nearly all of them, however, view *Traditionis Custodes* as a very bad document, bad for all kinds of reasons. This book is not, and makes no pretense of being, a presentation of "both sides of the argument." It offers a variety of critiques of this profoundly unwise and unpastoral decree, which suffers from incoherent doctrinal foundations, grave moral and juridical defects, and impossible ecclesiological implications.

Peter A. Kwasniewski
Feast of Our Lady of the Most Holy Rosary
450th Anniversary of the Battle of Lepanto
October 7, 2021

PRELUDE

Anticipating the Coming Document

On Liturgical Wars
and Rumors of Wars

DOM ALCUIN REID, O.S.B.

Catholic World Report
June 13, 2021

DISQUIET ABOUNDS AT PRESENT IN THE MILIEU WHICH celebrates the *usus antiquior*—the more ancient use—of the Roman rite of the Sacred Liturgy. Seemingly the Holy See is considering issuing new norms limiting its celebration, at least in parishes. Some bishops appear to be acting in this vein already, taking measures against good clergy and healthy apostolates which do not present any reason for concern—except that (1) they exist; (2) they are growing; and (3) they are fruitful in leading to good Catholic marriages and new families as well as significant numbers of vocations to the priesthood, monastic and religious life—all indications that this phenomenon is not going away any time soon.

We are in a peculiar age when these are seen as concerns. But for some, who are ideologically committed to "the changes," the rites and ecclesiastical reforms put in place following the most recent ecumenical Council of the Church as *means* to bring about a new Springtime in the life of the Church have become *ends* in themselves. For such persons, these means must be adhered to even if it has long since become clear that their ends — the profound renewal they were meant to usher in some decades ago — have simply not been achieved. They can become idols, occluding anything but their own worship.

Charity, prayer and patience are the weapons with which to confront such myopia. Please God people thus afflicted can become open to the signs of the times in which we actually live, which include the richness, beauty and fruitfulness of the *usus antiquior* in the life of the Church, and indeed to the fact that their celebration today often evinces far more of that full, conscious, actual (active) and fruitful participation in the liturgical rites for which the Second Vatican Council called than one can readily find elsewhere (to be sure, there are notable exceptions in both directions). Many bishops who have celebrated the older rites for communities in their dioceses have come to appreciate this reality. Acrimony in the face of its incomprehension will simply reinforce prejudices.

So too, we *usus antiquior* communities need to examine our consciences. To sustain a sectarian attitude or create a ghetto, whilst perhaps understandable in the heady years following the Council, is untenable today. The liturgical and pastoral riches our communities treasure are for the good of all the Church, not the privilege of a few gnostic "elect." The Christian lives of those who draw from them must be all the more credible, particularly in respect of the social teaching of the Church. The light of our communities must — each according to its proper charism — "so shine before men, that they may see [our] good works and give glory to [our] Father who is in heaven" (Mt. 5:16).

Clericalism has no place anywhere, and the seminaries of institutes which celebrate the *usus antiquior* must ensure that they form men whose apostolic zeal is concomitant with the love they have for the Sacred Liturgy. They must be men who live and work for the conversion of the world to Christ in the twenty-first century, not ones content to live in a gilt cage decorated according to the tastes of their preferred century in history. Ecclesiastical authorities are right to be concerned when they detect a self-serving narcissism in clergy — a reality that is by no means exclusively found in devotees of the older liturgical rites, or solely in junior clergy.

One of the first tests of a young man seeking to enter the monastic life is to see whether he is capable of hard manual work without complaint. Most aspirants have little difficulty in attending the liturgical Hours (with the possible exception of Matins) but almost all of us need to learn that whilst faithfully observing the norms of the liturgical books is integral to giving due glory to Almighty God, so too bathrooms and chicken sheds need cleaning. The candidate who is able to do both, or who at least becomes conscious that he must grow in his ability so to do, each at their appropriate time, will become a good monk.

Our *usus antiquior* communities and houses of formation need this same balance and moderation. Young people need space and time and patience, and they need love and understanding, in which to grow and mature. Older people, above all those in authority or with responsibility for formation, need to give them all of this and more, even if they themselves bear the scars of having been denied the same. So too, *usus antiquior* communities need to form candidates to be men of the Church rather than indulgent self-defined "rad trads" or *à la carte* laptop-liturgists who, in their fear, isolation or pride, inhabit a virtual world — or Church — of their own construction.

4

It is to be hoped that the anxieties and fears that have been aroused about a restriction of the older rites can be calmed and that no authority issues peremptory precepts which will, in all likelihood, simply undermine their own authority — blind obedience is no longer the daily bread of Catholic clergy or laity and cannot be relied upon as it was a half-century ago. The positive proscription of something true, good and beautiful is likely to intensify, not heal, enmity, clericalism and alienation within the Church.

In addition, to ban the *usus antiquior* because of its increasing popularity some fifty years after it was supposedly replaced by a liturgical reform that, according to St. Paul VI, involved the necessary sacrifice of the venerable liturgy for the pastoral good of the Church would, ironically, risk being nothing less than an "own goal"; an historic, eloquent and ultimately embarrassing admission of the colossal failure of that reform by those committed to its ideological perpetuation no matter what the cost.

"You will hear of wars and rumors of wars; see that you are not alarmed; for this must take place, but the end is not yet," Our Lord warns us in Saint Matthew's Gospel. "All this is but the beginning of the birth-pangs," He continues (Mt. 24:6,7). The Apocalyptic realities of which Our Lord was speaking end in the definitive triumph of good over evil, of God over the Devil. Our times may be difficult and may become more so. Misunderstanding and suffering, even persecution, may become our lot once again. But the same ultimate triumph awaits us if we are patient, charitable and faithful throughout whatever may arrive. *Oremus!*

Immemorial Tradition versus Legal Positivism

A CATHOLIC PRIEST[1]
Rorate Caeli
July 11, 2021

EVERYONE KNOWS THAT THE CENTERPIECE OF THE Catholic religion is the holy Mass. The Mass is a proper sacrifice in which the true Body and Blood of the Lord are offered to God under the outward appearances of bread and wine through the ministry of an ordained priest. The holy Mass renews — you could say it prolongs and perpetuates — the sacrifice Our Lord offered once and for all on the cross. In fact, it is the self-same sacrifice; only the outward manner of the offering differs.

This holy sacrifice, moreover, does not exist in a void but it is encased in a sublime sequence of prayers and ceremonies called the rite or the liturgy of the Mass. The ancient axiom of the Church Fathers *lex orandi, lex credendi* — "the law of praying is the law of believing" — reminds us that our liturgical prayers must be an accurate expression of our faith and must inculcate true reverence for God. That is why, especially at the time of the Protestant Reformation, the faith of the people was changed precisely by disrupting the ancient forms of Catholic worship. For example, John Calvin, a radical reformer who denied the Real Presence of Our Lord in the Eucharist, once wrote, "God has given us a table at which to feast, not an altar on which to offer sacrifice" (*Institutes*; IV, xviii, 12, col. 1059), and so by removing the old high altars and replacing them with a common table, the faith of the people in the sacrifice of the Mass was undermined and soon destroyed.

I mention these things because today [July 11] falls right between two important anniversaries related to the sacred liturgy: the papal letter *Summorum Pontificum* from Pope Benedict XVI on July 7, 2007 and the papal bull *Quo Primum* from Pope Saint Pius V on July 14, 1570. The Council of Trent had met from 1545 to 1563 to address the challenges of the Protestant

---

1 The author belongs to a traditional institute whose existence is threatened by *Traditionis Custodes*.

Reformation, above all by clearly defining the Catholic dogmas denied by the heretics[2] and by promoting sound reforms in the life of the Church to root out the abuses which had first sparked the Reformation — things like the poor training and immorality of some of the clergy and the shoddy manner of celebrating Mass in many places.

The Roman missal which Saint Pius V published after the Council of Trent was not cobbled together; it was a codification of the existing liturgy that had developed centuries earlier and been celebrated at the papal court for just as long. It was and is a bulwark against error. In promulgating the Roman Missal, Pope Pius V decreed:

> We grant and concede in perpetuity that, for the chanting or read-ing of the Mass in any church whatsoever, this Missal is hereafter to be followed absolutely, without any scruple of conscience or fear of incurring any penalty, judgment, or censure, and may freely and lawfully be used. Nor are superiors, administrators, canons, chaplains, and other secular priests, or religious, of what-ever title designated, obliged to celebrate the Mass otherwise than as enjoined by Us.

In order to remedy the decadence that existed in some places, this holy pope allowed his Roman missal to be used everywhere, even in those churches which also had their own local form of the liturgy. But this prudent saint, with his delicate respect for tradition, still allowed all local variations, such as the usages of the diocese of Toledo or of his own Dominican order, to continue in use if desired. The only condition was that such liturgies had to have a pedigree of at least 200 years. In other words, anything that was a recent fabrication could not be considered worthy of use in God's temple. Whereas Pius V abolished all liturgies less than 200 years old, we can note for comparison that the Novus Ordo, the new rite of Mass devised after Vatican II, has been around only for fifty years.

These fifty years have been troubled years, and it would be distasteful to review the heavy-handed policies of those who tried illegally and immorally

---

2 Such as these condemnations of errors relating to the Eucharist from Session XXII of the Council: "If any one saith, that in the Mass a true and proper sacrifice is not offered to God; or, that to be offered is nothing else but that Christ is given us to eat; let him be anathema" (canon 1); "If any one saith, that the sacrifice of the Mass is only a sacrifice of praise and of thanksgiving; or, that it is a bare commemoration of the sacrifice consummated on the Cross, but not a propitiatory sacrifice; or, that it profits him only who receives; and that it ought not to be offered for the living and the dead for sins, pains, satisfactions, and other necessities; let him be anathema" (canon 3).

to stamp out the timeless Catholic rite of Mass. The Collect today [for the Seventh Sunday after Pentecost] tells us that God's providence never fails, and the last several decades have witnessed the providential revival of the ancient rite. Thus it was in 2007 that Pope Benedict XVI made an act of justice and declared that the old liturgy had never been abolished: every Roman Catholic priest has the right to say this Mass even without special permission, and the people have the right to request and attend this Mass. There is a right to the right rite. *Summorum Pontificum* is emphatically not an "indult," which means a special exemption from a prevailing law. It is a recognition that no indult is necessary. Even if a tyrannical stroke of the pen were to rescind *Summorum Pontificum*, technically that would change nothing. Reality would not be altered. The right to celebrate the perennial Mass of the Roman Church is based on immemorial tradition and not on legal positivism.

You may have seen in the Catholic press that anxious dissidents are now openly drawing their knives against the traditional liturgy. They had never been able to swallow the liberation of the Mass. Take these words of an Italian bishop uttered in July of 2007; he said: "This day is for me a day of grief. I have a lump in my throat and I do not manage to hold back my tears. . . . It is a day of grief, not only for me, but for many who lived and worked in the Second Vatican Council. Today, a reform for which so many labored . . . has been cancelled." And only a few months ago, a Jesuit editor, sensing favorable winds, opined: "The church needs to be clear that it wants the unreformed liturgy to disappear and will only allow it out of pastoral kindness to older people who do not understand the need for change. Children and young people should not be allowed to attend such Masses" (*Religion News Service*, April 13, 2021). I must not be bright enough to understand why, at a time when most young people have stopped practicing, a priest would want to forbid them from attending Mass. Since the Mass is the centerpiece of the Catholic religion, you could not ask for a clearer illustration than this of the false prophets Our Lord warns of in today's Gospel [Mt. 7:15 – 21]. The old Mass is a threat to their new religion. Once you've understood that, you've understood everything.

The objection is made that we should not care too much about the outward form of the liturgy — all that really counts is that Mass is offered validly. It is true that it would be wrong to entertain a punctilious attachment to the outward forms of the liturgy only for their own sake. This would be an empty ritualism, the sort of thing that under the Old Covenant was distorted into Phariseeism. But it would be very wrong to conclude that the liturgy is therefore unimportant. Fifty years ago, when the new missal was promulgated, the General Instruction accompanying it had to be withdrawn and rewritten because its definition of the Mass was so off the mark. It read: "The Lord's Supper, or Mass, is the sacred meeting or congregation of the people of God assembled, the priest presiding, to celebrate the memorial of the Lord," a definition which the great Cardinal Ottaviani decried as "a striking departure from the Catholic theology of the Mass as it was formulated in . . . the Council of Trent." And this should hardly surprise us, when we recall that the architect of the reform, Monsignor Bugnini, stated: "We must strip from our Catholic prayers and from the Catholic liturgy everything which can be the shadow of a stumbling block for our separated brethren, that is, for the Protestants." And indeed, six Protestant ministers served as advisors to the committee which produced the new rite.

You all know that the Church is indefectible — meaning she cannot ever lose anything pertaining to her essence, such as the seven sacraments. This does not mean that Church leaders are prevented from occasionally making disastrous blunders in practical policies. The Holy Ghost protects the Church from approving for use a form of Mass that would be actually invalid or overtly heretical: the validity of a sacrament is either/or, not a spectrum, so of course the reformed Mass is still valid. Valid just means the sacrament "works." But in terms of *receiving* grace from a sacrament, there is also the question of *fruitfulness*: this goes beyond validity and depends on the personal dispositions of the recipient and also on the liturgy itself. That is a question of more or less. When I offer Mass or when Padre Pio offered Mass, there is no difference in validity, but certainly he offered Mass more fruitfully. Likewise, a form of Mass hemmed in with careful and precise signs of reverence for the Blessed Sacrament causes the participants to be better disposed than a liturgy from which signs of adoration and reverence have been systematically removed.

The liturgy should also express our faith accurately, and although the modern rite does not deny the Catholic faith, which would be impossible at least in the officially approved liturgical books, nonetheless it does obscure and attenuate the faith;[3] not to mention the abuses and real sacrileges which

---

3 Compare, for example, the Offertory prayer for the offering of the host from the traditional Mass: "Receive, O holy Father, almighty and eternal God, this unspotted host, which I, Thy unworthy servant, offer unto Thee, my living and true God, for my innumerable sins, offenses, and negligences, and for all here present: as also for all faithful Christians, both living and dead, that it may avail both me and them for salvation unto life everlasting," with the offering of the bread from the Preparation of the Gifts in the New Mass: "Blessed are you, Lord God of all creation, for through your goodness we have received the bread we offer you: fruit of the earth and work

easily slip in when a liturgy is riddled with options. The Lord in today's Gospel gives us a criterion of judgment: *by their fruits you shall know them.* The fruits we see are decimated Mass attendance, plummeted vocations, and almost universal disbelief in the Real Presence.

Our attachment to the traditional Mass, therefore, is not born of nostalgia or aesthetics, but because it is a more perfect expression of the Catholic faith, one which gives greater glory to God and better prepares us for fruitful reception of the sacrament. Come what may, it is a treasure we shall never be willing to forego.

---

of human hands, it will become for us the bread of life," a text based on a Jewish meal prayer, with all references to the sacrificial nature of the Mass expurgated.

Responses to
Traditionis Custodes

3

Best, Worst, and Middle Case Scenarios in the Short Term

CHRISTOPHER R. ALTIERI

Catholic World Report

July 16, 2021

DEFENDERS OF POPE FRANCIS'S DECISION TO ABRO-gate his predecessor's liberalization of the Traditional Latin Mass have been long on the sad necessity of the move, but vanishingly few of them have touted its prudence. Moderates in the Church find the pope's claims of necessity unconvincing, while they doubt the prudence of the measures almost to a man. Traditionalists and other Catholics devoted to the older form of worship are mostly shocked, though they are also hurt and insulted.

Whatever else Pope Francis's decision has done, it has done two things: (1) it has vindicated the Society of Saint Pius X — the SSPX — the chief Traditionalist outlier in the Church, whose leaders for years warned that Rome could not be trusted; (2) it has punished the Catholics who were loyal sons and daughters of the Church through long decades of needless suffering.

Benedict's liberal reform achieved significant détente, which allowed Francis to advance even greater rapprochement between Rome and Écône, where Archbishop Marcel Lefebvre founded the Society of St. Pius X and eventually "performed a schismatic act" when he consecrated four bishops without Rome's permission, to carry on his work. By the middle of the last decade, the movement toward canonically regular expression of substantial unity between the Vatican and the SSPX — which appeared geologically slow at times, even well into the 21st century — had made such progress that Francis first temporarily and then indefinitely granted SSPX clerics faculties to hear confessions, and also granted conditional faculties to them to witness marriages. Basically, Pope Francis used gradual, piecemeal legislation to make SSPX structures at least minimally functional as communities. Things were going so well that, by 2017, he had decided to fold the Pontifical Commission *Ecclesia Dei*, which dealt with the SSPX and other groups and persons and congregations devoted to the older liturgical forms, into the Congregation for the Doctrine of the Faith.

Traditionalists howled at that, while cooler heads — including this wizened Vatican Watcher — saw little to justify the alarm. "[P]rogress has been made in communion," wrote Nicola Gori for L'*Osservatore Romano* at the time, "and therefore the current [2017] motu proprio [by which Francis transferred Ecclesia Dei's responsibilities to the CDF] offers an implicit recognition to the Pontifical Commission which has carried out its tasks with its efforts and activity."

Speaking to the *Catholic Herald* on condition of anonymity because he was not authorized to discuss the subject, one Vatican official summarized the matter this way: "The motu proprio [of 2017] explains the reasons for the suppression pretty well: the nature of the dialogue with the SSPX has changed; the kind of oversight and promotion needed for traditional communities is different, now that they are firmly established, in their own right, in the life of the Church."

So much for that.

Pope Francis himself notes that his new law flies directly in the face of Benedict XVI's older but still newish law. One of the most head-scratching things about Francis's new new law, however, is that it flies directly in the face of Francis's own old new laws.

It also strikes one not quite as a solution without a problem, but more like a drastic remedy for a relatively minor annoyance. It is more like amputating a finger to treat a hangnail than it is anything else. Right now, there is no schismatic Traditionalist movement to speak of — none that really threatens the unity of the Church. Sure, there are angry and maladjusted people with strange theological notions and dubious political ideas out there, but they've been around since dirt was the next big thing. These days, they like mostly to haunt internet comboxes on websites they themselves own and operate. There's not a "movement" yet, but Francis's ham-fisted move on Friday made it a lot more likely that one will develop in short order. There is a real danger of one developing. Its leaders could very well be more powerful, funded, and organized than the bogeymen frequently touted as leaders of the opposition.

Cardinal Burke is — not a nobody, or an ex-nobody — but a marginal figure who was never a mover, shaker, or powerbroker in Rome. Bishop Athanasius Schneider is an auxiliary in Kazakhstan. Archbishop Carlo Maria Viganò is basically a disgruntled former employee who became a minor internet celebrity whistleblower and then never quite cottoned to the fact his fifteen minutes were up more than fifteen months ago. Cardinal Burke and Bishop Schneider are also fiercely loyal to the pope, whose governance they criticize. They are the very paragon of the *parrhesia* for which the Holy Father has repeatedly called in speeches and consistently punished in action. Neither is a leader, let alone a rebel leader. No, it won't be any of them.

If a movement does take shape, it is more likely we'll see a leader emerge from the SSPX, whose hardliners will be able — rightly, it happens, or at least plausibly — to say, "We told you so." They will steamroll the moderates in their ranks. They will fire up the base. They will bring in money, hand over fist. Their ranks will swell with the disaffected. It will make the late '80s and early '90s look like the ecclesiastical equivalent of Glasnost and Perestroika.

That, by the way, is not the worst case. That is the middle case.

The worst-case scenario would see the fractured groups of radical Traditionalist incorruptibles join forces with the SSPX irreducibles and overtake the moderate traditional groups entirely, while bishops enthusiastically exercise their new inquisitorial powers to punish the incorrigible laity who cling to their old books and purge the seminaries of any man who gives the slightest fleeting glance at tradition, and Roman offices broadly interpret the new law to mean more than it says and also more than it doesn't say. In fact, the new motu proprio is silent on the status of other Rites like the Dominican, Benedictine, Carthusian, or the Gallican Rites — Braga, Mozarabic, Carthusian, even the Ambrosian — and all that stands in the way of a general destruction is the absence of an authoritative interpretation from the Council for Legislative Texts.

If *Summorum Pontificum* could fall, is *Anglicanorum Coetibus* safe?

The point isn't that the worst case — or even the middle case — is bound or even likely to obtain. The point is: This is what people are afraid of — even those who recognize the problems one frequently finds in Traditional communities — and with some good reason.

Pope Francis has shown himself capable of wielding the great power of his office, but little evident interest in wielding it safely or with care for who gets hurt. The doomsayers aren't right, one hopes, but they're not obviously wrong just for thinking what they think. Pope Francis, in other words, has made it reasonable to think the worst. He has made it plausible.

The fact of the matter is that the law Pope Francis promulgated on Friday is cumbersome and unwieldy. It will require bishops to dedicate time and energy — sometimes enormous quantities of both — to a thankless project for which they didn't really ask, and from which they cannot expect any measure of good will. Most laity in most parishes don't care either way, while the faithful who are devoted to the older forms of worship are highly motivated. Now, they have their dander up. The bishops of the world know it, and as they measure the potential gains against certain losses, may well decide that a new Inquisition to rid the Church of false conversos is not worth the effort.

If enough bishops decide this is a fight they do not want, traditional communities may survive — in some places, at least — with minimal disruption. The devotees of traditional forms of worship may even decide to toe whatever lines they must in order to escape the purge, and then the danger will pass before too many fall. The best case scenario, in other words, is that the bishops ignore the pope.

4

The New Atom Bomb

PETER A. KWASNIEWSKI

The Remnant

July 16, 2021

SEVENTY-SIX YEARS AGO, ON JULY 16, 1945, THE FIRST atomic bomb was detonated in a lonely desert 210 miles south of Los Alamos, New Mexico. Today, on July 16, 2021, Pope Francis has dropped an atom bomb on the Catholic Church that will harm not just those who "adhere to the Latin liturgical tradition" but everyone who values continuity and coherence, reverence and beauty, our heritage and our future.

As I opened up *Traditionis Custodes* this morning, my eyebrows rose at the improbable title (*Traditionis Perditores*, "Destroyers of Tradition," would have been far more accurate). My incredulity rose with each paragraph. By the time I had finished the accompanying letter, I was deep into the ideological fantasy-world inhabited by Pope Francis and other enemies of the traditional liturgy in today's Church. It felt as if a budding George Orwell had been commissioned to compose the text. The document is dripping with condescension and heartlessness, designed like a Swiss Army knife to equip bishops with as many ways of inconveniencing or hounding tradition-loving Catholics as possible. And the contents were declared to be effective *immediately*, all other "norms, instructions, permissions, and customs" be damned.

It's as if — for all the world — as if we are dealing with a global pandemic of traditionalism that must be stopped by any and every method. The language of the motu proprio suggests that the traditional Latin Mass is being regarded very much like an ecclesiastical version of COVID-19: it is a disease which must be carefully quarantined, monitored, and limited by whatever social engineering is deemed necessary by central authority. Indeed, since the Latin Mass is supposed to be removed from parishes and no more personal parishes are to be set up for it, those who attend might as well wear yellow stars and ring a bell as they walk around. The ghettoization that Benedict XVI labored mightily to overcome has not only returned but received a ringing endorsement.

It is, needless to say, the antithesis of the highly-touted "pastoral" approach, the warm inclusiveness that accompanies everyone on their journey (even if that means they dissent from Catholic teaching on any number of major matters), the romanticized "peripheries" to which the shepherds are to show "mercy"— all the political rhetoric with which this pontificate has festooned itself. In the new motu proprio, it is not the shepherd who comes to smell like the sheep, but the sheep who are told how they must smell in order to be shepherded — or else.

Was it naivety on my part, or just a misplaced belief that simple respect for human beings and for fellow Catholics might still animate this Peronist pope's heart, that led me to be unprepared for the monstrous and mendaciously-named *Traditionis Custodes*? It is far worse than I had expected: a text that drips with contempt, miserliness, and vindictiveness, lacking even a rhetorical attempt to provide a context or (however insincerely) cushion the blow: a lack of rudimentary grace that has never been seen in a document of such magnitude, affecting so many Catholics. It is a historic slap in the face to Francis's pontifical predecessors, from St. Gregory the Great to St. Pius V, even to all the popes after the Second Vatican Council who, seeing that the love for the traditional liturgy had not and would not die out, made provisions for meeting the spiritual needs of Catholics nourished by these venerable rites. For countless souls this great liturgy has become a new motivation to live the demands of the Gospel, a sturdy foundation for family and community life, a source of precious priestly and religious vocations.

Francis cares for none of that. All he cares about is an artificial "unity" that ought to be called uniformity, or better, ideology. A uniformity characterized by every diversion and aberration (in spite of effete calls for reining in the party now running for over five decades), but intolerant of the seriousness, sobriety, and transcendence of an ageless act of worship.

Let's not mince words: this is a declaration of total war, and must be courageously resisted every step of the way, "anything else to the contrary notwithstanding." The true "guardians of tradition" will be the clergy, religious, and laity who carry on with the traditional liturgy in the face of the infernal hatred directed against it. If Francis wants war, I hope and pray there will be enough men ready to enlist, and enough men capable of leading them. And by the latter, I mean *priests* ready to give themselves 100% to the needs of the faithful who rightly adhere to tradition — come what may. There are souls at stake, including the priest's own soul; for he cannot "unknow" what he has come to know, cannot "unlove" what he has come to love. The stifling of one's conscience is too high a price to pay for obedience to a soul-crushing regime, whatever trappings of authority it claims to wear.

KWASNIEWSKI: *The New Atom Bomb*

This new motu proprio will be as bad as it seems only if we allow ourselves to think and act as if we are bound by it, as if its provisions are licit. If, however, we recognize that it is inherently anti-Catholic, and that no pope can rightfully trample on the members of the Church and on her venerable rites as Francis is attempting to do, then we will see it more as an external burden, like a plague, a war, a famine, or an evil government to be overthrown or borne with until its demise. Does the pope have the authority to issue such a diktat? No. It is worth even less than the paper on which it is written.

Those who love the traditional liturgy and recognize in it the focal point of the Church's inheritance will carry on as best they can. They will not beg for permission to offer the immemorial Mass. They will not do the readings in the vernacular, with "approved editions" (*New American Bible*, anyone?). They would rather perish as martyrs than die in the ignominy of lapsation.

I believe at least *some* bishops will be nonplussed by how cold, harsh, and foolish is Francis's anti-TLM motu proprio, which has all the charm of a decree by Stalin ordering the purge of Ukrainian dissidents. Of course, there are others who will run with it, but I can't imagine that bishops who have seen the many good fruits of *Summorum Pontificum* — not least, the steady and often generous financial contributions that flow in from traditional groups — and who enjoy good relationships with priests and parishes that peacefully celebrate the TLM will want to disturb them for the sake of falling in line with a temporary tyrant. Any bishop who genuinely loves the Catholic Faith, any bishop aware of the burgeoning love of tradition among the young and its power to revitalize the Church after the doldrums (not to say freefall) of recent decades, will quietly set aside this painful document and proceed as if nothing has changed — or rather, proceed in the certain knowledge that, as *Rorate Caeli* tweeted, "Francis will die and the traditional Mass will live on."

On the pragmatic side, most bishops do not have a superabundance of clergy such that they could afford to alienate a sizeable number of their presbyterate. If enough priests in the more conservative dioceses stick to the Latin Masses to which they have an inalienable and unabrogatable right, what are the bishops going to do — throw them all out? Where will they get pastors? Where will they get future vocations? Do bishops need another huge headache on their hands, a civil war, a smoldering discontent that saps time and energy on all sides? Benedict XVI brokered a fragile peace, one under which a certain measure of non-polemical normalcy was possible. Many will want to keep that peace, such as it is, in preference to renewed hostilities.

19

The "logic" of *Traditionis Custodes* is tortured, to say the least. Guardians of tradition . . . who attack the Roman tradition of divine worship spanning the centuries. Bishop are empowered . . . but only to limit and suppress; they may not invite, support, and multiply places of growth. The pope promotes unity . . . by doing one of the most unity-destroying actions imaginable. The pope praises his predecessor . . . by utterly and completely contradicting his teaching and revoking what he did. And since you have received from Catholic tradition the truth that the pope is in charge, remember that you must unconditionally obey him when he commands you to reject whatever traditions he personally dislikes, no matter how much they have been sustained by his predecessors whose authority is no less than his, and whose cumulative endorsement is vastly greater than his.

Recall that the pope was once asked point blank about the possibility of the salvation of a man who gave every evidence that he went to his grave denying God as an atheist. The pope replied in positive terms about the salvation of this man. By contrast, the pope in his letter worries about the salvation of Catholics attached to the Holy Tradition of the Church. He invokes unconditional obedience to his person when he ordains that their attachment to that Tradition be severed. Let's juxtapose the scenarios. If people deny God altogether and die as atheists, we have nothing but hopeful words; in fact, let's just admit they are saved because "mercy." But if people have the temerity to be attached to the Church's Tradition in spite of being told to sever that attachment, they are prospective schismatics on their way out of the Church and on the road to perdition. Can we not see here the utter breakdown of the hyperpapalism that makes the pope a mortal god, a divine oracle, who gets to rewrite liturgy, theology, morals, and even the record of history in pursuit of ideology?

Pope Francis reminds one of modern architects like Le Corbusier who build from ideology and are surprised when everything leaks, stains, buckles, and falls apart. The residents reasonably want to move back to the elegant, sturdy, tranquil old buildings.

Is there any silver lining on the menacing cloud? Perhaps it is this: the final stripping-away of all pretense about the deadly game the modernists wish to play.

The contrast between the feast of Our Lady of Mount Carmel and the detonation of the most destructive weapon ever invented by man — one that harms the guilty and the innocent alike, and sows sickness for years after — gives us a key to understanding today's significance. The sign of the Virgin, the one who received the Word and magnified God, stands opposed the sign of the Serpent, the one who proudly disdains God's gifts and exalts his own will. The primordial *non serviam* echoes in the voice of one who refuses to be the *servus servorum Dei*.

"By their fruits ye shall know them": this was the message of the Gospel this past Sunday, the Seventh Sunday after Pentecost in the quondam Extraordinary Form, better known as the Mass of Ages. The fruits of this new motu proprio will be widespread confusion and increased division; temptations to bitterness, discouragement, and despair; tensions and headaches for bishops across the globe; crippling hesitations in the minds of young men who had considered becoming seminarians under the provisions of *Summorum Pontificum*; a large migration of Catholics to the Society of St. Pius X (for which I judge no one!) and to sedevacantist groups (which, on the contrary, is nothing other than tragic), simply because ordinary Catholics cannot — and should not have to be able to — understand how a pope can act against the Church, her tradition, and her common good as Francis does and has done, again and again. All this, and more, will Jorge Bergoglio be called upon to answer for at the dread judgment seat of Christ.

Let us not only call upon Our Lady of Mount Carmel on this dark day and wear her brown scapular, but also see in that scapular a reminder of her protecting mantle that covers all her children and all things Catholic, including the traditions that unite us to one another and to all generations of believers, stretching back to Our Lady. For it was she who said, in words we must cling to in faithful perseverance: "He hath shewed might in his arm: he hath scattered the proud in the conceit of their heart. He hath put down the mighty from their seat, and hath exalted the humble."

5

Let Not the Past or the Present Get in the Way of the Future[†]

PIETRO DE MARCO

Settimo Cielo di Sandro Magister

July 17, 2021

A COLLECTION OF ESSAYS FROM THE MID-1960S (GROOT, van Hess, Poeisz and others, *Study of Dutch Catholics*) already contained the whole Catholic drama. "One of the first things," A. van der Weyer wrote, "is the exclusion of all that is not essential in order to lay bare the fundamental structure of the liturgical event." The new prayers were conceived according to these premises: "It is no longer the transcendent God but the Father who is close to us in Christ; no longer the God who appears in his glory but the hidden God of the Gospel; no longer the objective sacral relationship with God, but the human love in which we unite ourselves with the man Jesus Christ." No objective mystery, no sacrament in all this, of course, only an irrational "event." In addition, the Church must become "aware of being one with humanity as a whole and realizing itself [this thing alone] in the sacraments, in God, and in the faith."

I believe the interpretation I have to make here is that it is humanity as such that "realizes itself" in the sacraments, according to the mystical evolutionism widespread in the 1960s, boosted by the success of Teilhard de Chardin. Almost sixty years later, this seems to be the basic theology (humanistic without transcendence and without supernatural life), much more than liturgical, among the majority of Catholic clergy and theologians, in part by virtue of the astute ambiguity of those formulas — an ambiguity so suitable for justifying any subjectivism in convictions and practices that it has been deliberately cultivated by theological dissemination and is now spreading among the unwitting clergy and laity.

One moment of resistance (aware of the ongoing degradation) on the part of the living liturgical tradition was the pontificate of Benedict XVI. One act, seen as timid by many and deplorable by others — an act not of

† The translation of the Italian original was prepared by and for *Settimo Cielo* and published under the title "'Traditionis Custodes.' The commentary of Pietro De Marco."

magnanimity but of right governance and shrewd theological balance — was the 2007 motu proprio *Summorum Pontificum*. Pope Joseph Ratzinger entrusted to the protection of the Holy Spirit a dialectic between "vetus ordo" and "novus ordo" in the Church, so that the presence of the canon could act as corrective experience and theology for the universe of abuses small and large, and of dominant, shameful superficiality produced not by the Council but by the liturgical reform of the late 1960s (a true betrayal of the Liturgical Movement).

It is against this holy balance that the publication now comes, dated July 16, of the threatened and feared repeal of *Summorum Pontificum*. It will have to be carefully re-examined, but at first reading here is what appears: as usual in the current pontificate, a cover *letter* with a mild and at times heartfelt appearance accompanies a normative act entitled *Traditionis Custodes* whose partisan and destructive motivation (which perhaps escapes the pope himself) cannot deceive anyone. Naturally there is room for a juridical defense of the rights of the faithful, and this must be mounted.

The two documents, in addition to broadening the legitimate power (and burden) of the bishops to supervise the manner and content of celebrations according to the 1962 Missal, speak, in symptomatic and aberrant terms, of "groups" to be monitored and prevented from multiplying. Why is the term "group" aberrant? Because it suggests that fidelity to the "vetus ordo" is a matter of organized minorities leaning toward schism: a hypothesis far from reality and devoid of any discernment. It is alleged that persons and practices are treacherously stirring up a nefarious state of affairs: "groups" are cultivating hostility toward the Council and presenting themselves as "the true Church." Where this is not the case, persons and groups are referred to as "*minus habentes*" who put off, or struggle, to accept conciliar innovation. Two observations, in the face of this display of diagnostic obtuseness, which is more worrisome than disloyalty.

The first. The blame for the widespread, growing, and studied resistance, and its increasing entrenchment, lies to a large extent with the rhetoric and liturgical practice that proclaims itself as "conciliar." The theological flimsiness, as we know, and the main objective — the "participation" to which everything was sacrificed — of the liturgical reform, so far removed from *Sacrosanctum Concilium*, are stubbornly traced back to the will of the Council Fathers. This has also been happening in the same way, for decades and today even more blindly (who reads the conciliar texts?), with the varied and chaotic theological, pastoral, and missionary dynamics, all of which claim always to be implementing the Council. How could the Council not consequently appear to more vigilant believers as the source of all evil? In this context, a certain dishonesty typical of every intelligentsia is also operating among the theologians who have become intelligentsia: it is well known that the Council (its texts, its "*intentio*") justifies almost none of the current practices, except as "event," or rather as a purported "*caesura*" that can be interpreted at will. One knows but keeps it quiet.

The second. Feeling like the "true Church" or catacomb or monastic Church is certainly an error, or at least a form of naivety that is circulating through the widespread ecclesial resistance. It surprises me in some friends whose sincerity and longsuffering I still admire. But what display of missing or uncertain or betrayed preaching of the Christian mystery — that is, of Christ the true Son of God — is made by many parishes in the world, not a little of the hierarchy, in short, much of the Church "*in capite et in membris*"? Into what humiliating disaster are the remains of the national Churches that helmed the Council not wandering? What flood of parlor gossip is overwhelming the essence of the faith?

With what authority, then, will a "*quidam*" — as prescribed in the motu proprio — present himself to oversee the practices and beliefs of a community that I would call "*summorum pontificum*"? Latin will not be enough for him, for what would he do with it? Verify the orthodoxy of the "*Nobis quoque peccatoribus*"? Wouldn't it rather be the case that, before letting him in, the parish priest or the rector of that church should ask this conciliar commissioner (to be presumed as having too many powers and too little understanding of the facts) if he believes in something? For example, in the divinity of Jesus, in the supernatural action of the sacraments, in grace, in the saving sacrifice, in the Trinitarian mystery? What will the investigator of the faith of others answer, since, focused as he is on life and love, he has not been used to thinking on this center of the faith for a long time? But of course commissioners are not asked questions.

The point is important: the common layman who applauds the pope or his likable pastor or the latest writer of theological things does not know how many distortions and ruins of Catholic truth clutter the heads of priests and laymen and saturate documents and articles. To the injury (resulting from the incomprehension that Rome shows for the Catholic reality as a whole) is therefore to be added the insult that the motu proprio has for its title, "*traditionis custodes*." Since when does Pope Jorge Mario Bergoglio want to be "*traditionis custos*"? Undoubtedly, we expect our bishops, the bishops of the whole world, to be so. But if they are to be so (and I add with sorrow: if many of them had been so in recent decades), they cannot help but notice where "*traditio*" really is, and where it is ignored or explicitly mocked. Isn't everything new and different in the Church after the Council? Isn't everything in the faith and in the Church entrusted to the future, so that the past and the present may not get in the way? Isn't the liturgy a happy and creative performance? In short: who, if not this class, this *société de pensée* of reckless and overly influential people, is mainly responsible for "widening the gaps, reinforcing the divergences, and encouraging disagreements that injure the Church and block her path"? It is not long since I read the calembour (from an abyss of Catholic self-destruction) according to which the time of Lent is not a time of "mortification" but of "vivification."

The present writer does not belong to any ecclesial group. Memberships long ago were, if anything, in progressive groups. I have long been a simple Catholic believer, a "*civis*" of the "*civitas Dei*," theologically equipped, I presume, but (what matters more) from my early years, a firm believer in what my lips professed. "*Lex orandi, lex credendi.*" I evaluate what happens in the Church, who is truly my Mother, not owing to some right — a "constitutional" perspective on the Church that doesn't thrill me — but out of duty, the impulse of a believer. This is why I have agreed with those who dared to warn His Holiness of the risk of grave errors in his positions and statements. This is why I will be closer than ever to priests and "*Christifideles*" laity who grasp and live in the Mass of the *vetus ordo* in its 1962 *editio typica*: the fullness of the confession of faith and the apex of sacramental life in the Eucharistic Christ. Under the age-old guidance of the saints, not of pedagogists and organizers — nor of liturgists. I fear that the Holy Father will regret having succumbed, while still ill, to the pressure of anti-Ratzinger groups, to extremists of dubious doctrine and with no discernment of the damage they (for their part) have been causing for decades.

6

An Incomplete Argument and False Information[†]

CHRISTOPHE GEFFROY

La Nef

July 17, 2021

INCOMPREHENSION IS THE DOMINANT FEELING UPON reading the motu proprio *Traditionis Custodes* and the accompanying letter to bishops. It is impossible to understand either the justification or the necessity of the text, especially because the pope has legislated on the basis of an incomplete argument and false information.

INCOMPLETE ARGUMENT

It is not correct that John Paul II's motu proprio *Ecclesia Dei* was only motivated by "the ecclesial intention of restoring the unity of the Church." Of course, that was a major reason, but there was another Francis left out: "However, it is necessary that all the Pastors and the other faithful have a new awareness, not only of the lawfulness but also of the richness for the Church of a diversity of charisms, traditions of spirituality and apostolate, which also constitutes the beauty of unity in variety: of that blended 'harmony' which the earthly Church raises up to Heaven under the impulse of the Holy Spirit" (*Ecclesia Dei* 5a).

FALSE INFORMATION

Pope Francis claims that John Paul II's and Benedict XVI's generosity was used by trads as a means of opposing the Mass of Paul VI and the Second Vatican Council, thereby imperiling the unity of the Church. He writes: "An opportunity offered by St. John Paul II and, with even greater magnanimity, by Benedict XVI, intended to recover the unity of an ecclesial body with diverse liturgical sensibilities, was exploited to widen the gaps, reinforce the divergences, and encourage disagreements that injure the Church, block

† Translated from the French by Zachary Thomas and published at *Catholic World Report* on July 19 under the title "Reflections from France on the motu proprio *Traditionis Custodes* of Pope Francis."

her path, and expose her to the peril of division. . . . But I am nonetheless saddened that the instrumental use of the *Missale Romanum* of 1962 is often characterized by a rejection not only of the liturgical reform, but of the Vatican Council II itself, claiming, with unfounded and unsustainable assertions, that it betrayed the Tradition and the 'true Church'. . . . Ever more plain in the words and attitudes of many is the close connection between the choice of celebrations according to the liturgical books prior to Vatican Council II and the rejection of the Church and her institutions in the name of what is called the 'true Church.'"

The vocabulary Francis uses here is taken straight from the Society of St. Pius X's playbook: the "true Church" indeed! No traditionalist faithful to Rome uses that expression! His observation is true enough if limited to the Society of St. Pius X. But applied to the vast majority of the *Ecclesia Dei* movement, it is false. True, there are cases that correspond to the pope's accusations, but they are a minority: why deal out a collective punishment for the faults of a few? Wouldn't it have been enough to crack down on these few? Clearly, we are not looking at the same traditional world as the pope and his advisers, because their picture has no correspondence to reality. They paint it as a homogenous world, when the attitude they describe is actually found only within the Society of St. Pius X! Who is advising and informing the pope on these subjects?

If we base our view on real-world information, we suspect that the pope is responding to the demand of a tiny minority in the Church who have always been fiercely hostile to the extraordinary form.

THE POPE'S OBJECTIVE — AND THE DRAMATIC CONSEQUENCES WE CAN EXPECT

"In defense of the unity of the Body of Christ, I am constrained to revoke the faculty granted by my Predecessors. The distorted use that has been made of this faculty is contrary to the intentions that led to granting the freedom to celebrate the Mass with the *Missale Romanum* of 1962." In the interest of unity, this motu proprio will bring incomprehension, disarray, and conflict, and in the end will widen divisions instead of reducing them: the opposite of its stated objective! With the stroke of a pen, he overturns thirty-five years of efforts by John Paul II and Benedict XVI to calm the situation and establish a certain level of imperfect but genuine peace. Even the statement of the French Bishops' Conference, which is hardly well disposed to the traditionalist world, recognizes that *Summorum Pontificum* has led globally to a "peaceful situation," which our investigation has largely confirmed (cf.

the article on traditionalists in *La Nef* n°338, July–August 2021).

It will reignite the liturgy wars, exacerbate traditionalist resistance, and especially lead many to leave for the Society of St. Pius X (which will rejoice to see this motu proprio swell their ranks, confirming what they have warned about ever since 1988, namely that Rome cannot be trusted, a conviction that underlies their refusal of any reconciliation). This is precisely what John Paul II and Benedict XVI were able to avoid with their attentiveness to the traditionalist world. Francis's new decision risks creating a huge mess.

An important historical and psychological remark: Paul VI was ready to make concessions over the Mass if Mgr Lefebvre had not rejected Vatican II (his famous November 21, 1974, declaration against the "modernist Rome" of the council is what got him into trouble). But John Paul II and Benedict XVI understood that liturgical appeasement was a necessary condition for getting those traditionalists who were most reserved about Vatican II to open up to the council and assimilate. By tightening the vice around the Mass, Francis will end up with a result opposite of the one that has been legitimately sought so far.

A DOUBLE-STANDARD?

The tone of the motu proprio and letter is so harsh and severe toward traditionalists that one cannot help but think that there is a double standard at work: while Francis insists so often on mercy, humility, forgiveness, and is so patient with the German Church which is on the verge of schism, he, our common Father, shows not a trace of love or understanding for those who are only a tiny fraction of his flock! In these texts, trads comes across as a threat, barely tolerated on their "Indian reservation" until they can get back in line. The explicit goal is to make them disappear, without even stopping to wonder if they might have something to offer the Church, in terms of youth, dynamism, vocations, etc. Are there so many convicted, practicing Catholics in the West that it has to be a priority to drastically limit one group of them?

Recent experience has shown that to despise and persecute traditionalists in this way does not help them evolve; on the contrary, it fuels the resistance of hard-liners, they become more rigid: which goes against the sought-for goal of favoring unity.

The French Bishops' Conference deserves credit for their communiqué of July 17th, which conveys their respect for traditionalists: "The bishops wish to express to the faithful who regularly celebrate according to the

Missal of John XXIII and to their pastors, their attentiveness and the respect they have for the spiritual zeal of these faithful and their determination to continue the mission together in the communion of the Church and according to the norms in force."

DISRESPECT FOR THE GREAT WORK OF BENEDICT XVI

These two texts [of Francis] return without nuance to John Paul II's and especially Benedict XVI's efforts at reconciliation in an erroneous analysis of the facts. And they go so far as to annul the essential contribution of the Pope Emeritus when he distinguished two forms, ordinary and extraordinary, of the same Roman Rite. In so doing, the pope suppresses the juridical existence of the ancient extraordinary form in one fell swoop, treating it as if it does not exist. This plunges the Church back into the endless liturgy wars over the juridical status of the Mass of St. Pius V. We are going back to the regime of toleration on terms even more severe than those of 1988, a sort of "merciful parenthesis," but there is nothing merciful about it! A single decree sets us back more than thirty years.

WHAT CAN WE DEDUCE ABOUT ROME'S STRATEGY, READING BETWEEN THE LINES?

Francis's two texts show clearly that the pope wants to eradicate the traditionalist world from the Church and to ensure that the Mass of St. Pius V disappears. It prevents the movement from taking shape, forbidding any new groups and setting up obstacles for any diocesan priest who wants to celebrate with the old *ordo missae*. The motu proprio envisions those devoted to the extraordinary form one day using the new missal. The stage is set for a future in which the traditional Mass will be celebrated only by the Society of Pius X and its satellites. The pope's strategy seems to be to push the resistance toward the Society of St. Pius X so that the whole traditional world concentrates there, where they will be isolated and controlled on their little reservation, cut off from Rome and the dioceses, maintaining just enough connection to avoid formal schism. This explains why the pope is not seeking full reconciliation with the Society of St. Pius X, but has shown great generosity toward them by recognizing the full validity of their marriages and confessions, encouraging people to welcome them into the churches during pilgrimages, etc. It all makes sense, and flies in the face of John Paul II's and Benedict XVI's efforts toward Church unity.

LITURGICAL EXCLUSIVITY?

This motu proprio is a chance for the institutes who refuse to celebrate the ordinary form — and let's be clear, they are a minority in the *Ecclesia Dei* world — to seriously examine the liturgical, theological, and ecclesial basis for this refusal. Since 1988, the popes have invited them not to refuse the celebration of the new Mass in principle. (Although the position of the *Ecclesia Dei* Commission has fluctuated on this point, resulting in a certain lack of clarity.) This does not detract in any way from the special charism of these institutes to say the old Mass. Benedict XVI was very explicit in his letter to the bishops in 2007. Admittedly, the battle-lines haven't budged since. If they obey the pope on this sensitive point, won't these institutes demonstrate by their example that Francis's analysis is flawed?

All this is sad, because it's unjust. It is therefore legitimate to complain, to argue, and to relentlessly demand a reform of this motu proprio or for the most flexible possible application, while respecting the pope's role and authority. The bishops will have a pivotal role to play. Everything will depend on how they choose to apply this motu proprio. Early reactions have been encouraging: a big thank you to bishops who care for their whole flock. It's their responsibility to make sure that Rome is more justly apprised of reality on the ground in the traditional world. Traditionalists have proved unwilling to just roll over: let us hope that most do not fall back into a "resistance" that verges on revolt and open disobedience. Mgr Lefebvre and the Society of St. Pius X are not the examples to follow. We know where that leads. Suffering for the Church is never easy, but it is always fruitful.

7

A Pontifical Act
Lacking *Auctoritas*

FR. JOHN HUNWICKE

Mutual Enrichment

July 16–17, 2021

IN NOVEMBER OF 2001, PREBENDARY MICHAEL MORE-
ton wrote a letter to me in which he said:

> I regard the Roman Canon as part of the complex of traditions
> which characterized the life of the Church as it emerged from the
> centuries of persecution: a shared rule of faith in the creeds, a
> shared rule of what constituted Scripture, a shared rule of holy
> order, and a shared rule of prayer. I do not believe that any part of
> the Church in later centuries has any authority to alter these canons.

Cardinal Ratzinger held a similar view:

> Rites ... are forms of the apostolic Tradition and of its unfolding
> in the great places of the Tradition. . . . After the Second Vatican
> Council, the impression arose that the pope really could do any-
> thing in liturgical matters. . . . The First Vatican Council had in
> no way defined the pope as an absolute monarch. On the contrary,
> it presented him as the guarantor of obedience to the revealed
> Word. . . . The authority of the pope is not unlimited; it is at the
> service of Sacred Tradition.

So much, then, for Bergoglianist autocracy. In passing on, we can applaud
the insight and determination of the Moscow Patriarchate in resisting papist
ambitions in the See of Constantinople.

But if the hyperübersuperultrapapalism of Bergoglianity will not serve
God's People, what will? Conciliarism? You just have to be joking. After
the fiasco of Vatican II (yes; genuine, valid, canonical Ecumenical Councils
can be disasters for the Church, as both St. John Henry Newman and Cardinal Ratzinger had no trouble discerning)? And, on the other side of the
fence, how about the megafiasco of the "Great and Holy Council" a few
years ago in Crete? 'Nuff Said!

Holy Tradition. Holy Tradition, which, of course, has Holy Scripture as one of its ruling structures. Holy Tradition, the foremost manifestation of which, day by day, is in the Liturgy. Holy Tradition is our truest Mistress. Holy Tradition is the ultimate and overruling *auctoritas* in the life of the Household of God. No *auctoritas* can subsist in enactments which manifestly subvert Holy Tradition.

*   *   *

I wonder how far Pope Francis's power to obstruct his Predecessor's legislation extends. And exactly where he would cross the boundary into the *ultra vires*. A defense of a pope's capacity to do what Pope Francis claims to have done would find its strongest support in *Legalism*; in canonical enactments about papal authority. But, curiously, the rigidities of *Legalism* have sometimes elicited critical observations from the Holy Father's mouth!

However, to advocate a chaotic free-for-all is not the answer. I think it is important for us better to understand the concept of *auctoritas*. Which does not always have same parameters as Canonical Lawfulness. So what is this *auctoritas*?

A liturgical form can have full canonical status; and when it does, it is clear that a cleric is (for example) fulfilling his obligation to the Divine Office by using it. But the Latin term *auctoritas* has a more subtle sense than mere canonical liceity. It might suggest the personal influence which a player in Roman politics had, quite distinct from any *imperium* which he might enjoy as a result of a magistracy which he held. Or a sense of authoritativeness or impressiveness, of personal prestige or repute; we all know the sort of person who, perhaps in a committee or gathering, is listened to the moment he opens his mouth and whose interventions invite a respect out of all proportion to his merely legal status. (It is a characteristic of the Good Woman in Proverbs 31 that her husband is great among the elders at the gate; when such people are moved to utterance, other people put their hands to their mouths!) In our modern secular politics, the policies which were embodied in the manifesto of a government which has won power by a sweeping majority have *auctoritas* greater than the ideas dreamed up last night by a premier who is holding onto power by his fingertips . . . although the constitutional power may be formally the same in each case.

Auctoritas as opposed to mere canonical liceity has always had a place in Liturgy. When manualists such as the admirable O'Connell wrote about a custom which is even *contra legem* enjoying, by virtue of its longevity, not merely liceity but even prescription above the letter of the rubric, it is in a way *auctoritas* that they are talking about.

But I contend that the radical changes that followed Vatican II raise the question of *auctoritas* in new, difficult, and acute forms. One reason for this is the most striking novelty involved in post-Conciliar liturgical texts: multiple choices facing a celebrant or a worshipping community as they prepare to celebrate a rite. Previously, what every celebrant had said daily at every altar of the Roman Rite throughout the world for centuries obviously had enormous *auctoritas*. A novel formula which has just been put on some menu from which choices are to be made, manifestly has very much less. Whereas, *before* the Council, something that *auctoritas* urged one to do was broadly in line with what was canonically licit, *after* the Conciliar "reforms" *auctoritas* and liceity, lawfulness, might find themselves standing further and further apart from each other.

I strongly agree with Joseph Ratzinger's strongly expressed view that there is something highly questionable about the idea that a Roman Pontiff can "do anything, especially if backed by a mandate of an ecumenical council." I would contend that what is wrong with that idea is, among other things, its forgetfulness of liturgical *auctoritas*. And my inclination is to believe that, in many and important respects, the "reforms" went beyond the conciliar mandate of *Sacrosanctum Concilium* (*praeter Concilium*) and, even more problematically, in some cases directly contradicted it (*contra Concilium*). In my view, changes *praeter Concilium* have less *auctoritas* than those which do rest on a conciliar mandate.

Vatican II was an Ecumenical Council (albeit, a pastoral Council), just as much as all the other Ecumenical Councils. What it mandated, possessed *auctoritas*. What it did not mandate, but what subsequent committees put in place, has much less claim on our consciences. And where a clear instruction of the Council was categorically contradicted by committee-men only two or three years later, I think we have duties of discernment.

So changes *contra Concilium* raise, as Benedict XVI perceived, extremely acute difficulties with regard to their *auctoritas*.

The Catholic Church, more than many ecclesial bodies, has a deeply ingrained sense of Law. This makes it easy for Roman Catholics to underestimate the force of *auctoritas*. But Benedict XVI was appealing directly to *auctoritas* when he wrote "What earlier generations held as sacred, remains sacred and great for us too, and it cannot be all of a sudden entirely forbidden or even considered harmful."

In so teaching — in so using the word "cannot" — he was not speaking in terms of canonical or legislative details; he was arguing *theologically and ecclesiologically*.

And Benedict was right.

And... as Pope Francis forces us to face new Liturgy Wars... this has practical implications.

8

There Can Be No "Unity" through the Rejection of Tradition

LEILA MILLER

July 17, 2021

YESTERDAY, POPE FRANCIS ISSUED A MOTU PROPRIO, ironically named *Traditionis Custodes* ("Guardians of the Tradition"), which, in the name of "unity," seeks to bring the hammer down on the Traditional Latin Mass (TLM). This act, which some say rests on shaky legal grounds, attempts to undo Pope Benedict's *Summorum Pontificum*, which gave generous latitude for the use of the TLM. I want to be very clear that although I have attended a TLM only about eight times in my entire life, I throw my full support and sympathies behind the Church's TLM communities and priests, many of whom are my dear friends.

For today, I'd like to discuss the goodness and importance of tradition in general and the disaster that occurs when we toss it out — whether we are breaking with Church traditions, cultural traditions, national traditions, or family traditions. (Clearly, I am not speaking of any evil "traditions" or sins — and I hope that goes without saying.)

I was born in 1967, and I have no memory of anything prior to Vatican II. I was horribly catechized (essentially uncatechized), like the rest of my generation, and when I found out how much had been kept from me, I felt robbed. I even initially called my reversion story "I Was Robbed!" The break with Church tradition in the past fifty-plus years has been catastrophic by any objective measure. The Roman Catholic world was *unified* prior to that break, and sharing the same universal and ancient liturgy was key. We went from unity and a shared identity to disunity and a loss of identity. A break from Church tradition led to division and alienation.

The disjointing that occurred in the Body of Christ also happens in the other social spheres — family, culture, nation — when we renounce our traditions. For example...

FAMILY

The most obvious and common way that a family severs its members from its own tradition is through divorce. Here's how one man described his childhood to me, both before and after the dismantling of his family:

> What hits me the hardest is that there is no "going home" any-more. . . . There is no childhood place to which I can return. When parents in intact families move to a new house after the children grow up, there is still that place to go where the two parents act as they always have: Dad chops the firewood while Mom cooks dinner, the same Christmas decorations go up (albeit in different places), Dad cuts the ham, and so on. Familiar smells with familiar activities. For children of divorce, all those reminders of the home they grew up in are gone. "Home" isn't really a place, after all, but an experience. With divorce, that experience is immediately gone, with no warning or preparation.

The family went from unity and a shared identity to disunity and a loss of identity. A break from family traditions leads to division and alienation.

CULTURE

When a society breaks from its timeless traditions and innate understandings, it's also to devastating effect. Consider my dear friend and pro-life warrior Obianuju (Uju) Ekeocha's brilliant and scorching response to a Danish abortion activist.[1] It was like a master-class in schooling a pro-abort who seeks to destroy the ancient traditions of the naturally pro-life African people:

> I'd like to just address the Danish lady who had spoken about comparing African women not having "the right to choose what to do with her body," and it being "colonization." It's actually quite amazing how you were able to, kind of, twist that into shape, to [get to] that thought. But I must say this to you: I am from a tribe called the Igbo tribe in Nigeria. If I tried to translate in my native tongue what it means for a woman "to choose what to do with her body," I couldn't. Most of the African native languages don't even have a way of phrasing abortion to mean anything good.
>
> Now, as communities of people, and as societies, where it actually then becomes colonization and neo-colonization is that people from the Western world come to Africa and try to give us these

---

1 "Best practices for maternal health in Africa Q&A Session (United Nations Side Event)," https://www.youtube.com/watch?v=LZ6nioMimCc&t=165s.

kinds of language that we could never translate into our native tongue. They tell us that it actually can mean something for a woman to "do something with her body [abortion]" which isn't really morally bad. But anyway, the first thing that we have to think of and remember is that as communities . . . culturally most of the African communities actually believe by tradition, by their cultural standards, that abortion is a direct attack on human life. So, for anybody to convince a woman that abortion is good [long pause while the audience applauds loudly] . . . . So for anyone to be able to convince any woman in Africa that abortion is actually a good thing and can be a good thing, you first of all have to tell her that what her parents and her grandparents and her ancestors taught her is actually wrong; you're going to have to tell her that they have always been wrong in their thinking. And that, Madame, is colonization. [loud applause]

Our Western culture is in danger as well, due to sudden and jarring turns from our own tradition. From a US census report: "Millennials in the United States have a different set of values on social and economic topics than the generations before them," and "more than half — 55% — believe marrying and having children is not very important." This is a cataclysmic, and unnatural, break from the past. No society can survive its young people not wishing to form families through marriage and procreation. And it's not just the United States, of course; it is most of Western culture at this point.

A culture that breaks from its ancient traditions and understandings goes from unity and a shared identity to disunity and a loss of identity. A break from societal traditions leads to division and alienation.

NATION

The traditions of a nation, and the virtue of patriotism, unify its citizens. In the seventies and eighties, I attended public schools, K–12, in a heavily Democrat city (Tucson, AZ). And yet, as all American schoolchildren in the past, we were taught to love our country. Patriotic expression through stories, songs, poems, and flag-waving was a good thing, a given. We learned about the founding of America with pride, and we were profoundly, happily connected to what came before us. My husband says the same about his own schooling at the time, and he was a mostly secular, liberal Jewish kid growing up in the South.

In recent years, however, things have radically changed. We know well that the average school kid today is taught to suspect and even despise this nation and its founding, and traditional patriotism is seen as racist. We have cut off American children from their patrimony, their history, their traditions — and thus a part of themselves. (And please don't tell me that immigrant children have no such connection. My father was a refugee immigrant, and he's the first one who taught me to be a proud American! There has never been a stronger American patriot than Farouk Habra.)

The change in our nation's young people has been shocking to observe, particularly because of how quickly the change has come. Once a person is persuaded to rail against his own homeland, when he is convinced to hate what his own parents and grandparents cherished, the future of that nation is in peril. Marxists, even under the name of BLM and "progressivism" in our own land, know that to take a nation, they must first separate the people of a nation from their past, rupturing their revered cultural and religious traditions, in order to disorient, demoralize, and reprogram them, erasing the "collective memory" that formed the bonds of the generations.

A nation that breaks from its traditions and foundations goes from unity and a shared identity to disunity and a loss of identity. A break from national traditions leads to division and alienation.

You get the point, and the pattern. Without the connections of our traditions, we humans are adrift and vulnerable; isolated from each other and our past, we can be re-made into whatever evil image a malicious actor may impress upon us. Without our traditions, we lose — and even begin to despise — our families, our cultures, our nations, and our Church.

In the life-changing book, *What We Can't Not Know*, Professor J. Budziszewski (a former atheist) describes tradition as: "a sort of apprenticeship in living, with all of the previous generations as masters, [which] includes not only ways of doing things, but ways of raising questions about things that matter" (p. 174). And G. K. Chesterton famously stated in *Orthodoxy*: "Tradition means giving votes to the most obscure of all classes, our ancestors. It is the democracy of the dead. Tradition refuses to submit to the small and arrogant oligarchy of those who merely happen to be walking about."

Tradition is good and necessary. Tradition is not to be disdained, fought against, or cast off like Grandma's old chotskies. Tradition unifies; it does not divide. I love the traditions of my family, my culture, my nation, and especially my Church. If loving Catholic tradition, defending Catholic tradition, advocating for Catholic tradition makes me a "traditionalist" — then so be it. I can think of many worse things to be.

9

The Pope's Merciless War against the Old Rite

TIM STANLEY

The Spectator

July 17, 2021

I AM GOING TO HAVE TO BOIL THIS DOWN AS CRUDELY as I can, because it's a complex subject with a simple message, but the Pope is attempting to make it as hard as possible to say, and thus attend, the Old Rite Mass. This is the form of Mass most Catholics went to before the 1970s. It was replaced with a New Rite and the Old was driven more-or-less underground. In 2007 Pope Benedict XVI decided that priests who wanted to say the Old should be allowed to. Francis has rescinded that: now you must get the bishop's permission and things will be weighed heavily in favor of the bishop saying no.

Why does this matter for Catholics and non-Catholics alike? Because it's a lesson in how liberalism in this gerontocratic, Brezhnev-esque stage behaves — utterly intolerant of anyone who breaks from the party line. It is not enough to be quiet or even submit. You must conform.

Francis's case is flawed on three levels. First, he is known as the Pope of mercy, but this is decidedly unmerciful to those parts of his flock who love the Old Rite. He routinely attacks rigidity in the faithful, meaning conservatism, but can be as rigid as steel. He has pushed for a more decentralized church but is now invading people's very consciences. And he says he wants unity, but his decree is most likely to promote schism. In short: this is a classic case of hypocrisy, of a politician being everything they accuse their opposition of.

Second, I'm reluctant to accuse the pontiff of outright lying, but his proclamation is disingenuous. He claims that all Benedict wanted to do was provide for the handful of dying traditionalists who wanted the Old Rite, but we all know there was more to it than that — that there was a hope of modernizing the Old Rite while clearing up abuses in the New, while acknowledging that the Old is a perfectly valid expression of the Catholic faith (which is a recipe for mutual enrichment and genuine unity).

Moreover, practice of the Old is one of the few areas of growth in the Western Church — to the embarrassment of those who hate it — and the reasons for its success are obvious. For many attending it for the first time, stripped of its social context in the 1960s, it is refreshingly novel and it strikes them as prayerful and beautiful, an antidote to the noise of the twenty-first century. Francis claims that it has become a rallying point for critics of the modern church, that it is a threat to unity — and that's true in parts, but not in the vast majority of dioceses. Indeed, the best effect of Benedict's action was to divorce practice of the Old Rite from schismatics: it meant that if you wanted to enjoy it, you no longer had to attend a dubious underground church in Bayswater. It is Francis who has made it controversial again, pushing it to the margins and then accusing it of being marginal.

Third, we all know deep down that this is a desperate last stand by the 1960s generation of clerics, a generation that is about ten years from losing its grip on power. The seminaries are full of young men who want to say the Old Rite. In many cases, Francis's action will seem like a terrible blow to their vocations because it strips them of a right they assumed they would be free to exercise, sending the message that they cannot trust the Vatican not to change the rules of the game at a moment's notice (what's next?!). But they should stand their ground and persevere, because that Sixties generation, the type that go weak at the knees when you whisper the words "Robert F. Kennedy," are not long for this world, and when they finally go, all the baggage of their era goes with them. What they do not realize with this last ditch attempt to kill the Old Rite is that they are poisoning the legacy of their own agenda. There's a lot that Francis is correct about: he has changed my mind on the environment and nudged me back to the Left in economics. But by tying that progressive agenda to a narrow cultural politics, liberals will alienate natural allies.

They will also leave the wider world scratching its head in confusion. Why, in the middle of a pandemic — with child abuse dogging the church and communist China suppressing religion — launch a crusade against a pretty liturgy that is said in very few places and does no harm to anyone? Because liturgical wars, like debates over art or architecture, are a cover for ideological obsession. We betray ourselves by our priorities.

Liberalism once promoted diversity; now it is in power, it has hardened into orthodoxy, a design for life that we must all follow. The conservatives used to run the Church and were often nasty with it, that's true: but they lost the war. Now that they are out of power, all they want is the right to be left alone. Well, they can't have it, and it's naive to think peace is an option.

The reason why what Francis has done matters is because some day the kind of liberalism he embodies will come for you — for the simple, sweet thing you were doing that wasn't bothering anyone else but, by its mere existence, was an existential threat to the governing regime. You are next.

10

The Hat and the Head[†]

JUAN MANUEL DE PRADA

ABC

July 18, 2021

CHESTERTON ASSERTED THAT "THE CHURCH ASKS US
to take off our hats, not our heads when entering it." Taking off one's hat
can, however, be an act of mortification when the church lacks a roof or
if its roof is leaky, not to mention when shitting pigeons nest therein. But
through mortification a Catholic completes the Passion of Christ in his
flesh, as St. Paul asked of us.

In order to mortify myself, I have humbly endured Masses that vio-
lently assault my artistic sensibility and devotional preferences: Masses
with revolting little ditties based on Simon & Garfunkel tunes, Masses with
empowered laywomen who read the epistles stumbling over every phrase,
Masses with thick-headed priests who stuff the liturgy with a tacky filling
of improvisation till it overflows, Masses with sermons that stink of forgettable politicking.

And I have endured all these mortifications because I believe that a Catholic should go to Mass in his parish, even if the Masses he slurps leave him
disgusted and sodden with their hideousness. This painful awareness of their
hideousness stings even more when I compare them with the awareness of
beauty I have felt in the few traditional Masses I have participated in. There
I have recognized myself as another link in the chain of a living tradition
that has inspired the most eminent artists.

For the sake of my faith I have often taken off my hat, putting up with
a shower of revolting little ditties, tacky improvisations, empowered laywomen, and forgettable sermons.

However, my faith cannot demand that I take off my head, and this —
precisely this — is what Bergoglio has just asked of me. Only a few years
ago, Benedict XVI explained in a motu proprio that "the Roman Missal promulgated by Pope Paul VI is the ordinary expression of the *lex orandi* of the
Catholic Church of the Latin rite. The Roman Missal promulgated by Saint

---

[†] Translated from the Spanish by Gerhard Eger and published at *Rorate Caeli* on July 22.

Pius V and revised by Blessed John XXIII is nonetheless to be considered an extraordinary expression of the same *lex orandi*." And now Bergoglio affirms in another motu proprio that "the liturgical books promulgated by Saint Paul VI and Saint John Paul II, in conformity with the decrees of Vatican Council II, are the unique expression of the *lex orandi* of the Roman Rite."

I am a Catholic, but I cannot be irrational. I cannot accept one thing and its opposite; I cannot split my head in half. I cannot obey contradictory instructions, as if I were a corpse or a robot that reacts to electric impulses. The virtue of obedience does not exempt us from the obligation to use our reason correctly, since obedience, as St. Thomas teaches us, is "a reasonable offering ratified by a vow to submit one's will to another in order to submit it to God for the sake of perfection." Obedience cannot assent to an absurdity, nor can it submit to contradictory commands just to avoid annoyances or complications.

The God in whom I believe is the *Logos*, and therefore I cannot be asked to take off my head. Bergoglio's motu proprio asks me to do just that, and I have no intention of doing it.

11

Pope Francis and the Tridentine Mass

DOUGLAS FARROW

First Things
July 18, 2021

TRADITIONIS CUSTODES, POPE FRANCIS'S MOTU PRO-prio "on the use of the Roman Liturgy prior to the Reform of 1970," appears at first glance to be business as usual in the prudential work of governing the Church. Having consulted his fellow bishops, the bishop of Rome has decided to reverse the provisions of his predecessor in *Summorum Pontificum*, in which Benedict encouraged use of the traditional Latin Mass by way of a general permission for priests to say it.

This, writes Francis in his accompanying letter, may now be deemed a failed gesture toward greater ecclesial unity. In practice, it created enclaves of dissent from the reforms pursuant to Vatican II: "An opportunity offered by St. John Paul II and, with even greater magnanimity, by Benedict XVI, intended to recover the unity of an ecclesial body with diverse liturgical sensibilities, was exploited to widen the gaps, reinforce the divergences, and encourage disagreements that injure the Church, block her path, and expose her to the peril of division." The decision must therefore be reversed and the opportunity withdrawn.

On Friday it was withdrawn, but in a manner that is hardly business as usual. For whatever the truth of the charge he levels, Francis himself seems to have weaponized the Latin Mass in the very act of suppressing it. The obvious goal of the motu proprio is to dissolve certain communities devoted to it, communities that have been a thorn in his side for too long. In the waning days of his pontificate, the thorn is being plucked.

It is rumored that earlier drafts were less charitable than the final documents. Yet the measures are draconian and the tone, though dignified, remains severe. To make matters worse, Francis has assigned to diocesan bishops the difficult task of suppression while reserving to Rome the right to veto particular acts of clemency, including (at article 4) any permission granted new ordinands to say the Latin Mass. For this, few of his brethren will thank him. Some, who themselves love and respect the *vetus ordo*, will resist him.

Others are better equipped to discuss the problems this will pose on the ground, and to untangle any knots that appear in the light of canon law. For my part, I will venture only two further observations.

First, Francis takes comfort "from the fact that, after the Council of Trent, St. Pius V also abrogated all the rites that could not claim a proven antiquity, establishing for the whole Latin Church a single *Missale Romanum*" which for four centuries was "the principal expression of the *lex orandi* of the Roman Rite." He thinks he is doing something analogous. Francis does not explain, however, how the form promulgated by Pius — then regarded as the perfect embodiment of venerable tradition and now itself possessing a proven antiquity — can be suppressed without implying that it was fundamentally defective. Nor does he explain its relation to the modern rite.

In *Summorum*, Benedict declared the Roman Missal promulgated by Paul VI to be the ordinary expression of the *lex orandi* and that promulgated by Pius V (as revised by John XXIII) to be an extraordinary expression, "duly honored for its venerable and ancient usage." While his terminology is not unproblematic, the crucial point is that Benedict did not believe that these two expressions of the *lex orandi* could divide the Church's *lex credendi*. As "two usages of the one Roman rite," they articulate a common faith. Hence there was no abrogation of the latter when the former came into existence. The law of prayer is indeed the law of faith, in other words, but both are at work in the Mass, not identical to it in some particular form. Let us not forget that the two forms of the Roman rite stand alongside a variety of Eastern rites, each embodying in its own way the faithful Church at prayer.

Francis has thrown all this into question. According to his motu proprio, the form promulgated by Paul VI is not merely the ordinary or even the principal expression of the *lex orandi* of the Roman Church; it is the "unique" expression and will soon be the sole expression. This goes beyond prudence to principle. Are we to understand that the new sublates and eliminates the old? Or even to suspect that Rome finds a moment of truth in what certain Latin Mass proponents claim; namely, that the *novus ordo* is not really compatible with the *vetus ordo*, that one or the other must give way?

This, of course, Francis denies. It is just the sort of thing he finds problematic about the communities he means to discipline and dissolve. But if actions speak louder than words and if realities, as he likes to say, are more important than ideas, his move to suppress the *vetus ordo* tends only to reinforce the repudiated claim.

Second, Francis speaks of being "saddened by abuses in the celebration of the liturgy on all sides." Quoting Benedict, he deplores "the fact that 'in many places the prescriptions of the new Missal are not observed in celebration, but indeed come to be interpreted as an authorization for or even a requirement of creativity, which leads to almost unbearable distortions.'" Amen! Yet Francis deplores; he does not address. If his grief over sloppy or instrumentalized celebrations of the ordinary form is genuine, surely he ought to have attended first of all to that problem and only afterward to the other.

Here too he has reversed his predecessor's course, hastening in the opposite direction. The Synod on the Amazon leaps quickly to mind, and those Pachamama rituals in which he participated. Or the ongoing exercises on the Rhine, to which he appears rather cooler but has not put a stop. Is the "creativity" of the Amazonian or the German church somehow less a concern than the "rigidity" of scattered Latin Mass congregations? What exactly does he have in mind when he asks his brother bishops to beware "the eccentricities that can easily degenerate into abuses"?

In sum: *Traditionis Custodes*, alas, confirms that the old Mass has indeed become a proxy in the fight over the legacy of Vatican II, as much on the one side as on the other. It also confirms that in Rome rigidity is the order of the day. But now some advice, directed to those tempted to find in this motu proprio a justification for schism, as some of their opponents doubtless hope they will.

I preface the advice with a warning. No one can legitimately erect a shadow Church. That is the Protestant error and a rejection (not a revision) of the Petrine office as such. Those who wish to follow in the footsteps of the Old Catholic Church by some new claim to that title will fare no better, as the sorry history of the SSPX illustrates.

What then? Those whose bishops do not provide adequately for the Latin Mass, and who cannot find a place *pro tempore* where the ordinary form is celebrated with extraordinary respect and dignity, might consider a third option: learning to appreciate an Eastern rite celebration that is available to them. That could be liberating in more ways than one.

Should they find themselves stymied, none of these options being open to them, they can take some comfort from the fact that the present trials and tribulations are just that — *present* trials and tribulations, which can be put to good use spiritually even if they cannot be enjoyed. Not for long will things remain in the Church as they are now.

12

On the Unity of the Church in Our Times

DOM ALCUIN REID, O.S.B.

Homily at the Monastère Saint-Benoît

July 18, 2021

OUR HOLY FATHER POPE FRANCIS HAS, LAST FRIDAY, enacted legislation in respect of the *usus antiquior* of the Roman rite — the more ancient form of the liturgy — in the light of his grave concerns that its celebration has endangered the unity of the Church and fostered division within it, including a rejection of the legitimacy of the Second Vatican Council and of the Magisterium of the popes following it. These are grave concerns, and any pope is right to address them when he believes they exist. The service of the unity of the Church is one of the particular duties of the Petrine ministry for which each pope must answer before Almighty God on the day of judgement. It is beholden to us, therefore, as faithful Catholics, to take his concerns very seriously indeed.

The Church teaches that her unity comes through our each being immersed in the life of the Blessed Trinity — the *principalis Unitas* of our Saturday Vespers hymn — through baptism in Our Lord Jesus Christ, who is Himself the principle of the Church's unity.[1] She also teaches that the Church's unity embraces "a great *diversity*," the "great richness" of which "is not opposed to the Church's unity."[2] The bonds of this unity are "the profession of one faith received from the apostles," the "common celebration of divine worship," and the "apostolic succession through the sacrament of Holy Orders, maintaining the fraternal concord of God's family."[3]

In respect of the celebration of the Sacred Liturgy, unity in diversity has been the norm for the Church since her beginning, with Eastern and Western liturgical rites growing up from Apostolic times on. The Eastern Churches enjoy a rich diversity of liturgical forms within the bounds of Catholic unity. Even in the light of the (relatively recent) centralization of liturgical matters in the West following the Council of Trent, different uses

---

1 See *Catechism of the Catholic Church* [CCC], n. 813.   2 CCC 814.
3 CCC 815.

of the Roman rite (Lyon, Braga, the religious orders) and even whole rites (Ambrosian, Mozarabic) have been seen as rich expressions of the legitimate diversity that is possible within the One True Church of Christ. In 2007 Pope Benedict XVI established that the *usus antiquior* of the Roman rite — which was never abrogated — rightly takes its place in this unity in diversity, and a generation of Catholics have now grown up in that light.

It is certainly true that some of our brethren have — very noisily — adopted some of the sectarian and divisive positions about which the Holy Father is so rightly concerned. I sought to address some of these issues, and others also, in our "Time after Pentecost 2021" monastery newsletter. For those who celebrate the *usus antiquior* have no excuse to perpetuate division and strife in the Church. Our Christian lives must be exemplary, each according to our particular vocation.

So too, we have no business other than to affirm the Second Vatican Council as a legitimate Ecumenical Council of the Church and to hold as true that which any Ecumenical Council, including the most recent one, defines to be a matter of faith. The authoritative disciplinary decisions of a Council and the prudential judgements they contain, however, are not *themselves* articles of faith that are included in the profession of faith required of those being received into full communion with the Church: "I believe and profess all that the holy Catholic Church believes, *teaches*, and proclaims *to be revealed by God*."[4]

For example, one *could* hold the opinion that the Second Vatican Council's call for full, conscious, actual and fruitful participation in the Sacred Liturgy in its Constitution on the Sacred Liturgy,[5] which echoed the same call made by St. Pius X in 1903 (in *Tra le sollecitudini*) and by the liturgical movement of the first half of the twentieth century, was bad and that it should not have done so, and still remain a Catholic in good standing. The adoption of this policy by the Council is a prudential judgement, not a doctrine of the faith. I hasten to add that in my considered opinion, and in my scholarly and pastoral judgement, such a stance would be downright stupid, unhelpful and indeed destructive of what is one of the soundest liturgical principles enunciated in the twentieth century. Our Holy Father's letter last Friday underlines its importance. We must, however, be clear that it is possible to disagree on matters such as this within the unity of the Church and in the liberty which we each enjoy within her.

Our Holy Father has, seemingly, decided that the *usus antiquior* of the Roman rite no longer rightly has any place in the unity in diversity that is the life of worship of the Catholic Church. The reasons he gives are, as

---

4 *Rite of Christian Initiation of Adults*, n. 491. 5 See *Sacrosanctum Concilium* 14.

mentioned above, very grave indeed. Where these aberrations exist, they must rightly be corrected.

However, it must be said plainly that the *usus antiquior* of the Roman rite as it is celebrated and lived in many if not most communities throughout the world is by no means coterminous with the errors which our Holy Father seeks to correct. On the contrary, as it has been my privilege to experience many times and in many countries, and as I wrote in our last newsletter, full, conscious, actual and fruitful participation in these rites flourishes in these communities, particularly amongst the young. I encourage those who doubt this to visit them and to immerse themselves in their life with open hearts and minds. The reality they will discover is one of faith, beauty and joy — something of which the Fathers of the Second Vatican Council (and indeed, of which its peritus-become-pope) would be proud. I invite those who wish, to do so here, as our guests.

In this context, the command to discard the riches of the *usus antiquior* — about which Pope Benedict wrote so eloquently in his Letter of July 7, 2007 — is disconsonant. In stating that "What earlier generations held as sacred, remains sacred and great for us too, and it cannot be all of a sudden entirely forbidden or even considered harmful," Pope Benedict articulated a truth that is no less true for the passing of a mere fourteen years.

A son who is disobedient or worse will, howsoever grudgingly, accept rebuke and just punishment. But when a father coldly commands his son, under obedience, immediately to commit suicide, he must — and shall rightly — be disobeyed. Should an enraged father lunge at his son with a knife in order to sever his arteries, he must be resisted with means that are proportionate to the danger posed.

Our bishop, our Father in God, who as the Holy Father reminds us is the "visible principle and foundation of unity" of this particular Church, and to whom he assigns the "exclusive competence" to authorize the *usus antiquior* in his diocese, would do neither. He knows perhaps more than many how the *usus antiquior* rightly takes its place in the unity in diversity of the Church, and of the substantial spiritual and pastoral fruits that flow from respecting this reality.

Our little monastery was established because our bishop desired it as a valuable enrichment for his diocese. He will not uproot the vine he has planted. The monastery lives and grows in hierarchical communion with him and through him with the bishop of Rome.

Our community is resolved to pursue its vocation of seeking God through a life or prayer and work according to the *Rule* of Saint Benedict within that unity, and we are confident that our Father in God understands and shall respect and protect the integrity of our life. If we are able to observe the fidelity, charity and patience of which I have recently written, our life shall bear much fruit here, now and in the future.

The fact remains that these are difficult times and that we may see some turbulence in the life and unity of the Church as a result of this new legislation. Because of this I have decided that the monastery, henceforth, each Friday where it is liturgically possible, shall offer a votive Mass *pro Ecclesiæ unitate*. The first shall be on Friday of this week. I invite you to be present, or if that is not possible, I encourage you to pray some of the prayers of this ancient and beautiful Mass. I encourage others to take up this initiative: our first recourse must be to that liturgical worship and adoration of the Blessed Trinity which is the fundament of all prayer. So too I invite you with us to offer your Friday fasting and penance for this intention.

So too, we must continue our work, building up this House of God as an oasis of liturgical integrity and peace amidst the thorns of the world for those who wish to serve the Lord here as monks, and for those who wish, in different ways, to participate in our life regularly or from time to time. As heretofore, we rely on the kindness and generosity of our extended monastic family and friends for the material support necessary to achieve this — a support that is perhaps now all the more urgent.

Saint Benedict instructs his sons that "nothing is to be put before the work of God."[6] My friends, we shall never cease to be faithful to that injunction in our celebration of the daily round of the Sacred Liturgy as beautifully and as richly as we are able, in hierarchical communion with our Bishop and through him with the Successor of Peter, the Bishop of Rome.

We shall continue to pray and work for the unity of the Church in our times and, please God, shall be an instrument of reconciliation for those whose communion with her is somehow impaired. We shall witness to the ongoing pastoral and evangelical value of the liturgical "riches which have developed in the Church's faith and prayer," and of the reality that it is possible, right and good — indeed necessary — "to give them their proper place" in the unity of the Church today.[7]

We place these aspirations at the foot of this altar in this Mass. We beg the intercession of the saints in winning for us the grace of perseverance unto the end. And we ask your prayers and your practical help in achieving them, for the Glory of Almighty God and the salvation of souls.

---

6 Holy Rule, ch. 43.   7 Benedict XVI, Letter *Con Grande Fiducia*, July 7, 2007.

13

Nine Reflections on
Traditionis Custodes

PHILLIP CAMPBELL

Unam Sanctam Catholicam

July 19, 2021

PAPA FRANCESCO SURE STIRRED UP SOME LÍO WITH his new motu proprio. If Francis is concerned about the growth of traditionalism that rejects the postconciliar Church, giving the SSPX their single biggest marketing boost of all time is certainly a strange way to show it. Many people more astute than I have already commented on *Traditionis Custodes* extensively, so I will try not to repeat their talking points. Here are nine reflections on it.

First, the antithesis between Francis and Benedict. Some are saying this isn't a repudiation of Benedict XVI's *Summorum Pontificum*. They are arguing that those who are saying so are being unnecessarily partisan and dramatic. Have these people even read these documents? We need to start by realizing that *Summorum Pontificum* did not "legalize" or "allow" or "liberalize" the Traditional Latin Mass. It did not make the Latin Mass available by positive decree; rather, it stated the principle that the Latin Mass could never truly have been abrogated and, therefore, by consequence was (and is) always allowed. *Traditionis Custodes*, on the other hand, completely repudiates that principle. It's not just that it suppresses something that Benedict XVI allowed; it's that by presuming to suppress the traditional liturgy by papal dictate, it contradicts the principle elucidated in *Summorum Pontificum* while giving no explanation of why or how that is possible. But that's par for the course these days; the modern magisterium creates continuity by merely declaring it.[1] We are to accept that continuity and harmony exist merely because we are told they do.

Second, Francis's motu proprio was issued out of an expressed concern that traditional communities foster a divisive spirit, believing that they alone are "the true church." What does this even mean? Does this refer to traditionalists who literally think the Church presided over by Francis is

---

1 See "The Phantasm of Fiat Continuity," *Unam Sanctam Catholicam*, May 6, 2016.

a false church? That Francis is a false pope? Or perhaps it merely means the belief that the Traditional Latin Mass reflects the authentic heart of our faith? It's hard to say. *Traditionis Custodes* does not elaborate on what the false premises affirmed by these divisive traditionalists actually consist of. It is impossible to determine when and whether someone is guilty of thinking they are "the true church," as the document provides no explanation of this new and dangerous schism, which is nevertheless so grave as to justify suppressing an entire rite. It is meant to cast suspicion on an entire subsection of the Church.

The crux of the matter is this: there is a subtle transmutation being wrought upon word "schism," morphing it from a canonical status into an *attitude*. It is very difficult to pin the canonical state of schism upon somebody; it is extremely easy to accuse someone of having a "schismatic attitude." I think most uses of the word "schism" I see on social media these days are in the context of an attitude rather than an objectively existing canonical state. Basically, "schismatic attitude" has become the catchphrase to denote anyone who posts mean things online about the current regime. Its definition is so broad it means nothing; its used the way Wokies use the word "racism." Also, the fact that the Holy Father is taking punitive action against an *attitude* is horrifying. And this isn't even speculation; Francis says plainly in his accompanying letter that his edict is prompted by "words and attitudes."

As for real schism, the number of traditionalist groups or parishes that have gone into schism during the pontificate of Francis is zero.

Third, if there *are* traditional Catholics who literally believe that they and they alone are the "true Church," they must number only a few thousand worldwide. And apparently we are to believe that this tiny sliver of a demographic poses an existential threat to the unity of a communion of one billion believers? But fear not! As a remedy, we shall herd every Catholic who loves the Latin Mass into one or two parishes in a diocese, place draconian restrictions on them, functionally ban them celebrating in new parishes or even with new priests, and then we're going to let them stew in an age of social media. Sounds like a winning plan for unity. The harshness of this diktat is surpassed only by its sheer imbecility.

Fourth, even if there is a real threat of schism, it is exceptionally bizarre to suppress a legitimate rite because of such concerns. Canonically speaking, it is *persons*, not rites, who are the objects of legislation in such cases. Consider this nugget of history: during the pontificate of Bl. Pius IX, Chaldean Patriarch Joseph VI Audo was frequently at odds with the Vatican. Most notable were his efforts to bring the Syro-Malabar Catholics of India under his jurisdiction, sending the Bishop of Aqra, Mar Elias Mellus, to India as his envoy in 1874 to accomplish this. Mar Elias was actually excommunicated for fomenting schism there. This did not stop Joseph Audo, who continued to consecrate various bishops without prior consultation with Rome in the following years, effectively setting up a rival hierarchy in India. In September 1876, Pope Pius IX eventually threatened to excommunicate the Patriarch and the bishops he had consecrated if they remained disobedient. Patriarch Audo finally submitted to the pope, who then commended him for his compliance and recognized all his episcopal appointments outside of India. Bishop Mellus also reconciled with the Holy See and went on to become the Bishop of Mardin.

This story is noteworthy because the promotion of the Chaldean rite in India was directly linked to the establishment of a rival and schismatic hierarchy in a blatant usurpation of ecclesiastical jurisdiction. Nevertheless, Pius IX made no attempt to limit the use of the Chaldean rite, despite the serious threat of schism. Canonical penalties were imposed against the persons fomenting schism. A rite itself is not the proper subject of these types of canonical penalties. I hope more commentators and canonists start pointing out how truly bizarre the rationale of *Traditionis Custodes* is in this regard.

Fifth, Francis's accompanying letter says, "Most people understand the motives that prompted St. John Paul II and Benedict XVI to allow the use of the Roman Missal, promulgated by St. Pius V and edited by St. John XXIII in 1962, for the Eucharistic Sacrifice. The faculty granted by the indult of the Congregation for Divine Worship in 1984 and confirmed by St. John Paul II in the motu proprio *Ecclesia Dei* in 1988 was above all motivated by the desire to foster the healing of the schism with the movement of Mons. Lefebvre." This is demonstrably false. The indult was not set up to heal the schism with the SSPX. Rather, the indult was set up to create a home for the faithful who loved the Latin Mass but nevertheless did not want to follow the SSPX into formal schism. That is to say, the object of John Paul II's legislation was the faithful who did *not want* to join the SSPX; but Pope Francis says that the object of John Paul's legislation was the SSPX. This is a colossal blunder.

Sixth, despite the motu proprio's insistence that the abuses in the Novus Ordo be checked, we all know that that will never happen. If Francis is really concerned about Catholics dissenting from Church teaching, then *Traditionis Custodes* is like pulling the speck from the traditionalists' eye without removing the plank in the eye of the Novus Ordo. Polls consistently show that 89% of Catholics reject papal authority to teach on the immorality of contraception; 51% reject papal teaching on abortion. And 69% of Catholics do not believe in transubstantiation.[2] Is the Holy Father distressed about this? Is he going to take decisive action against these people?

Of course not. The double standard does not invalidate the weight of *Traditionis Custodes* (whatever that may be), but it does destroy any pretense of good will on the part of the Holy Father, and it destroys any likelihood that the faithful will receive this with docility. In the face of such brazen injustice, the prospect of traditional Catholics just rolling over and accepting this is ridiculous. This is just going to cause more trouble. And it was 100% avoidable. What a waste. Talk about fights that did not need to happen.

Seventh, as for you self-hating trads who are saying, "We asked for this and we're getting what we deserved," and "the Holy Father's assessment of traditionalism must be correct," I can't imagine what sort of mental torture you must put yourself through to square these circles. I understand that traditional Catholics can be toxic; I've whined about it just recently. But if you think the bad attitudes of a few online traddies merit the global suppression of an entire rite — and not just any rite, but the preeminent historical rite of Latin Christendom — then you are infinitely more unbalanced than the boogey-man trads you are wringing your hands about. This is akin to amputating a hand to fix a hangnail.

Eighth, one of the most laughable passages in the accompanying letter is where the pope says, "Whoever wishes to celebrate with devotion according to earlier forms of the liturgy can find in the reformed Roman Missal according to Vatican Council II all the elements of the Roman Rite, in particular the Roman Canon which constitutes one of its more distinctive elements."

This is a frighteningly reductionist view of the liturgy. There is a certain attitude amongst conservative Catholics that the only thing that matters in the liturgy is a valid Eucharist. "It's still Jesus!" they would predictably intone, as the balloons ascended, and the sanctuary was filled with the strumming of guitars. This represents a radical minimalist view of the liturgy, reducing the Mass down to its most barebones component and rejoicing that we at least still have the *sine qua non* of the liturgy. Pope Francis evidences a similar view with his statement that boils down the entire liturgical tradition of the West to just the Roman Canon. "What are you complaining about? You have the Roman Canon." If that's the pope's view of continuity, then literally nothing in the Church is safe from his novelty. I hope more people

---

2   See Gregory A. Smith, "Just one-third of U. S. Catholics agree with their church that Eucharist is body, blood of Christ," *Pew Research Center*, August 5, 2019.

realize what a horrifically reductionist hermeneutic this is. It's as if after years of feeding my children healthy, balanced meals, I suddenly throw them outside and tell them to eat insects. And when they complain that they can't survive on insects, I dismissively say, "It's still protein."

Ninth, "what are we to do?" That's really what everyone wants to know. To this I shrug. I don't know. But I will say two things:

1. Traditional Catholics have a tendency towards scrupulosity. We worry *way* too much about rules, about minutiae, about jots and tittles. And the current situation just exacerbates scrupulous anxieties. This development has put many of us in extremely challenging dilemmas that no Catholic should ever have to be in. No Catholic should have to pit pope against liturgy, obedience against worship, fidelity to tradition against the living magisterium. In these dilemmas, we cannot afford to be overly scrupulous. I'm speaking to laypeople, but also bishops and priests. We are way too litigious in the West. With everything that's going on in the world and the Church, with civilization falling apart and the Church in total chaos, with all the confusion and misinformation and lies and double-standards being vomited forth from the hierarchy on a daily basis, do you *really* think God is laying the responsibility entirely on your shoulders for determining the precise canonical status of that independent chapel? Just do what you need to do and don't worry too much about the fine print.

2. As awful as this situation is, I always try to remember that the Mass is not my faith. It's an integral part of how I live my faith, but my faith is much bigger than the Mass. I make this point because people will message me and say "This is damaging my faith." I don't know if they really mean that, in the sense that this is making them believe in God less; sometimes I think they just mean "This is making it challenging for me to live my faith." The Latin Mass is an absolute treasure. But God doesn't owe you the Mass. He gives it, and He can remove it. If deprivation of access to the Latin Mass actually makes you lose your faith, what would you have done in Japan all those centuries when the Catholics there had no Mass? Or in Elizabethan England? Would you have simply lost faith? Many of the Desert Fathers didn't even go to Mass at all; nor immured nuns in the Middle Ages, nor many of the hermits.

God is still on the throne. Jesus is still risen from the dead. I am still redeemed by His blood and incorporated into His body through the sacred font of baptism. Has any of that changed? No. None of it has changed, and therefore my faith is unchanged. I don't mean to diminish the importance of the Mass in any way; but if your actual faith in God is predicated upon a certain level of access to the Traditional Mass, where will your faith be when it becomes even more difficult in ages to come? I am not insulting you if your faith is being challenged. Rather, I am challenging you to go back to the basics, the unchanging truths that no prelate can touch. Have faith in God. And I'm not talking about "Have faith that the Traditional Latin Mass will triumph!" or "Have faith that some future pope will reverse all this." I mean have faith that God is with us, that the blood of Christ had freed us from sin, and that in Him we can live a life of grace and holiness — even if these disorders are never remedied unto the very ending of the world.

Even if the hierarchy has control over the exterior forms of our worship, it has no control over my spiritual life. Even though those forms of worship are meant to nourish my spiritual life, they can't ultimately be identified with it. The life I have in Christ is "an inheritance which is imperishable, undefiled, and unfading, kept in heaven" (1 Pet. 1:3–4). And that will never be touched, even though a pope worse than Francis should destroy ten times as much. *Christus regnat.*

14

Making the Celebration of the Eucharist a Battleground†

MARTIN GRICHTING

LifeSiteNews

July 19, 2021

AS A PRIEST BORN IN 1967, WHO HAS NEVER CELE-
brated the Extraordinary Form of the Holy Mass and who, because of his
rather sober character, has no intention of ever doing so, it is perhaps easier
for me than it is for those directly concerned to give an assessment of the
situation that has arisen following the publication of the motu proprio
Traditionis Custodes of July 16, 2021.

This legal decree is an expression of fear, the fear that in free circumstances
a form of liturgy could be preserved and even expanded in the younger
generation (priests and laity). The legal text is at the same time an admission
that the liturgy created after the Second Vatican Council has apparently not
sufficiently reached the hearts of the faithful, so that many more want to
return to a form that is not only intellectualistic, but also gives a spiritual
home to the reasons of the heart of which reason knows nothing. As martial
as the decree of law comes across, it is a sign of weakness. It proves against
its own wishes that serious mistakes were obviously made in the reform of
the liturgy after Vatican II and that one must now try by force to prevent its
definitive derailment. It seems to be a bad state of affairs for the reformed
liturgy if one thinks that one has to protect it in this draconian form.

This decree definitely makes the celebration of the Eucharist, "the
source and summit of the whole Christian life" (*Lumen Gentium* 11), a bat-
tleground — the heart of Christian life, of all things! For this legal text, in
its rigidity, after all that has happened in the last fifty years, is so hurtful
and humiliating for those involved that it can only provoke resistance,
hopefully peaceful and spiritual, and different from the spirit of exclusion
and hardening by which it is generated.

---

† The German original (which appeared at *kath.net* on July 20) was translated by Maike
Hickson and published at *LifeSiteNews* under the title "How should we continue after
Traditionis Custodes?"

The banishment of this form of the liturgy from parish churches, where in some cases it had been peacefully at home for decades, means giving an incentive for an Underground Church of a new kind. One should have learned by now what the consequences of abrogating edicts of tolerance can be. The split brought about by the decree will first be a local one. However, since the faithful of different liturgical forms will now meet even less often physically, there will subsequently be an increased social, pastoral, and even ecclesiological segregation of the faithful. Moreover, chapels will not be available everywhere. There will not always be enough space in such [non-parochial] churches, which are by nature rather small. Holy Mass will most probably therefore be celebrated more often in private houses, in secret, or in secular halls. The spirit of conspiracy thus fostered will give rise all the more to conspiratorial groups.

It will be difficult in the future for those affected by the motu proprio not to live in a hardening of feelings. To them, guidance might be therefore given by a letter the Prophet Jeremiah sent to the people who had been led into Babylonian captivity. They are words of wisdom and foresight, in the face of humiliation and exclusion:

> These are the words of the letter that the prophet Jeremiah sent from Jerusalem to the remaining elders among the exiles, and to the priests, the prophets, and all the people, whom Nebuchadnezzar had taken into exile from Jerusalem to Babylon. . . . Thus says the Lord of hosts, the God of Israel, to all the exiles whom I have sent into exile from Jerusalem to Babylon: Build houses and live in them; plant gardens and eat what they produce. Take wives and have sons and daughters; take wives for your sons, and give your daughters in marriage, that they may bear sons and daughters; multiply there, and do not decrease. But seek the welfare of the city where I have sent you into exile, and pray to the Lord on its behalf, for in its welfare you will find your welfare. (Jer. 29:1, 4–7)

In his work *Zeitfragen und christlicher Glaube* [Questions of the Time and the Christian Faith] (1983), Joseph Ratzinger remarked on this letter of Jeremiah that it was "by no means an instruction for action, for political resistance, for the destruction of the slave state." And the future Pope commented on the letter in this way: "It is rather an instruction for the preservation and strengthening of the good. It is thus an instruction for survival and at the same time for the preparation of the better, the new."

15

Francis:
The Pope of Exclusion†

JEAN-PIERRE MAUGENDRE

Renaissance Catholique

July 19, 2021

THE TRUCE WAS SHORT-LIVED: 2007–2021. WITH THE motu proprio *Traditionis Custodes*, Pope Francis has re-launched the liturgical war that his predecessor, with the motu proprio *Summorum Pontificum*, had suspended. Everyone agrees on the subject: the measure is brutal. Henceforth, the liturgical books subsequent to Vatican II become "the only expression of the *lex orandi* of the Roman Rite"; the missal prior to the reform of 1970 cannot be used regularly in parish churches; no new group can be established; the Apostolic See must give diocesan priests authorization to celebrate according to the *usus antiquior*, etc. Jean-Marie Guénois has nicely formulated the objective of these measures: "to reduce the influence of traditionalists."

This influence, in fact, continues to grow. The traditionalists regularly furnish about 20% of the annual priestly ordinations in France and constitute a notable presence in the dioceses, 5 to 6% of the total number of churchgoers in our country according to Guillaume Cuchet (*La Nef* n°338), and certainly more in reality because of the massive dropping off (30% according to Bishop Chauvet) of many "conciliar" faithful, noticeably older than their traditionalist counterparts, as a result of the coronavirus pandemic.

THE REASONS FOR EXCLUSION

Everyone is asking questions. Why such a harsh measure from a pope who, to say the least, has a lot of other work to do: repeated financial scandals, the quasi-schismatic situation of the German Church, immense doctrinal and liturgical confusion, the collapse of Peter's Pence, the aftermath of the pedophilia scandals in the Church, the sexual orgies in the Vatican, etc.?

The argument put forward by the Holy Father is that these communities "doubting the Council" would jeopardize the unity of the Church of which

---

† Translated from the French by Zachary Thomas and Peter Kwasniewski for this anthology.

the Pope is the guarantor. Were it not for the seriousness of the subject, this argument would be laughable. What "unity" is there in a Church where:
- no two Masses celebrated in two different churches are identical;
- in one diocese, remarried divorcees are admitted to Holy Communion, but not in another;
- 69% of American Catholics say they do not believe in the substantial presence of Christ under the appearances of bread and wine after consecration (Pew Research Center Survey, August 2019);
- with impunity, German priests bless homosexual unions in their churches, decorated with rainbow colors, etc.

The pope who signed the Abu Dhabi declaration affirming that "the diversity of religions is willed by God in his wisdom" writes in the letter to the bishops accompanying the motu proprio: "To remain in the Church not only 'with the body' but also 'with the heart' is a condition of salvation." One thinks of La Fontaine's fable of the Bat and the Two Weasels: "I am a bird: see my wings . . . I am a mouse: long live the rats!" A far cry from the "yes, yes, no, no" of the Gospel.

Moreover, how do those who often attend the traditional Mass and wish to benefit from a sacramental and catechetical pastoral ministry that has proven its worth, harm the unity of the Church? Why should we stigmatize them? "They would refuse to accept the Council." To be frank, the vast majority of them could not care less about the Council, which does not interest them and which seems to them to be a whim of ideological and nostalgic old men. What these faithful are asking for is a liturgy that leads them to God and a moral and doctrinal teaching that allows them to remain faithful to Christ and thus to resist the seductions of an apostate society.

"LET US TRY THE EXPERIMENT OF TRADITION"

In the 1970s, Archbishop Lefebvre's original and founding intuition was summed up in one formula: "Let us try the experiment of Tradition." This experiment has been made and the fruits are before our eyes. The traditional apostolate, whatever its institutional framework, is undeniably fruitful. The communities have grown and spurred many conversions. Young and large families keep them alive — the famous "rabbits" who try to remain faithful to the requirements of Christian marriage, whom Francis mocked with distasteful humor.

Note that, according to the pope, the objective of the liturgical concessions of his predecessors was to bring back the lost Lefebvrist sheep "in due course to the Roman rite promulgated by Saints Paul VI and John Paul II." This is clearly not what happened, contrary to what some feared, denouncing the inexorable "*ralliement*" of traditional priests and laity who would seek a legal agreement with the Roman authorities. The experiment having been a success, it was decided to . . . end the experiment?! Christ asked us to judge the tree by its fruit and to throw the *barren* fig tree into the fire — not the tree that bears fruit. Fifty years after its conclusion, the good fruits of the Council (according to its supporters) still haven't appeared, yet the harvest will be coming soon . . .

WHO ACTUALLY BELIEVES THIS?

Basically this motu proprio seems to mark the end of Benedict XVI's attempt to establish a hermeneutic of continuity between the Second Vatican Council and the Church's earlier teaching. His belief in the continuity between preconciliar and postconciliar teaching explains his form of benevolence toward the traditional Mass. In contrast, Francis's militant hostility to the traditional Mass manifests the conviction that "the conciliar Church" (to use Cardinal Benelli's expression) is of a different nature from the Church that preceded it. One does not reject with such violence those whose only fault is to be fifty years behind. On the other hand, one fights fiercely against those who are believed to be the followers of another Church. Thus, paradoxically, Pope Francis agrees on this point with the positions of the Society of Saint Pius X.

EVERYTHING HAS TO CHANGE SO THAT NOTHING WILL CHANGE

In reality, it seems that not much will change. This motu proprio is inapplicable. It will freeze the situation but will not reduce the influence of the traditionalist communities. Indeed:

• the Pope is 85 years old and his position is very weakened;

• a certain number of bishops are happy with the activity of the traditionalist communities;

• some bishops, especially in France, have enough to worry about. They know, for example, that withdrawing the use of parish churches from traditionalist communities would inevitably lead to demonstrations, church occupations, etc. Several cautious bishops immediately said that nothing would change in their dioceses.

Finally, we must not overlook the fact that public opinion, Catholic or not, does not understand the reasons for this ostracism by a Supreme Pontiff who talks only of mercy, acceptance, forgiveness, respect for the other, etc. The sparkling editorial by Michel Onfray, a self-proclaimed atheist ("Ite missa est," *Le Figaro*, July 19 [1]), is a clear sign of this incomprehension.

In a conference in Paris on June 25, Bishop Schneider, when asked about the possible suppression of *Summorum Pontificum*, did not hesitate to declare: "The faithful and the priests have the right to a liturgy that is the liturgy of all the saints.... In consequence the Holy See does not have the power to suppress a heritage of the whole Church. That would be an abuse, even on the part of bishops. In this case, you can continue to celebrate the Mass in this form: it is a form of obedience ... to all the popes who have celebrated this Mass."

One cannot conclude without observing the feeling of betrayal experienced by priests and laity attached to the traditional liturgy, who had trusted the Roman authorities, who had been promised freedom of worship and respect for their convictions. They probably did not imagine that they would be treated like Indians on a reservation...

Without bitterness or revolt, we assume this new trial in prayer, serene, confident, and determined, strengthened each day in our fidelity by the first words of the traditional Mass: *Introibo ad altare Dei, ad Deum qui laetificat juventutem meam.* "I will go up to the altar of God: to God who gives joy to my youth."

---

1 See chapter 17.

16

Distinguishing Unity from Uniformity[†]

CARDINAL GERHARD MÜLLER

The Catholic Thing

July 19, 2021

THE POPE'S INTENTION WITH HIS MOTU PROPRIO TRA-*ditionis Custodes* is to secure or restore the unity of the Church. The proposed means for this is the total unification of the Roman Rite in the form of the Missal of Paul VI (including its subsequent variations). Therefore, the celebration of Mass in the Extraordinary Form of the Roman Rite, as introduced by Pope Benedict XVI with *Summorum Pontificum* (2007) on the basis of the Missal that existed from Pius V (1570) to John XXIII (1962), has been drastically restricted. The clear intent is to condemn the Extraordinary Form to extinction in the long run.

In his "Letter to the Bishops of the Whole World," which accompanies the motu proprio, Pope Francis tries to explain the motives that have caused him, as the bearer of the supreme authority of the Church, to limit the liturgy in the Extraordinary Form. Beyond the presentation of his subjective reactions, however, a stringent and logically comprehensible theological argumentation would also have been appropriate. For papal authority does not consist in superficially demanding from the faithful mere obedience, i.e., a formal submission of the will, but, much more essentially, in enabling the faithful also to be convinced with consent of the mind. As St. Paul, courteous towards his often quite unruly Corinthians, said, "in the church I would rather speak five words with my mind, so as to instruct others also, than ten thousand words in tongues" (1 Cor 14:19).

This dichotomy between good intention and poor execution always arises where the objections of competent employees are perceived as an obstruction of their superiors' intentions, and which are, therefore, not even offered. As welcome as the references to Vatican II may be, care must be taken to

---

† Originally published in English under the title "Cardinal Mueller on the New TLM Restrictions." Translated from the text of His Eminence by Robert Royal and Msgr. Hans Feichtinger.

ensure that the Council's statements are used precisely and in context. The quotation from St. Augustine about membership in the Church "according to the body" and "according to the heart" (*Lumen Gentium* 14) refers to the full Church membership of the Catholic faith. It consists in the visible incorporation into the body of Christ (creedal, sacramental, ecclesiastical-hierarchical communion) as well as in the union of the heart, i.e., in the Holy Spirit. What this means, however, is not obedience to the pope and the bishops in the discipline of the sacraments, but sanctifying grace, which fully involves us in the invisible Church as communion with the Triune God.

For the unity in the confession of the revealed faith and the celebration of the mysteries of grace in the seven sacraments by no means require sterile uniformity in the external liturgical form, as if the Church were like one of the international hotel chains with their homogenous design. The unity of believers with one another is rooted in unity in God through faith, hope, and love and has nothing to do with uniformity in appearance, the lockstep of a military formation, or the groupthink of the big-tech age.

Even after the Council of Trent, there always was a certain diversity (musical, celebratory, regional) in the liturgical organization of Masses. The intention of Pope Pius V was not to suppress the variety of rites, but rather to curb the abuses that had led to a devastating lack of understanding among the Protestant Reformers regarding the substance of the sacrifice of the Mass (its sacrificial character and Real Presence). In the Missal of Paul VI, ritualistic (rubricist) homogenization is broken up, precisely in order to overcome a mechanical execution in favor of an inner and outer active participation of all believers in their respective languages and cultures. The unity of the Latin rite, however, should be preserved through the same basic liturgical structure and the precise orientation of the translations to the Latin original.

The Roman Church must not pass on its responsibility for unity in cult to the Bishops' Conferences. Rome must oversee translation of the normative texts of the Missal of Paul VI, and even of the biblical texts, that might obscure the contents of the faith. Presumptions that one may "improve" the *verba Domini* — e.g., *pro multis* ("for many") at the consecration, the *et ne nos inducas in tentationem* ("and lead us not into temptation") in the Our Father — contradict the truth of the faith and the unity of the Church much more than celebrating Mass according to the Missal of John XXIII.

The key to a Catholic understanding of the liturgy lies in the insight that the substance of the sacraments is given to the Church as a visible sign and means of the invisible grace by virtue of divine law, but that it is

64

up to the Apostolic See and, in accordance with the law, to the bishops to order the external form of the liturgy (insofar as it has not already existed since apostolic times).[1]

The provisions of *Traditionis Custodes* are of a disciplinary nature, not a dogmatic one, and can be modified again by any future pope. Naturally, the pope, in his concern for the unity of the Church in the revealed faith, is to be fully supported when the celebration of Holy Mass according to the Missal of 1962 is an expression of resistance to the authority of Vatican II, which is to say, when the doctrine of the faith and the Church's ethics are relativized or even denied in the liturgical and pastoral order.

In *Traditionis Custodes*, the pope rightly insists on the unconditional recognition of Vatican II. Nobody can call himself a Catholic who either wants to go back behind Vatican II (or any other council recognized by the pope) as the time of the "true" Church or wants to leave that Church behind as an intermediate step towards a "new Church." One may measure Pope Francis's will to return to unity the deplored so-called "traditionalists" (i.e., those opposed to the Missal of Paul VI) against the degree of his determination to put an end to the innumerable "progressivist" abuses of the liturgy (renewed in accordance with Vatican II) that are tantamount to blasphemy. The paganization of the Catholic liturgy — which is in its essence nothing other than the worship of the One and Triune God — through the mythologization of nature, the idolatry of environment and climate, as well as the Pachamama spectacle, were rather counterproductive for the restoration and renewal of a dignified and orthodox liturgy reflective of the fullness of the Catholic faith.

Nobody can turn a blind eye to the fact that even those priests and laypeople who celebrate Mass according to the order of the Missal of St. Paul VI are now being widely decried as traditionalist. The teachings of Vatican II on the uniqueness of redemption in Christ, the full realization of the Church of Christ in the Catholic Church, the inner essence of the Catholic liturgy as adoration of God and mediation of grace, Revelation and its presence in Scripture and Apostolic Tradition, the infallibility of the magisterium, the primacy of the pope, the sacramentality of the Church, the dignity of the priesthood, the holiness and indissolubility of marriage — all these are being heretically denied in open contradiction to Vatican II by a majority of German bishops and lay functionaries (even if disguised under pastoral phrases).

---

1 *Sacrosanctum Concilium* 22 § 1.

And despite all the apparent enthusiasm they express for Pope Francis, they are flatly denying the authority conferred on him by Christ as the successor of Peter. The Congregation for the Doctrine of the Faith's document about the impossibility of legitimizing same-sex and extramarital sexual contacts through a blessing is ridiculed by German (and not only German) bishops, priests, and theologians as merely the opinion of under-qualified curial officials. Here we have a threat to the unity of the Church in revealed faith, reminiscent of the magnitude of the Protestant secession from Rome in the sixteenth century. Given the disproportion between the relatively modest response to the massive attacks on the unity of the church in the German "Synodal Way" (as well as in other pseudo-reforms) and the harsh disciplining of the old rite minority, the image of the misguided fire brigade comes to mind, which, instead of saving the blazing house, first saves the small barn next to it.

Without the slightest empathy, one ignores the religious feelings of the (often young) participants in the Masses according to the Missal of John XXIII (1962). Instead of appreciating the smell of the sheep, the shepherd here hits them hard with his crook. It also seems simply unjust to abolish celebrations of the old rite just because it attracts some problematic people: *abusus non tollit usum.*

What deserves special attention in *Traditionis Custodes* is the use of the axiom *lex orandi—lex credendi* ("rule of prayer—rule of faith"). This phrase appears first in the anti-Pelagian *Indiculus* ("Against superstitions and paganism") which spoke about "the sacraments of priestly prayers, handed down by the apostles to be celebrated uniformly all over the world and in the entire Catholic Church, so that the rule of prayer is the rule of faith" (Denzinger-Hünermann, *Enchiridion symbolorum* 3). This refers to the *substance* of the sacraments (in signs and words) but not the *liturgical rite*, of which there were several (with different variants) in the patristic era. One cannot simply declare the latest missal to be the only valid norm of the Catholic faith, without first distinguishing between the "part that is unchangeable by virtue of divine institution and the parts that are subject to change" (*Sacrosanctum Concilium* 21). The changing liturgical rites do not represent a different faith, but rather testify to one and the same Apostolic Faith of the Church in its different expressions.

The pope's letter confirms that he allows the celebration according to the older form under certain conditions. He rightly points to the centrality of the Roman Canon in the more recent Missal as the heart of the Roman rite. This guarantees the crucial continuity of the Roman liturgy in its essence, organic development, and inner unity. To be sure, one expects the lovers of the ancient liturgy to recognize the renewed liturgy, just as the followers of the Paul VI Missal also have to confess that Mass according to the Missal of John XXIII is a true and valid Catholic liturgy — that is, it contains the substance of the Eucharist instituted by Christ and, therefore, there is and can only be "the one Mass of all times."

A little more knowledge of Catholic dogmatics and the history of the liturgy could counteract the unfortunate formation of opposing parties and also save the bishops from the temptation to act in an authoritarian, loveless, and narrow-minded manner against the supporters of the "old Mass." The bishops are appointed as shepherds by the Holy Spirit: "Keep watch over yourselves and all the flock of which the Holy Spirit has made you overseers. Be shepherds of the church of God, which he bought with his own blood" (Acts 20:28). They are not merely representatives of a central office, with opportunities for further advancement. The good shepherd can be recognized by the fact that he worries more about the salvation of souls than about recommending himself to a higher authority by subservient "good behavior" (1 Pet 5:1–4). If the law of non-contradiction still applies, one cannot logically castigate careerism in the Church and at the same time promote careerists.

Let us hope that the Congregations for Religious and for Divine Worship, with their new authority, do not become inebriated with power and think they have to wage a campaign of destruction against the communities of the old rite, in the foolish belief that by doing so they are rendering a service to the Church and promoting Vatican II.

If *Traditionis Custodes* is to serve the unity of the Church, that can only mean a unity in faith, which enables us to "come to the perfect knowledge of the Son of God," which is to say, unity in truth and love (cf. Eph 4:12–15).

17

"Ite missa est"†

MICHEL ONFRAY

Le Figaro

July 19, 2021

I AM AN ATHEIST. IT IS WELL KNOWN. BUT I AM INTER-ested in the life of the Catholic Church because it gives us the heartbeat of our Judeo-Christian civilization, now in bad shape.

God is not part of my world, but my world was made possible by the God of the Christians. *Pace* anyone who thinks France began with the Declaration of the Rights of Man — a notion as stupid as the belief that Russia was born in October 1917 — Christianity has built the civilization I call my own and that I feel I can love and defend without beating my breast, without having to ask forgiveness for its faults, without waiting for redemption after confession, contrition, and getting on my knees.

How foolish they who despise Christianity and pretend it never happened, yet are as soaked in it as rum cakes!

Benedict XVI was a philosopher pope, formed in German hermeneutics and phenomenology. He also read the French Catholic authors directly. His *Jesus of Nazareth* (2012) is part of the history of German idealism, notably of "right" Hegelianism, so-called to distinguish it from the "left" Hegelianism that led to the young Marx.

Pope Francis is not on the same level theologically, far from it. But he is amply supplied with a Jesuitical cunning evident in his choice, though he is a member of the Society of Jesus, of a papal name worlds apart from the intrigues and anterooms of power where Jesuits love to linger: that of Saint Francis of Assisi. Jorge Mario Bergoglio is a chemist by training and comes out of Peronism; Joseph Ratzinger a theologian who comes from anti-Nazism.

The major act of Pope Benedict XVI's pontificate, to my mind, was his address at Regensburg. There, on September 12, 2006, in the German university where he had once been a professor, he did his job as a pope, evaluating the antinomic relationship that exists between Christianity and Islam on a

---

† Freshly translated from the French by Zachary Thomas for this anthology. © Michel Onfray / Le Figaro / 18.07.2021.

textual level, particularly over the question of faith and reason, but also on the question of violence in general and that of jihad in particular. I say "on the textual level" because, in fact, he presented his own interpretation of a dialogue written at the beginning of the fifteenth century between the Byzantine Emperor Manuel II Paleologus and a learned Persian. His invitation to reflection on this question was received as a global insult against Islam...

Pope Francis's major act, again in my opinion, has been to be photographed in front of a crucifix on which Jesus is wearing the orange safety vest of the migrants.[1] Here we have the triumphant icon of Vatican II — that council that pitched everything sacred and transcendent in exchange for a meager moraline sent out on a planetary scale like a girl-scout cookie.

This is the context in which we need to understand Pope Francis's decision to abrogate (to use a profane word) the decision taken by Benedict XVI to permit the use of the Mass in Latin, known as the Tridentine Mass, for those who desire it. In *Summorum Pontificum*, Benedict XVI liberalized the Mass of Pius V. In *Traditionis Custodes*, Francis cancels this liberality. Benedict XVI wanted to overcome the schism with the traditionalists, Francis is going to restore it. Once a Jesuit, always a Jesuit, he'll do it on the pretext that he is actually uniting what he is separating. Vocations collapsed after Vatican II. But the religious who have kept the Latin rite do not suffer this malaise. Their seminaries are full. Pope Francis prefers to have churches empty, as long as they're under the sway of his ideas, than full under those of Benedict XVI.

Division ... is that not the prerogative of ... the devil? It's in the etymology. If I had the Catholic faith, I couldn't help but think of the Letter of John where it says: "Every spirit that dissolveth Jesus, is not of God: and this is Antichrist, of whom you have heard that he cometh, and he is now already in the world" (1 John 4:3).

What is at stake in this affair is the aftermath of Vatican II, or to put it simply, the abolition of the sacred and the transcendent. The laicization of the rite, reduced to a liturgy in which *Life is a long quiet river*,[2] has proven its compelling power, with its hip pastor who plays the guitar while inanely cooing: "Jesus, Je-e-e-e-sus, come!" I suppose one is allowed to prefer Gregorian chant without nostalgia for Vichy...

The genius of Christianity, with its differing opinions about the possibility of representing Christ, was to render possible a civilization of allegory, symbolism, and metaphor. The Jewish genius lay in hermeneutics, that of

---

1   See Ines Angeli Murzaku, "The Cross, the Life Jacket, and the Dangers of Idolatry," *Catholic World Report*, December 22, 2019.
2   See https://en.wikipedia.org/wiki/Life_Is_a_Long_Quiet_River.

Christianity in the explication of parables. The Jews invented hermeneutics for the learned, and rabbis wrote lectures on the Kabbalah. Christians worked out a popular hermeneutic, and told stories for the faithful to make sense of in the context of sacred history. Our civilization of the image, of explanatory reason, of philosophy separated from theology, is a product of that world.

The Latin Mass is the patrimony of our civilization. It is the historical and spiritual heir of a long sacred lineage of rituals, celebrations, and prayers, all crystallized in a form that offers a total spectacle: a *Gesamtkunstwerk*, to use a word from German Romantic aesthetics.

For believers in God, the Latin Mass is to the Mass of the *Long quiet river* (for which Francis has such warm affection) what the Roman basilica of St. Augustine's era is to a multi-purpose hall in a high-rise apartment complex in Aubervilliers: not a place one looks for sacrality and transcendence.

What room is there for spirituality in such places?

Let's put it enigmatically: Pope Francis is doing exactly what he is there to do...

To close with another enigma, but not only that: Why are we living in a time when there are two popes?

18

Francis Reverses Benedict's Legacy

MATTHEW SCHMITZ

The American Conservative

July 19, 2021

POPE BENEDICT HAS OUTLIVED HIS LEGACY. HIS SIG-
nature achievements were moral and liturgical. First as head of the doctrinal congregation under John Paul II and then as pope, he made clear that
Catholics would be expected to live by the Church's unchanging teaching.
When Catholics urged the Church to permit divorce and remarriage, Benedict said no. He rejected the idea that new times call for a new morality.

In liturgical matters, he promoted pluralism and beauty. His outreach to
the Anglicans and opening to traditionalists were the most dramatic parts
of this program. He believed that those attached to the words of Cranmer
or the austere beauties of the Roman Rite should be free to use them. He
hoped that "mutual enrichment" would allow all Catholics to experience
a liturgy that was beautiful.

Almost since the moment of Pope Francis's election, there has been a
steady attack on this twin legacy. But it received its clearest blow on Friday, when Francis issued *Traditionis Custodes*, a document that places fresh
restrictions on the Latin Mass. Back in 2007, Benedict issued *Summorum
Pontificum*, a document that made the use of the Latin Mass, suppressed after
Vatican II, easier. "What earlier generations held as sacred, remains sacred
and great for us too, and it cannot be all of a sudden entirely forbidden or
even considered harmful," he declared.

Francis has now made clear that he disagrees. He writes that the Latin Mass
as it is practiced "contradicts communion, nourishing [a] drive to division."
For the health of the Church, he believes, its use must be restricted, especially among younger priests. This is the legal consummation of his frequent
suggestions that traditionalists are notably nasty, vain, and querulous. If
true, this makes them exactly like all other Catholics. Indeed, all other men.

Benedict is often called a conservative and Francis a liberal. These descrip-
tions are not fully satisfying. Especially in his youth, Benedict could be

theologically adventurous. And despite his closeness to liberals, Francis has often said strikingly reactionary things.[1] There is a better way to understand the differing approaches of the two popes. Benedict believes that Catholic beauty and Catholic morals are not beyond the common man's comprehension. Francis, to all appearances, does not.

This difference first became clear in 2016, when Pope Francis said "the great majority of our sacramental marriages are null" because most Catholics simply do not understand Church teaching. If Catholics don't know what marriage is, they cannot enter it. Some have accused Francis of having a low view of marriage, but the opposite is true. His view of marriage is so high that he places it above the reach of most men.

Contrast this with Benedict, whose papacy reflected a confidence that Catholics can understand what the Church teaches and live by it. For however harsh Benedict may sometimes have seemed, it was precisely this confidence that lay behind his public defense of Catholic truth. The two men do not differ in any substantial way in their understanding of marriage and sexual morality. They differ only in their estimation of whether others can grasp the truths they both believe.

One can see the same divide in the two popes' approach to Catholic liturgy. Benedict is the Pope most associated with classical music. He loves Mozart, a fact the media rarely failed to mention when presenting him as a comic-book villain. But Francis's appreciation for music is far more refined. This was revealed in 2013, when Francis not only listed some of his favorite composers and works, but named his favorite recordings. As Damian Thompson (an accomplished music critic and papal critic alike) has noted,[2] these selections reveal exquisite taste and countless hours of careful listening. Only a man keenly appreciative of beauty and committed to the highest standards of art would engage in such an undertaking.

And yet it is Benedict who devoted the most effort to reviving Catholic music and promoting the liturgy. This is not because he loves music more than Francis does (by all indications, he does not) but because he believes that all Catholics can and should be caught up in the riches of beauty. Francis may listen to the most glorious recordings in his private chambers, but he has been far less concerned to promote the liturgical arts that would make beauty accessible to Catholics at large.

---

1 See, e.g., Jamie Manson, "Pope Francis, women and 'chauvinism with skirts,'" *National Catholic Reporter*, April 24, 2013.

2 See Damian Thompson, "The Mystery of Pope Francis's Infallibly Good Taste in Classical Music," *The Spectator*, March 25, 2021.

Benedict and Francis both believe in the true, good, and beautiful. But Benedict believes that truth, goodness, and beauty are things that can and should be shared. Francis often seems to disagree. One view is more narrow, the other more encompassing. Those who believe that all Catholics can enjoy the riches of the Church's teaching and liturgy will lament the destruction of Benedict's legacy.

19

Does *Traditionis Custodes* Lack Juridical Standing?

PETER A. KWASNIEWSKI

LifeSite News

July 20, 2021

ARTICLE 1 OF THE MOTU PROPRIO *TRADITIONIS CUS-todes* reads: "The liturgical books promulgated by Saint Paul VI and Saint John Paul II, in conformity with the decrees of Vatican Council II, are the only expression [*l'unica espressione*] of the *lex orandi* of the Roman Rite."

The pope here claims that the Novus Ordo is the *only* law of prayer for the Roman Rite. It is impossible to see how this is compatible with the history of the Church and with her reverence for the venerable rites of antiquity and the Middle Ages, epitomized in the *Missale Romanum* of 1570 and its subsequent integral editions. They, too, are the *lex orandi* and cannot be otherwise. Instead, the motu proprio fumblingly makes "*lex orandi*" do duty as a juridical, canonical term, able to be applied *ad libitum*, as if it were an extrinsic label. In reality, the *lex orandi* is the whole complex of historical prayer texts, ceremonies, and music that make up the Roman Rite.

The only way to sustain the fiction of Article 1 is to claim that there is so great a continuity between the old missal and the new missal that the new one is simply an updated version of the old one — that the Novus Ordo is substantially the same as the traditional Roman Rite that preceded it. Francis's letter to the bishops makes just this move:

> It must therefore be considered that the Roman Rite, adapted several times over the centuries to the needs of the times, has not only been preserved but also renewed "in faithful obedience to Tradition." Those who wish to celebrate with devotion according to the previous liturgical form will not find it difficult to find in the *Roman Missal*, reformed according to the mind of the Second Vatican Council, all the elements of the Roman Rite, especially the Roman Canon, which is one of its most characteristic features.

One can only stare in amazement at the flagrant falsehood of this pair of sentences.

As Michael Fiedrowicz has unanswerably demonstrated in his recent book *The Traditional Mass: History, Form, and Theology of the Classical Roman Rite*, the Roman Rite has witnessed many changes over the centuries, but its development has been slow, steady, and continuous, a truly organic body of texts, ceremonies, and music. It was never "adapted" for a particular century by a super-committee treating all the material of the liturgy as raw matter at their disposal to be reorganized, rewritten, and innovated *ad libitum*, with a papal fiat for ensoulment. St. Pius V did not create a new set of liturgical books but codified as carefully as possible the historical practice of the Church of Rome, a *lex orandi* fully expressive of the Catholic Faith that was then under attack by the Protestants. He solemnly established this rite of Mass as a *regula fidei* by his Apostolic Bull Quo Primum of July 14, 1570. This Bull was republished in subsequent editions of the missal by his papal successors, as a sign of continuity in the *lex orandi*, precisely so that the *lex credendi* might be fully preserved and handed down. [1]

In stark contrast, the liturgical books promulgated by Paul VI were fashioned out of bits and pieces of older Western books and non-Western sources, spliced in with new compositions, and unmoored from a linguistic, rubrical, and musical heritage that was shared, with local variations, by all Western Catholics prior to the Reformation. His missal was the first since 1570 *not* to be prefaced with Quo Primum, an eloquent absence that testifies to its discontinuity from the preceding tradition. Call it what you will, this interruption of transmission is what made possible in the first place the confusing situation to which *Summorum Pontificum* was directed as a pastoral response.

Therefore, when Francis asserts that "all the elements of the Roman Rite" will be found in the modern Roman Missal of Paul VI and John Paul II, he is asserting a falsehood, and we need to call him out on that as clearly and

---

1 Quo Primum, after all, is the authoritative declaration that the 1570 missal is the monument of tradition par excellence for the Roman Rite, the definitive expression of the *lex orandi* of the Catholic Church in the sphere that makes use of the Latin rite of Rome. It is the Mass of the Western Fathers. As such, it can never be rendered illegitimate in the Catholic Church. If Pius V was simply "modifying the Missal for the needs of the present day" as has been inanely alleged, why would he dream of giving a permanent sanction for the use of his Missal? He obviously believed this was the core of the Roman liturgical tradition, which no earthly power could undo. People say "Oh, that's just boilerplate language." They should pause and read Quo Primum slowly over again, and ask: Why would any pope describe a liturgical rite in such repeated, emphatic, and solemn language, if he had no intention of conveying with utmost seriousness that this rite is a canonical liturgical expression of the Roman Church's faith of all time, for all time? That does not exclude additions or minor modifications, but it surely renders impossible the idea of replacing it or abolishing it altogether.

as boldly as possible. How vastly the two missals, traditional and modern, contrast and diverge has been the subject of voluminous scholarly studies. [2] I have contributed to this body of work with several lectures that would make for useful reading as we endeavor to respond to the badly-argued and factually erroneous motu proprio:

- "Beyond 'Smells and Bells': Why We Need the Objective Content of the *Usus Antiquior*" (*Rorate Caeli*, November 29, 2019)
- "Two 'Forms' of the Roman Rite: Liturgical Fact or Canonical Fiat?" (*Rorate Caeli*, September 14, 2020)
- "Beyond *Summorum Pontificum*: The Work of Retrieving the Tridentine Heritage" (*Rorate Caeli*, July 14, 2021)
- "The Byzantine Liturgy, the Traditional Latin Mass, and the Novus Ordo — Two Brothers and a Stranger" (*New Liturgical Movement*, June 4, 2018)

Since the claim of substantive continuity and merely superficial revisions cannot be maintained against evidence to the contrary, Pope Benedict in a spirit one might call charitable pragmatism decided to let both of these "traditions" — the one that was centuries old and the one newly-crafted in the sixties — coexist in an unprecedented situation. He could not think of another way to break through the impasse Paul VI's decision had created, and he wished to be as generous as possible to those who continued to adhere to the traditional liturgy, which could not be held against them as a moral fault or in any way opposed to the Faith without simultaneously calling into question the Church's internal coherence. He himself had had many second thoughts about the liturgical reform and saw it as necessary to let the older form — really, a different rite, by all standards — continue in force.

In keeping with the judgment of a commission of cardinals appointed years before by Pope John Paul II, Pope Benedict XVI asserted that the Tridentine rite, which he dubbed "the Extraordinary Form," was "never abrogated." [3] The deeper reason why it was not abrogated, however, is not that Paul VI just forgot to do so, or flubbed the right steps. Rather: "What earlier generations held as sacred, *remains* sacred and great for us too, and

---

2 For a stark example of the rupture and discontinuity, see Matthew Hazell: "'All the Elements of the Roman Rite'? Mythbusting, Part II," *New Liturgical Movement*, October 1, 2021. Hazell demonstrates, with detailed documentation, that only 13% of the orations of the old Missal were preserved intact in the new Missal.

3 *Summorum Pontificum*, Article 1; cf. *Con Grande Fiducia*, "this Missal was never juridically abrogated and, consequently, in principle, was always permitted."

it *cannot* be all of a sudden entirely *forbidden* or even *considered harmful*. It *behooves* all of us to *preserve* the riches which have developed in the Church's faith and prayer, and to give them their proper place."[4]

These are statements of ecclesiological fact: they tell us how things actually are. When he speaks thus, Pope Benedict is not addressing a matter of discipline but expressing truths about the nature of Catholic liturgy in history and its inherent authority as a monument of tradition.

So thoroughly does Francis evacuate Benedict's motu proprio of its theological sense that it seems the new motu proprio "has legislated on the basis of an incomplete argument and false information," as Christophe Geffroy observes.[5] Francis's contradiction of his predecessor on this point is obvious, for *Traditionis Custodes*'s fundamental message is: "What earlier generations held as sacred does *not* remain sacred and great for us too, and it *can* be all of a sudden entirely forbidden and considered harmful. It does *not* behoove all of us to preserve the riches which have developed in the Church's faith and prayer, or to give them any place at all."

What are we to make of this contradiction? One pope or the other is correct, and again, only one can be right, because these are universal truth claims, not prudential determinations. Let's say it again: We are not dealing here with this or that liturgical preference, with giving or withdrawing particular permissions. What is at stake is a theological claim about the objective status of the monuments of liturgical tradition — something that does not depend on a papal decision, unless papal authority is now deemed to extend to rewriting the past, something that theologians maintain not even the omnipotent God can do.

There are at least three falsehoods that play a pivotal role in *Traditionis Custodes*:

1. As we have just discussed, the New Mass is not what he says it is. Valid, to be sure; but by no ingenuity of reasoning, by no metric whatsoever, can it be said to be just another "adaptation" of the same *Missale Romanum*.

2. The motives of John Paul II and Benedict XVI are blatantly misrepresented in Francis's pair of documents, and their theological premises are directly contradicted.

3. The traditional world is not what he says it is — and the results of the touted survey have not been honestly submitted to the public. We know of bishops, especially from the United States, who

---

4   *Con Grande Fiducia*, emphasis added.
5   See chapter 6.

submitted positive reports, something one would never be able to glean from the stern tone of the papal letter. An inside source who works at the Congregation for the Doctrine of the Faith summed up for me the entirety of the survey: "cautiously positive." That sounds nothing like the picture painted by Francis and by the notoriously hostile episcopal conferences of France and Italy. Who are we to trust? The McCarrick scandal was investigated only because of outside pressure; the examination went at a snail's pace; and the final report was inadequate. The Vatican's transparency or penchant for truth-telling does not inspire confidence. Yet bishops are asked to throw flourishing congregations of faithful Catholics under the bus because of supposedly negative survey results — on a "just trust us" basis?

Let me offer a comparison: imagine that a civil authority ordered a beloved city zoo closed because of "frequent and saddening reports" of incidents of animals harming visitors, and because the only people who go to zoos hate animals anyway. But if such incidents were in fact not taking place with any regularity, and the latter claim was outright falsehood and calumny, in what sense would subordinates be *obliged* to close the zoo?

These fallacious claims are the columns upon which Francis's disciplinary directives stand. But common sense and logic bid one to ask: Can a document based on falsehoods have juridical standing? How can it be taken seriously as a juridical instrument? An instrument is vitiated if it is promulgated on a false basis, resulting from the legislator's lack of due knowledge and regnative prudence. In logical form: "Given X, one should do Y. But X is demonstrably false; therefore we refrain from doing Y."

Another hallowed principle from canon law is relevant: a doubtful law does not bind. Many bishops have already indicated the need for careful study before implementing the motu proprio, despite the document going into effect immediately. As they deliberate on what to do, let them keep this in mind: as it stands, between errors, contradictions, and ambiguities, *Traditionis Custodes* is so full of doubtfulness that it is hard to see how one could responsibly act upon it. Given its systemic weaknesses, those who *do* act upon it risk committing sins of imprudence and injustice, sins against charity and ecclesial communion. We cannot fail to note with sorrow how consistently the new provisions fit into the whole pattern of Francis's pontificate, with its fruits of ambiguity and anarchy.

20

A Cry from the Heart about Traditionis Custodes and the Latin Mass[†]

MSGR. CHARLES POPE

National Catholic Register

July 20, 2021

MANY HAVE ALREADY WRITTEN WELL OF THE CONcerns and heartache elicited by the Pope's motu proprio, *Traditionis Custodes*, which sets strict norms limiting the celebration of the Traditional Latin Mass. I have celebrated in this "extraordinary form" (as well as the ordinary form) for more than 32 years and written often of it. Hence, I seek to add my voice.

I must say that I am grieved and stunned by this document and the letter to the bishops that accompanied it. I think not so much of my own potential loss but of the many Catholics I have served who love the extraordinary form. For so long and in so many places they have often been treated harshly and have been marginalized for their love for the form of the liturgy that most of the saints knew.

Pope Benedict and Pope St. John Paul II sought to heal the rift by gradually normalizing the celebration of the older form of the Roman Rite in the life of the Church. In effect they said to such Catholics, "You are important to us. You are our sons and daughters. Your love for the tradition is legitimate and understandable and we have obligations to care for your spiritual needs and well-being."

Here in Washington, D. C., the extraordinary form has existed peacefully alongside the ordinary form in approximately ten of our parishes. We have no parishes exclusively devoted to the celebration of the Latin Mass. While people on both "sides" may have preferences, even strong preferences, there has been mutual respect and a willingness to make room for one another. Whatever tensions do exist, they are minor and not so different than the tensions that emerge from the diverse mosaic of ethnic communities. In

---

this diocese Mass is celebrated in dozens of languages. Some of our Eastern Rite liturgies are also celebrated in our Roman Rite parish churches. We also have one parish that hosts the Anglican liturgical tradition and nearly a dozen who host the Neocatechumenal Way liturgy with all its adaptations. Somehow, we all make room for one another and deal with the logistical challenges well enough.

Apparently, Pope Francis does not see this rich and peaceful diversity when it comes to the Traditional Latin Mass. Instead, he writes to the world's bishops in his cover letter that he sees something very different: "An opportunity offered by St. John Paul II and, with even greater magnanimity, by Benedict XVI, intended to recover the unity of an ecclesial body with diverse liturgical sensibilities, was exploited to widen the gaps, reinforce the divergences, and encourage disagreements that injure the Church, block her path, and expose her to the peril of division." Even if other expressions of diversity may be tolerable or agreeable to him, the Latin Mass seems to be the fly in the ointment. With a special focus that seems overly harsh he attributes blame for divisions to traditional Catholics who attend the Latin Mass.

To be sure, there are some well-known personalities in traditionalist circles who stir up passions about liturgical and other matters, including the authority of the Second Vatican Council. But it is not reasonable to attribute the sins of a vocal minority to an entire movement. Yes, some people advance the superiority and glory of the extraordinary form. But I know many Catholics from Eastern Rites who think their liturgies are vastly preferable and even superior to the Roman Rite. Many Catholics in the Neocatechumenal Way assert that the Church will not experience reform until their liturgy and their "way" is embraced by all. In African American Parishes where I serve there is a great pride in the joy of their worship and a wonderment at why so many other parishes seem to have "dead" and short liturgies.

People are passionate about what they love, sometimes to a fault, but for the majority, this is human and generally kept within a tolerable range of sparring and bluster rather than disgust and deep division. I fear the Pope is using a cannon to kill a fly. I also fear that aspects of the motu proprio have caused great hurt and discouragement to many of the faithful and will intensify the very divisions the Pope laments.

Consider the following aspects.

First, it carries a harsh and heavy-handed tone. Is it really necessary for the Holy Father to write in such a blunt and authoritarian manner? Consider two quotes, one from the letter, the other from the motu proprio:

I take the firm decision to abrogate all the norms, instructions, permissions and customs that precede the present motu proprio, and declare that the liturgical books promulgated by the saintly Pontiffs Paul VI and John Paul II, in conformity with the decrees of Vatican Council II, constitute the unique expression of the *lex orandi* of the Roman Rite.

Everything that I have declared in this apostolic letter in the form of motu proprio, I order to be observed in all its parts, anything else to the contrary notwithstanding, even if worthy of particular mention, and I establish that it be promulgated by way of publication in *L'Osservatore Romano*, entering immediately in force and, subsequently, that it be published in the official commentary of the Holy See, *Acta Apostolicae Sedis*.

This is not the language of mercy. It "abrogates" all prior permissions and "declares" that there is only one form of the liturgy that qualifies for the *lex orandi* (in opposition to the magisterium of Benedict). It is "ordered" to be observed in all of its parts and nothing is to withstand it. Even worthy arguments must give way. In effect this matter is settled and brooks no delay. It took effect immediately and is now in force. Pope Francis has seldom addressed any other group this harshly. To others such as unbelievers, dissenters and wayward politicians there is to be mercy, understanding and tolerance. He speaks of "going to the margins" and of compassion for the poor and morally lost. But to those attached to the Latin Mass comes this strong rebuke, with almost no room to maneuver in the Church they love. It is very shocking and saddening to me as a pastor of souls that such vitriol be directed at the flock I have long cared for.

Second, it imposes impossible requirements. On the one hand the Pope delegates to bishops any decision about locations, but then he ties their hands. He writes: "[The diocesan bishop] is to designate one or more locations where the faithful adherents of these groups may gather for the eucharistic celebration (not however in the parochial churches and without the erection of new personal parishes)." But if not in parish churches, then where? What is a bishop to do in understanding, let alone applying, this statute? It is hard to interpret the Pope's instruction in any benign way. He seems to be saying to Latin Mass Catholics, "You are not welcome in our churches." If so, this is a stunning lack of pastoral solicitude and love and it is very dismaying.

Third, it displays a strange treatment of bishops. While referring the implementation to the local ordinary, he also restricts their pastoral judgment in numerous ways. Not only are they to forbid the Mass in parish churches, but they also cannot confer faculties on new priests to celebrate the Latin Mass without permission from Rome (Article 4). Furthermore, they cannot establish new communities (Article 3). Does this refer to locations, oratories, guilds or something else? It's difficult to determine what this means at all. So, the bishops are given authority, but with their hands tied, with confusing language and with nearly impossible guidelines to follow.

Now we must look to our bishops and beseech them to exhibit the pastoral solicitude this document seems to lack. They have been given a hard and awkward task. Be careful to pray for them, and try not to embitter them with predictions or presumptions of bad treatment. Many of them have already shown the pastoral sense to avoid the rash and "immediate" implementation of this motu proprio.

Dear bishops, as a pastor of souls, I ask you for a gentle and kind interpretation of it. Traditional Catholics are among the sheep of your flock, and they need a shepherd's care. Even if the document suggests that they be shuffled off to the margins, I beg you not to do it. This is a vibrant and growing section of the flock. Many young families and young adults, as well as young priests and older folks are depending on you to do what is truly pastoral. If greater unity is needed, teach us what this means, but please, do not drive us to the margins to live in rejection. Some of us are ornery but most of us are just trying to be good, decent Catholics and stay close to the heart of the Church. Keep us close to you and find room for us in your hearts.

Dear Holy Father, I beg you to reconsider what you have written and to hear the unnecessary pain you have caused. You rightly desire unity in the Church, but I fear that, by this action, you may end up causing far more serious division. Since my opinion means nothing, I ask you to consider the words of the great rabbi Gamaliel, who said in the Acts of the Apostles (5:38 – 39): "So in the present case I advise you: Leave these men alone. Let them go! For if their purpose or endeavor is of human origin, it will fail. But if it is from God, you will not be able to stop them. You may even find yourselves fighting against God."

21

Pope Francis Takes Aim at the Latin Mass— and His Own Faithful

MICHAEL BRENDAN DOUGHERTY

National Review

July 21, 2021

LAST WEEK, POPE FRANCIS COMPLETELY REVERSED the policy of his living predecessor, Pope Benedict XVI, when it comes to the traditional Latin Mass. And he did it without warning his bishops, and while showily exhibiting his personal animosities and neuroses. One friend, commiserating with me, tried to make sense of what was happening in the Church. He wrote to me: "Some boomers got mad about Twitter and decided to abolish the Mass of the Ages. Extraordinary."

Here's the background. In 2007, Benedict declared that the liturgy as it had existed before the Second Vatican Council was sacred and good for Catholics today. He affirmed that it had never been forbidden, implying strongly that it never could justly be forbidden. He instructed bishops to make generous use of it, and to allow any of their priests to say it if they were serving a stable group of faithful who requested it. Numerically, this tiny movement grew a great deal, but it also remains small. Perhaps 4 percent of Catholic parishes in the United States have a regular traditional Latin Mass.

In 2021, Pope Francis now revokes all this permission, because he says that the traditional Latin Mass threatens the unity of the Church and is being used to weaken adherence to the Second Vatican Council. (What this adherence consists of is maddeningly unclear, and always has been.) In the recent apostolic letter *Traditionis Custodes*, he takes the extraordinary step of requiring every diocesan priest to essentially "reapply for permission" to his bishop. He obliges the bishops to be suspicious of Catholic laymen and priests who like the traditional Latin Mass. He demands that bishops who want to expand its use to another parish in their diocese first get permission from Rome. It's almost impossible to overstate how audacious and invasive this regime of micromanagement and heresy-hunting is. It's clerical McCarthyism. And his vision is to see the celebration of the old Mass eventually abolished.

Stunning, sad, weird, baffling, vengeful, and crazy barely begin to describe this situation. But the main thing to point out is that it's abusive and paranoid. Pope Francis is abusing a group of Catholics, most of whom do not harbor ill will toward him, and most of whom don't have any real doubts or opposition to the Second Vatican Council. He's doing so because a few handfuls of radical Traditionalist Catholics have criticized him, or opposed his efforts to "evolve" the faith once delivered to the saints. He's doing this to this small band of zealous, faithful Catholics at precisely the moment that German bishops are openly contemplating a revolution in moral teaching in their nation.

It's true that there are handfuls of crusty old "Traddy" Catholics like me, who do have reservations about the Second Vatican Council and the new liturgy. But, contra Francis, Benedict's peace terms drastically diminished our influence. Or at least our influence on this point.

We became drowned out of our own Latin Mass movement by young people who largely didn't care about our old battles about ecumenical councils. That seems healthy. The Council of Vienne's fourteenth-century ranting about the Knights Templar, when read today, evokes little more than a mood you'd associate with Dungeons & Dragons. Similarly, the Second Vatican Council's ruminations on nuclear arms, or on modern man's relationship to community life, are about as riveting as a slow-motion stage-reading of *Hair*. Sure, this was once important to some septuagenarians out there, somewhere. But a sensible reader now can only marvel at the obscene amount of money spent on the travel and accommodations that were used to produce and exhibit this guff. It's irrelevant to most people.

Francis writes: "I am nonetheless saddened that the instrumental use of the *Missale Romanum* of 1962 is often characterized by a rejection not only of the liturgical reform, but of the Vatican Council II itself, claiming, with unfounded and unsustainable assertions, that it betrayed the Tradition and the 'true Church.'"

As a factual matter, this is almost provably wrong. The majority of priests who say the traditional Latin Mass are now diocesan priests, serving in ordinary parishes. They almost all say the new liturgy, which is precisely the thing that Pope Francis deems proof of adherence to the Church.

Francis argues that the liturgical books of Pope Paul VI and John Paul II "constitute the unique expression of the *lex orandi* (law of prayer) of the Roman Rite."

In 2007, Benedict XVI had proposed a rather legible principle for allowing the celebration of the traditional Latin Mass. "What earlier generations held as sacred, remains sacred and great for us too, and it cannot be all of a sudden entirely forbidden or even considered harmful." Francis's principle for abolishing it is simply a word salad. What does "unique expression" even mean? It has no legal or theological substance or weight. It's just a giant "because we said so."

The bishops do have some power to at least preserve the permission that their priests already have to say this Mass. For now. But is this the Church progressives want? Constant henpecking and paranoia from Rome? There is so much more to say in the days and months ahead; for now it's enough to say this is unseemly and ugly. This may be the most significant act of Francis's pontificate; and it's nothing more than bullying iconoclasm. He needs help.

The Worst Papal Document in History

GERHARD EGER INTERVIEWS
PETER A. KWASNIEWSKI
The Remnant
July 21, 2021

GE: *I am very grateful, Dr. Kwasniewski, that you are willing to take the time to answer my questions. What is your overall assessment of the motu proprio* Traditionis Custodes?

PAK: It is the worst document promulgated by a pope in the history of the Roman Church. Full stop. Why do I say this? Because although popes have changed this or that aspect of the legislation of their predecessors, none has ever tried to stamp out one of the greatest liturgical rites in Christendom by putting its adherents under siege and starving them until they die or capitulate. It's a mentality of warfare applied to members of the Mystical Body. Totally unworthy of a successor of the Apostle Peter, who, like the Apostle Paul with whom he is always depicted in iconography, would have counseled us to "hold fast to the traditions" (2 Thess 2:15).

Its publication had been expected, but not its harshness.

And this harshness, this meanness of spirit, this willingness to punish everyone for the (supposed) sins of a few, has cemented the motu proprio's evil reputation. If the old Mass and especially its vocal proponents — who also tend to be the opponents of his progressivism — are a thorn in the side of Pope Francis, his motu proprio is a thorn in the side of all bishops who, over the past fourteen years, may have felt relieved to find a bit of liturgical peace in their dioceses and some growing communities of young people as well as families who are generously open to life and zealous in faith (and, let's not forget, generous when it comes to the collection basket). The pope's action has insulted the episcopacy by implying they have been incompetent in doing their work (which sadly is often true, but in a way contrary to what Francis has in mind) and that they are, moreover, incompetent to handle the problem of a perceived lack of docility to the Magisterium. For we must note that the motu proprio gives bishops only power to destroy, not to build up: they may limit or eliminate Latin Mass groups but they may not authorize new groups, new parishes, or newly-ordained priests to learn the Mass. This is like tying the hands of over 4,000 bishops and then expecting them to be grateful for it.

Traditionis Custodes comes across as payback, dressed in sweeping charges that have embarrassingly little substance — a settling of scores with conservative and traditional Catholics, especially in the United States, for their steady resistance to the pope's progressivism and modernism.

What practical consequences might it have in the life of the Church?

It will return us straight back to the bitter days of the 1970s. This step puts the entire project of seeking an "inner reconciliation" (as Benedict XVI expressed it) back fifty years. But with this difference: there are now millions of Catholics who either love or are supportive of the TLM, and they are often well-organized and well-educated. Therefore, the civil war the pope has unleashed will involve many more people than there were in the early days of traditionalism. In those early post-Council days, when the faithful were still in the grip of a naive ultramontanism, nearly everyone went along with the new program (or, sadly, voted with their feet and left the modernizing Church behind). Today, fifty years later, faithful Catholics have been shocked so many times by abuses and corruption that they are not so willing to be blind followers who simply obey the commands of the Great Leader.

In reality, there should be a peace treaty as soon as possible, to mitigate the casualties. The effects will be dire: many will be tempted to despair and discouragement; some will find a permanent home among Eastern-rite Catholics or even the Eastern Orthodox; a large number may go over to the SSPX (not that I would blame them!), effectively giving up on a Vatican that seems more interested in purging its own faithful than in purging heresy, financial scandal, and sexual abuse. In all of these cases, we can see how hypocritical it is for the pope to say he is doing all this in the service of unity. It is rather in the service of ideological uniformity.

It is striking that it came into force immediately, without a prudential interval between the announcement and its entry into force (vacatio legis).

Yes: this too is unprecedented, and it may turn out to be one of the ways in which this move by Bergoglio is suicidal, since evil has a way of overreaching itself in its ambitions, and falling into catastrophe. It's clear that the lack of *vacatio legis* was due to fears over the pope's health: serious surgery presents the risk of a sudden end to the pontificate, and if a pope happens to die during the *vacatio legis* of a law, the legislation never goes into effect.

Already reports are flowing in from all sides of bishops who are irritated and indeed angry that they were given such a difficult and draconian document the very day it was supposed to be put into effect. One bishop said he learned about it first on social media! The general response has been either to say "things will not be changed" or "we need more time to study how to implement the document." In other words, the bishops are giving *themselves* a *vacatio legis* — and who knows, maybe after this "vacation" many will decide not to implement it, or to implement it as minimalistically as possible, so as to not have more turbulence and bureaucratic headaches in their dioceses.

We must remember that it was not 99% of the world's bishops who asked for this motu proprio, but perhaps 1% who seethe with a hatred of the enduring witness of the traditional Latin Mass. I do not believe for one moment the pope's assertion that the results of the CDF survey were predominantly negative, as contrary evidence is abundantly at hand, and the narrative irresistibly reminds one of other notorious cases of information control and suppression. The strategy of "just trust us" has really run out of gas in the Age of McCarrick.

Is this a disappointment for those for whom the traditional liturgy is a "just aspiration" and who believe it provides great richness to the Church?

No, it's not a disappointment. It's a cause of righteous anger, a scandal, a form of clerical abuse from a father who has kicked his children in the gut for the "crime" of loving what the saints have loved for so many centuries, and who then waits for their grateful return to the Novus Ordo.

I had always thought Jesuits were supposed to be clever, but this one seems not to know basic rules of human psychology: (1) the underdog always wins the sympathy of the many; (2) harsh tactics directed against minorities will draw lots of attention to their cause; (3) forbidden goods become more desirable; (4) if you try to take away something that people love as dearly as life itself, you will only succeed in intensifying their love of it and increasing their distance from or violence against those who would take it away. If you want a man to show his love for his family, all you have to do is threaten his wife and children with harm, and he will either take them far away or fight to the death. This is the right reaction on a natural

88

level and on a supernatural level. After all, St. Thomas Aquinas said that in the face of injustice "the lack of anger is a sign that the judgment of reason is lacking" (ST II-II.158.8 ad 3).

Its negative judgment of the traditional Mass and the faithful who assist in its celebration seems entirely unjustified. Moreover, it speaks of bishops having to evaluate whether TLM groups do not question the validity and legitimacy of the liturgical reform, of the decrees of Vatican II, and of the magisterium of the supreme pontiffs.

The document is (and can't help being) vague about what "adherence to" or "acceptance of" the Second Vatican Council would actually *mean*, and after so many decades of discussion, it is still not entirely clear what it means. Take *Dignitatis Humanae*, for example: scholars have been arguing for decades about what it says and what it obliges us to do or not to do, and still the matter is far from clear. John XXIII and Paul VI both said the Council taught nothing fundamentally new, but presented the same Catholic Faith to the modern world. There is legitimate room for debate about how effectively and clearly that Faith was in fact presented, but surely no Catholic should be required to receive Vatican II in a way that runs contrary to Vatican I, Trent, the first seven councils, or any of the preceding Magisterium.

It is therefore arbitrary and ideological (as Ratzinger noted more than once) to isolate Vatican II as a "super-council," a litmus test of orthodoxy, when one would be able to find heresies galore in the Novus Ordo environment — *meaty* heresies, things that have been anathematized, whereas Vatican II defined nothing and anathematized nothing. My point here is that the way Francis speaks makes it seem as if adherence to Vatican II were somehow more important than adherence to Trent, from the teaching of which huge numbers of clergy, religious, and laity dissent or distance themselves. We are seeing, in short, the weaponization of the Council. No observant person can fail to note the irony that traditionalist Catholics accept the "traditional" content of Vatican II far more than their Novus Ordo brethren tend to do, especially among academics and clergy. By that standard, Pope Francis should be taking action against the Novus Ordo world, but he doesn't, and he can't, owing to his ideological blinders.

The same sort of thing could be said about making the liturgical reform into a gauge of orthodoxy. Unless there is an outright *contradiction* between the *lex orandi* of the old Roman rite and the *lex orandi* of the modern rite of Paul VI, such that the one is orthodox and the other heretical — a few hold this view, but the vast majority of traditionalists do not — there

FROM BENEDICT'S PEACE TO FRANCIS'S WAR

is no reason why a Catholic who accepts the one should be thought to reject the other's theological content as such. Many (including Francis's own living predecessor) have criticized the weaknesses and omissions of the new liturgical books, but very few call their sacramental validity into question. On top of this, no liturgical reform could ever be "irreversible," since it's inherently a disciplinary matter subject to prudential evaluation and practical modification.

So the shibboleths imposed by the pope seem to have to do with something other than their surface meaning. Here, "Vatican II" and "the liturgical reform" *stand for something else*, something that cannot be said openly.

But let's be honest: high-level theological discussions do not appeal to most of the faithful. They go to the TLM because they love its reverence, its beauty, its transcendent orientation, its rich and always-reliable prayers (the lack of "optionitis"), its atmosphere of timelessness that pulls us out of and above our ordinary life, as does its cousin from the East, the Byzantine Divine Liturgy, which chants: "Let us all who mystically represent the cherubim and sing the thrice-holy hymn to the life-creating Trinity now set aside all earthly cares." Venerable liturgies like these bring us to the brink of heaven. And they do so in ways that either do not exist in the reformed liturgy of Paul VI or find a place there awkwardly and rarely.

The document states that the liturgical books promulgated by the holy pontiffs Paul VI and John Paul II, in conformity with the decrees of Vatican II, are the sole expression of the lex orandi *of the* Roman rite. *Does this mean that the* Missale Romanum *of 1962 is, in a way, abolished?*

It would be impossible in principle for a pope to abolish the venerable Roman rite, the Mass of Ages. I have explained the reason why in an article published at LifeSiteNews. [1] Francis in this motu proprio never dares to say "the rite in force before the liturgical reform is abrogated," as neither did Paul VI before him. Rather, he abrogates Summorum Pontificum, and attempts to exclude the old Roman rite from being a legitimate lex orandi of the Catholic Faith. This is bizarre, untenable, and ultimately incoherent. The document is full of contradictions and mental fog. It never mentions the Ordinariate liturgy, which is also part of the Roman rite but has a distinctive lex orandi, or the various uses of the Roman rite that are again not identical with it (e.g., the Dominican or the Norbertine). The vitriolic spirit of Traditionis Custodes is betrayed by its poor composition — the result of haste, lack of intelligence, and profound ignorance of liturgical history and theology.

1   See chapter 19.

We might add that flagrantly contradicting theological stances of one's predecessor is about as sensible as sawing with vigor at the branch one is sitting on. It discredits either the current pope or all popes.

At the same time, however, it affirms that diocesan bishops have the exclusive competence to authorize the use of the Missale Romanum *of 1962 in their dioceses, following the instructions of the Holy See.*

Right: another of the contradictions. As of this past Sunday, when I attended a Latin Mass, I was (according to the motu proprio) no longer praying with the *lex orandi* of the Roman Church. And yet the Mass was a Roman rite Mass offered by a priest in good standing and with full permission of the Church. It seems to me that the motu proprio is a perfect expression of nominalism and voluntarism, in that it thinks by applying the labels of words to certain realities we make those realities to exist, and they exist if we want them to, but not if we don't want them to. It is of a piece with the relativistic philosophy that can be detected in so many acts of this pontificate, a sort of union of infidelity and irrationality that parodies the Catholic harmony of faith and reason.

In point of fact, a very good case can be made — I have begun to make it in that *LifeSite* piece — that this document is so full of errors, ambiguities, and contradictions that it lacks juridical standing. It is illicit from the get-go. That won't prevent some hierarchs from feeling compelled to put it into effect with a speed that does credit to their unity of spirit with the reigning pontiff. One need only recall, in contrast, how *Ex Corde Ecclesiae* of John Paul II, the document that tried to clean up Catholic higher education, remained nearly universally unimplemented.

We can see some hopeful signs, however: Bishop Paprocki of Springfield, Illinois, canonically dispensed his diocese from some elements of the motu proprio; Archbishop Fisher of Sydney told his diocese that the TLM will continue and the faithful need have no fear of losing it. I heard of a diocese where the bishop within 24 hours had granted renewed permission to 27 priests to keep saying the Latin Mass. Reports like this, which keep reaching me, indicate that the number of friends of tradition, or at least diplomatic partners, is perhaps larger than we realized. The motu proprio has drawn them out of the woodwork. Stark alternatives have a way of doing that.

In any case, regardless of what the motu proprio says to the contrary, no priest needs any permission to offer the Tridentine Mass. Inevitably and prudently, most priests will wish to be or to remain in their bishops' good graces and will seek their blessing (and even play along with calling it "permission"), but it is crucial to remember that this is only a formality, a matter of clerical *politesse*.

Although the traditional Mass continues to be permitted under certain circumstances, is this a step towards its outright suppression?

The neo-modernists of our time desire nothing more than this, precisely because they recognize the truth of the axiom *lex orandi, lex credendi, lex vivendi*. Traditional Catholics are inoculated, in a way, against the destruction and reconstruction of Catholicism that has been pursued for some time now, in the "long march through the institutions." Such Catholics are the "iconophiles" of our time who revere the images of Christ and His holy ones — the primary image being the liturgy itself! — and who therefore make a central place for ritual, culture, memory, history. The iconoclasts would rid the Church of these things and replace them with their own humanistic substitutes. The faction in power right now will do their utmost to suppress the old Mass altogether. It's worse: they want the extinction of the *usus antiquior* in its entirety — all the sacramental rites, the *Breviarium Romanum* of Pius X, the *Rituale Romanum*, the *Pontificale Romanum*, the whole works. They're starting with the Mass because it's the "font and apex," but their end game is to see the historic Roman rite confined to encyclopedia entries. We will have to work and pray very much to oppose their efforts, and it is going to get very messy in many places.

In closing, is there any advice you would like to give to our readers, Dr. Kwasniewski?

In the three days that followed the publication of the motu proprio, I realized anew the magnitude of the spiritual warfare in which we are engaged as traditional Catholics. Let's not kid ourselves: this is a battle for souls, a battle for clergy and religious, a battle for the future of the Church, for our descendants. We're all in — or it's all over. We need to be driven by faith, not by fear.

My wife and I decided to commit to a daily Holy Hour at an adoration chapel near our house, to pray for a resolution to this crisis, to pray for all the priests and laity it will affect, for all the bishops and, of course, for the pope. I would urge everyone to take some concrete step, even if it's as simple as explicitly praying daily in the Rosary for the restoration of tradition to its rightful place. Enroll in the Brown Scapular of Our Lady of Mount Carmel if you haven't already done so. Choose a day or days for fasting: Our Lord says some demons are driven out only through prayer and fasting. And finally, remember that this crisis is not likely to clear up quickly. We may not even live to see it resolved, but it will be our children and grandchildren who reap the fruits of what we sow today by the prayers, labors, and sufferings we offer up. We do all this because God deserves our faithful love and rewards it with admission to the heavenly liturgy.

A friend reminded me recently of some timely verses from St. Peter's First Epistle: "Now who is there to harm you if you are zealous for what is right? But even if you do suffer for righteousness' sake, you will be blessed. Have no fear of them, nor be troubled, but in your hearts reverence Christ as Lord. Always be prepared to make a defense to anyone who calls you to account for the hope that is in you, yet do it with gentleness and reverence; and keep your conscience clear, so that, when you are abused, those who revile your good behavior in Christ may be put to shame. For it is better to suffer for doing right, if that should be God's will, than for doing wrong" (1 Pet 3:13–17).

May St. Gregory the Great, St. Pius V, and all holy popes intercede for us!

23

Revolution and Repudiation: Governance Gone Awry†

SEBASTIAN MORELLO

The European Conservative

July 21, 2021

LAST WEEK, POPE FRANCIS ISSUED A MOTU PROPRIO — an edict—whose aim is that of dramatically restricting the celebration of the Roman Rite liturgy according to its ancient use, and declaring its 1960s "reformed" use to be the only true "expression" of the Roman Rite liturgy. This is a massive assault on the tradition of the Catholic Church by one whose office is that of foremost guardian of that tradition. The document was not without its humor, however, as the Holy Father picked an ironic title for the edict: "Guardians of the Tradition."

From the outset, I wish to state that what follows is not a theological analysis, for which I am untrained (that has, in any case, been provided by Cardinal Gerhard Müller[1]). I am a conservative philosopher who has researched mainly on the early conservatives: Maistre, Burke, Bonald, Chateaubriand, Cortés and others. Ordinarily, I analyze the content of political and social topics. Nonetheless, the Church is analogous to a political society, is admixed with natural society, and is a true society in its own right, being both a nation (the New Israel, according to *Lumen Gentium* 9) and possessing a government, namely the bishops. A conservative analysis of events may be applied to the Church and its government, especially for the task of detecting and criticizing revolutionary activity.

In his new edict, Pope Francis claims to foster "ecclesial communion," but in order to achieve such unity in the Church he calls for the marginalization of a specific group within the body of the faithful. An odd way of achieving communion, to be sure. By so doing, the Pope makes a grave mistake of government, that of using his power to damage that which his power exists to protect, namely the Church's tradition.

---

† Originally published with the title "Reflections on Pope Francis's motu proprio *Traditionis Custodes*."
1   See chapter 16.

Perhaps nothing can so undermine the authority of government than such an obvious blunder. During the Soviet terror, in places like Hungary, Czechoslovakia and Romania, for example, "the people" were told that they were being liberated by the commissars who were systematically abolishing the traditions and ways of life of those very people. They were being "emancipated" without choice from their very own cultural inheritance. When *the people* reacted negatively, they were told that they were *the enemy of the people*. That this was all being done with the best of intentions was hardly convincing then, as it isn't now.

Civil society is a logically pre-political entity, as there can be no societal ordering principle (the State) if there is no society of which State officials are already members. So too, the whole faithful of the Church, as a community, is logically prior to the episcopacy, even if the episcopacy and the wider ecclesial community are correlative and brought into being together. The reason for a Church government (as leaders, rather than sacrificial priests) is found in the community of faithful for which such government exists.

Government exists per se for the protection of society and its way of life, so that society may achieve the ends for which human communities are formed; government is not the *creator* of society. So too, the pope and bishops are mandated to guard and pass on the tradition that has been handed down to them (2 Thess. 2:15), and are not to repudiate or abrogate it, or concoct their own novel version. The Church's tradition, both belief and practice, is not theirs, with which they may do as they wish. The Church's tradition belongs to the whole faithful. Of this tradition, the bishops (including the pope) are the guardians and servants. They can never be the creators nor the owners of the Church's doctrine, practice or liturgical life, but are charged with protecting and promulgating the common religious inheritance of the whole faithful. For popes and bishops to behave as if the Church's tradition is their belonging, with which they may do as they please, with the rest of the faithful just having to accept it, marks the crudest form of clericalism.

By his edict, the Pope has simultaneously committed a second blunder of government. He has set an even stronger precedent than that which already existed regarding the repudiation of papal predecessors.

In his Letter accompanying the motu proprio, Pope Francis writes that his (living) predecessor "granted freedom to celebrate" the ancient liturgy because he had good intentions. In fact, Pope Benedict XVI did not so much *grant* freedom as simply *acknowledge* that such freedom had always existed within the Church. In any case, these good intentions were then purportedly exploited by people attending traditional Masses to foster disunity in the Church. Due to this alleged appropriation of the ancient liturgy to create disunity in the Church — it seems we just have to take Pope Francis's word for this — the Pope tells us that he is moved out of necessity to reverse the liberties that were "granted" by Pope Benedict to the Church's faithful. Pope Francis goes further, however, and states a point of principle in his edict: Pope Benedict had advanced the theory that there are two equally valid "forms" of the Roman Rite, the "ordinary" (1960s) and "extraordinary" (ancient) forms; Pope Francis has declared this to be untrue.

According to Pope Francis, the 1960s reformed liturgy is the "unique expression of the *lex orandi* of the Roman Rite." The word "unique" in this sentence is the official Vatican translation of the original Italian *l'unica*. The sentence is better understood, then, as "the *only* expression of the . . . Roman Rite." It is clear how extreme Pope Francis's position really is. He claims that a new liturgy concocted by a committee (one led by a rather shady character) half a century ago is to be understood as the *only* legitimate expression of a liturgical tradition with a pedigree going back to apostolic times. How can this be so? We are given no explanation beyond, "Because I say so."

Now, presumably, if Pope Francis can reject the claims of his predecessor by the click of his fingers, his successor will be free to do the same to him. Catholic faithful attached to the traditional liturgy may derive comfort from this, as there remains the possibility that the whole thing could be reversed by a future edict. Do not be consoled, for here lies the path to ever intensifying ecclesiastical tyranny. For example, the reason why revolutionary governments become so draconian when they attain power by the overthrowing of government, immediately requiring a secret police and increasingly severe punishments, is because the revolutionary government has, in acquiring government, legitimized revolution against government. So too, in the game of predecessor repudiations, ever more draconian measures are needed to prevent any reversal by a future edict. In the case of the new motu proprio, the measures are so harsh that it is clearly hoped that by the time any future pope is inclined to reverse them, the faithful attached to the traditional liturgy will have been scattered and purged.

According to the motu proprio, priests who already know how to offer the ancient Mass may continue to do so only *if* they obtain permission from their bishops. If a priest does not have a sympathetic bishop, tough luck. If a priest obtains permission, he cannot choose the days on which he offers this Mass — that is now for the bishop to decide — and it is forbidden to offer it in his parish church (thankfully, this last detail is being ignored by some bishops who have already responded to the edict). So, occasionally, with permission, a priest with this newly invented "faculty" may visit the catacombed faithful for a gathering that is only just tolerated by the regime if completely out of sight. Any priest who wants to *learn* the traditional liturgy, however, must now ask permission from his bishop, who in fact (despite the edict asserting that the bishop is the "moderator . . . of the whole liturgical life of the particular Church entrusted to him") cannot grant such permission. The bishop must first consult the Holy See, and I have a suspicion that the Holy See (as in, the office whose incumbent is trying to suppress the ancient liturgy) will be reluctant to grant such permission. One thing is clear: Pope Francis's new "collegial Church" does not look very collegial.

The themes of revolution and repudiation have troubled me for some time in regard to Pope Paul VI. Pope Paul seemed to abrogate the ancient liturgy (though Pope Benedict claimed he never actually did so, seemingly because that would have been beyond his authority — take note, Pope Francis) after he issued his brand new "reformed" liturgy called the New Order of the Roman Rite. Pope Paul claimed that the Second Vatican Council had called for this new liturgy, but in fact the reforms proposed by the Council did not correspond to Pope Paul's final liturgical product, which I am informed even he eventually grew to regret.

I have wondered for some time: if a pope can bring out his very own liturgy, and force it on the whole Church's faithful, and foster a culture that makes life very difficult for those who wish to worship as did their forefathers in the Faith, why cannot every one of his successors, in principle, do the same? Presumably, in principle, the faithful could be forced to radically change the practice of their religion every ten years or so, which, if the effects of the 1960s reform is anything to go by, would be catastrophic for faith-retention and faith-induction.

What essentially has been established is a program of ongoing repudiation and revolution, which, from the perspective of basic governmental competence and regnative prudence, is a spectacularly unwise way to govern the Church. The subterranean presence in such a program is that of a hyper-voluntarism: I *want it to be so, therefore it will be so.* The motu proprio, for example, has no explanation contained within it. It is a list of demands without reasons. The accompanying letter offers no further explanation beyond a list of observations that Pope Francis says makes him "sad." As things stand, until further explanation is offered, including some account of how the principled claims of his new edict can be squared with those of previous documents of the same authority (if they cannot be, we have no reason for taking this edict seriously), all we have is a pope saying, "*This is how I feel. This is what I want. I demand obedience!*" Behaving in such a way not only lacks the maturity expected of a leader, but turns the papacy into exactly what Protestants have accused it of being for centuries: an arbitrary authority demanding mindlessness of its subjects.

This is the terrible effect of this revolutionary voluntarism: the exercise of arbitrary power. Arbitrary power, free from accountability, is what Edmund Burke in his *Speech on the Impeachment of Warren Hastings* characterized as "wholly satanic." Now, the Catholic Church's faithful may have to adopt new teachings and practices of piety, and do so regularly, solely because the emotional states and cultural preferences of the reigning pope have been announced. Such a situation is so abusive of the religious life of the faithful that, in the climate it creates, the religion itself cannot be expected to persist.

The legacy of Pope Paul VI is important, for Pope Francis's edict is not about the liturgy, but about that legacy. Pope Francis has said as much. It is about the Second Vatican Council and its effects. This is indeed the major theme of the accompanying Letter.

I will say nothing about the legitimacy of the Second Vatican Council. It is, however, important to understand the *role* of the Second Vatican Council in the life of the Church. Councils had previously been called to condemn threats to doctrinal orthodoxy. Councils were not for scrutinizing the Church itself. It was stated from the outset that the Second Vatican Council was not to have error as the object of its concern, but the Church itself, which it was to re-organize and re-configure by its novel principles. In turn, the historical *role* of the Second Vatican Council has been that of giving to the Church something like a written constitution. As the celebrated Cardinal Leo Jozef Suenens ecstatically proclaimed after the closing of the Council, "Vatican II is the French Revolution in the Church!" Since the Council, Church leaders have not been able to speak authoritatively without concurrently claiming to be furthering the Council's cause. For this reason, no bishop, including the pope, can publicly teach without beginning most of his sentences, "As Vatican II taught us . . ."

The Council was received as the *author* of a new Church. Ever since, the preoccupation of the Church's government has been that of implementing the principles of the Church's new constitution. As the existent reality fails to conform itself to the new ideas, ever more draconian measures must be put in place, especially against those most noticeable hotbeds of resistance, the traditional Masses. They have enjoyed a decade or so without persecution, and now the Church's government deems that to have been a grave mistake. The congregations attending such Masses could not avoid drawing attention to themselves; they are frequently made up of young families with many children whose parents succeed in passing on the Faith — a rare spectacle in the Catholic Church today. Such signs of life are always quashed by revolutionaries, who see things only from the deconstructive perspective.

In a conservative analysis, employed to detect the presence of revolution, one must distinguish the revolutionaries from all others. Revolutions always mark the overthrowing of an established order in favor of a new system. Revolutions can come from society, as is the case with plebeian uprisings, or from the government, as was the case with our very own King Henry VIII, who launched a revolt against the religious inheritance of his people.

Those Catholics who are anxiously conserving their inherited religious beliefs and practices are not the revolutionaries, and they are not the disobedient. Shamefully, such Catholics will be accused — indeed, already are being accused — of disobedience. In reality, such Catholics simply do not want to be part of a revolutionary cause. It is precisely their *obedience* and *fidelity* to their tradition, in the face of the abusive exercise of arbitrary power, that makes them the targets of revolution and disobedience. Such Catholics must be clear about this in their minds: they are not the revolutionaries; they are not the disobedient; they are the faithful.

24

The Devotion of Families to the Traditional Mass[†]

JOSEPH SHAW
Voice of the Family
July 21, 2021

THE PRACTICAL EFFECTS OF POPE FRANCIS'S NEW Apostolic Letter will no doubt vary from place to place, but one thing is clear: at the highest level, the pastoral solicitude of Pope John Paul II and above all of Pope Benedict XVI towards Catholics attached to the ancient liturgical tradition has been replaced at the highest level of the Church by an attitude of suspicion, and even of hostility.

I started attending the Traditional Mass in 2002, and so I had a taste of life before Pope Benedict. Ordinary Catholics, even quite conservative ones, would literally recoil in horror when they heard that I was attending the ancient Mass, regardless of the fact that it had the approval of the local bishop and was celebrated by a priest in good standing in the Church. Ferocious attacks on us appeared in mainstream and, again, conservative Catholic publications. This continued for some time even after 2007, but as time has worn on it has become less and less of a problem.

What effect does this kind of hostility have, particularly on families? Positively, it makes for a strong sense of solidarity and *esprit de corps* among the Traditional faithful. But it also causes harm. Parents are driven out of the natural social network of the wider Catholic community; children feel as though they are growing up in a persecuted cult. For a number of years my own family had a choice — if we wanted to attend the Traditional Mass — between getting our small children up in the dark, in the winter months, to attend a Low Mass before breakfast, where for a long time we were not allowed to gather for a cup of tea afterwards, or spending the best part of three hours in the car on a Sunday. Many others, I know, were not so fortunate.

Readers may wonder why we bothered. Why not simply go to the ordinary English Mass? As a matter of fact, for many people locally available alternatives to the Traditional Mass are especially unattractive. Pope Francis does not

---

[†]   Originally published with the title "*Traditionis Custodes* and Families."

disagree. In his Letter to Bishops, which accompanied the Apostolic Letter *Traditionis Custodes*, he wrote: "In common with Benedict XVI, I deplore the fact that 'in many places the prescriptions of the new Missal are not observed in celebration, but indeed come to be interpreted as an authorization for or even a requirement of creativity, which leads to almost unbearable distortions.'"

It seems, however, that the Holy Father has no plans to do anything about the issue of liturgical abuses. No one watching him washing the feet of Muslim women on Maundy Thursday, in advance of changing liturgical law to allow the feet of women (but not non-Catholic women) to be washed on Maundy Thursday, will imagine that he is deeply concerned about liturgical rules.

Indeed, while Pope Francis acknowledges the problem of liturgical "distortions," he nevertheless insists that there is no such problem. Later in the same document he declares: "Whoever wishes to celebrate with devotion according to earlier forms of the liturgy can find in the reformed Roman Missal according to Vatican Council II all the elements of the Roman Rite, in particular the Roman Canon which constitutes one of its more distinctive elements."

As a matter of fact, in many places the Roman Canon, or Eucharistic Prayer I, is simply never used. In any case, Pope Francis is far from encouraging a style of celebration of the Novus Ordo which accentuates its continuity with the older Missal. Those who have been trying to do this — the "Reform of the Reform" movement — have come in for particularly heavy criticism by Pope Francis. Cardinal Robert Sarah was both publicly and privately rebuked[1] in 2016 for promoting the celebration of Mass facing liturgical East (the priest facing the same way as the people), and using the reformed Missal in Latin can generate a hostile reaction from bishops who take their cue from Pope Francis.[2]

However, the desire to attend the Traditional Mass goes beyond a hope to escape liturgical abuses in the Novus Ordo: it springs from positive as well as negative considerations. We are motivated, ultimately, by a desire to have for ourselves, and to pass on to our children, something which has incomparable spiritual value. Indeed, this treasure is our birthright as Catholics of the Latin Rite. If we might feel obliged to preserve an ancestral home, or the cultural artifacts of a minority ethnic group of which we are members, all the more do those of us who recognize the value of this Mass feel obliged to preserve it. This sense of obligation implies that we must be prepared to suffer for it.

---

1   See "Did Pope Francis rebuke Cardinal Sarah?," *California Catholic Daily*, July 12, 2016.
2   See https://tdpelmedia.com/costa-rican-bishop-suspends-priest-for-saying-novus-order-mass-in-latin-and-ad-orientem.

Families attached to the Traditional Mass feel particularly committed to the project of preserving the ancient liturgy, both because it comes naturally to a family to consider the next generation, and because the ancient Mass has a particular value for children. As children, especially younger ones, do not engage as readily as adults with words, this liturgy's use of non-verbal communication — symbolic actions, incense, silence, vestments, chant — has special value for them. It is commonly observed that small children are better-behaved in the Traditional Mass, because (I believe) it is easier for them to absorb an atmosphere of recollection there.

At the same time, families are particularly vulnerable in the liturgical realm. It is more difficult for families to attend Masses at peculiar times and in peculiar places. A lack of parking spaces or facilities at a church makes a much greater difference for families taking small children to church with them than it does for single adults. The cost of fuel in a family car can be a serious impediment to a family's attendance at a distant Mass, as is the disappearance of so much of the time when families can enjoy common recreation, on Sundays, into staring at the back of the car in front on a motorway. Over many years, many families have made great sacrifices in these and other ways to attend the ancient Mass. Many others, who might have liked to try the older Mass out a few times, have not done so because of such obstacles, and lost the chance to discover it.

Nevertheless, I do not believe the situation in the coming months and years will be as bad as it was in the 1970s and 1980s. All that has been said since that time, by Popes and by others, cannot now be unsaid. Pope Benedict made clear that depriving Catholics of the old Mass was unjust, and that the attempt to banish the Church's own past creates a theological problem which, as he put it, "calls her very being into question."[3] The appeal of the Mass to families and to young people cannot now be doubted: indeed, it seems to be the very fact that it is so appealing that has stimulated these repressive actions. The energy and zeal of the reforming 1960s generation, the ones who smashed the altars and the stained glass windows, and bullied and mocked the faithful who objected, is long gone. In its place there is today a generation of young priests and lay Catholics who are highly motivated to hold fast to the Tradition.

If it proved impossible to suppress the ancient Mass between 1969 and 1988, it will certainly not be done starting in 2021.

---

3   Joseph Ratzinger, *Salt of the Earth: The Church at the End of the Millennium* (San Francisco: Ignatius Press, 1996), 176.

25

"They Will Throw You out of the Synagogues" (John 16:2)

THE HERMENEUTIC OF CAIN'S ENVY AGAINST ABEL[†]

MASSIMO VIGLIONE

Duc in altum
July 21, 2021

THERE HAVE BEEN MANY COMMENTS, ONE AFTER THE other, in these days following the official declaration of war—a war made by Francis himself—of the ecclesiastical hierarchy against the Holy Mass of the Ages. And more than one comment has revealed the not-at-all concealed contempt and the simultaneous absolute clarity of content and form that marks the motu proprio *Traditionis Custodes*, written in a style and formality that is political more than theological or spiritual. It is, in effect, a declaration of war.

It is noteworthy that there is a formal difference and also a difference in tone found in the various documents with which Paul VI, beginning in 1964, announced, planned, and implemented his liturgical reform, which was finally made official with the Apostolic Constitution *Missale Romanum* issued on 3 April 1969, by which the ancient Roman Rite was *de facto* replaced (this is the most appropriate term both from the point of view of intentions as well as facts) with the new vulgar Rite. In the Montinian documents we find, on several occasions, hypocritical but evident pain, regret, and remorse, and paradoxically the beauty and sacredness of the ancient Rite are celebrated. In short, it is as if Montini had said: "Dear Rite of all time, I am sending you away, but you were so beautiful!" In contrast, in the Bergoglian document, as many have noted, sarcasm and hatred for the ancient Rite shine through. A hatred such that it cannot be contained.

Naturally, Francis is not the initiator of this war, which was begun by the modernist liturgical movement (or, if you like, with Protestantism), but

---

† Translated from the Italian by Robert Moynihan and published as the *Moynihan Letter* #62 on July 22. The text was subsequently published at *LifeSiteNews* and *Rorate Caeli*.

rather, on the official and operative level, it was Paul VI himself. Bergoglio has only — to use the strong and popular metaphor — "shot madly" in an effort to kill once and for all a mortally wounded thing that in the course of the post-conciliar decades not only did not die but returned to life, dragging along with it, with an exponential crescendo in the last fourteen years, an incalculable number of faithful all over the world.

And this is the crux of the whole matter.

The progressive and more convinced modernist clergy had to suffer Benedict XVI's motu proprio, dragged by the neck, but at the same time they constantly worked against the Mass of the Ages through hostile resistance by the majority of the world episcopate, which has always openly disobeyed what *Summorum Pontificum* established, beginning right in the years of the Ratzingerian pontificate, and then all the more so after the resignation up until today. The hostility of the bishops meant that in the end the task of putting the motu proprio into action very often fell to the courage of a few priests celebrating it anyway, even without the permission of the bishop (which was specifically not necessary according to the provisions of *Summorum Pontificum*).

Now, those bishops who have been constantly and undauntedly disobedient to the Supreme Pontiff of the Catholic Church and one of his motu proprios, now in the name of obedience to the Supreme Pontiff of the Catholic Church and one of his motu proprios will be able not only to continue but even to intensify their censorship, in the war that is no longer hidden but is now blatant, as is in fact already happening.

But Francis has not limited himself to "shooting" the immortal victim. He wanted to take a further step, that of a fast and furious — to say nothing of monstrous — "burying alive" of the ancient rite, affirming that the new rite is the [sole] *lex orandi* of the Catholic Church. From which it should be deduced that the Mass of the Ages is no longer the *lex orandi*.

It is well known that Our Friend [Bergoglio] doesn't have a clue about theology (which is a bit like saying that a doctor doesn't have a clue about medicine, or that a blacksmith doesn't know how to use fire and iron). The *lex orandi* of the Church, in fact, is not a "precept" of positive law voted on by a parliament or prescribed by a sovereign, which can always be retracted, changed, replaced, improved, or worsened. The *lex orandi* of the Church, furthermore, is not a specific and determined "thing" in time and space, as much as it is the collective whole of theological and spiritual norms and liturgical and pastoral practices of the entire history of the Church, from evangelical times — and specifically from Pentecost — up to today. Although it obviously lives in the present, it is rooted in the entire past of the Church. Therefore, we are not talking here about something human — exclusively human — that the latest boss can change at his pleasure. The *lex orandi* comprises all twenty centuries of the history of the Church, and there is no man or group of men in the world who can change this twenty-century-old deposit. There is no pope, council, or episcopate that can change the Gospel, the *Depositum Fidei*, or the universal Magisterium of the Church. Nor can the Liturgy of all time be [decisively] changed.

And if it is true that the ancient Rite had an essential apostolic core that then harmoniously grew over the course of the centuries, with progressive modifications (even up to the time of Pius XII and John XXIII), it is also true that these modifications — at times more appropriate, at other times less so, and sometimes perhaps not appropriate at all — have nevertheless always been harmoniously structured in a *continuum* of faith, sacredness, tradition, and beauty.

The Montinian reform broke all this apart, improvisedly inventing a new rite adapted to the needs of the modern world and transforming the sacred Catholic Liturgy from being theocentric to being anthropocentric. From the Holy Sacrifice of the Cross repeated in an unbloody manner through the action of the *sacerdos*, we transitioned to the assembly of the faithful led by its "presider." From a salvific and even exorcistic instrument, we passed to a horizontal populist gathering, susceptible to continual autocephalous and relativistic changes and adaptations that are more or less "festive" and whose supposed "value" is based on winning mass consensus, as if it were a political instrument aimed at the *audience* — an audience that is, however, progressively completely disappearing.

It is useless to continue on this path: the very results of this liturgical subversion speak to minds and hearts and cannot lie.

What it is important to clarify, however, is the reason for this transition from Montinian hypocrisy to Bergoglian sincerity. What has changed?

The general climate has changed. It has literally turned upside down. Montini believed that in a few years no one would remember the Mass of the Ages. Already John Paul II, faced with the evidence that the enemy did not die at all, was constrained — he, too, dragged by the neck — to grant an "indult" (as if the Sacred Catholic Liturgy of all time needed to be forgiven for something in order to continue to exist), which (no one ever says this) was even more restrictive than this latest Bergoglian document, although devoid of the hatred that characterizes the latter. But above all, it was the uncontainable success of the Mass of the Ages among the people — and in particular, among young people — following upon Benedict XVI's motu proprio that was the triggering factor for this hatred.

The "new Mass" has lost in the face of history and the evidence of the facts. The churches are empty, ever more empty; the religious orders — even, and perhaps above all, the most ancient and glorious ones — are disappearing; monasteries and convents are deserted, inhabited only by religious who are now very advanced in years, and upon whose death the doors will be shuttered; vocations are reduced to nothing; even the "otto per mille" [Italian church tax] has been cut in half, despite the obsessive cloying and pathetic third-worldesque publicity it receives; priestly vocations are scarce — everywhere we see pastors with three, four, or at times even five parishes to run. The mathematics of the Council and of the "new Mass" is the most merciless thing that can exist.

But the failure is above all *qualitative*, from the theological, spiritual and moral point of view. Even the clergy that exists and resists [the decay] is in large part openly heretical or in any case tolerant of heresy and error in the exact measure that it is intolerant towards the Tradition, no longer recognizing any objective value in the Magisterium of the Church (except for what pleases it), living instead on theological and dogmatic improvisation, and liturgical and pastoral improvisation as well, all based on doctrinal and moral relativism, accompanied by an immense flood of chatter and empty and inane slogans; nor have we even mentioned the devastating — when it is not monstrous — moral situation of a good part of this clergy.

It's true, there are the so-called "movements" that save the situation a little. But they save it at the cost, once again, of doctrinal relativism, liturgical relativism (guitars, tambourines, entertainment, "participation"), and moral relativism (the only sin is to go against the dictates of this society — today, to go against the vaccine; everything else is more or less permitted). Are these movements still *Catholic?* And in what measure and quality? If we were to analyze their fidelity with theological and doctrinal precision, how many would pass the examination?

"*Lex orandi, lex credendi*," the Church teaches. And in fact, the *lex orandi* of the nineteen centuries prior to Vatican II and the Montinian liturgical reform have produced one type of faith, and the fifty years following it have produced another type of faith — and another type of Catholic. "*You will know them by their fruits*" (Mt 7:16), the Founder of the Church taught.

Exactly.

The fruits of the total failure of modernism (or, if you like — for the most attentive and intelligent — the triumph of the true purposes of modernism), the fruits of the Second Vatican Council, the fruits of the post-council. Where did the hermeneutic of continuity shipwreck? It shipwrecked, along with "Mercy," in the hermeneutic of hatred.

The Mass of the Ages, on the other hand, is the exact antithesis of all this. It is disruptive in its propagation, despite all of the constant hostility and episcopal censorship; it is sanctifying in its perfection; it is engaging precisely because it is the expression of the Eternal and Unchanging, of the Church of all time, of the theology and spirituality of all time, of the liturgy of all time, of the morality of all time.

It is loved because it is divine, sacred, and hierarchically ordered, not human, "democratic" or liberal-egalitarian. It is both divine and human together, like its Founder on the day of the Last Supper. It is loved above all by young people, both the laity who frequent it as well as among those who are approaching the priesthood. While the seminaries of the new rite (the *lex orandi* of Bergoglio) are dens of heresy and apostasy (and it is better to be silent about what else...), the seminaries and novitiates of the world of Tradition overflow with vocations, both male and female, in an unstoppable stream.

The explanation of this incontrovertible fact is found in the one *lex orandi* of the Catholic Church, which is the one willed by God Himself and from which no rebel may escape.

Here is the root of the hatred. It is the worldwide and multi-generational consensus against the enemy who must die, in the face of the failure of that which was supposed to bring new life and instead is withered and dying, because the lifeblood of Grace is missing. It is hatred of kneeling girls wearing white veils, hatred of ladies with many children wearing black veils; hatred of men kneeling in prayer and recollection, perhaps with the rosary in their hands; hatred of priests in cassocks who are faithful to the doctrine and spirituality of all time; hatred of families that are large and peaceful despite the difficulties of this society; hatred of fidelity, of seriousness, of the thirst for the sacred. It is hatred of an entire world, ever more numerous, that has not fallen — or no longer falls — into the humanistic and globalist trap of the "New Pentecost."

At its root, that mad shooting is nothing other than a new murder of Abel by an envious Cain. And in fact, in the new Rite what is offered to God is "the fruit of the earth and the work of human hands" (Cain), while in the Rite of all time what is offered is "*hanc immaculatam Hostiam*" (the first-born Lamb of Abel: Gen 4:2–4). Cain always wins momentarily through violence, but then without fail he suffers the punishment of his hatred and his envy. Abel dies momentarily, but then he lives forever in the *sequela Christi* [following of Christ].

* * *

What will happen now? This is a more interesting and inevitable question than anyone can believe, and at many levels. Since we cannot know the future, let's ask ourselves some fundamental questions in the meantime.

Will all the bishops obey? It seems not.

Apart from the great majority of them, who will fall in line quite willingly either because they share their boss's hatred (almost all of them) or because they are afraid for their personal future, we think that there will be not a few of them who could also oppose the Bergoglian "machine gun," as already appears to be happening in various cases in the USA and in France (we have little hope for the Italians, who are the most fearful and flattened as always), either because they are not hostile in principle [to the ancient rite] or else out of friendship with the various orders tied to the Mass of the Ages, or else perhaps — is this a vain hope? — out of a jolt of just pride in response to the humiliation, which could even be called grotesque, that they have received at the hands of this document, wherein first it says that the decision regarding the granting of permission falls to them, but then not only does it restrict every liberty of action, placing conditions on any minimal possibility of choice, but it also falls into the most blatant contradiction, affirming that in every case they must receive the permission of the Holy See! Will everyone really obey blindly, or will some cracks start to make the system of hatred shake?

And what will happen in the so-called "traditionalist" world? "We will see some good ones," to use a popular expression. Without excluding historical twists. There are those who will fall, who will survive, who perhaps will benefit from it (but beware of the poisoned meatballs of the servants of the Father of Lies!).

Instead, let us trust in divine Grace, so that the faithful not only remain faithful but also grow.

All this will be confirmed above all by an aspect that until now no one has highlighted: the true goal of this multi-decade war against the Sacred Catholic Liturgy, which then is the true goal of the creation of the New Rite *ex nihilo* (better to say *a tavolino*[1]), is the dissolution of the Catholic Liturgy in itself, of every form of the Holy Sacrifice, of doctrine itself, of

---

1   Improvised at a little table.

the Church herself in the great globalist current of the universal religion of the New World Order.

Concepts like the Most Holy Trinity, the Cross, Original Sin, good and evil understood in the Christian and traditional sense, the Incarnation, the Resurrection and thus the Redemption, the Marian privileges and the very figure of the Mother of God who is the Immaculate Conception, the Eucharist and the Sacraments, Christian morality with its Ten Commandments and the doctrine of the universal Magisterium (defense of life, of the family, of rightly-ordered sexuality in all its forms, with all the consequent condemnations of today's follies) — all of this must disappear into the universal and monist cult of the future.

And, in this perspective, the Mass of the Ages is the first element that must disappear, since it is the absolute bulwark of all that they want to make disappear: it is the first obstacle to every form of ecumenism. Over time, this will inevitably involve a gradual movement closer to the Sacred Liturgy of All Time by the body of the faithful who still linger in attendance at the new Rite, perhaps trying to go to those priests who celebrate it with dignity. Because in the end, sooner or later, even those priests will find themselves at the crossroads of having to choose between obedience to evil or disobedience to evil in order to remain faithful to the Good. The comb of the Revolution, in society as in the Church, does not leave any knots: sooner or later they all fall out — if not here, then there. And this will involve the search by the good ones, who are still confused, for Truth and Grace — that is, for the Mass of the Ages. Those who still linger today [at the new rite], so as not to have to deal with these "questions," following these bishops and parish priests, know that, if they want to remain truly Catholic and truly avail themselves of the Body and Blood of the Redeemer . . . their days are numbered. Soon, they will have to choose.

We have now touched on the central problem of this entire situation: How do we behave in the face of a hierarchy that hates the True, the Good, the Beautiful, the Tradition, which fights against the one true *lex orandi* in order to impose another one that is pleasing not to God but to the prince of this world and his "controller" servants (in a certain sense, his "bishops")?

It is the key problem of obedience, over which even in the world of Tradition a dirty game is often played, often incited not by a sincere search for what is best and for the truth but by personal wars, which have today become more acute in the face of the rift caused by health totalitarianism and vaccination.

Obedience — and this is an error that finds its deepest roots even in the pre-conciliar Church, it must be said — is not an end. It is a means of sanctification. Therefore, it is not an absolute value, but rather an instrumental one. It is a positive value, very positive, if it is ordered towards God. But if one obeys Satan, or his servants, or error, or apostasy, then obedience is no longer a good, but rather a deliberate participation in evil.

Exactly like peace. Peace — the divinity of today's subversion — is not an end, but rather an instrument of the good and the just, if it is aimed at creating a good and just society. If it is ordered towards creating or favoring a society that is Satanic, malignant, erroneous, and subversive, then "peace" becomes the instrument of hell.

We must be *"pleasing not to men, but to God, who tests our hearts"* (1 Thess 2 : 4). Exactly! Therefore, whoever obeys men while being aware of facilitating evil and obstructing the Good, whoever they may be — including the ecclesiastical hierarchy, including the pope — in reality becomes an accomplice of evil, of lies, and of error. Whoever obeys in these conditions disobeys God. *"Because no slave is greater than his master"* (Mt 10 : 24). Even Judas was part of the apostolic college. Or else he falls into hypocrisy.

As if — just to give an example from academia — a Catholic traditionalist, self-erected as the dispenser and judge of the seriousness of others, would openly criticize the present pontiff for *Amoris Laetitia* or this latest document, but then, as regards the submission — even obligatory submission! — to vaccinism in itself and the acceptance of the use of human cell lines obtained from fetuses that are the victims of voluntary abortion, he would declare, in order to defend himself in the face of just and obvious general indignation, that he is obedient to what the "Sovereign Pontiff" says on this matter.

The *conditio sine qua non* of all seriousness lies not so much in the "tones" used (also, this is an important aspect but absolutely not primary and above all it remains subjective) but first and foremost in the doctrinal, ideal, and intellectual coherence of the Good and the Truth in their integrity, in every aspect and circumstance.

In other words, we must understand whether the one who guides the Church today wishes to be a faithful servant of God or a faithful servant of the Prince of this world. In the first hypothesis, obedience is due to him and obedience is the instrument of sanctification. In the second, the consequences have to be drawn out. Clearly, with due respect for the norms codified by the Church and as children of the Church and also with the proper education and serenity of tone. But one must always draw out the consequences: the first concern ought to be to always follow and defend the Truth, not the cloying, obsequious, and scrupulous groveling which is the spoiled fruit of a misunderstood Tridentinism. Neither pope nor hierarchy can be used as a referent of truth, in fits and starts, according to one's personal ends.

*   *   *

We are in the most decisive days of human history and also of the history of the Church.

All of the authors who have commented in these days invite their readers to prayer and hope. We will obviously do this too, in the full conviction that everything that is happening in these days and, more generally, since February 2020, is the unequivocal sign that the times are drawing near in which God will intervene to save His Mystical Body and humanity, as well as the order that He Himself has given to creation and to human coexistence, in the measure He wishes to give it, in the way and time of His choosing.

Let us pray; let us hope; let us keep vigil, and let us choose to be on the right side. The enemy helps us in the choice: in fact, he is always the same everywhere.

26

A Bitter Surprise[†]

CARDINAL JOSEPH ZEN

July 21, 2021

WHY DO THEY SEE A PROBLEM WHERE THERE IS NONE, and close their eyes to the problem for which they are also responsible?

Concerns about a much discussed document "against" the Tridentine Mass (see my blog on June 12, 2021) have come true, and the blow has been no less severe because expected. Many tendentious generalizations in the documents wound the hearts of so many good people more than expected, who never gave the slightest reason to be suspected of not accepting the liturgical reform of the Council, much less of not accepting the Council as a whole. Moreover, they remain active members in their parishes.

It came as a bitter surprise to me personally that the "thorough" consultation did not reach me, a cardinal and former member of the Congregation for Divine Worship and the Discipline of the Sacraments. Furthermore, during the years 2007–2009, I was bishop of Hong Kong, and therefore responsible for the implementation of *Summorum Pontificum*, and until now, a well-known supporter of the group.

Not having known either the questionnaire or the responses to the questionnaire, I cannot judge, but only suspect that there was much misunderstanding (or perhaps even manipulation) in the process.

As I read the two documents, I notice (1) an incredible ease (or tendentiousness) in linking the desire to use the *vetus ritus* to the non-acceptance of the *ritus novus* and (2) in associating the non-acceptance of the liturgical reform (which often concerns the way in which it was carried out with its many serious abuses) with a total and profound rejection of the Council itself (for the proponents of this rejection, the diversity of the rite of the Mass is but a small corollary, so much so that the concession regarding the rite did not undo the schism).

The Vatican authorities should ask themselves (and perhaps even make a thorough investigation) why the persistence and perhaps (recent) worsening of the second phenomenon [is occurring].

[†] The Italian original on His Eminence's blog was translated by Bree Dail and published in slightly modified form at New Liturgical Movement on July 21.

The problem is not "which rite do people prefer?," but it is "why don't they go to Mass anymore?" Some surveys show that half of the Christian population in Europe no longer believes in the Real Presence of Jesus in the Eucharist, no longer believes in eternal life! Certainly, we do not blame the liturgical reform; but we just want to say that the problem is much deeper. We cannot evade the question: "Has not the formation of faith been lacking?" "Has not the great work of the Council been wasted?" Isn't the root of evil that attitude of believing that everything can now be changed? Is it not that attitude of believing that this Council cancels out all previous ones, and that the Council of Trent is like the dirt accumulated on the fresco of the Sistine Chapel (as a "liturgist" in our diocese put it)?

The Document obviously sees not only disturbances in the execution of *Summorum Pontificum*, but considers the very existence of a parallel rite to be an evil. Don't paragraphs § 5 and § 6 of Article 3 and Articles 4 and 5 clearly wish for the death of the groups? But, even with that, can't the anti-Ratzinger gentlemen of the Vatican patiently wait for the Tridentine Mass to die along with Benedict XVI, instead of humiliating the venerable Pope Emeritus in this way?

27

The Wonderful Gift of the Usus Antiquior[†]

RAYMOND LEO CARDINAL BURKE

Feast of Saint Mary Magdalene, Penitent
July 22, 2021

MANY FAITHFUL — LAITY, ORDAINED, AND CONSE-crated — have expressed to me the profound distress which the motu pro-prio *Traditionis Custodes* has brought them. Those who are attached to the *Usus Antiquior* (More Ancient Usage) [UA], what Pope Benedict XVI called the Extraordinary Form, of the Roman Rite are deeply disheartened by the severity of the discipline which the motu proprio imposes and offended by the language it employs to describe them, their attitudes, and their conduct. As a member of the faithful, who also has an intense bond with the UA, I fully share in their sentiments of profound sorrow.

As a Bishop of the Church and as a Cardinal, in communion with the Roman Pontiff and with a particular responsibility to assist him in his pastoral care and governance of the universal Church, I offer the following observations.

1. In a preliminary way, it must be asked why the Latin or official text of the motu proprio has not yet been published. As far as I know, the Holy See promulgated the text in Italian and English versions, and, afterwards, in German and Spanish translations. Since the English version is called a translation, it must be assumed that the original text is in Italian. If such be the case, there are translations of significant texts in the English version which are not coherent with the Italian version. In Article 1, the important Italian adjective, "unica," is translated into English as "unique," instead of "only." In Article 4, the important Italian verb, "devono," is translated into English as "should," instead of "must."

2. First of all, it is important to establish, in this and the following two observations (nos. 3 and 4), the essence of what the motu proprio contains.

† Published at Raymond Leo Cardinal Burke's personal website (www.cardinalburke. com) under the title "Statement on the motu proprio *Traditionis Custodes*."

It is apparent from the severity of the document that Pope Francis issued the motu proprio to address what he perceives to be a grave evil threatening the unity of the Church, namely the UA. According to the Holy Father, those who worship according to this usage make a choice which rejects "the Church and her institutions in the name of what is called the 'true Church'," a choice which "contradicts communion and nurtures the divisive tendency . . . against which the Apostle Paul so vigorously reacted."

3. Clearly, Pope Francis considers the evil so great that he took immediate action, not informing Bishops in advance and not even providing for the usual *vacatio legis*, a period of time between the promulgation of a law and its taking force. The *vacatio legis* provides the faithful and especially the Bishops time to study the new legislation regarding the worship of God, the most important aspect of their life in the Church, with a view to its implementation. The legislation, in fact, contains many elements that require study regarding its application.

4. What is more, the legislation places restrictions on the UA, which signal its ultimate elimination, for example, the prohibition of the use of a parish church for worship according to the UA and the establishment of certain days for such worship. In his letter to the Bishops of the world, Pope Francis indicates two principles which are to guide the Bishops in the implementation of the motu proprio. The first principle is "to provide for the good of those who are rooted in the previous form of celebration and [who] need to return in due time to the Roman Rite promulgated by Saints Paul VI and John Paul II." The second principle is "to discontinue the erection of new personal parishes tied more to the desire and wishes of individual priests than to the real need of the 'holy People of God.'"

5. Seemingly, the legislation is directed to the correction of an aberration principally attributable to the "the desire and wishes" of certain priests. In that regard, I must observe, especially in the light of my service as a Diocesan Bishop, it was not the priests who, because of their desires, urged the faithful to request the Extraordinary Form. In fact, I shall always be deeply grateful to the many priests who, notwithstanding their already heavy commitments, generously served the faithful who legitimately requested the UA. The two principles cannot help but communicate to devout faithful who have a deep appreciation and attachment to the encounter with Christ through the Extraordinary Form of the Roman Rite that they suffer from an aberration which can be tolerated for a time but must ultimately be eradicated.

6. From whence comes the severe and revolutionary action of the Holy Father? The motu proprio and the Letter indicate two sources: first, "the

wishes expressed by the episcopate" through "a detailed consultation of the bishops" conducted by the Congregation for the Doctrine of the Faith in 2020, and, second, "the opinion of the Congregation for the Doctrine of the Faith." Regarding the responses to the "detailed consultation" or "questionnaire" sent to the Bishops, Pope Francis writes to the Bishops: "The responses reveal a situation that preoccupies and saddens me, and persuades me of the need to intervene."

7. Regarding the sources, is it to be supposed that the situation which preoccupies and saddens the Roman Pontiff exists generally in the Church or only in certain places? Given the importance attributed to the "detailed consultation" or "questionnaire," and the gravity of the matter it was treating, it would seem essential that the results of the consultation be made public, along with the indication of its scientific character. In the same way, if the Congregation for the Doctrine of the Faith was of the opinion that such a revolutionary measure must be taken, it would seemingly have prepared an Instruction or similar document to address it.

8. The Congregation enjoys the expertise and long experience of certain officials — first, serving in the Pontifical Commission Ecclesia Dei and then in the Fourth Section of the Congregation — who have been charged to treat questions regarding the UA. One must ask whether the "opinion of the Congregation for the Doctrine of the Faith" reflected the consultation of those with the greatest knowledge of the faithful devoted to the UA?

9. Regarding the perceived grave evil constituted by the UA, I have a wide experience over many years and in many different places with the faithful who regularly worship God according to the UA. In all honesty, I must say that these faithful, in no way, reject "the Church and her institutions in the name of what is called the 'true Church.'" Neither have I found them out of communion with the Church or divisive within the Church. On the contrary, they love the Roman Pontiff, their Bishops and priests, and, when others have made the choice of schism, they have wanted always to remain in full communion with the Church, faithful to the Roman Pontiff, often at the cost of great suffering. They, in no way, ascribe to a schismatic or sedevacantist ideology.

10. The Letter accompanying the motu proprio states that the UA was permitted by Pope Saint John Paul II and later regulated by Pope Benedict XVI with "the desire to foster the healing of the schism with the movement of Mons. Lefebvre." The movement in question is the Society of Saint Pius X. While both Roman Pontiffs desired the healing of the schism in question, as should all good Catholics, they also desired to maintain in continuance

the UA for those who remained in the full communion of the Church and did not become schismatic. Pope Saint John Paul II showed pastoral charity, in various important ways, to faithful Catholics attached to the UA, for example, granting the indult for the UA but also establishing the Priestly Fraternity of Saint Peter, a society of apostolic life for priests attached to the UA. In the book, *Last Testament in His Own Words*, Pope Benedict XVI responded to the affirmation, "The reauthorization of the Tridentine Mass is often interpreted primarily as a concession to the Society of Saint Pius X," with these clear and strong words: "This is just absolutely false! It was important for me that the Church is one with herself inwardly, with her own past; that what was previously holy to her is not somehow wrong now" (pp. 201–2). In fact, many who presently desire to worship according to the UA have no experience and perhaps no knowledge of the history and present situation of the Priestly Society of Saint Pius X. They are simply attracted to the holiness of the UA.

11. Yes, there are individuals and even certain groups which espouse radical positions, even as is the case in other sectors of Church life, but they are, in no way, characteristic of the greater and ever increasing number of faithful who desire to worship God according to the UA. The Sacred Liturgy is not a matter of so-called "Church politics" but the fullest and most perfect encounter with Christ for us in this world. The faithful in question, among whom are numerous young adults and young married couples with children, encounter Christ, through the UA, Who draws them ever closer to Himself through the reform of their lives and cooperation with the divine grace which flows from His glorious pierced Heart into their hearts. They have no need to make a judgment regarding those who worship God according to the *Usus Recentior* (the More Recent Usage, what Pope Benedict XVI called the Ordinary Form of the Roman Rite) [UR], first promulgated by Pope Saint Paul VI. As one priest, member of an institute of the consecrated life which serves these faithful, remarked to me: I regularly confess to a priest according to the UR, and participate, on special occasions, in the Holy Mass according to the UR. He concluded: Why would anyone accuse me of not accepting its validity?

12. If there are situations of an attitude or practice contrary to the sound doctrine and discipline of the Church, justice demands that they be addressed individually by the pastors of the Church, the Roman Pontiff and the Bishops in communion with him. Justice is the minimum and irreplaceable condition of charity. Pastoral charity cannot be served, if the requirements of justice are not observed.

13. A schismatic spirit or actual schism are always gravely evil, but there is nothing about the UA which fosters schism. For those of us who knew the UA in the past, like myself, it is a question of an act of worship marked by a centuries-old goodness, truth and beauty. I knew its attraction from my childhood and indeed became very attached to it. Having been privileged to assist the priest as a Mass Server from the time when I was ten years old, I can testify that the UA was a major inspiration of my priestly vocation. For those who have come to the UA for the first time, its rich beauty, especially as it manifests the action of Christ renewing sacramentally His Sacrifice on Calvary through the priest who acts in His person, has drawn them closer to Christ. I know many faithful for whom the experience of Divine Worship according to the UA has strongly inspired their conversion to the Faith or their seeking Full Communion with the Catholic Church. Also, numerous priests who have returned to the celebration of the UA or who have learned it for the first time have told me how deeply it has enriched their priestly spirituality. This is not to mention the saints all along the Christian centuries for whom the UA nourished an heroic practice of the virtues. Some have given their lives to defend the offering of this very form of divine worship.

14. For myself and for others who have received so many powerful graces through participation in the Sacred Liturgy, according to the UA, it is inconceivable that it could now be characterized as something detrimental to the unity of the Church and to its very life. In this regard, it is difficult to understand the meaning of Article 1 of the motu proprio: "The liturgical books promulgated by Saint Paul VI and Saint John Paul II, in conformity with the decrees of Vatican Council II, are the only (*unica*, in the Italian version which seemingly is the original text) expression of the *lex orandi* of the Roman Rite." The UA is a living form of the Roman Rite and has never ceased to be so. From the very time of the promulgation of the Missal of Pope Paul VI, in recognition of the great difference between the UR and the UA, the continued celebration of the Sacraments, according to the UA, was permitted for certain convents and monasteries and also for certain individuals and groups. Pope Benedict XVI, in his Letter to the Bishops of the World, accompanying the motu proprio *Summorum Pontificum*, made clear that the Roman Missal in use before the Missal of Pope Paul VI "was never juridically abrogated and, consequently, in principle, was always permitted."

15. But can the Roman Pontiff juridically abrogate the UA? The fullness of power (*plenitudo potestatis*) of the Roman Pontiff is the power necessary

to defend and promote the doctrine and discipline of the Church. It is not "absolute power" which would include the power to change doctrine or to eradicate a liturgical discipline which has been alive in the Church since the time of Pope Gregory the Great and even earlier. The correct interpretation of Article 1 cannot be the denial that the UA is an ever-vital expression of "the lex orandi of the Roman Rite." Our Lord Who gave the wonderful gift of the UA will not permit it to be eradicated from the life of the Church.

16. It must be remembered that, from a theological point of view, every valid celebration of a sacrament, by the very fact that it is a sacrament, is also, beyond any ecclesiastical legislation, an act of worship and, therefore, also a profession of faith. In that sense, it is not possible to exclude the Roman Missal, according to the UA, as a valid expression of the lex orandi and, therefore, of the lex credendi of the Church. It is a question of an objective reality of divine grace which cannot be changed by a mere act of the will of even the highest ecclesiastical authority.

17. Pope Francis states in his letter to the Bishops: "Responding to your requests, I take the firm decision to abrogate all the norms, instructions, permissions and customs that precede the present motu proprio, and declare that the liturgical books promulgated by the saintly Pontiffs Paul VI and John Paul II, in conformity with the decrees of Vatican Council II, constitute the unique [only] expression of the lex orandi of the Roman Rite." The total abrogation in question, in justice, requires that each individual norm, instruction, permission and custom be studied, to verify that it "contradicts communion and nurtures the divisive tendency . . . against which the Apostle Paul so vigorously reacted."

18. Here, it is necessary to observe that the reform of the Sacred Liturgy carried out by Pope Saint Pius V, in accord with the indications of the Council of Trent, was quite different from what happened after the Second Vatican Council. Pope Saint Pius V essentially put in order the form of the Roman Rite as it had existed already for centuries. Likewise, some ordering of the Roman Rite has been done in the centuries since that time by the Roman Pontiff, but the form of the Rite remained the same. What happened after the Second Vatican Council constituted a radical change in the form of the Roman Rite, with the elimination of many of the prayers, significant ritual gestures, for example, the many genuflections, and the frequent kissing of the altar, and other elements which are rich in the expression of the transcendent reality — the union of heaven with earth — which is the Sacred Liturgy. Pope Paul VI already lamented the situation in a particularly

dramatic way by the homily he delivered on the Feast of Saints Peter and Paul in 1972. Pope Saint John Paul II labored throughout his pontificate, and, in particular, during its last years, to address serious liturgical abuses. Both Roman Pontiffs, and Pope Benedict XVI, as well, strove to conform the liturgical reform to the actual teaching of the Second Vatican Council, since the proponents and agents of the abuse invoked the "spirit of the Second Vatican Council" to justify themselves.

19. Article 6 of the motu proprio transfers the competence of institutes of the consecrated life and societies of apostolic life devoted to the UA to the Congregation for Institutes of Consecrated Life and Societies of Apostolic Life. The observance of the UA belongs to the very heart of the charism of these institutes and societies. While the Congregation is competent to respond to questions regarding the canon law for such institutes and societies, it is not competent to alter their charism and constitutions, in order to hasten the seemingly desired elimination of the UA in the Church.

There are many other observations to be made, but these seem to be the most important. I hope that they may be helpful to all the faithful and, in particular, to the faithful who worship according to the UA, in responding to the motu proprio *Traditionis Custodes* and the accompanying Letter to the Bishops. The severity of these documents naturally generates a profound distress and even a sense of confusion and abandonment. I pray that the faithful will not give way to discouragement but will, with the help of divine grace, persevere in their love of the Church and of her pastors, and in their love of the Sacred Liturgy.

In that regard, I urge the faithful to pray fervently for Pope Francis, the Bishops and priests. At the same time, in accord with can. 212, § 3, "[a]ccording to the knowledge, competence, and prestige which they possess, they have the right and even at times the duty to manifest to the sacred pastors their opinion on matters which pertain to the good of the Church and to make their opinion known to the rest of the Christian faithful, without prejudice to the integrity of faith and morals, with reverence toward their pastors, and attentive to common advantage and the dignity of persons." Finally, in gratitude to Our Lord for the Sacred Liturgy, the greatest gift of Himself to us in the Church, may they continue to safeguard and cultivate the ancient and ever new More Ancient Usage or Extraordinary Form of the Roman Rite.

28

Pope Francis and the Latin Mass: A Mistake?

DAVID DEAVEL

The Imaginative Conservative

July 22, 2021

POPE FRANCIS'S TRADITIONIS CUSTODES LANDED WITH a thud this past week. The legal document *motu proprio* ("on his own initiative") effectively reversed *Summorum Pontificum*, Pope Benedict XVI's 2007 legal document that made it clear that the older form of the Roman liturgy, what many people call the Traditional Latin Mass, was never abrogated and that priests had the legal right to celebrate this form of the liturgy. Pope Francis ruled that priests may not say this form of the liturgy without the permission of their bishops, that these liturgies may not happen in parish churches, that any priest celebrating this liturgy must profess the validity of the Second Vatican Council (1962–65) and acknowledge the legitimacy of the newer form of the Roman Liturgy (known colloquially as the Novus Ordo, or new order), and that any priest ordained from henceforth must have his application to his bishop approved by Rome in order to say it.

These new restrictions are made, Francis writes, in the name of the "concord and unity" of the Church since, according to a letter to bishops accompanying the legal document, Pope Benedict's own decision to allow a freer use of the traditional rite was abused: "Ever more plain in the words and attitudes of many is the close connection between the choice of celebrations according to the liturgical books prior to Vatican Council II and the rejection of the Church and her institutions in the name of what is called the 'true Church.'"[1] In other words, many people who celebrate the older rite reject the Novus Ordo and possibly Vatican II; thus it must be reined in.

Now there are a great number of problems with the thinking behind this. Several years ago Fr. Donald Kloster teamed up with some statisticians to look at how those who regularly go to Traditional Latin Mass compare with statistics on American Catholics derived from various surveys taken

---

1 Pope Francis, Letter of the Holy Father to the Bishops of the Whole World, Accompanying *Traditionis Custodes*, July 16, 2021.

by CARA (a Georgetown institute dedicated to studying Catholic life), Pew Research, and others who are surveying American Catholics in general, who are most likely to attend the Novus Ordo. What they showed was that Traditional Latin Mass Catholics were much more likely to adhere to Catholic teaching on abortion, same-sex marriage, and contraception by wide margins. They also have on average about 1.5 times the number of children as do Novus Ordo attendees, have a weekly Mass attendance rate over 90% (as opposed to 25% of NO), and give five times as much to Church or charity. [2] If the association between liturgies and rejections of Catholic teaching is enough justification for a papal crack down on the Traditional Latin Mass, then those who favor that Mass have a far better case for the abolition of the Novus Ordo. Even ignoring Francis's one-sided application of a principle, this document will affect only those Catholics who are attending the traditional rites in churches that are in full communion with the Church where priests have followed all the legal prescriptions. Those in schismatic churches or in the legally problematic (but not schismatic) Society of St. Pius X are not affected at all.

In other words, Pope Francis seems intent on punishing those most faithful to Catholic teaching and most desirous of being in the good graces of the bishops and the bishop of Rome by making it more difficult for them to celebrate in the rite that they believe best represents and most allows them participation in the fullness of Catholic teaching. In the name of unity, he is willing to marginalize this group of Catholics while large sectors of the Roman Catholic Church, particularly many German clerics and even bishops, continue to publicly cast doubt on Church teaching and indicate their willingness to disobey the pope on matters such as blessing same-sex unions.

There are deeper problems with the coherence of his reasoning. Pope Francis's assertion in his document that the liturgical forms of the Novus Ordo "are the unique expression of the *lex orandi* [law of prayer] of the Roman Rite" seems a bit strained. The Anglican Use liturgy, approved by Pope Benedict for those who came into the Catholic Church from Anglicanism, also differs from the Novus Ordo and yet is considered (as its name indicates) a "use" of the Roman Rite, thus presuming that it participates in the same *lex orandi*. But the pope is given to hyperbole here, it seems, because he associates the revised rites with the will of the Holy Spirit and wants to end celebration of the older rites.

---

2   Brian Williams, "National Survey Results: What We Learned About Latin Mass Attendees," *Liturgy Guy*, February 24, 2019.

Quoting the Vatican II document on the liturgy, *Sacrosanctum Concilium*, he implies that attendees of the Traditional Latin Mass are necessarily "strangers and silent spectators in the mystery of faith" whereas those who attend the Novus Ordo can have "a full understanding of the rites and prayers" and "participate in the sacred action consciously, piously, and actively." He quotes Pope Paul VI, the pope under whose watch the Roman Rite was revised in 1969, who "declared that the revision of the Roman Missal, carried out in the light of ancient liturgical sources, had the goal of permitting the Church to raise up, in the variety of languages, 'a single and identical prayer,' that expressed her unity." Despite these stark weaknesses of the older rite, which can apparently only a) produce passivity and a sense of exile from the liturgy and b) result in a disunified bunch of private prayers (the reasoning is not stated, but it seems to be the old canard that all worshipers at the older rite simply pray their rosaries or other devotions and do not actually pray along with the priest), Francis is still willing to provide for those who prefer the older rite. Though he assures us that these people "need to return in due time to the Roman Rite promulgated by Saints Paul VI and John Paul II."

Let me say with confidence that this universal return will not happen. And that is because Pope Francis's assertions are very problematic, starting with the idea that only the reformed rites are or can be associated with active, conscious participation. Those who have attended both the Traditional Mass and the Novus Ordo know that a simplified rite in vernacular languages, even with a great many verbal responses and physical actions, does not in any way guarantee "active, conscious participation" in liturgy. I primarily assist (a much better term for a conscious, active participation than "attend") at the Novus Ordo but have done so many times at the Traditional Latin Mass and several Eastern Liturgies. In all liturgical celebrations I am perfectly capable of and have been guilty of indulging in anxious worry about other matters, preoccupation with work, daydreams, and anything else rather than active, conscious participation in the prayer of Christ the high priest. If anything, a simplified rite in my own language provides an environment more conducive to being a stranger to the Lord since I can zone out and pop back in more easily. I'm guessing that many people like the older rites such as the Traditional Latin Mass or the Liturgy of St. John Chrysostom (used by many Eastern Catholics and Eastern Orthodox), whether in an ancient language or in English, because one must pay more attention in order to follow along with the services. The paradox of modern liturgical reform is that liturgical rites made less complicated render active, conscious participation more difficult. The same problem attends his argument that returning to the liturgical books of the Novus Ordo, revised under the authority of the canonized popes Paul VI and John Paul II, will show the "singular" and "identical" nature of the Roman liturgical tradition. First of all, the insistence on the use of vernacular languages betrays this notion right off the bat. One can attend the Traditional Latin Mass anywhere and follow along in one's missal (or Mass book), whatever language is being spoken. Will one understand the sermon, which is given in the vernacular? No, but the rest of the Mass can be followed when one is in Tokyo just as easily as when one is in Peoria — or vice versa. It is much more difficult to follow a Mass in a language one does not know than it is to follow the Latin. And given the nature of the Novus Ordo Mass, in which there are at least four canons (or Eucharistic prayers) that are in regular use, it is ever so much harder to figure out what is going on when traveling.

In fact, the question of Eucharistic prayers is only the beginning of it, for there are countless legitimate options for priests celebrating the newer rite. Even putting aside the question of illicit liturgical practices, the "single and identical" nature of the Roman Rite is largely a fiction. Throw in all the liturgical illegalities (most of which are banal and many of which are heterodox) that are practiced and Francis's argument is pretty self-defeating. Though he makes a stab at balance in the letter to the bishops with some stock phrases about stopping such liturgical freewheeling, he is only writing legislation against one form of liturgy. And the liturgy he is legislating against is the one likely to give a vivid sense that there is one "single and identical" liturgy for those who attend it in different parishes around the diocese, country, or world.

Many Vatican observers do not think Pope Francis is all that interested in liturgy, or that if he is, it is only in relation to ecclesio-political issues. I cannot say in what his interest lies. But the document issued under his guidance bears the arguments of an older and slightly out-of-touch generation of clerics and scholars who have never accepted that their "reforms" were not really popular with the vast Catholic body. Or, if "popular," they were popular in the way that a substitute teacher who lets you use your notes for the test is popular. They make things easy, but ease does not breed love. As the statistics cited above show, they certainly have not increased faith among modern people. If anything, those who have experienced conversion in which Catholic liturgy is a part of the process have most often experienced it under the Traditional Latin Mass or one of the Eastern liturgies.

Those who love the Latin Mass say that this power the older liturgy has is not merely because it is foreign or makes one work a bit harder at prayer; they make the further claim that the "reforms" of the modern liturgy were not just ineffective at some level, but that they marred the Roman Rite. While some traditionalists will claim that the Novus Ordo is an invalid liturgy (i.e., it is not a real Mass; no transformation of the elements of bread and wine into the Lord's body and blood, soul and divinity occurs), most claim that although it is valid it is an objectively inferior rite, one that cut out important parts of the Roman Rite as it developed from the age of Gregory the Great until 1962 and added elements that are theologically weaker and not as coherent. As Cardinal Ratzinger observed, the new liturgical books "occasionally show far too many signs of being drawn up by academics and reinforce the notion that a liturgical book can be 'made' like any other book."[3]

There is not really a good case that the Novus Ordo is per se invalid, but even to make claims about its weakness or inferiority is supposedly beyond the pale for many of these clerics and scholars. Never mind that even non-traditionalist scholars such as Lauren Pristas have shown how the theological edges have been sawed off some of the prayers that were "reformed" in the newer rite. How could the Holy Spirit allow a bad or lesser liturgy to be foisted on them? Lost on them is the irony that they think the same thing of the earlier rites. Why would those earlier rites have needed "reform" if they had not somehow lost their true or better form? What would be the point of all the changes if the changes were not for the better?

Defenders of modern liturgy often appeal to the authority of Vatican II's documents. To reject the reforms of the Mass, they say, is to reject a Church Council. This seems to be the implication of Pope Francis's accompanying letter. Yet the Novus Ordo liturgy was not created by the Second Vatican Council but by a committee under Pope Paul VI. One does not even need to criticize Vatican II to criticize the liturgy; one just needs to criticize the popes in charge for approving it. Some object that this criticism is heterodox, but papal infallibility only applies to doctrinal definitions authoritatively made in the name of the Church. There is no teaching that popes will always make wise decisions with regard to the life of the Church. Any cursory skimming of the Catholic Church's history will make that clear.

Even if one criticizes the Vatican II documents on the liturgy that inspired the supposed reforms, it is not clear how, from a Catholic perspective, this is a problem either. Ecumenical Councils (and the Catholic Church considers

---

3   Joseph Ratzinger, *The Feast of Faith* (San Francisco: Ignatius Press, 1981), 85.

Vatican II such) are also only infallible when they authoritatively teach doctrines. Setting out goals for future liturgy or even making disciplinary decisions do not count as defining doctrine. As noted, one of those goals — full, conscious, and active participation in liturgy — is accepted by all Catholics. One might think that the Traditional Latin Mass both allows and encourages it and that the Novus Ordo does not do as well at this goal and be orthodox. Catholic history is full of failed reform councils. As Pope Benedict once noted, it is an open question as to whether Vatican II will be considered a failed council as the Fifth Lateran Council was. He said this despite having been a participant at and a proponent of most of the decisions of Vatican II.

What *Traditionis Custodes* boils down to practically is a decision to marginalize one group of Catholics, tempting many of them to leave the unity in whose name the decision was made. But it is also a decision to attempt to foreclose on the question of whether the Catholic reforms of the late twentieth and early twenty-first centuries were actually successful. Pope Benedict's decision to free the older rite and his terminology of the Novus Ordo as the Ordinary Form of the Roman Rite and the Traditional Latin Mass as the Extraordinary Form was designed, he said, for a mutual enrichment of the two rites. Perhaps, he thought, there could be a development where the two rites met somewhere in the middle someday.

That mutual enrichment business might have been a pipe dream. Perhaps like the immortals in the *Highlander* films, "there can be only one" Roman Rite. But Francis's decision to forego that co-existence and attempt to legally squash the Traditional Latin Mass seems like the move of a man, afraid that he cannot win by persuading others, who flees to legal authority to stop the voices of the competitors. It may also reflect the fact that where the enrichment happened, it was not so mutual. Many, especially younger priests and laypeople, are more likely to seek out Novus Ordo liturgies that look more like the Traditional Latin Mass. And when they did, even simply by following the letter of the Novus Ordo law, they were treated with suspicion anyway. "Nobody can turn a blind eye," wrote Cardinal Gerhard Müller in an essay on the document, "to the fact that even those priests and laypeople who celebrate Mass according to the order of the Missal of St. Paul VI are now being widely decried as traditionalist."[4]

It is quite possible that the next pope will reverse Francis's decision. In the meantime, however, Francis's ham-handed move is much more likely to steel the resolve of those who make the argument that the Roman Rite should return to its earlier form. The pope whose motto is that the Church

4   See chapter 16.

should "make a mess" has betrayed the weakness of his arguments by resorting to a bullying use of the law in order to shut down an argument that is messy for those attached to the 1960s and unwilling to admit they have made mistakes. The Holy Spirit is certainly progressive. But sometimes true progress involves, as Chesterton noted, admitting you've gone down a wrong road and retracing your steps. At the very least, it involves taking seriously the evidence that you might have done so. This would be a good step for a pope who has spoken at length about the need for humility even in leaders of the Church.

29

In Defence of the
Traditional Latin Mass

DANIEL MCGLONE

The Tablet

July 22, 2021

THE APOSTOLIC LETTER TRADITIONIS CUSTODES recently issued by Pope Francis provides local bishops with new powers to regulate and restrict access of the faithful to the Extraordinary Form of the Mass. The Extraordinary Form often attracts a degree of uncertainty and sometimes hostility from those not familiar with it. This is one person's experience of it.

In the 1986 film *The Mission*, the papal emissary Cardinal Altamirano is sent to report on the eighteenth-century Jesuit missions in the Paraguayan jungle. He surveys the missions, learning of their work, the numbers they care for and how they have brought the faith to people. In writing about new restrictions imposed against the Extraordinary Form I am tempted to begin the same way, pointing out the number of Mass centers, the number of Catholics they care for, their extensive social and spiritual work, the good they do. Instead I will write on a more personal note.

First it is important to appreciate Catholic life in my particular part of the world. I live in the Ballarat diocese, Australia, a place devastated by the experience of sexual abuse of the laity by priests and religious. Between 1980 and 2015 there were 139 people raped by 21 abusers, 17 of which were priests, just under ten per cent of the priest population of the diocese.

The fences of the main Catholic churches and institutions are festooned with ribbons, each symbolizing the experience of an individual who was broken by this experience of sexual abuse either directly or as a friend or a family member of a victim. The current bishop, in a ritualistic manner, attempted to take down the ribbons on the fences of the local cathedral, placing them all in an iron box to be set in a memorial garden. The people of Ballarat would have none of that. It had been previous Bishops of Ballarat who had allowed the abuse to happen. They had moved priests on to new parishes when complaints of sexual abuse were received. It was part of a strategy to hush things up, placing the interests of the clergy involved before that of ordinary people. So the ribbons were put back the very next day in greater numbers. People were tired of the contempt clerics held them in and did not want the bishop to forget.

I am 52, married, with two daughters, one thirteen, the other seventeen. I work as a legal advocate. My wife is 48 and teaches literature and language. We moved to Ballarat eight years ago when the girls were five and nine. It was a difficult transition. We had come from a rich parish in Melbourne that was in the care of Opus Dei. Ballarat was a spiritual desert. Apart from the school Masses, attendance at Mass seemed to be the reserve of the very old clinging to a culture of folk hymns I found cringeworthy even when they were first rolled out forty years ago. It seemed to be a church in a time warp, stuck in the 1980s when the enormity of the sexual scandal here first began to hit home, striking at the heart of the faith of many and killing it dead. I felt that there were no people my children's age. We were raising them Catholic. They wanted to know why things felt so different to Melbourne. I didn't want to lie to them but how could I explain to them that this faith I had said was a vital source of love and hope had been associated with such evil?

There was an out. A little enclave of laity that organized Masses following the pre-1970 rubrics. This was an oasis. People were open and kind. Prior to Mass there was confession and rosary. After there were cups of tea, cakes and warm-hearted conversation. My girls could see these people were genuinely devout and able to take the faith they expressed so reverently at Mass into their daily lives. That was immediately clear in the kindness these people showed once they stepped outside the church into the world outside. I got involved.

During my time assisting with the pre-1970 Mass here in Ballarat I have watched it grow. It seemed to have an attraction for other young families in the same way it had had for us when were first arrived. Numbers grew. People of all sorts of backgrounds: mechanics; council workers; lawyers; physiotherapists; farmers; laborers; teachers; cleaners; nurses; students; unemployed. I have always thought that a parish is not a parish unless there is a baby crying during Mass. We have a small chorus of young people making this kind of racket. The place is vital and alive.

I have found that the Latin Mass, as they call it here, has never been popular with clergy. I have heard all sorts of uncharitable caricatures described by priests about the pre-1970 ceremonies and the people who support it. They seem particularly hostile to it, especially priests who were less committed to the faith generally, or so it seems to me. But like many I tired of the performing wanna-be celebrity priests some time ago. At university, Mass had started to feel like a kindergarten assembly presided over by a fragile individual whom I had to put at ease rather than someone I could turn to with my own spiritual needs. I needed to go deeper. I studied philosophy in my undergraduate degree. I began to explore different traditions that the Church had to offer. Then I came across the Tridentine form. Through it I discovered the extraordinary mysticism that the Catholic tradition had to offer. I learnt about curious figures like Augustine, Roy Campbell, John Dobree Dalgairns, Huysmans and Caryll Houselander. This experience of the Mass became a spiritual anchor when my experience of the secular world was drawing me away from the Church. I attend both forms of the Mass but I remain deeply attached to the Latin Mass. It is like an old friend that has guided me through a dark time. I go to it regularly and I was not surprised in such a damaged place like Ballarat it was there offering me and my family solace.

A little about myself. I am perhaps not typical of what people think of as a Latin Mass attendee. I was a student activist with a particular concern for social justice and the environment. I regularly volunteered working with the poor living on the streets. I have taken that into my work where I have worked with indigenous Australians and the socially marginalized. I ran for parliament for the Australian Labor Party, the social democratic party here. At the same time I have done work for the Church having been a consultant on legal matters and presented policy submissions to government bodies on behalf of Catholic organizations. I have attempted to live my faith as publicly and fully as possible.

The reality is I am not atypical. Latin Mass attendees come from all walks of life, from a wide variety of social backgrounds and occupations. Yet despite our differences we all come together in a wonderful spirit of fellowship as Catholics.

I would like to say as a Catholic I feel regularly cut down by the Church. I have spoken of the horror of sexual abuse. I have also seen terrible financial abuse. Parishes that families helped build and gave money to at great personal expense over many years sold off without much notice and for not much money. Pastoral programs launched to great fanfare with expensive publicity ending up being an expensive waste of time for little benefit. And now the extraordinary financial scandals coming out of Rome. But the most depressing thing of all is the contempt so many clergy seem to have for the quiet devotions of ordinary people. It is difficult not to think you hate us. We have done you no harm so the only thing I can think of to explain this animosity is a distaste for vulnerable people and the obligation to care for them. Many people hate their job after a time but this is a devastating experience for the average Catholic when it is a priest who hates his job.

Moves against the Latin Mass seem to me typical of a clerical hate towards the laity. I do not understand it. Those who attend the Latin Mass love the Church. We love God. We try to live good lives as Catholics. As ordinary people attending Mass we should be to bishops and priests nothing less than the face of Christ. I am not sure why we warrant such contempt.

At the end of The Mission the success of the Jesuit Fathers meant nothing. The missions were closed. This led to different responses. The Robert De Niro character, Rodrigo Mendoza, attempts violent resistance. Jeremy Irons' character, Father Gabriel, chooses instead to walk towards the soldiers solemnly carrying a monstrance, Christ in the Blessed Sacrament. The response of Rome was the same. Both characters are brutally pushed aside for agendas far removed from the people they cared for.

30

An Evil Ukase from Pope Francis[†]

BISHOP ROB MUTSAERTS

Paarse Pepers
July 22, 2021

POPE FRANCIS PROMOTES SYNODALITY: EVERYONE should be able to talk, everyone should be heard. This was hardly the case with his recently published motu proprio *Traditionis Custodes*, an ukase that must put an immediate termination on the traditional Latin Mass. In so doing, Francis puts a big bold line through *Summorum Pontificum*, Pope Benedict's motu proprio that gave ample scope to the old Mass.

The fact that Francis here uses the word of power without any consultation indicates that he is losing authority. This was already evident earlier when the German Bishops' Conference took no notice of the Pope's advice regarding the synodality process. The same occurred in the United States when Pope Francis called on the Bishops' Conference not to prepare a document on worthy Communion. The pope must have thought that it would be better [in this case] not to give advice any more, but rather a writ of execution, now that we're talking about the traditional Mass!

The language used looks very much like a declaration of war. Every pope since Paul VI has always left openings for the old Mass. If any changes were made [in that opening], they were minor revisions — see, for example, the indults of 1984 and 1988. John Paul II firmly believed that bishops should be *generous* in allowing the Tridentine Mass. Benedict opened the door wide with *Summorum Pontificum*: "What was sacred then is sacred now." Francis slams the door hard through *Traditionis Custodes*. It feels like a betrayal and is a slap in the face to his predecessors.

By the way, the Church has never abolished liturgies. Not even Trent [did so]. Francis breaks completely with this tradition. The motu proprio contains, briefly and powerfully, some propositions and commands. Things are explained in more detail by means of an accompanying longer statement. This statement contains quite a few factual errors. One of them is the claim

---

† The Dutch original at the bishop's blog (https://vitaminexp.blogspot.com/2021/07/een-kwaadaardige-oekaze-van-paus.html) was translated by Peter Kwasniewski and published at *Rorate Caeli* on July 26.

that what Paul VI did after Vatican II is the same as what Pius V did after Trent. This is completely far from the truth. Remember that before that time [of Trent] there were various transcribed manuscripts in circulation and local liturgies had sprung up here and there. The situation was a mess.

Trent wanted to restore the liturgies, remove inaccuracies, and check for orthodoxy. Trent was not concerned with rewriting the liturgy, nor with new additions, new Eucharistic prayers, a new lectionary, or a new calendar. It was all about ensuring uninterrupted organic continuity. The missal of 1570 harks back to the missal of 1474 and so on back to the fourth century. There was continuity from the fourth century onwards. After the fifteenth century, there are four more centuries of continuity. From time to time, there were at most a few minor changes — an addition of a feast, commemoration, or rubric.

In the conciliar document *Sacrosanctum Concilium*, Vatican II asked for liturgical reforms. All things considered, this was a conservative document. Latin was maintained, Gregorian chants retained their legitimate place in the liturgy. However, the developments that followed Vatican II are far removed from the council documents. The infamous "spirit of the council" is nowhere to be found in the council texts themselves. Only 17% of the orations of the old missal of Trent can be found [intact] in the new missal of Paul VI.[1] You can hardly speak of continuity, of an organic development. Benedict recognized this, and for that reason gave ample space to the Old Mass. He even said that no one needed his permission ("what was sacred then is still sacred now").

Pope Francis is now pretending that his motu proprio belongs to the organic development of the Church, which utterly contradicts the reality. By making the Latin Mass practically impossible, he finally breaks with the age-old liturgical tradition of the Roman Catholic Church. Liturgy is not a toy of popes; it is the heritage of the Church. The Old Mass is not about nostalgia or taste. The pope should be the guardian of Tradition; the pope is a gardener, not a manufacturer. Canon law is not merely a matter of positive law; there is also such a thing as natural law and divine law, and, moreover, there is such a thing as Tradition that cannot simply be brushed aside.

What Pope Francis is doing here has nothing to do with evangelization and even less to do with mercy. It is more like ideology.

Go to any parish where the Old Mass is celebrated. What do you find there? People who just want to be Catholic. These are generally not people who engage in theological disputes, nor are they against Vatican II (though

1 [In fact, the actual figure is 13%: see the study mentioned in note 2 on pg. 76. — Ed.]

they *are* against the way it was implemented). They love the Latin Mass for its sacredness, its transcendence, the salvation of souls that is central to it, the dignity of the liturgy. You encounter large families; people feel welcome. It is only celebrated in a small number of places. Why does the pope want to deny people this? I come back to what I said earlier: it is ideology. It is either Vatican II — including its implementation, with all its aberrations — or nothing! The relatively small number of believers (a number growing, by the way, as the Novus Ordo is collapsing) who feel at home with the traditional Mass must and will be eradicated. That is ideology and evil.

If you really want to evangelize, to be truly merciful, to support Catholic families, then you hold the Tridentine Mass in honor. As of the date of the motu proprio, the Old Mass may not be celebrated in parish churches (where then?); you need explicit permission from your bishop, who may only allow it on certain days; for those who will be ordained in the future and want to celebrate the Old Mass, the bishop must seek advice from Rome. How dictatorial, how unpastoral, how unmerciful do you want to be!

Francis, in Article 1 of his motu proprio, calls the Novus Ordo (the present Mass) "the unique expression of the *lex orandi* of the Roman Rite." He therefore no longer distinguishes between the Ordinary Form (Paul VI) and the Extraordinary Form (Tridentine Mass). It has always been said that *both* are expressions of the *lex orandi*, not just the Novus Ordo. Again, the Old Mass was never abolished! I never hear from Bergoglio about the many liturgical abuses that exist here and there in countless parishes. In parishes everything is possible — except the Tridentine Mass. All weapons are thrown into the fray to eradicate the Old Mass.

Why? For God's sake, why? What is this obsession of Francis to want to erase[2] that small group of traditionalists? The pope should be the guardian of tradition, not the jailer of tradition. While *Amoris Laetitia* excelled in vagueness, *Traditionis Custodes* is a perfectly clear declaration of war.

I suspect that Francis is shooting himself in the foot with this motu proprio. For the Society of St. Pius X, it will prove to be good news. They will never have been able to guess how indebted they'd be to Pope Francis . . .

---

2   The bishop here uses the German word *ausradieren*, which was used by Hitler when he was speaking of erasing cities off the map: "Wir werden ihre Städte ausradieren."

31

Pope Francis Is Losing His Culture War

TIM STANLEY

The Spectator

July 22, 2021

SINCE I WROTE ABOUT THE POPE'S DECLARATION OF war on the Old Rite,[1] something unexpected and beautiful has happened. Many bishops have held the line. Far from all: some have gleefully welcomed the opportunity to extinguish the pretty rite, and intellectual justification has come, predictably, from the Jesuits, who haven't been sound since *The Exorcist*. But so many other bishops have judiciously, almost seditiously, chosen to interpret the Pope's instruction to the letter while ignoring its spirit, and given immediate dispensation to the priests who already say it to continue. Others, I'm told, have written or telephoned Old Rite-saying priests to offer personal comfort and reassurance. This is how you quietly turn the tide in a culture war. Ignore the bullies.

Why would the bishops — including friends of Francis — do this? Because he took them by surprise. He insulted them. Francis always said he wanted a "synodal church" that proceeded by debate and consensus, but this was a bolt from the blue: could it be that all along synodality was a way of imposing liberal reform from the center under the guise of consultation?

Second, whatever these men thought of the Old Rite fourteen years ago, it's been active in their dioceses for a while now and they can no longer see any harm in it. In fact, so-called traddy priests are some of the hardest working. Why should an overburdened bishop want to upset or antagonize good priests or laity over a debate that was resolved yonks ago — or so the Vatican has long insisted?

Some readers of my previous column complained that I didn't explain for a non-Catholic the distinctions between Old and New Rites, but that's sort of the point. Beyond the externals, the official line is that they don't exist. The Old Rite is all-Latin, the priest faces away from the people, the congregation, one might say, witnesses rather than actively participates,

1   See chapter 9.

yadayada — but though much of the liturgy was reformed in the 1970s, the genius of Catholic tradition is to keep and advance ancient principles through new methods, to tweak the outward appearance of a liturgy, by saying it in English or facing the congregation, while maintaining internal meaning and historical coherence.

This was Benedict XVI's reading of it, anyway. In 2007, when he issued *Summorum Pontificum*, permitting wider use of the Old Rite, he didn't mean it as a comment on the New Rite but, on the contrary, to reassert that the two Rites have the same heritage, the same validity, and can even enrich one another — and Heaven knows, aspects of Church life had grown utilitarian and sterile. I am personally of the view that one of the best qualities of Catholicism, one of the things that attracted me to it, is that it is beautiful. This is not mere aesthetics: like St. Thomas digging his finger into Christ's side, humans have a desire to see in order to believe, and religious beauty helps us come closer to God through sensual experience. This is the philosophy of most of the Catholic priests saying the Old Rite: far from being *Looney Tunes* schismatics, as Francis seems to imagine, they want to restore and revivify the whole Church, and by encouraging the Old Rite in a whole new social context, add something to our appreciation of the New.

Benedict, in short, gifted the Church the conditions for greater unity. It is Francis who has threatened disunity by assuming there is controversy where for 99 per cent of Catholics there was none, and Francis who has reignited debate about the liturgy, not the trads. The Benedictine consensus was that the New Rite had strong roots in the Old, but if one disinherits the Old, then what is the basis for the New? Are we saying that sometime in the 1970s the Catholic Church just invented an entirely new liturgy, that this was Year Zero in the history of Catholicism? Such an idea has profound implications for the Church's authority today.

Francis behaves like a man in a tree, angrily sawing off the branch upon which he sits. It all defies common sense. He could've wedded Benedict's theory of the development of tradition to his own superb project of stressing the Church's pastoral role, but he turned out to have limited regard for the pastoral needs of priests and no intention whatsoever of "accompanying" those who want the Old Rite, or probably even those who simply want a bit of beauty. Throughout history, theological radicals have assumed that they know what the poor want better than they do themselves, and in their eagerness to remake the world to suit the image in their mind of a poor person's utopia, one always ends up making everything look drab and depressing (consider Stevenage). The end of history, if the progressives have anything to do with it, will have no color, no perfume, no gilt, no joy. I am reminded of Mark Twain's insistence that if there's no smoking in Heaven, he'd rather not go.

The bishops have shown greater sensitivity for human need, particularly that of their priests, some of whom — I know this because they've told me — feel their relationship with their bishop has been renewed. More bishops, I hope, will proceed in this fashion. There is, however, one very important extra thing to do.

They must commit to giving the Old Rite a future. The diplomatic response to the Pope's instruction is to preserve it in the present by giving the green light to priests who already say it, but the seminaries are bursting with young men who want to say it, too — and if Benedict was right, and if tradition flows like the River Tiber from the Old to the New Rite, one cannot logically deprive them of the right to do just that. Cardinal Zen made the crucial point that what rite people attend is far less significant than the fact that fewer and fewer Western Catholics attend church at all,[2] and reversing that trend will require genuine unity, pastoral care and a much greater concern for liturgical excellence. The Church should draw people to it, like the sun.

---

2   See chapter 26.

32

Competing Concepts of Unity[†]

DR. TOMASZ DEKERT

Christianitas

July 23, 2021

MARK SEARLE, A WELL-KNOWN AMERICAN LITURGIST, in one of his books wrote that someone who was theologically formed, or more precisely, accustomed to thinking about liturgy in the first place in terms of sacramental "matter and form," can approach real rituals from the position of one who "already knows what is significant and what is not," and who views "the rest, whether it be the rite or people, as dispensable."[1] These words came to mind when I reflected on the motu proprio *Traditionis Custodes* and its background. Well, I have the impression that they say something very important about the deep causes of the present situation, causes that are in no way limited to Rome's usual reaction to the alleged destruction of the Church's unity by the presence and development of groups centered around the liturgy in the classical Roman Rite, but that are stuck in a kind of mental alienation of parts of the Church elites, both academic and hierarchical. And not only the present ones, but above all those from half a century ago.

Early critics of the post-conciliar liturgical changes, who, in addition to being Catholic, were also prominent figures in sociology and anthropology — I mean Mary Douglas and Victor Turner — pointed out that from their professional perspective, the way in which the reform was carried out was burdened with the error of misdiagnosing the true needs of the masses of believers in terms of things such as the consistency, repetitiveness, and archaic nature of the ritual. As in the famous case study of the "bog Irish" in Douglas's *Natural Symbols*, the elites turned out to be insensitive to "dense" and ritualized symbolic communication, which in turn built a whole world of religious references, not necessarily conceptualized, for people from classes of lower cultural capital. Therefore, the changes in the

---

[†] The translation from the Polish original, by the author, was published at *New Liturgical Movement* on August 5.

[1] Mark Searle, *Called to Participate: Theological, Ritual, and Social Perspective*, ed. Barbara Searle and Anne Y. Koester (Collegeville, MN: Liturgical Press, 2006), 20.

structure of the Catholic ritual system forced by intellectuals and hierarchs constituted, as in the parable of the prophet Nathan, taking the poor
man's last sheep. The point, however, is not to reduce the problem to the
relationship between different social classes. It is more about noticing the
fact that the beginning of a specific split in the Church lies at the moment
when her elites began to think of themselves as omnipotent regulators of
the life of this huge and very internally diversified social body, based on
their own intellectual competences and possessed power.

In an article from 1969, Yves Congar describes in an almost surprising way
the importance of the permanence and traditionality of the liturgical ritual:

> The conservative character of the liturgy makes it possible for it
> to preserve and transmit intact the values whose importance one
> epoch may have forgotten, but which the next epoch is happy
> to find intact and preserved, so that it can live from them again.
> Where would we be if this liturgical conservatism had not resisted
> the late medieval taste for sensory devotions, the eighteenth cen-
> tury's individualistic, rational, and moralizing imperatives, the
> nineteenth century's critique, or the modern period's subjective
> philosophies? Thanks to the liturgy everything has been retained
> and transmitted. Ah! Let us not expose ourselves to the reproach
> sixty years hence that we squandered and lost the sacred heritage
> of the Catholic communion as it is deployed in the slow flow of
> time. Let us keep a healthy awareness that we carry in ourselves
> only a moment, the tip of the iceberg in relation to a reality which
> is beyond us in every way. [2]

I would add one more to these values. Wherever ritual is a widely accepted
medium and — at the same time — an object of *traditio* (a content handed
on) in which all members of the community participate, regardless of social
class, political affiliation, cultural capital, etc. (which does not mean that it
has to be the same everywhere), there the foundations of unity are so deep
that they transcend all particularisms that are abundant in such a vast social
organism. The necessary condition, however, is not the "uniformity," which
is, by the way, often mythologized in traditionalist thinking, but precisely
the *traditionality*, a certain "organicity" (at least on the perception level)
of the relationship between the community and its ritual system. In the
circumstances in which this relationship found itself in the Roman Church
after the reforms of St. Pius V, the above-mentioned condition required
that a possible reform process should not in any way violate the visible

---

2   Yves Congar, O. P., "Autorité, Initiative, Coresponsabilité," *La Maison-Dieu* 97 (1969): 55.

and experiential traditional liturgical forms. At the level of the Conciliar Constitution on the Sacred Liturgy *Sacrosanctum Concilium*, the awareness of this fact was expressed in one of the sentences of section 23: "there must be no innovations unless the good of the Church genuinely and certainly requires them; and care must be taken that any new forms adopted should in some way grow organically from forms already existing."

As we know, in the end the liturgical reform proceeded in a way that differed greatly from the fulfillment of this condition. Fr. John Baldovin, S. J., an ardent supporter of reform and critic of traditionalist tendencies, expressed it with endearing and at the same time brutal simplicity:

> The implementation of the reform, under Bugnini's tutelage and involving dozens of experts in the fields of history, theology and pastoral practice, resulted in the complete vernacularization of the liturgy, reorientation of the presiding minister vis-à-vis the assembly, an extensive and even radical reform of the order of Mass, and a major overhaul of the liturgical year, not to mention a complete revision of every sacramental liturgy and daily liturgical prayer. [3]

It should be added that the liturgy subjected to such a total "makeover" could not be introduced in the entire Church solely on the basis of the authority of the professors' titles or even the cardinal hats of its creators, but it required the involvement of the supreme authority, i.e. the Pope. Paul VI, although there are known cases when he vetoed the proposals of the Consilium, was himself actively involved in the reform process, and willing to use his power to this end. The reformed Roman Rite was proclaimed, and the Church was obliged to accept it, with the simultaneous — administratively ordered and almost non-exceptional — suspension of the functioning of the previous ritual. And this was precisely the situation in which the Church elites, or at least some of the dominant part of them at the time, manifested their sense of omnipotence as regulators of religious life throughout the Church from the position of those who "know better" and "can do more." The Church as a whole was to embody in her new liturgy a series of concepts and beliefs of a certain particular group of her members about what she and her liturgy were to be.

The founding sin of the breakdown of unity, for which Francis declares such concern in *Traditionis Custodes*, is the very fact of the reform understood and carried out in this way. Introducing into the bloodstream of the Church

---

3   John F. Baldovin, "The Twentieth Century Reform of the Liturgy: Outcomes and Prospects," *Institute of Liturgical Studies Occasional Papers* 126 (2017): 4–5.

rituals that are "non-traditional" in a very visible and experiential way, but enforced by the power of the highest authority (in fact, as a result of the transition from a kind of self-steering to manual control, this act made the rites dependent on this authority and its bureaucratic agendas) has practically abolished the "naturally" and profoundly unifying influence of the liturgy. In a sense, *the liturgy itself was problematized*; it put before each of the faithful the need to respond to the proposal of a new ritual submitted to him — albeit in an "irrefutable" mode.

Of course, for a large part of the members of the Church, the mandate of the papal seal was enough for them, and the fact that today they participate in rituals other than the day before yesterday, became the order of the day. Many elements of this new liturgical reality were attractive to some Catholics, and even gave a sense of a new quality of participation. But there were also those who deeply understood and felt the meaning and importance of the traditional Catholic liturgy, and who saw in the Vatican's "proposal" a number of things that were dubious or even wrong; and the fact that, as Archbishop Bugnini argued, the actions of the reformers were accompanied by "the scrutiny of hundreds of experts and of the Church's hierarchy,"[4] and that everything had been approved by the Pope, did not provide sufficient justification in the eyes of tradition-loving faithful. Here, in fact, we have a whole spectrum of attitudes, from trust in Church authority, saturated with deep sadness and the more or less rationalized submission to authority's orders, to the complete refusal of such submission in the name of the "true Roman Church" and other products of overwhelming cognitive dissonance. Finally, there were those who could be described as victims of the Church's modernization process, that is, people who simply drifted away in the post-conciliar period, or at least stopped attending church. It is not known just how many people in this large crowd who, during and after the Council, in one way or another departed from the Church[5] did so because of the liturgy. In this very group the motivations were certainly varied. Some people were affected by the loss of the sense of the Church's credibility, others by fatigue with destabilization and permanent fluctuations, others by disgust due to the invasion of pop culture in the liturgical space or other such phenomena. Some of the faithful have also fallen victim to the discouragement resulting

---

4 Annibale Bugnini, "The Consilium and Liturgical Reform," *The Furrow* 19.3 (1968): 177.
5 Two sociological works, on France and the English-speaking world respectively, have been recently devoted to this topic: Guillaume Cuchet, *Comment notre monde a cessé d'être chrétien. Anatomie d'un effondrement* (Paris: Éditions de Seuil, 2018), 95–141; Stephen Bullivant, *Mass Exodus: Catholic Disaffiliation in Britain and America since Vatican II* (New York: Oxford University Press, 2019).

from an excessively progressive approach (interestingly described by James Hitchcock),[6] that is, the inability to find "something" appropriately "relevant" in ever new experimental para-ritual forms. Nevertheless, although the post-conciliar losses of the Church have never been comprehensively established, it is difficult to imagine that the liturgical factor would be irrelevant here; in fact it seems to have played a key role.

Since history is written by the victors, the dominant narrative in the post-conciliar Church makes reform a providential, even theological movement, and a great pastoral success, proclaimed in probably every subsequent document on the liturgy. There is no doubt that, in the scale of the entire Church, the reform campaign was successful. As a result, a new face of "unity" was obtained, which is not rooted in the organic totality of the traditional ritual — this is practically non-existent in the reformed liturgy — but which is based on trust and obedience to the ecclesiastical authority (especially the Pope) and the post-conciliar liturgical order introduced by it. In the victors' narrative, the fraction of the dissatisfied or dissenters and their activity are either ignored in silence or accused of schism, that is, for nothing but active disobedience. However, from the perspective of the above-presented argument, one has to look at it differently. Opposition does not simply arise from disobedience, as if the opponents were just rude brats or prideful hotheads, but from a different understanding of the fundamental principle of unity itself. And the fact that there has been a radical change in this area and the controversy it sparked was *not* caused by "traditionalists," but by the post-conciliar reform itself. It was what destroyed, or at least greatly violated, the foundations of the unity of the Church. This fact tends to be overlooked in current Catholic discourse.

Traditionis Custodes consciously operates within the strictly narrowed framework of the above-mentioned new face of "unity," which it elevates to the rank of absolute, central value. The projects of the "post-conciliar" Church and liturgy, precisely because of their foundation in acts of power, are understood here as a reality without alternative — ultimately ("in due time," as Francis puts it in his letter to the bishops), one who will not accept them (= who will not obey), has no right to be in the Church and call himself Catholic — even if he or she was baptized, believes in all dogmas, leads a full prayer life and sacramental life, tries to do works of mercy and live the gospel. Sounds absurd? But that's what the Pope announced to us.

---

6   See James Hitchcock, *Recovery of the Sacred: Reforming the Reformed Liturgy* (San Francisco: Ignatius Press, 1974).

33

A Drastic and Tragic Act

DIANE MONTAGNA INTERVIEWS
BISHOP ATHANASIUS SCHNEIDER
The Remnant
July 23, 2021

DM: *Your Excellency, Pope Francis's new apostolic letter, issued motu proprio on July 16, 2021, is called* Traditionis Custodes (Guardians of Tradition). *What was your initial impression of the choice of this title?*

AS: My initial impression was of a shepherd who instead of having the smell of his sheep, is angrily beating them with a stick.

What are your general impressions of the motu proprio and of Pope Francis's accompanying letter to the bishops of the world, in which he explains his rationale for restricting the Traditional Latin Mass?

In his programmatic Apostolic Exhortation, *Evangelii Gaudium*, Pope Francis advocates "certain attitudes which foster openness to the message: approachability, readiness for dialogue, patience, a warmth and welcome which is non-judgmental" (n. 165). Yet in reading the new motu proprio and accompanying letter, one has the opposite impression, namely, that the document, as a whole, exhibits a pastoral intolerance and even spiritual rigidity. The motu proprio and accompanying letter communicate a judgmental and unwelcoming spirit. In the document on Human Fraternity (signed in Abu Dhabi on February 4, 2019), Pope Francis embraces the "diversity of religions," whereas in his new motu proprio he resolutely rejects the diversity of liturgical forms in the Roman Rite.

What a glaring contrast in attitude this motu proprio presents, compared to the guiding principle of Pope Francis's pontificate, i.e., inclusiveness and a preferential love for minorities and those on the peripheries in the life of the Church. And what an astonishingly narrow-minded stance one discovers in the motu proprio, in contrast to Pope Francis's own words: "We know that we are tempted in various ways to adopt the logic of privilege that separates, excludes and closes us off, while separating, excluding and closing off the dreams and lives of so many of our brothers and sisters" (Homily at the Vespers, December 31, 2016). The new norms of the motu

143

proprio demean the millennial form of the *lex orandi* of the Roman Church and, at the same time, close off "the dreams and lives of so many" Catholic families, and especially of young people and young priests, whose spiritual lives and love for Christ and the Church have grown and greatly benefited from the traditional form of the Holy Mass.

The motu proprio establishes a principle of a rare liturgical exclusivity, by stating that the new promulgated liturgical books are the only [*unica*] expression of the *lex orandi* of the Roman Rite (Art. 1). What a contrast this position, too, is with these words of Pope Francis: "It is true that the Holy Spirit brings forth different charisms in the Church, which at first glance may seem to create disorder. Under his guidance, however, they constitute an immense richness, because the Holy Spirit is the Spirit of unity, which is not the same thing as uniformity" (Homily of Pope Francis at the Catholic Cathedral of the Holy Spirit, Istanbul, Saturday, November 29, 2014).

What are your greatest concerns about the new document?

As a bishop, one of my chief concerns is that, instead of fostering a greater unity by the coexistence of diverse authentic liturgical forms, the motu proprio creates a two-class society in the Church, i.e., first-class Catholics and second-class Catholics. The privileged first-class are those who adhere to the reformed liturgy, i.e., the Novus Ordo, and the second-class Catholics, who will now barely be tolerated, include a large number of Catholic families, children, young people and priests who, in the last decades, have grown up in the traditional liturgy and experienced, with great spiritual benefit, the reality and mystery of the Church thanks to this liturgical form, which earlier generations held as sacred and which formed so many saints and outstanding Catholics throughout history.

The motu proprio and accompanying letter commit an injustice against all Catholics who adhere to the traditional liturgical form, by accusing them of being divisive and of rejecting the Second Vatican Council. In fact, a considerable portion of these Catholics keep far away from doctrinal discussions regarding Vatican II, the new Order of Mass (Novus Ordo Missae), and other problems involving ecclesiastical politics. They just want to worship God in the liturgical form through which God has touched and transformed their hearts and lives. The argument invoked in the motu proprio and accompanying letter, i.e., that the traditional liturgical form creates division and threatens the unity of the Church, is disproven by the facts. Furthermore, the disparaging tone taken in these documents against the traditional liturgical form would lead any impartial observer to conclude that such arguments are merely a pretext and a ruse, and that something else is at play here.

How convincing do you find Pope Francis's comparison (in his accompanying letter to bishops) between his new measures and those adopted by St. Pius V in 1570?
The time of Second Vatican Council and the so-called "conciliar" Church has been characterized by an openness to a diversity and inclusivity of spiritualities and local liturgical expressions, along with a rejection of the principle of a uniformity in the liturgical praxis of the Church. Throughout history, the true pastoral attitude has been one of tolerance and respect towards a diversity of liturgical forms, provided they express the integrity of the Catholic Faith and the dignity and sacredness of the ritual forms, and that they bear true spiritual fruit in the lives of the faithful. In the past, the Roman Church acknowledged the diversity of expressions in its *lex orandi*.

In the apostolic constitution promulgating the Tridentine Liturgy, *Quo Primum* (1570), Pope Pius V, in approving all those liturgical expressions of the Roman Church that were more than two hundred years old, recognized them as an equally worthy and legitimate expression of the *lex orandi* of the Roman Church. In this bull, Pope Pius V stated that he in no wise rescinds other legitimate liturgical expressions within the Roman Church. The liturgical form of the Roman Church that was valid until the reform of Paul VI did not arise with Pius V, but was substantially unchanged even centuries before the Council of Trent. The first printed edition of the *Missale Romanum* dates back to 1470, thus one hundred years before the missal published by Pius V. The order of Mass of both missals is almost identical; the difference lies more in secondary elements, such as the calendar, number of prefaces, and more precise rubrical norms.

Pope Francis's new motu proprio is also deeply concerning in that it manifests an attitude of discrimination against an almost one thousand-year-old liturgical form of the Catholic Church. The Church has never rejected that which, over the span of many centuries, has expressed sacredness, doctrinal precision, and spiritual richness, and has been exalted by many popes, great theologians (e.g., St. Thomas Aquinas), and numerous saints. The peoples of Western and, in part, of Eastern Europe, of Northern and Southern Europe, of the Americas, Africa, and Asia were evangelized and doctrinally and spiritually formed by the traditional Roman Rite, and these peoples found in that rite their spiritual and liturgical home. Pope John Paul II gave an example of a sincere appreciation of the traditional form of the Mass when he said: "In the Roman Missal, called 'of St. Pius V,' as in various Eastern Liturgies, there are beautiful prayers with which the priest expresses the deepest sense of humility and reverence before the holy mysteries: they reveal the very substance of any liturgy" (Message to Participants in the Plenary Assembly of the Congregation for Divine Worship and the Discipline of the Sacraments, September 21, 2001).

It would go against the true spirit of the Church of all ages to now express contempt for this liturgical form, to label it as "divisive" and as something dangerous for the unity of the Church, and to issue norms aimed at making this form disappear in time. The norms enshrined in Pope Francis's motu proprio seek to unmercifully rip out of the souls and lives of so many Catholics the traditional liturgy, which in itself is holy and represents the spiritual homeland of these Catholics. With this motu proprio, Catholics who today have been spiritually nourished and formed by the traditional liturgy of Holy Mother Church will no longer experience the Church as a mother but rather as a "stepmother," consistent with Pope Francis's own description: "A mother who criticizes, who speaks ill of her children is not a mother! I believe you say 'stepmother' in Italian. . . . She isn't a mother" (Address to Consecrated Men and Women of the Diocese of Rome, May 16, 2015).

Pope Francis's apostolic letter was issued on the feast of Our Lady of Mount Carmel, patroness of Carmelites (such as St. Thérèse of Lisieux), who pray especially for priests. In light of the new measures, what would you say to diocesan seminarians and young priests who had hoped to celebrate the Traditional Latin Mass?

Cardinal Joseph Ratzinger spoke about the limitation of the powers of the pope regarding the liturgy, with this illuminating explanation: "The pope is not an absolute monarch whose will is law; rather, he is the guardian of the authentic Tradition and, thereby, the premier guarantor of obedience. He cannot do as he likes, and he is thereby able to oppose those people who, for their part, want to do whatever comes into their head. His rule is not that of arbitrary power, but that of obedience in faith. That is why, with respect to the Liturgy, he has the task of a gardener, not that of a technician who builds new machines and throws the old ones on the junk-pile. The 'rite,' that form of celebration and prayer which has ripened in the faith and the life of the Church, is a condensed form of living Tradition in which the sphere using that rite expresses the whole of its faith and its prayer, and thus at the same time the fellowship of generations one with another becomes something we can experience, fellowship with the people who pray before us and after us. Thus the rite is something of benefit that is given to the Church, a living form of *paradosis*, the handing-on of Tradition."[1]

The traditional Mass is a treasure that belongs to the entire Church, since it has been celebrated and deeply regarded and loved by priests and saints for at least a thousand years. In fact, the traditional form of the Mass was almost identical for centuries before the publication of the Missal of Pope Pius V in 1570. An almost one thousand-year-old valid and highly esteemed liturgical treasure is not the private property of a pope, which he can freely dispose of. Therefore, seminarians and young priests must ask for the right to use this common treasure of the Church, and should they be denied this right, they can use it nevertheless, perhaps in a clandestine manner. This would not be an act of disobedience, but rather of obedience to Holy Mother Church, who has given us this liturgical treasure. The firm rejection of an almost one thousand-year-old liturgical form by Pope Francis represents, in fact, a short-lived phenomenon compared to the constant spirit and praxis of the Church.

Your Excellency, what has been your impression thus far of the implementation of Traditionis Custodes?

Within a few short days, diocesan bishops and even an entire bishops' conference have already begun a systematic suppression of any celebration of the traditional form of the Holy Mass. These new "liturgy inquisitors" have displayed an astonishingly rigid clericalism, similar to that described and lamented by Pope Francis, when he said: "There is that spirit of clericalism in the Church, which one feels: the clerics feel themselves superior, the clerics turn away from the people, the clerics always say: 'this is done like this, like this, like this, and you go away!'" (Daily meditation in the Holy Mass from December 13, 2016).

Pope Francis's anti-traditional motu proprio shares some similarities with the fateful and extremely rigid liturgical decisions made by the Russian Orthodox Church under Patriarch Nikon of Moscow between 1652 and 1666. This eventually led to a lasting schism known as the "Old Ritualists" (in Russian: *staroobryadtsy*), who maintained the liturgical and ritual practices of the Russian Church as they were before the reforms of Patriarch Nikon. Resisting the accommodation of Russian piety to the contemporary forms of Greek Orthodox worship, these Old Ritualists were anathematized, together with their ritual, in a Synod of 1666 – 67, producing a division between the

---

1   Preface to Dom Alcuin Reid, *The Organic Development of the Liturgy. The Principles of Liturgical Reform and Their Relation to the Twentieth-Century Liturgical Movement Prior to the Second Vatican Council* (San Francisco: Ignatius Press, 2004), 10 – 11.

Old Ritualists and those who followed the state church in its condemnation of the Old Rite. Today the Russian Orthodox Church regrets the drastic decisions of Patriarch Nikon, for if the norms he implemented had been truly pastoral and allowed the use of the old rite, there would not have been a centuries-long schism, with many unnecessary and cruel sufferings.

In our own day we are witnessing ever more celebrations of the Holy Mass that have become a platform for promoting the sinful lifestyle of homosexuality — the so-called "LGBT-Masses," an expression which in itself is already a blasphemy. Such Masses are tolerated by the Holy See and many bishops. What is urgently needed is a motu proprio with strict norms suppressing the practice of such "LGBT-Masses," since they are an outrage to the divine majesty, a scandal to the faithful (the little ones), and an injustice towards sexually active homosexual persons, who by such celebrations are confirmed in their sins, and whose eternal salvation is thereby being put in danger.

And yet a number of bishops, particularly in the United States but also elsewhere, such as in France, have supported the faithful of their dioceses who are attached to the Traditional Latin Mass. What would you say to encourage these your brother bishops? And what attitude ought the faithful to have toward their bishops, many of whom were themselves surprised by the document?

These bishops have shown a true apostolic and pastoral attitude, as those who are "shepherds with the smell of the sheep." I would encourage these and many other bishops to continue with such a noble pastoral attitude. Let neither the praises of men nor the fear of men move them, but only the greater glory of God, and the greater spiritual benefit of souls and their eternal salvation. For their part, the faithful should demonstrate gratitude toward these bishops, and filial respect and love.

What effect do you think the motu proprio will have?

Pope Francis's new motu proprio is ultimately a pyrrhic victory and will have a boomerang effect. The many Catholic families and ever-growing number of young people and priests — particularly young priests — who attend the traditional Mass will not be able to allow their conscience to be violated by such a drastic administrative act. Telling these faithful and priests that they must simply be obedient to these norms will ultimately not work with them, because they understand that a call to obedience loses its power when the aim is to suppress the traditional form of the liturgy, the great liturgical treasure of the Roman Church.

In time, a worldwide chain of catacomb Masses will surely arise, as happens in times of emergency and persecution. We may in fact witness an era of clandestine traditional Masses, similar to that so impressively depicted by Aloysius O'Kelly in his painting, "Mass in Connemara (Ireland) during Penal Times." Or perhaps we shall live through a time similar to that described by St. Basil the Great, when traditional Catholics were persecuted by a liberal Arian episcopate in the fourth century. St. Basil wrote: "The mouths of true believers are dumb, while every blasphemous tongue wags free; holy things are trodden under foot; the better laity shun the churches as schools of impiety, and lift their hands in the deserts with sighs and tears to their Lord in heaven. Even you must have heard what is going on in most of our cities, how our people with wives and children and even our old men stream out before the walls, and offer their prayers in the open air, putting up with all the inconvenience of the weather with great patience, and waiting for help from the Lord" (*Letter* 92).

The admirable, harmonious and quite spontaneous spread and continuous growth of the traditional form of the Mass, in almost every country of the world, even in the most remote lands, is undoubtedly the work of the Holy Spirit, and a true sign of our time. This form of the liturgical celebration bears true spiritual fruits, especially in the life of the youth and converts to the Catholic Church, since many of the latter were attracted to the Catholic faith precisely by the irradiating power of this treasure of the Church. Pope Francis and the other bishops who will execute his motu proprio should earnestly consider the wise counsel of Gamaliel, and ask themselves if they actually are fighting against a work of God: "In the present case I tell you, keep away from these men and let them alone; for if this plan or this undertaking is of men, it will fail; but if it is of God, you will not be able to overthrow them. You might even be found opposing God!" (Acts 5:38–39). May Pope Francis reconsider, with a view to eternity, his drastic and tragic act, and courageously and humbly retract this new motu proprio, recalling his own words: "In truth, the Church shows her fidelity to the Holy Spirit in as much as she does not try to control or tame him" (Homily at the Catholic Cathedral of the Holy Spirit, Istanbul, Saturday, November 29, 2014).

For the time being, many Catholic families, young people and priests on every continent are now weeping, for the Pope — their spiritual father — has deprived them of the spiritual nourishment of the traditional Mass, which has so greatly strengthened their faith and their love for God, for Holy Mother Church and for the Apostolic See. They may, for a time, "go out weeping, bearing the seed for sowing, but they shall come home with shouts of joy, bringing their sheaves with them" (cf. Psalm 126:6).

These families, young people and priests could address to Pope Francis these or similar words: "Most Holy Father, give us back that great liturgical treasure of the Church. Do not treat us as your second-class children. Do not violate our consciences by forcing us into a single and exclusive liturgical form, you who always proclaimed to the entire world the necessity of diversity, pastoral accompaniment, and of respect for conscience. Do not listen to those representatives of a rigid clericalism who counseled you to carry out such an unmerciful action. Be a true family father, who 'brings out of his treasure what is new and what is old' (Mt 13:52). If you will hear our voice, on the day of your judgment before God, we will be your best intercessors."

34

A Cannon Shooting at Sparrows[†]

PETRA LORLEBERG INTERVIEWS
FR. GERO P. WEISHAUPT

Kath.net
July 23, 2021

PL: *Dr. Weishaupt, how urgent would you have considered a motu proprio in the sense of* Traditionis Custodes *in this early summer?*

GW: In my opinion, *Traditionis Custodes* oversteps the mark. This motu proprio is disproportionate and seems like a cannon with which the Pope shoots at sparrows.

I do not want to deny that here and there after *Summorum Pontificum* there have been undesirable developments that were not the intention of Pope Benedict XVI. For example, *Summorum Pontificum* was misunderstood when groups of faithful formed in parishes or were joined by faithful who celebrated Mass in the Tridentine form exclusively but avoided Mass in the "Pauline" form. If *Summorum Pontificum* and the explanatory instruction *Universae Ecclesiae* had been consistently implemented, such groupings would not have occurred in one parish or another, and Pope Francis's most recent motu proprio would have been superfluous. But such undesirable developments stayed within limits. The motu proprio *Traditionis Custodes* and its accompanying letter, however, generalize, fail to distinguish, and ignore the many tradition-loving faithful who have found their spiritual home in both forms. Instead of a word of appreciation, the Pope kicks them and drives them back into the ghetto. And the traditional, classical liturgy ends up in the museum.

Pope Francis, through his radical legal restrictions, is indiscriminately sanctioning all the faithful, including the majority of those who hold the traditional liturgy dear without calling the new liturgy into question. And also the majority of priests who celebrate Mass in the Tridentine rite have strictly adhered to the prescriptions of *Summorum Pontificum* and its implementing provisions in the Instruction *Universae Ecclesiae*. In both legal texts,

---

† The German original was translated by Peter Kwasniewski and published at *Rorate Caeli* on the same date.

the conditions and limits for celebrating according to the classical rite have been clearly indicated.

The divisions that Pope Francis deplores can therefore be avoided in another way — for example, by a supplementary instruction to the motu proprio *Summorum Pontificum* or by a papal or episcopal decree. For instance, without changes to *Summorum Pontificum*, it could have been decreed that bishops who have heard of schisms in their dioceses remind the responsible priests and faithful of the strict observance of the prescriptions of *Summorum Pontificum* and punish violations. This did not require a new legislative act, and certainly not drastic, disproportionate restrictions that are completely incomprehensible with regard to the intended purpose, as in *Traditionis Custodes*.

In any case, the Pope's latest law remains completely incomprehensible and highly controversial with regard to its purpose, namely reconciliation and unity. I fear that this motu proprio will achieve the opposite of what it seeks precisely to prevent, namely division; it will not reconcile. The reservations that tradition-bound Catholics already have about Pope Francis will even be strengthened by *Traditionis Custodes*. I fear that with this motu proprio, Pope Francis has immensely damaged himself and his office and done a disservice to the [legitimate] intention of *Traditionis Custodes*.

Critical voices on Traditionis Custodes *ask the question whether Pope Francis, in his serious pastoral effort for those sheep who stray, has now struck with his shepherd's crook, of all things, those sheep who, despite some hardships, faithfully rally around him and are not willing to give up communion with him. What is your opinion of this?*

In any case, I see neither in the motu proprio nor in the accompanying letter to the bishops the signature of a mild, gracious, and merciful father, let alone that of a shepherd who has taken on the "smell of the sheep." Rather, I recognize a shepherd who uses his shepherd's crook as a cudgel. Pope Francis, who like no other pope before him constantly preaches mildness and mercy, who rightly castigates clericalism and talks about the "smell of the sheep" that shepherds are supposed to take on, proves exactly the opposite of all this with the motu proprio *Traditionis Custodes*. I see the Pope's credibility and authenticity damaged.

Can bishops dispense or exempt from the motu proprio Traditionis Custodes?

Of course they can. In the meantime, there are also bishops, especially in the USA, who have already dispensed from some of its norms. That is gratifying. And it is to be hoped that the bishops in the German-speaking countries will do the same. It is also gratifying to see that the younger generation of bishops is more likely than their predecessors to have a change of heart and an open mind about the old liturgy. This gives hope for a generous dispensational practice in this matter.

Thank God for this legal institution of dispensation, i.e., exemption from a law in a concrete case for the good of the faithful. However, it applies only to purely ecclesiastical laws, to which *Traditionis Custodes* belongs. From laws that formulate divine law — that is, from law derived from revelation or from natural law — the pope, let alone any other bishop, can never dispense. Thus, for example, the law that only men can validly receive ordination (a truth intrinsically connected with revelation) can never be dispensed with, just as little as the married can be from the indissolubility of marriage (a truth of the natural law).

The purpose of a dispensation from a purely ecclesiastical law is to avert the harshness of the law — and *Traditionis Custodes* is undoubtedly unexpectedly harsh — in a concrete case or in several cases of the same kind among those subject to the law. Although the law as such remains, the enormous force of *Traditionis Custodes* can thus still be cushioned in individual cases, since the person or persons affected are exempted from it by the dispensation.

It is to be hoped that the bishops, as mild and merciful shepherds who have taken on the "smell of the sheep" and use their shepherd's crook not as a cudgel but to lead, gather, and unify, will generously exhaust the legal possibilities of a dispensation. Indeed, if they did not do so, they would irresponsibly destroy in one fell swoop the good fruits for the Church that the motu proprio *Summorum Pontificum* has demonstrably produced so far. Unfortunately, Pope Francis's ill-fated law has the potential to do just that. Pastoral-mindedness and benevolence look different. Recognition of the good fruits of *Summorum Pontificum*, appreciation for Catholics who are faithful to the papacy and bound by tradition, and (not least) respect for Pope Benedict XVI, are not at all evident in Pope Francis's latest legislative act.

What happens now on the ground for the priests, faithful, and communities affected?
In any case, one should not refrain from trying to ask the Pope to withdraw the controversial law altogether or to amend it in such a way that the breach with *Summorum Pontificum* is reversed, because the purpose of *Traditionis Custodes* can legally be achieved in another, more respectful way. Moreover, if one considers that some bishops have not received at all the questions from the survey initiated by the Congregation for the Doctrine

of the Faith on the implementation of *Summorum Pontificum* in their dioceses, then it becomes clear that this law is already highly doubtful in its genesis. However, as long as *Traditionis Custodes* has legal force, legally there is nothing left to do but to seek from the respective diocesan bishop the already-mentioned possibility of dispensations from the hard norms and to hope for his pastoral and benevolent spirit.

If you were allowed to give the Pope some advice — let's just play this out as a fantasy — would you advise him to have a Traditionis Custodes II, *which then tries to take other [problematic] currents in the Church by the reins? Where do you currently see "processes," especially in the German-speaking world, which you consider to be extremely dangerous for church unity?*

Clearly in the Synodal Way and the actions accompanying it, which are indeed directed against the Pope, the doctrine, and the unity of the Church. But also in the liturgical abuses in the post-conciliar liturgy, which are partly to blame for the present disintegration of the Church. Here it would be urgent for the Pope to remind the bishops that they are, in fact "*traditionis custodes*" and to take a firm stand against schismatic tendencies in their particular Churches in order to avert a schism. However, I am convinced that a schism has already occurred, but has not yet been formally established. The danger to the unity of the Church does not come from the old liturgy and those who value it, quite the contrary. The danger threatens from a world of thought that has made the Synodal Way what it is now.

35

Illuminating Comparisons: Pius V, John XXIII, Paul VI, and Francis

FR. JOHN HUNWICKE[1]

Mutual Enrichment

July 22, 23, and 24, 2021

DEAR FATHER,

Thank you for your email about whether you are bound *in conscience* to adhere to *Traditionis Custodes*. The answer is No; certainly Not; and Of Course Not.

We need to look at the document of 1570 *Quo Primum*, which St. Pius V put right at the front of his own edition of the *Missale Romanum*. Sometimes traddy people quote stuff towards the end where St. Pius V appears to condemn anybody who makes *any* changes in his 1570 Missal. But he cannot have meant to forbid a gentle evolutionary process . . . an additional Festival here, an occasional new Preface there . . . because every pontiff since his time has made such changes . . . if they have lived long enough. It's what happens in traditional lived Liturgy. What St. Pius V ordered does, however, bear strongly on the issues in play today. But we need to be quite clear what St. Pius *actually* said. Please bear with me.

Both Bergoglians and some Traddies are currently writing as if St. Pius V in 1570 "permitted" rites with more than 200 years behind them to continue. He *did not*. He *ordered* such old rites to be continued. Nequaquam *auferimus* were his words . . . *auferimus* means "we take away," *nequaquam* means "not at all." What he *did* allow was his own new 1570 Edition to be brought into use if a bishop and his entire Chapter agreed.

Just imagine this scene in 1570. New Trendy bishop wants to bring in the 1570 Missal . . . The Chapter, a load of cringing cowards, say "Yes Bishop Of course Bishop Anything you say Bishop What shall we lick next Bishop." But over there sitting in the corner, sociably passing wind, is old Canon Lostitzio. He's pretty gaga . . . senile, almost . . . and drunk most of the day from breakfast onwards. Not even his wife can keep him off the bottle. But

---

1 The author wishes to remind his readers that Irony is among the literary genres upon which he has drawn.

he won't agree to the 1570 *Missal.* Last time the bishop very coaxingly spoke to him about "Our Diocesan Mission Strategy," he just blew some snuff right up the episcopal nostrils and said some unusual words in an obscure Ligurian dialect. So, in *that* diocese, there was no *Capituli universi consensus.* Therefore, in that diocese, there can be no 1570 Missal . . . Bishop Trendino and the rest of them will have to stick with their old rite. Oh D*mn!

That's what St. Pius V mandated.

Even if Canon Lostitzio dies tonight, Bishop Trendino still isn't *obliged* to bring in the new Missal. What St. Pius V says is *permittimus.* That means "we permit." (*Permitto* is nice old-fashioned Latin verb that popes quite often used, once upon a time. It's still in some of the more old-fashioned dictionaries.) So: one single off-message old man and his veto could preserve the local tradition of his particular church. That's how strongly St. Pius V believed in tradition.

When Papa Ratzinger issued *Summorum Pontificum,* he explained to his brother bishops that "What earlier generations held as sacred, remains sacred and great for us too, and it cannot be all of a sudden entirely forbidden or even considered harmful." Observe that Benedict XVI did not say "It *should not* be forbidden"; he said "it *cannot* be . . . "

From 1570 until 1970, *Quo Primum* stood at the beginning of every Missal of the Roman Rite. Pope Benedict XVI, in his own words, in our time, has reiterated its assertion of the essential, *theological,* primacy of Tradition. "*Cannot* be." Is anything else needed to make clear that this is the settled doctrine of the Catholic Church?

Are you obliged, then, to obey Pope Francis if he attempts to prevent you from using the Traditional Form of the Roman Rite? Most certainly not. He is only the Pope; he has no right to overrule Holy Tradition. A pope cannot "do anything." (I think I've remembered that from somebody else's words . . . I must try to identify the quotation . . .) He has no more right than I do. He has no more right than your Aunt Mavis does. He has no more right to order you to set aside Holy Tradition than do Aunt Mavis's little twins Nicolas and Nicola (who, so you tell me, have just started at their kindergarten and are learning to lithp thothe thublime wordth *Amo Amath Amat Amamuth Amatith Amant*). Even if all six of us order you to dump Tradition . . . Me; Mavis; Nicola; Nicolas; Nicola's teddy-bear Wilfrid; and Pope Francis . . . and if we all order you simultaneously . . . while waggling, each of us, a great big nasty club with a nail in it . . . we are all acting *ultra* our *vires.*

I expect you will have noticed Cardinal Burke's words on this subject.[2]
Father: May God bless you in His and your most holy priesthood.
Remember always that it does not belong to the pope. *Mei in sacrificiis tuis sis memor.*

Yours *in Domino*
John

*   *   *

Liberation!

I have long been uneasy about the arbitrary provision in *Summorum Pontificum* that the normative form of the Authentic Version of the Roman Rite should be that of 1962. I suppose Benedict XVI was being kind to Archbishop Lefebvre, who, after some variations, settled, in the mid-seventies, for 1962.

But now!... marvelous!!... Pope Francis, with his generously reiterated abrogations, has liberated us from all the Ratzinger provisions!!! We are now in a happy period of freedom. Broad Sunlit Uplands territory! Bound no longer to "1962," we are at liberty to use . . . for example . . . the 1939 rite as provided in the St Lawrence Press Ordo. Or any other . . .

Readers will remember the provisions of St. Pius V in *Quo Primum*. This is often misquoted — indeed, it was by Pope Francis himself — as if St. Pius *permitted* the continuation of rites with more than 200 years' prescription. He did nothing of the sort. He *ordered*, he *mandated* the continued use of such rites — *unless* the Bishop and the *unanimous* Chapter of a diocese should agree to adopt instead his own edition of the Roman Rite. The *fallback* position bequeathed by *Quo Primum* was (and *is*) that those old rites stay firmly in place.

I think it is fairly safe to state, despite the difficulties of asserting and proving historical negatives, that in no English diocese, in the years after 1559, did the Bishop, with his unanimous, rejoicing, Chapter, agree to abrogate the old rites of Sarum, York, Hereford, Lincoln, Bangor . . . or do I mean Bognor . . . Ergo . . .

I think Sarum is the rite with which (in our new-found loyalty to Pope Francis) we should begin our restorations. Within the last year, an admirable and learned priest has edited and published an Altar Edition of the Sarum Missal — the "unique expression," one might say, of the Sarum Rite. And Mr. Urquhart has done a fine and painstaking "O'Connell" to go with it:

---

2   See chapter 27.

Ceremonies of the Sarum Missal. I expect the poor fellow will be nagged to edit an annual *Ordo recitandi Officii Divini Sacrique peragendi secundum usum insignis et praeclarae Ecclesiae Sarisburiensis* so as to help us through *the nombre and hardnes of the rules called the pie.* Sarum is, as our Mr. Johnson would cry, Oven Ready and Awaiting Lift Off.

Whereabouts to begin? In Puginopolis, clearly (Ramsgate, as *hoi polloi* call it). Just think how it will rejoice the heart of dear Augustus Welby. There is evidence that Dr. Wiseman celebrated "according to the rite of Sarum" there. Historians will undoubtedly come to call this the Pugin Pontificate.

Then, perhaps, the ruins of Glastonbury . . . in honor of the Blessed Abbot Richard Whiting, and his martyred Companions; on Tower Hill, honoring the Cardinal Bishop of Rochester . . . What glorious events *those* Pontifical High Masses will be! We must pray for fine weather! *Viva il Papa!*

*   *   *

Many of you will be too young to remember the infamous events of 1962. They led to famine and public disorder; to mobs of crazed people jostling in the streets as they struggled in the queues to register for their unemployment benefit and for hand-outs of public foodstuffs. Gaunt and famished, in country after country the hungry men, driven to despair, protested in the only way they knew. The barricades . . . the street massacres . . .

The cruel decree *Veterum Sapientia* had ordered the sacking of thousands of men, and some women, from Catholic seminaries throughout the world. Papa Roncalli, "Good Pope John XXIII" as he had ironically been called, in full consciousness of His authority, Decreed and Commanded eight important rules. Rule 5 ordered that the major sacred sciences should be taught *in Latin,* that the professors of these sciences in universities or seminaries be required to speak *Latin* and to make use of textbooks written *in Latin.* "Those whose ignorance of *Latin* makes it difficult for them to obey these instructions shall be gradually *replaced* by professors who are suited for this task. Any difficulties which may be advanced by students or professors must be overcome . . ." Hence the world-wide sackings. The Pope had spoken. *Petrus locutus est. Fiat Latinitas, ruat caelum.*

St. John XXIII ended with the impressive words "In virtue of our Apostolic Authority, We will and command that all the decisions, decrees, proclamations and recommendations of this Our Constitution remain firmly established and ratified, "anything to the contrary notwithstanding, even things worthy of special note." Gosh! Nobody would disregard something as definite as that, would they?

What a persecution was then unleashed! Spies and informers abounded; Gestapo-like bands of thugs went around seminaries collecting evidence and listing names. Unspeakable cruelties were perpetrated upon these hungry, workless men; upon their unfed women and their emaciated catamites. Since the elimination by burning of the Cathars, nothing like it had been seen in the Catholic Church.

In Argentina, no bishop was more rigorous than Bishop Bergoglio in enforcing the decrees of St. John XXIII. If ever he heard of a seminary professor giving a single lecture in Spanish rather than Latin, he was instantly on the phone demanding that the man be sacked. He had the reputation of being the strictest bishop in Latin America in implementing *Veterum Sapientia.*

Of course, the relentless pressure of the Bishops and of the Seminary Management Boards proved . . . as they must . . . successful. Vernacular teaching totally disappeared from our seminaries; and as the succeeding Popes enforced the same rules, even the memory of Vernacular Seminary Teaching has disappeared. The world feels, somehow, so much *cleaner,* so much safer. And how right all this has been. *Veterum Sapientia* was an Apostolic Constitution, signed, for greater emphasis, on the High Altar of St. Peter's. Catholic clergy and laity know their duty of submission to the authority of the Roman Pontiff. When we hear the Pope's voice, it is St. Peter that we hear. This knowledge calls us to unquestioning obedience. "Do all your seminary teaching in Latin," he cries. Our response is "Certainly, Holy Father. Pronto!"

Our privilege today, in 2021, is that we are being given a very similar opportunity for total and unthinking obedience, Jesuit style. Pope Francis possesses precisely and exactly the same authority as St. John XXIII. When he decrees the extermination of the Old Mass, that decree comes to us with precisely and exactly the same force as the requirement of St. John XXIII that all Priestly Formation in seminaries should be done entirely in Latin . . . er . . . except that possibly a motu proprio may not have . . . um . . . *quite* the authority of an Apostolic Constitution . . . er . . . I wouldn't know about that sort of thing; I'm only a "convert."

Just suppose that 1962 decree had been ignored! Just suppose that the Rectors and the Episcopal Boards running seminaries had taken not the slightest bit of notice of those Decrees of St. John XXIII!

It just doesn't bear thinking about, does it?

36

The Upside-Down Church

GEORGE NEUMAYR

The American Spectator

July 25, 2021

POPE FRANCIS HAS OFTEN COMPARED THE CATHOLIC Church to a "field hospital." It is an odd analogy in his case, given his penchant for quackery and malpractice. The healthiest patients at his field hospital have their limbs hacked off while the sickest ones receive increased dosages of a medicine that doesn't work. The pope's conception of health in the body of Christ is the opposite of his predecessors. They saw the absence of orthodoxy as a cancer in the Church, whereas Pope Francis sees the persistent presence of orthodoxy as the poison.

According to this twisted view, the crisis in the Church derives not from the modernist heresy but from the unwillingness of Catholics to succumb to it. Laboring under this view, he has devoted much of his pontificate to undoing the post-Vatican II conservative retrenchment of Pope John Paul II and Pope Benedict XVI. In complaining about the Church's reluctance to embrace "modern culture," he has implicitly criticized those predecessors. Where they viewed the liberal "spirit" of Vatican II with concern, he welcomed it.

At the beginning of his pontificate, he lamented that the progressive promise of Vatican II hadn't been fulfilled — "very little was done in that direction" — but that he had the "ambition to want to do something."[1]

The pope's recent order curtailing the traditional Latin Mass is central to that ambition. He can't rest until all Catholics have submitted to his modernism. In the past, popes instituted oaths against modern errors. This pope is eager to impose an oath in favor of them. In urging the bishops to marginalize the traditional Latin Mass, the pope reveals the depth of his contempt for Catholic tradition and his desire to cement in place a modernist redefinition of Catholicism.

Pope Benedict XVI used to talk about the theologians at Vatican II who wanted to start a new religion from scratch. He called them anarchic utopians. He said that "after the Second Vatican Council some were convinced

---

1   Michael Sean Winters, "Pope Francis' latest bombshell interview," *National Catholic Reporter*, October 1, 2013.

that all would be made new, that another Church was being made, that the pre-conciliar Church was finished and we would have another, totally 'other' [Church]." That largely sums up the program of his successor. His decree against the traditional Latin Mass is designed to finish off the pre-conciliar Church. It severs any connection between the post-Vatican II Church and the pre-Vatican II Church, thereby allowing the modernists to monopolize the direction of the Church.

In order to take Catholicism out of Catholicism and turn it into an unspiritual and political quasi-religion, the modernists can't abide any competition from the orthodox. Because the traditional Latin Mass movement was growing, particularly among young people and young priests, the pope had to kill it. The onerous provisions in the decree will first ghettoize the old Mass, then snuff it out. The Church, already suffering from a vocations crisis, will lose even more vocations, as the decree in effect tells tradition-minded young men that the price of entry into the priesthood now is total submission to the pope's modernism.

For a religion predicated on tradition, the suppression of tradition makes no sense unless the goal is to change that religion fundamentally. By "unity," the pope means universal acceptance of that project. He is demanding that all Catholics view uncritically changes that have obviously weakened the faith. If they don't, they are "divisive."

The pope, of course, embodies the very division that he claims to deplore. He is dividing Catholics at the deepest possible level — from Catholic tradition itself. A "unity" rooted in heterodoxy is a sham. As the modernist Church stumbles from scandal to scandal, he dares to hold it up as the model of Catholicism to which all must aspire. His latest act of ecclesiastical tyranny is nothing more than an attempt to extract from the most faithful Catholics a pledge of allegiance to that crumbling Church.

The spectacle of a pope disloyal to Catholic tradition issuing loyalty litmus tests is an outrageous one. By disregarding the authority of past popes, Francis erases his own. He is not solving crises but creating them so that his modernist revolution can be fulfilled. In the past, orthodox Catholics defended the pope from enemies of the faith. Now they must defend the faith from a pope who has shown himself repeatedly to be their enemy.

37

The Faithful Are Entitled to Defend Themselves against Liturgical Aggression

JOSÉ ANTONIO URETA

American Society for the Defense of Tradition, Family and Property
July 25, 2021

WITH THE STROKE OF A PEN, POPE FRANCIS HAS TAKEN concrete steps to abolish in practice the Roman Rite of the Holy Mass. Substantially in use since Saint Damasus, at the end of the fourth century, and with additions by Saint Gregory the Great at the end of the sixth, the 1962 Missal promulgated by John XXIII is the most recent version of the Roman Rite.

In his letter to bishops around the world accompanying the motu proprio *Traditionis Custodes*, the sovereign pontiff is clear about his intent to restrict the use of this immemorial rite gradually, unto extinction. The pope urges bishops "to proceed in such a way as to return to a unitary form of celebration" with the liturgical books of Paul VI and John Paul II, which, he says, are "the unique expression of the *lex orandi* of the Roman Rite." The practical consequence is that Roman Rite priests are no longer entitled to celebrate the traditional Mass. They can only do so with their bishop's permission, and for those ordained after the motu proprio, that of the Holy See!

The obvious question that arises in the face of this drastic measure is: Does a pope have the authority to overturn a rite that has been used in the Church for 1,400 years and whose essential elements come from apostolic times? If, on the one hand, the Vicar of Christ has *plena et suprema potestas* in matters concerning "the discipline and government of the Church throughout the world,"[1] as the First Vatican Council teaches, on the other, he must respect the universal customs of the Church in liturgical matters.

The *Catechism of the Catholic Church* promulgated by John Paul II gives a definitive answer to this question in paragraph 1125: "no sacramental rite may be modified or manipulated at the will of the minister or the

---

1   See *Denz.-Rahner* 1827.

community. Even the supreme authority in the Church may not change the liturgy arbitrarily, but only in the obedience of faith and with religious respect for the mystery of the liturgy."[2] Commenting on this text, then-Cardinal Joseph Ratzinger wrote:

> It seems to me most important that the *Catechism*, in mentioning the limitation of the powers of the supreme authority in the Church with regard to reform, recalls to mind what is the essence of the primacy as outlined by the First and Second Vatican Councils: The pope is not an absolute monarch whose will is law, but is the guardian of the authentic Tradition, and thereby the premier guarantor of obedience. He cannot do as he likes, and is thereby able to oppose those people who, for their part, want to do whatever has come into their head. His rule is not that of arbitrary power, but that of obedience in faith. That is why, with respect to the Liturgy, he has the task of a gardener, not that of a technician who builds new machines and throws the old ones on the junk-pile. The "rite," that form of celebration and prayer which has ripened in the faith and the life of the Church, is a condensed form of living Tradition in which the sphere using that rite expresses the whole of its faith and its prayer, and thus at the same time the fellowship of generations one with another becomes something we can experience, fellowship with the people who pray before us and after us. Thus the rite is something of benefit that is given to the Church, a living form of *paradosis*, the handing-on of Tradition.[3]

Msgr. Klaus Gamber, whom Cardinal Ratzinger deemed one of the greatest liturgists of the twentieth century, develops this thought in a superb book entitled *The Reform of the Roman Liturgy*. He starts from the observation that the rites of the Catholic Church, taken in the sense of obligatory forms of worship, definitively date back to Our Lord Jesus Christ but gradually developed and differentiated from the general custom, being later confirmed by ecclesiastical authority. From this reality, the distinguished German liturgist draws the following conclusions:

1. If we assume that the liturgical rite evolved on the basis of shared traditions — and nobody who has at least some knowledge of

---

2 CCC 1125.

3 Preface to Dom Alcuin Reid, *The Organic Development of the Liturgy* (San Francisco: Ignatius Press, 2004), 10–11. *Paradosis*: a Greek term used thirteen times in the Bible and translated as tradition, instruction, transmission.

liturgical history will dispute this — then it cannot be developed anew in its entirety. . . . Just as the primitive Church gradually emerged from the Synagogue, so did the liturgical forms used by the young communities of Christians emerge from the liturgical rites of the Jews. . . .

2. Since the liturgical rite has developed over time, further development continues to be possible. But such continuing development has to respect the timeless character of all rites; and its development has to be organic in nature . . . never breaking with tradition, and with no directives emanating from the Church hierarchy. Plenary and local church councils concerned themselves only with eliminating abuses in the actual execution of liturgical rites.

3. There are different, independent liturgical rites in the universal Church. In the Western Church, in addition to the Roman rite, there are the Gallican rite (now defunct), the Ambrosian rite, and the Mozarabic rite; and in the East, among others, the Byzantine rite, the Armenian rite, the Syriac rite and the Coptic rite. Every one of these rites has gone through a process of independent growth and developed its very own characteristics. Thus, it is not appropriate to simply exchange or substitute individual liturgical elements between different rites . . .

4. Every liturgical rite constitutes an organically developed, homogeneous unit. To change any of its essential elements is synonymous with the destruction of the rite in its entirety. This is what happened during the Reformation when Martin Luther did away with the canon of the Mass and made the words of consecration and institution part of the distribution of communion. . . .

5. Restoration of early liturgical forms does not necessarily constitute a change in the rite, at least not if this is done on a case-by-case basis, and if it is done within certain constraints. There was thus no break with the traditional Roman rite when Pope St. Pius X restored the Gregorian chant to its original form, or when he reinstated the *per annum* calendar of Sunday Masses to its original precedence . . . [4]

The distinguished founder of the Regensburg Theological Institute goes on to comment that while "the revision made in 1965 did not touch the traditional liturgical rite . . . the publication of the *Ordo Missae* of 1969, however, created a new liturgical rite."[5] He calls it *ritus modernus*, since "the

4   Klaus Gamber, *The Reform of the Roman Liturgy: Its Problems and Background*, trans. Klaus D. Grimm (San Juan Capistrano, CA: Una Voce Press, n.d.), 27–31.
5   Ibid., 33–34.

assertion . . . that the inclusion of some parts of the traditional Missal into the new one means a continuation of the Roman rite, is insupportable."[6] To prove this point, from a strictly liturgical point of view,[7] it suffices to quote what Prof. Roberto de Mattei said about this devastation:

> In the course of the reform, a whole series of novelties and variants were in fact introduced, a certain number of which had been foreseen neither by the Council, nor by Paul VI's Constitution *Missale Romanum*. The *quid novum* certainly did not consist merely in the substitution of vernacular languages for the Latin used in worship; but in the altar being conceived as being a "table," so as to emphasize the aspect of the feast, in place of that of sacrifice; in the *celebratio versus populum* being substituted for that *versus Deum* — with, as a consequence, the abandonment of celebrating facing East, that is, towards Christ as symbolized by the rising sun; in the absence of silence and recollection during the ceremony, and in the theatrical quality of the celebration, often accompanied by songs which tended to desacralize the Mass, with the priest often being reduced to being the "president of the assembly"; in the exaggerated development of the Liturgy of the Word, as against the eucharistic Liturgy; in the "sign" of the Peace, which replaced the genuflections made by priest and faithful, as an action symbolizing the change from the vertical to the horizontal dimension in the liturgical action; in Communion being received by the faithful standing, and in the hand; in women being allowed to approach the altar; in concelebration, which tended towards the "collectivization" of the rite. Finally, and above all, it consists in the changing and replacing of the Offertory prayers and of the Canon. The elimination of the words *Mysterium Fidei* from the words of consecration, in particular, can be considered, as Cardinal Stickler has remarked, as a symbol of the demythologizing, and thus of the humanizing, of the central core of the Holy Mass.[8]

The greatest liturgical revolution took place in the Offertory and Canon. The traditional Offertory, which prepared and prefigured the unbloody

---

6 Ibid., 34.

7 Serious theological errors in the *ritus modernus* such as downgrading the sacrificial and propitiatory character of the Mass deserve a separate article.

8 Roberto de Mattei, "Reflections on the Liturgical Reform," in *Looking Again at the Question of the Liturgy with Cardinal Ratzinger: Proceedings of the July 2001 Fontgombault Liturgical Conference*, ed. Alcuin Reid, O. S. B. (Farnborough, UK: St. Michael's Abbey Press, 2003), 135–36.

immolation in the Consecration, was replaced by the Beràkhôth of the Kiddush, meaning the blessings of the Passover supper of the Jews. Father Pierre Jounel, from the Pastoral Liturgical Center and the Superior Institute of Liturgy in Paris, one of the experts of the Consilium that prepared the liturgical reform, described to the newspaper La Croix the fundamental element of reform in the liturgy of the Eucharist: "Creating three new Eucharistic prayers whereas hitherto only one existed, the first Eucharistic Prayer established in the Roman Canon since the fourth century. The second is taken from the Eucharistic Prayer of [St.] Hippolytus (3rd cent.), as discovered in an Ethiopian version at the end of the nineteenth century. The scheme of the Eastern liturgies inspired the third. The fourth was prepared in one night by a small team around Fr. Gelineau."[9]

Fr. Joseph Gelineau, S. J., was not mistaken when he enthusiastically greeted the reform stating, "Indeed, it is another liturgy of the Mass. It must be said bluntly: The Roman Rite as we knew it no longer exists; it has been destroyed."[10]

How can Pope Francis say in his letter to the bishops, that "Whoever wishes to celebrate with devotion according to earlier forms of the liturgy can find in the reformed Roman Missal according to Vatican Council II all the elements of the Roman Rite, in particular the Roman Canon which constitutes one of its more distinctive elements"? This seems as bitterly ironic as the title of the motu proprio, Custodians of Tradition.

If the Novus Ordo Missae is not a mere reform but implies a rupture with the traditional rite, then the latter's celebration cannot be prohibited. For, as Msgr. Gamber reiterates,

> [T]here is not a single document, including the Codex Iuris Canonici, in which there is a specific statement that the pope, as the supreme pastor of the Church, has the authority to abolish the traditional rite. In fact, nowhere is it mentioned that the pope has the authority to change even a single local liturgical tradition. The fact that there is no mention of such authority strengthens our case considerably.

---

9 See La Croix, April 28, 1999, 19. [The second Eucharistic Prayer is no longer considered to be by St. Hippolytus; indeed, the entire scholarly basis for E. P. II has collapsed. See John F. Baldovin, S. J., "Hippolytus and the Apostolic Tradition: Recent Research and Commentary," Theological Studies 64 (2003): 520–42; Michael Davies, Pope Paul's New Mass (Kansas City: Angelus Press, 2009), 368–70. — Ed.]

10 Joseph Gelineau, Demain la liturgie: Essai sur l'évolution des assemblées chrétiennes (Paris: Les Éditions du Cerf, 1977), 10.

There are clearly defined limits to the *plena et suprema potestas* (full and highest powers) of the pope. For example, there is no question that, even in matters of dogma, he still has to follow the tradition of the universal Church — that is, as [Saint] Vincent of Lérins says, what has been believed always, everywhere, and by everyone (*quod semper, quod ubique, quod ab omnibus*). In fact, there are several authors who state quite explicitly that it is clearly outside the pope's scope of authority to abolish the traditional rite.[11]

Moreover, if he did so, he would run the risk of separating himself from the Church. Indeed, Msgr. Gamber writes:

> Thus, the eminent theologian Suarez (d. 1617), citing even earlier authors such as Cajetan (d. 1534), took the position that a pope would be schismatic "if he, as is his duty, would not be in full communion with the body of the Church, as, for example, if he were to excommunicate the entire Church, or if he were to change all the liturgical rites of the Church that have been upheld by apostolic tradition."[12]

It was probably to avoid this risk that eight of the nine cardinals on the Commission appointed by John Paul II in 1986 to study the implementation of the 1984 Indult declared that Paul VI had not prohibited the ancient Mass. Furthermore, in answer to the question, "Can any bishop forbid any priest in good standing from celebrating the Tridentine Mass?" Cardinal Stickler replied, "the nine Cardinals unanimously agreed that no bishop may forbid a Catholic priest from saying the Tridentine Mass."[13] "There is no official ban, and I don't think the pope will issue one."[14]

However, in his motu proprio *Traditionis Custodes*, Pope Francis authorizes the bishops to ban its celebration. Indeed, the Bishops' Conference of Costa Rica hastened to decree collectively that "the use of the 1962 *Missale Romanum* or any expression of the liturgy before 1970 is not authorized," so that "no priest is authorized to continue celebrating according to the ancient liturgy."[15]

---

11 Gamber, *Reform of the Roman Liturgy*, 35.

12 Ibid., 35–36.

13 John Vennari, "Traditional Mass Never Forbidden: Cardinal Stickler Confirms," *Catholic Family News* (Feb. 1998), https://olrl.org/new_mass/latinmass_cfn.shtml.

14 Cardinal Stickler's statements were published first in *The Latin Mass* and were reproduced by the French magazine *La Nef* n°53 of September 1995.

15 Conferencia Episcopal de Costa Rica, "Mensaje de los Obispos de la Conferencia Episcopal de Costa Rica con relación al *motu proprio* del Papa Francisco sobre la liturgia

For all of the above, we fully subscribe to the conclusions drawn by Fr. Francisco José Delgado: "I think the smartest thing to do now is, ever so calmly, to defend the truth over iniquitous laws. The pope cannot change Tradition by decree or say that the post-Vatican II liturgy is the only expression of the lex orandi in the Roman Rite. Since this is false, the legislation stemming from this principle is invalid and, according to Catholic morals, should not be observed, which does not imply disobedience."[16]

No specialized knowledge in ecclesiology is needed to understand that papal authority and infallibility have limits and that the duty of obedience is not absolute. Numerous leading scholars explicitly recognize the legitimacy of public resistance to erroneous decisions or teachings of pastors, including the sovereign pontiff. They are widely cited in a study by Arnaldo Xavier da Silveira titled "Public Resistance to Decisions of Ecclesiastical Authority."[17]

In the current case, it is permissible not only to "not observe" Pope Francis's motu proprio but even to resist its implementation according to the example set by Saint Paul (Gal. 2:11). It is not a matter of questioning papal authority, before which our love and reverence must grow. It is love for the papacy itself that must lead to the denunciation of *Traditionis Custodes*, which seeks dictatorially to eliminate the most ancient and venerable rite of Catholic worship, from which all the faithful have the right to drink.

As the distinguished theologian Francisco de Vitoria (1483 – 1546) says:

> According to natural law it is licit to repel violence with violence. Now, with such orders and dispensations, the pope does violence because he acts against the law, as was proven above. Therefore it is licit to resist him. As Cajetan observes, we do not affirm all this in the sense that someone has the right to be judge of the pope or have authority over him, but rather in the sense that it is licit to

---

anterior a la Reforma de 1970" (July 19, 2021), 3a–b, https://prensacelam.org/wp-content/uploads/2021/07/Mensaje-Traditionis-Custodes-19.07.2021.pdf.

16   Walter Sánchez Silva, "Sacerdotes se pronuncian tras restricciones del Papa a Misa tradicional en latín," ACI *Prensa*, July 17, 2021, https://www.aciprensa.com/noticias/sacerdotes-se-pronuncian-tras-restricciones-del-papa-a-misa-tradicional-en-latin-68603.

17   See Arnaldo Vidigal Xavier da Silveira, "Resistência Pública a Decisões da Autoridade Eclesiástica," *Catolicismo*, no. 244 (Aug. 1969), 2–3, https://catolicismo.com.br/Acervo/Num/0224/P02-03.html; idem, *Can Documents of the Magisterium of the Church Contain Errors? Can the Catholic Faithful Resist Them?*, trans. John R. Spann and José Aloisio A. Schelini (Spring Grove, PA: The American Society for the Defense of Tradition, Family and Property, 2015), 127–46, https://www.tfp.org/can-documents-of-the-magisterium-of-the-church-contain-errors-can-the-catholic-faithful-resist-them/.

defend oneself. Anyone, indeed, has the right to resist an unjust act, to try to impede it and to defend himself.[18]

The model of resistance on which Catholics can base their reaction is the late Prof. Plinio Corrêa de Oliveira's declaration of resistance to the *Ostpolitik* of Pope Paul VI. This statement, firm but filled with respect for the supreme pontiff, states in its crucial paragraphs:

> The bond of obedience to the successor of Peter, which we will never break, which we love in the most profound depths of our soul, and to which we tribute our highest love, this bond we kiss at the very moment in which, overwhelmed with sorrow, we affirm our position. And on our knees, gazing with veneration at the figure of His Holiness Paul VI, we express all our fidelity to him. In this filial act, we say to the Pastor of Pastors: Our soul is yours, our life is yours. Order us to do whatever you wish. Only do not order us to do nothing in the face of the assailing Red wolf. To this, our conscience is opposed.[19]

---

18   *Obras de Francisco de Vitoria* (Madrid: BAC, 1960), 486–87, quoted in Xavier da Silveira, *Can Documents of the Magisterium,* 134.

19   Plinio Corrêa de Oliveira, "A política de distensão do Vaticano com os governos comunistas — Para a TFP: omitir-se? ou resistir? (*Folha de S. Paulo,* Apr. 10, 1974), available at PlinioCorreadeOliveira.info; "The Vatican Policy of Détente with Communist Governments — Should the TFPs Stand Down? Or Should They Resist?," available at TFP.org.

38

Pope Francis's Scarlet Letter

EDWARD FESER

Catholic World Report

July 26, 2021

CONSIDER TWO GROUPS OF CATHOLICS: FIRST, DIVORCED Catholics who disobey the Church's teaching by forming a "new union" in which they are sexually active, thereby committing adultery. And second, traditionalist Catholics attached to the Extraordinary Form of the Mass (i.e., the "Latin Mass"), some of whom (but by no means all) hold erroneous theological opinions about the Second Vatican Council and related matters. In *Amoris Laetitia*, Pope Francis radically altered the Church's liturgical practice in order to *accommodate* the former group. And in *Traditionis Custodes*, he has now radically altered the Church's liturgical practice in order to *punish* the latter group.

Nathaniel Hawthorne's novel *The Scarlet Letter* famously portrays an unmerciful society in which adulterers are forced to mark themselves off from others by wearing a scarlet A on their clothing. Pope Francis clearly would disapprove of such cruelty, and rightly so. Yet the cruel treatment of the community of those attached to the old form of the Mass — the *innocent majority* of them no less than the minority with problematic theological opinions — amounts to something analogous to the affixing on them of a scarlet letter: the letter T for "traditionalist," the one group to which the pope's oft-repeated calls for mercy and accompaniment appear not to apply.

ACCOMPANYING ADULTERERS?

Let us consider just how radical each of these papal moves is. The Church has consistently taught that a valid sacramental marriage does not end until the death of one of the spouses, and has condemned as gravely sinful any sexual relationship with anyone except one's spouse. Hence those in such a marriage who divorce a spouse and then form a sexual relationship with someone else are guilty of grave sin, and cannot be absolved in confession without a firm resolution not to continue the sexual relationship. This is grounded in Christ's teaching on marriage and divorce in passages like Matthew 19:3–12 and Mark 10:2–12.

The gravity of this teaching cannot possibly be overstated. Christ acknowledges that "*Moses* allowed" for divorce. But then he declares: "And I say to you" that divorce is forbidden. Now, the law of Moses was given to Moses by God himself. So who has the authority to override it? Who would have the audacity to declare: "*Moses* allowed" such-and-such but "I say" differently? Only God himself. *Christ's teaching against divorce is therefore nothing less than a mark of his very divinity.* To put ourselves in opposition to that teaching would thus implicitly be either to deny Christ's divinity or, blasphemously, to put our authority above even his. It would be to declare: "*Christ* said such-and-such, but I say differently." Absolutely no one other than God himself, not even a pope (whose mandate is precisely only ever to *safeguard* Christ's teaching), has the right to do that.

If the teaching in question sounds "rigid," blame Christ. His own disciples thought it so, going so far as to opine that if that is how things are, it would be better not to marry (Matthew 19:10).

Now, no Catholic in a state of mortal sin is permitted to receive Holy Communion until he is validly absolved in confession. And no Catholic can be validly absolved who is aware of the Church's teaching on marriage and divorce, violates that teaching by having a sexual relationship with someone other than his spouse, and refuses to end this sexual relationship. Hence no Catholic who refuses to end such a relationship is permitted to receive Holy Communion.

This teaching too is extremely grave, grounded as it also is in Scripture, specifically in the words of St. Paul in 1 Corinthians 11: 27 – 29. According to St. Paul's teaching, to take Holy Communion while refusing to end such a sexual relationship is nothing less than to profane Christ's very body and blood and therefore to bring judgment upon oneself.

These doctrines are as clear, consistent, and authoritative as any Catholic teaching is or could possibly be. They are as ancient as the Church herself, are presented by her as infallible and absolutely binding, and have been unambiguously reiterated again and again and again. This is, of course, why *Amoris Laetitia* was so controversial. For it *seems* to allow that, in at least some circumstances, those who refuse to stop engaging in adulterous sexual activity can nevertheless take Holy Communion. To be sure, Pope Francis has not explicitly rejected any of the teachings summarized above. But he has also notoriously refused requests from several of his own cardinals (in the famous "dubia") explicitly to reaffirm that traditional teaching, and thereby decisively put to rest any worries about the consistency of *Amoris* with that teaching.

That the Holy Father himself is aware of how grave the issue is, and has even had his conscience troubled by it, is evident from a conversation recounted by one of his defenders, Cardinal Christoph Schönborn. *Crux* magazine (not exactly a traditionalist outlet) reported:

> Schönborn revealed that when he met the Pope shortly after the presentation of *Amoris*, Francis thanked him, and asked him if the document was orthodox. "I said, 'Holy Father, it is fully orthodox'," Schönborn told us he told the pope, adding that a few days later he received from Francis a little note that said: "Thank you for that word. That gave me comfort."

End quote. Note that the pope himself had at least *some* doubt about the document's orthodoxy — enough that he took "comfort" in being reassured about it — *even after* it had already been finalized and published! My point here is not to rehearse all the details of the controversy over *Amoris*. The point is simply to note the extreme lengths to which the pope was willing to go to try to accommodate the weaknesses even of those who obstinately refuse to obey the teaching of Christ and St. Paul. Even if you think *Amoris* itself does not cross the line of heterodoxy with regard to that teaching, it cannot be denied that the document is extremely gentle with and accommodating to those who *do* cross it.

SHAMING TRADITIONALISTS

The contrast with the treatment of traditionalist Catholics in *Traditionis Custodes* could not be more stark. Note first that, in the accompanying letter explaining his decision, Pope Francis claims that attachment to the old form of the Mass "is often characterized by a rejection . . . of the Vatican Council II itself, claiming, with unfounded and unsustainable assertions, that it betrayed the Tradition and the 'true Church.'"

The first thing to say about this is that, even if it is true that *some* people attached to the old form have this attitude, it is by no means true that *all* of them do. On the contrary, as Pope Francis himself notes in the same document, his predecessor Pope Benedict XVI affirmed that many who are attached to the old form "clearly accepted the binding character of Vatican Council II and were faithful to the Pope and to the Bishops." All the same, Pope Francis's severe restriction of the old form of the Mass punishes these innocent Catholics along with the guilty.

Secondly, we need to consider the precise nature of the purported heterodoxy and/or schismatic tendencies of which some of these traditionalists are accused. There are, of course, some extreme traditionalists who deny that we have had a valid pope for decades (namely the sedevacantists), and others who are in some less radical way in imperfect communion with the pope (such as the SSPX). But precisely because they are not in regular communion, the errors of these groups are irrelevant to the intended audience of *Traditionis Custodes* — namely, traditionalist Catholics who *are* in regular communion with the pope (such as the FSSP, and attendees at Extraordinary Form Masses offered at ordinary diocesan parishes).

By definition, the latter groups are not in schism. And though there are no doubt *some* among this small group within the Church who might nevertheless be said in some sense to have a "schismatic mentality," the same is true of the untold *millions* of liberal Catholics who casually dismiss the pope's authority to tell them what to believe or how to act — including the adulterous Catholics the pope accommodated in *Amoris*. Clearly, the pope feels no urgency about dealing with the schismatic mentality among countless liberals. So, why the urgency in dealing with the schismatic mentality of a small number of traditionalists?

Then there is the question of what it *means* exactly to "reject" Vatican II. Typically, with those traditionalists who are in full communion with the pope, what this means is that they reject some particular teaching of the Council, such as its teaching about religious liberty. Now, I disagree with those who reject that teaching. My view is that Vatican II's teaching on religious liberty can and should be reconciled with the teaching of the pre-Vatican II popes on the subject. (My favored way of doing so is the one developed by Thomas Pink.) But for one thing, the teaching of Vatican II on this subject is not one that has been proposed infallibly (even if, of course, that does not entail that we do not owe it assent); and for another, how exactly to interpret it in light of traditional teaching has been a matter of controversy among theologians faithful to the Magisterium. So, if the pope is going to be gentle and accommodating with those who obstinately defy the ancient and infallible teaching of Christ and St. Paul on marriage and Holy Communion, then how can he reasonably be *less* gentle and accommodating with those who have problems with a non-infallible teaching that is only a little over fifty years old?

So, the offense of which the traditionalists to whom *Traditionis Custodes* is addressed are accused is (a) not one of which all of them are guilty, and (b) manifestly less grave than that of Catholics who reject the Church's teaching on marriage, divorce, and Holy Communion. Yet those who reject that teaching are shown mercy, whereas traditionalists, the innocent as well as the guilty, are shown harshness.

And the punishment is very harsh. The pope aims to banish the

Extraordinary Form of the Mass from ordinary parish communities, to restrict future ordinations of priests interested in celebrating it, and effectively to quarantine from the rest of the Church those communities which are still permitted to use the old form of the Mass until such time as they are prepared to adopt the new form. As Cardinal Gerhard Müller observes, "the clear intent is to condemn the Extraordinary Form to extinction in the long run."[1] The pope is essentially telling traditionalist Catholics attached to the old form of the Mass that as individuals they are suspect, and as a group they are slated eventually to disappear. As Cardinal Müller writes:

> Without the slightest empathy, one ignores the religious feelings of the (often young) participants in the Masses according to the [old] Missal.... Instead of appreciating the smell of the sheep, the shepherd here hits them hard with his crook. It also seems simply unjust to abolish celebrations of the old rite just because it attracts some problematic people: *abusus non tollit usum*.

This is bad enough when the harm done to traditionalists alone is considered. But it is *the whole Church* that suffers from this decision, not just traditionalists. For one thing, Pope Benedict XVI made it clear that the preservation of the Extraordinary Form was by no means a matter merely of catering to the needs of a certain group within the Church. Rather, it had to do with reestablishing the connection of *the Church as a whole* with her own past in the liturgical context. That is why, though Benedict too hoped that there would in the future be only a single form of the Mass, he wanted the old form to exert an influence on the new no less than the new would exert influence on modifying the old. This was part of Benedict's general insistence on a "hermeneutic of continuity." *Traditionis Custodes* shows no sensitivity whatsoever to this dimension of the issue.

For another thing, while the pope says that he took this decision in order to foster greater unity in the Church, it is manifestly likely to foster instead only greater disunity. That is inevitable in any family when a father shows a double standard toward his children. Indeed, it is precisely this double standard, and not the old form of the Mass, that has generated the disunity of recent years. What has done more to lead some traditionalists to question Pope Francis's orthodoxy? The fact that they hear the Latin Mass every week? Or *Amoris Laetitia* and the pope's refusal to answer the dubia? To ask the question is to answer it. *Traditionis Custodes* will not put out the fire *Amoris* started. If anything, it will pour gasoline on it.

---

1   See chapter 16.

HE IS STILL THE HOLY FATHER

Some will say that the pope is merely acting like the father in the parable of the prodigal son (Luke 15:11–32). The resentful older son in the parable, on this interpretation, represents traditionalists, whereas the prodigal son represents Catholics who do not obey the Church's teaching on marriage and divorce.

But the analogy is ridiculous. For one thing, the prodigal son in the parable *repents and explicitly declines special accommodation.* He does not say "I intend to keep living an immoral life, but I demand some of that fattened calf anyway." For another, the father does not treat the older son at all harshly, but rather gently reassures him that he loves him no less than he loves the prodigal son.

All the same, the pope *is*, when all is said and done, a father — indeed, he is still the Holy Father of all Catholics, traditionalists included. And while the Church permits criticism of popes under certain circumstances, this cannot properly be done except with humility, respect, and restraint. [2] The pope is not some politician or corporate executive whom we might see fit to mock or to fire or vote out of office. He is the vicar of Christ, and he has no superior on earth. We may respectfully urge him to reconsider some course of action, but if he refuses, then we have to leave it to Christ to resolve the problem in the manner and at the time he chooses.

Moreover, because he is the pope, we must *in this case even more than in any other* follow Christ's command to turn the other cheek and pray for those who harm us. We must be willing to embrace the suffering this entails and to offer it up for others — including *for Pope Francis himself.*

---

2 See my article "The Church Permits Criticism of Popes under Certain Circumstances," *Edward Feser* (blog), May 20, 2018.

39

The Ungovernable Catholic Church[†]

ROSS DOUTHAT

New York Times

July 27, 2021

THE LATEST DRAMATIC MOVE BY POPE FRANCIS — HIS recent order abrogating the right of Roman Catholic priests to say their church's traditional Latin Mass — fits neatly within a historical analogy that's useful for understanding the larger drama of Catholicism: Namely, the church since the 1960s has been reliving the experience of France after 1789, with the arc of revolution and counterrevolution embodied in each successive pope.

This analogy belongs to a writer named Arturo Vasquez, a Catholic traditionalist turned disillusioned observer of the church, who teased it out in a short essay in 2019, expanding on an earlier reference by Joseph Ratzinger, the future Benedict XVI. In this story, the Second Vatican Council of the 1960s and its aftermath is the initial revolutionary moment — the apparent reconciliation with liberalism and modernity, the stripped altars and the reinvented liturgy, and the subsequent struggle of various factions to claim power, with apparent radical victories coexisting with the partial Thermidor of Pope Paul VI's encyclical forbidding artificial contraception.

Then John Paul II is Napoleon: the outsider — Polish rather than Corsican — who favors "rule by charisma and geopolitical power plays," who trades on the symbols of both the revolution and the previous regime, in a pontificate that displays "characteristics of a traditional mentality (Marian piety, conservative sexual morality, anti-communism)" but also ratifies important parts of the revolution, in personnel and rhetoric and canon law.

Then comes Benedict XVI, with a spirit closer to the royalist restoration that followed Napoleon: His appointments are more consistently conservative, his attitude toward the secular world and its "dictatorship of relativism" is more critical and embattled, and he restores not just certain costumes and gestures but also the pre-Vatican II liturgy itself, not in full but as an option with the same validity as the new liturgy, a tangible reminder of an older way of faith.

And now his successor — with Benedict alive to see it — seeks to suppress the old Mass once again, distilling in a single act Vasquez's suggestion that "Pope Francis is the 1848 revolution of the Catholic Church."

What the 1848 analogy illustrates isn't just Francis's role as a would-be liberalizer, his attempts to push forward with changes that were ruled out in the church's Napoleonic and restoration phases — most notably, changes to church regulations on marriage and divorce. It also points to the way that the Francis era has revealed, much as 1848 did to the conservative forces of order in nineteenth-century Europe, how fully the previous revolution had taken hold, so that a conservative or traditionalist pope can no more simply put the genie back into the bottle than nineteenth-century monarchists could reimpose an eighteenth-century political system.

Conservatives could ignore this reality as long as they felt they held the Vatican — even when, Vasquez argues, "the actual church in its vast majority was closer to Pope Francis than it ever was to Pope Benedict XVI or even John Paul II." But now that the majority has a pope in its own image, subverting or sweeping away some of his predecessors' most important acts, the weakness of the conservative party is laid bare.

Notably, though, apart from revealing the failure of the restoration, 1848 settled nothing about the future of France, let alone of Europe. It mostly revealed a political landscape that was ungovernable by either liberals or royalists and set the stage for ideological battles yet to come.

In a similar way, if the changes and reversals of the Francis era are breaking a particular narrative beloved of Catholic conservatives, in which the Roman pontiff guides the church through late-modern controversies with near-infallible wisdom, that breakage doesn't tell us where the church will end up fifty years or 100 years from now. The failure of the restoration is not the final victory of the revolution; it is only a sign of total uncertainty about what now lies ahead.

For instance, to say that Francis is closer to the spirit of mass Catholicism than his predecessors is not to say that mass Catholicism directly mirrors his complex mix of 1960s-era and Jesuit and Latin American ideas about the church, let alone the more thoroughgoing liberal Catholicism of some of his advisers. It's to say that mass Catholicism reflects his turbulent spirit, his impatience with ecclesial forms, his sense of church teaching as a zone of contest and debate, his idea of a decentralized and experimental Catholic system — all of which cashes out as its own kind of ungovernability, with many different forces empowered and contending all at once.

The attempted suppression of the old Mass is a good example. On the one hand, Francis is attempting to use centralized authority to complete the revolution of Vatican II, to consign definitively to the past a liturgy that's often a locus of resistance to the council's changes. (It's many other things as well, but Francis is not wrong to see it playing that role.)

At the same time, precisely because of the development of the revolution, his authority may not be strong enough to achieve this goal. The decentralization that liberals desire on doctrinal issues, the disillusioning impact of the sex abuse scandals, the doubts about a Vatican that keeps changing its mind from papacy to papacy, the role of the internet as a rallying point against disliked authority — these factors will make many bishops reluctant to act as Rome's enforcers and probably allow the old Mass to persist.

To put it another way, some of Francis's moves have seemed designed to restore the church as it looked in 1975, after the revolutionary decade and before John Paul II and Benedict. But the church of 1975 could actually suppress the old Mass, for a time, for the same reason that the church of 1975 could suppress, for a time, the evidence of priest sex abuse: It still had enough of its old authority, and the technological disruption was not yet ripe. Whereas in the church of 2021, conservative Catholic journalists just exposed the secret sex life of a notable American monsignor who was active on Grindr while he was responsible for formulating sexual misconduct policy. Whether you're theologically left or right, it's disruption all the way down.

Then there is also a crucial way the 1848 analogy breaks down. The grand ideological contests of the nineteenth century were battles to control an institution, the modern state, that was strong and growing stronger and from whose power and reach it was difficult for dissenters to escape. The contest for control of Catholicism is a battle for an institution that's been dramatically weakened by all sorts of trends and that people can simply exit — without having to emigrate or even dramatically change their weekday life — when they're disillusioned or defeated or just tired.

This creates a deep unpredictability about what counts as long-term strength within the church. Traditionalists proclaim that their Masses are full while many modernized parishes and dioceses decline, and accuse Francis of trying to choke off a growing and often youthful movement. Liberals counter that old-rite Massgoers are a tiny minority in the United States and Europe and an even tinier one in the context of the global church and that all the trend stories about young traditionalists mistake anecdotes for data.

Both have a point. The liberals are right that there is no great traditionalist groundswell among everyday Catholics. But the trads are right that there is a diverse cadre of younger Catholics, priests especially, who are traditionally inclined and likely to be increasingly influential in the otherwise diminished church of 2040, assuming the pope's attempt at suppression fails.

It's a condensed example of a larger trend, in which conservative Catholicism is weaker than conservatives imagined in the pontificates of John Paul II and Benedict, but liberal Catholicism shares in the crisis of confidence afflicting secular-liberal institutions and struggles to turn sympathy and soft affiliation into full religious zeal.

"Finding young candidates for the priesthood," a liberal Jesuit, Father Thomas Reese, wrote recently, "who support Francis and want to be celibate is like looking for Catholic unicorns" — an exaggeration but directionally correct. Which in turn explains why the most liberal precincts of Catholicism, the German church especially, feel that Francis hasn't gone nearly far enough toward a less priestly and more Protestantized church and that the only way to really serve the revolution is to push onward, from 1848 to 1871 or 1917.

In the divisions of the church, the pressure toward traditionalist and progressive extremes, both Latin Massgoers and German Protestantizers recognize the fact of Catholic decline. Both believe the other's vision would break the church in order to save it. Both have weaknesses and very different sorts of strength. The outcome of their struggle is — as good Catholics know — somehow foreordained. But more than at any other point in my lifetime, neither past analogies nor present trends supply much clarity about the church's future, and the better part of wisdom is to simply say, "God knows."

40

An Act of Weakness

CRISTIANA DE MAGISTRIS[1]
Voice of the Family
July 28, 2021

AFTER A CALM AND CAREFUL READING OF THE RECENT
motu proprio *Traditionis Custodes*, with none of the acrimony and indignation that a biased and draconian document like this one almost inevitably
arouses, the text seems not an act of strength but of weakness, a song of
the swan that, nearing his end, does not sing with a more beautiful voice
but with a louder one.

The document presents a number of canonical anomalies that jurists will
have to examine carefully. The priority for us is to dwell on a single point,
the liturgical, whose scope seems absolutely revolutionary and untenable.
Article 1 of the document, as if to set the tone for everything that follows,
states: "The liturgical books promulgated by Saint Paul VI and Saint John
Paul II, in conformity with the decrees of Vatican Council II, are the unique
expression of the *lex orandi* of the Roman Rite."

There is much that could be said about that "in conformity with the
decrees of Vatican Council II," seeing that the missal of Paul VI — as has
been amply demonstrated — went far beyond the conciliar dictate, coining
a liturgy from scratch, in complete discontinuity not only with the tradition
epitomized in the missal of St. Pius V but also with the will of the council
fathers themselves.

In any case, this liturgy made "at the drafting table" (Cardinal Ratzinger)
can no longer be considered part of the Roman Rite. No less a personality
than Monsignor Gamber affirmed this vigorously after the new missal went
into effect. The new liturgy is a "Ritus modernus," he said, no longer a
"Ritus Romanus." Fr. Louis Bouyer, a member of the Liturgical Movement,
who on the whole was in favor of the conciliar innovations, was forced
to affirm: "We must speak clearly: today there is in the Catholic Church
practically no liturgy worthy of this name." "Today," Monsignor Gamber
stressed, referring to the reformed liturgy, "we find ourselves before the

---

1   Cristiana de Magistris is the pen name of a traditional religious sister.

ruins of an almost bimillennial Tradition." Fr. Joseph Gelineau, one of the supporters of the renewal, was able to say: "Let those who, like me, have known and sung a solemn Gregorian Mass in Latin remember it, if they can. Let them compare it with the Mass we have now. It is not only the words, the melodies, and some of the gestures that are different. To tell the truth, it is a different liturgy of the Mass. This must be said without ambiguity: the Roman Rite as we knew it no longer exists (*le rite romain tel que nous l'avons connu n'existe plus*). It has been destroyed (*il est détruit*)."

That the Roman Rite no longer survives in the reformed missal of Paul VI is affirmed by liturgist friends and enemies of Tradition. Therefore, the reformed missal, as Klaus Gamber states, deserves the title of missal *modernus* but not *romanus*.

In the light of these elementary liturgical considerations, how is Article 1 of the motu proprio to be understood? To which is added the surprising and tendentious statement in the letter to the bishops: "It must therefore be maintained that the Roman Rite, adapted many times over the course of the centuries according to the needs of the day, has not only been preserved but renewed 'in faithful observance of the Tradition.' Whoever wishes to celebrate with devotion according to earlier forms of the liturgy can find in the reformed Roman Missal according to Vatican Council II all the elements of the Roman Rite." And it concludes: "in particular the Roman Canon which constitutes one of its more distinctive elements." Now it must be made quite clear that in the missal of Paul VI the Roman Canon is not — even in its *editio typica* — the Roman Canon of the missal of Saint Pius V. It is the one that most resembles it, but is by no means the same thing. Fr. R. T. Calmel, O. P., wrote a good four articles between 1968 and 1975, later grouped under the evocative title "Public reparation to the outraged Roman Canon" (in the new missal) to explain its beauty and immutability, as well as the antinomies existing between the Roman Canon of the missal of St. Pius V and that of Paul VI. We are saddened — yes, we too are saddened — to find in a pontifical document (moreover addressed to the bishops) such incompetence. But such it is. And it is not alone. It also remains to be explained what the missal of St. Pius V is now, since it is no longer an expression of the Roman Rite, the missal of Paul VI being the only expression of the *lex orandi* of the Roman Rite. After more than 400 years of life, has it perhaps ceased to be the Roman Rite?

The other serious problem that arises is the legitimacy of such an act. Again Klaus Gamber, in his study *The Reform of the Roman Liturgy*, wonders if a supreme pontiff can modify a rite. And he answers in the negative, since the pope is the custodian and guarantor of the liturgy (as well as of dogma), not its master. "No document of the Church," Gamber writes, "not even the Code of Canon Law, expressly says that the pope, as Supreme Pastor of the Church, has the right to abolish the traditional rite. The pope's *plena et suprema potestas* falls under clear limitations. . . . More than one author (Gaetano, Suarez) expresses the opinion that the pope's powers do not include the abolition of the traditional rite. . . . It is certainly not the task of the Apostolic See to destroy a rite of Apostolic Tradition, but its duty is to maintain it and pass it on." It follows that the Roman Rite presented in the missal of St. Pius V has not been abrogated or repealed, and all priests retain the right to celebrate the Mass and the faithful the right to attend it.

Finally, it is astonishing and painful to read in the Letter to the Bishops that the intent of this motu proprio is none other than that of St. Pius V after the Council of Trent: "I take comfort in this decision from the fact that, after the Council of Trent, St. Pius V also abrogated all the rites that could not claim a proven antiquity, establishing for the whole Latin Church a single *Missale Romanum*." But Saint Pius V did the exact opposite of what Pope Francis has done with this motu proprio. It is true that Saint Pius V established a single *Missale Romanum* for the whole Latin Church, but this missal — unlike that of Paul VI imposed by Francis — was only *restored*, in compliance with the Tridentine decrees, to be an instrument of unity for all Catholics *because it was older, not because it was newer*. How can the missal of Paul VI be an instrument of unity if (in addition to a myriad of other problems) it has reached a creativity, that is, a diversity, "almost unbearable," as the pontiff himself recognizes? Furthermore, the "proven antiquity" of the rites desired by the pope of Lepanto required an uninterrupted continuity of at least 200 years. This means that the modern rite of Paul VI, under the Grand Inquisitor, would have been elegantly crossed out, without any hope, not even a remote one, of being able to triumph as the sole rite of all Christendom. Not to mention that with the bull *Quo Primum*, St. Pius V armored his Missal *in perpetuum*, making it irrevocable. The motu proprio, therefore, invokes the authority of one who condemns it. Here too it is surprising to note such historical ineptitude in a pontifical document.

In conclusion, the motu proprio, if one wishes to read it in depth, is the recognition of a defeat. It is an apparent act of strength that covers a basic weakness and incompetence. The reformed missal has been a catastrophe on every level: liturgical, dogmatic, moral. The result, plain for all to see, is that it has emptied churches, convents, and seminaries. Not being able to impose it by virtue of tradition, which it does not convey, one wishes to impose it by dint of law. But this is an underhanded operation, founded on deception, and therefore destined to fail. It is not a fatal stroke dealt against the Roman Rite, but the euthanasia of the modern rite. It is not a death blow, but a life-giving pruning of the missal of St. Pius V, which — by the hatred it arouses among the modernist fringes of the hierarchy — confirms that it is "the most beautiful thing this side of Heaven," handed down to us by our fathers for us to pass on to our children, even if we should have to crimson it with our blood.

41

Scattering the Sheep[†]

ARCHBISHOP THOMAS E. GULLICKSON

ut ad Sancta sanctorum puris mereamur mentibus
July 28, 2021

I WONDER WHY SOME ARE SO TAKEN UP WITH TRYING to "scatter the sheep": *Quare fremuerunt gentes* . . . Why would anyone pretending to be of Christ's Church lash out at the lambs?

In his *New York Times* article of yesterday,[1] Ross Douthat seems to think that those who, regarding the motu proprio, prognosticate the "success" of this latest attempt at suppression of the Mass of the Ages do not have all of the present variables in hand. He expressed skepticism regarding his colleague's thesis that the present motu proprio, just like revolutionary activity in 1848 in France, could accomplish what no amount of violence in the 1970s was able to attain in its attempt to eradicate the timeless liturgical patrimony of the Roman Church. Part of Douthat's argument was that the hierarchical principle has been so undermined in the last 30 – 40 years that legislation like *Traditionis Custodes*, apart from its many flaws, is deader in the water than was *Veterum Sapientia* back in 1962.

Notwithstanding Douthat's incisive commentary, the situation is still terribly worrisome for me. This is not a tempest in a teapot. We need but take a closer look on the political side here in the United States at what the radical left seems to be achieving in undermining the family. People are not being convinced or even seduced by the left's dystopic propaganda, no; rather, the little ones are being cowed by threats and violence, too often supported by bureaucrats and even elected officials at city, state, and federal levels. They are being victimized and things are being torn down.

What has brought on this violence today in the Church? It is the same deep-seated hatred of the Apostolic Faith which was at work back in the sixties and seventies, and which still perdures among an ever-diminishing old guard and their clueless recruits. They seem to have imbibed that same

---

† A composite, approved by the Archbishop for the present publication, of material taken from two posts at his blog "ut ad Sancta sanctorum puris mereamur mentibus," July 28 and August 1.
1 See chapter 39.

hatred which "wreckovated" churches and burned books and vestments, with no respect for the devotion of a generation now mostly gone to their eternal reward.

This kind of violence cannot be met by counterviolence. Rather, it is met by the steadfast adherence to the truth and the love of the Old Mass, which has captured the love and imagination of not a few young people in our own day and time. The revolutionaries, the violent, are kicking against the goad, so to speak. These days I am inclined to see *Traditionis Custodes* as a scythe or a winnowing fan, which will further bring to light that good seed, which like the proverbial mustard seed will come to fruition and shelter a new world in its branches. Pacific, tranquil demographic growth does not fit the bill. Saint Michael the Archangel, defend us in battle!

When we were children, one of my mom's ultimate arguments against younger siblings throwing temper tantrums was to tell them to go look at themselves in the mirror and be covered with shame at their ugliness. It was an argument suited to a child, a very simple call to introspection, based on a fundamental conviction concerning the goodness of that child who stood before her stamping his or her little feet. It is a dialogue without much sophistication, but one shot through with love. At some point the fuming and railing against us and the *usus antiquior* will subside or stop altogether. It *has* to, for we have a world to claim for Christ. All else is less than to the point.

Another day is coming. Be of courage, little flock!

42

Was the Sacred Liturgy Made for the Pope, or the Pope for the Sacred Liturgy?

JOHN A. MONACO

Catholic World Report

July 28, 2021

THE PUBLICATION OF POPE FRANCIS'S MOTU PROPRIO, *Traditionis Custodes*, has once more lit the embers underneath ecclesiological and liturgical debates. Among the various reactions to this document include disbelief, shock, and hurt by those who love the traditional Latin Mass; while those favorable to the spirit of the Second Vatican Council express vindication, triumph, and glee.

As bishops scramble to their flocks and discern how best to implement the motu proprio, there seems to be more emphasis given to questions of a canonical and pastoral nature, such as the future of long-existing Latin Mass communities, the existence of religious congregations attached to the rite, and the rights of priests to offer Mass according to the 1962 missal. With traditionalists holding high Pius V's *Quo Primum* (1570) and progressives Paul VI's *Missale Romanum* (1969), the arguments rage on regarding the legal status of the traditional Roman Rite.

Amidst the clanging clamor and ubiquitous uproar, I suggest there be a collective pause, to allow space for a reflection of a more theological nature. Given the papal-centric nature of this discourse, it is important to ask the following: was the Sacred Liturgy made for the pope, or the pope for the Sacred Liturgy?

Knee-jerk reactions to this question might include a quotation from the First Vatican Council (1869 – 70) on the pope's unquestionable role on faith, morals, discipline, and government of the Church (*Pastor Aeternus*, III.2). Pope Pius XII's encyclical, *Mediator Dei* (1947), also comes to mind, in which he states that only the pope has "the right to recognize and establish any practice touching the worship of God, to introduce and approve new rites, as also to modify those he judges to require modification" (58).

Other reactions might quote the 1983 Code of Canon Law, which makes clear the pope's "supreme, full, immediate, and universal ordinary power in the Church" (Can. 331). As the administration of the sacraments falls within Church discipline, it is not surprising that canon law designates the ordering of the liturgy to the pope (Can. 838 § 2) and even grants him the power to "approve or define the requirements for their validity" (Can. 841).

Immediately, then, we are faced with disturbing questions. If the pope has the power over the liturgy, then what is stopping him from suppressing all of the Eastern rites and forcing the Eastern Catholic Churches to use the *Novus Ordo Missae*, if not a brand new liturgy crafted for postmodern man? If the pope can determine what is required for sacramental validity, what is preventing the Holy Father from replacing the bread and wine used for the consecration at Mass with rice and tea?

Some might argue that the pope would never do such a thing, and they rightfully point out the damage such an action could cause to the Church. Others might dismiss such hypotheticals as absurdities, claiming that the people of God would resist. But such protesting does not change the fact that, according to the aforementioned quotations, the pope indeed does have such power — whether or not he chooses to use it is an entirely different issue. To deny the pope this power would seemingly call the papal office itself into question.

Historically, Scholastic theologians were not afraid to tackle such hypotheticals. Cardinal Juan de Torquemada (1388 – 1468), while not dealing with this particular issue, nevertheless knew that there were limits to papal authority. The pope was constrained by divine and natural law, the order of the sacraments, and moral teachings (*Summa de ecclesia*, 3.57). For Torquemada, the pope's authority was tied to its purpose — there was no papal authority in the abstract, but only in relation to his relationship to the Church, which was one of confirming the Christian faith and preserving the proper order of the Church (*status ecclesiae*), whose mission is the salvation of souls. Elsewhere in his treatise on the Church, Torquemada also notes how, among all the things necessary for promoting the well-being of the Church, none is higher than those pertaining to divine worship (*maxime ad cultum divinum*).

Following in Torquemada's footsteps, the well-known Jesuit philosopher-theologian, Francisco Suarez (1548 – 1617), was quick to show how papal power is not absolute in an unqualified sense. For example, if the pope decided to excommunicate the entire Church, he would be in error. The pope would also err — as well as commit the sin of schism from the Church — if he were to overthrow or destroy (*evertere*) liturgical rites of apostolic origin (*De charitate*, 12.1).

Let us return to the original question: was the Sacred Liturgy made for the pope, or the pope for the Sacred Liturgy? If we affirm the former, then we acknowledge the fullness of power (*plenitudo potestatis*) belonging to the Supreme Pontiff, albeit at the expense of granting that the liturgy — in theory — could be his plaything. In this mindset, the pope is the ultimate arbiter of divine worship, and if he requires that priests offer the Mass while riding on a unicycle, there is nothing preventing him (save divine intervention) from doing so. Even the assurances of those who suggest that this is not probable does not quell the fear that it is possible. However, if we affirm the latter — that the pope was made for the Sacred Liturgy, we might have a firmer and more theological basis for his liturgical role, one that grants the pope's primacy without sacrificing the beauty and truth of ancient worship.

With all respect to all that the Catholic faith teaches regarding his office, the pope, above all, is a bishop, and a bishop is necessarily a priest. A priest is one who offers sacrifice to the LORD, and the only true and absolute priest is Christ Himself (Heb 7:25–28). All priestly acts flow from His priesthood, all holy sacrifices from His sacrifice. In his sacramental actions, the priest acts in the person of Christ (*in persona Christi*), not in the person of the pope. In many ways, the priest does indeed represent the bishop, who, as the *Catechism* notes, possesses the "fullness of the sacrament of Holy Orders" (#1557). In the early Church, the bishop was the primary celebrant of the Eucharist. The unity of the Church was expressed through the offering of Christ in the Eucharist, and the bishop represented Christ, offering the Divine Victim to the Father, the Head offering the Body made manifest through the gathering assembly (*synaxis*). Each local Church expressed its visible communion through gathering for liturgy celebrated by the bishop, and each bishop manifested his communion with the wider Church through his union with the Church of Rome, which held a true primacy in relation to the other Churches.

Why is the focus on the pope-as-priest important to our question? Let us imagine an undivided Church, in which all the bishops are gathered for the Eucharistic liturgy. By the very nature of the Mass, there can only be one main celebrant. Given its historical and theological importance, the Bishop of Rome would hold such primacy, just as St. Peter was known as the leader of the Apostles. But what does such primacy consist of? The pope would express his primacy in "presiding in love," as St. Ignatius of Antioch wrote. Such presiding would have its fullest sense in liturgical presidency. In the liturgy, we witness the offering of Christ to the Father, the same offering made on Calvary for the remission of sins. If primacy is regarded as "power over," then the pope's primacy — which, I suggest, is best seen in him serving the altar as bishop and priest — has no place in the liturgy.

The liturgy is not our pushing aside Christ and putting ourselves on the Cross, but instead our mystical participation in Calvary, which is a sacrifice we first must receive before participating. To speak of papal primacy as "power over" fails the litmus test by which we should measure our identity — in the Sacred Liturgy, the "source and summit of the Christian life."

If we think of the liturgy as a "thing," then it makes sense that it was made for the pope, whose supremacy was dogmatized at Vatican I. But if we understand the liturgy to be the divine drama of salvation made present, the saving acts of the LORD given to the Church as a mountain of treasure, then we cannot help but reject the notion that the guardian of such treasure has the right to dispose of it, for it did not originate with him, nor does it belong solely to him, but rather the treasure is given to the Church as its ransom and redemption.

The liturgy is not a "thing" which we can grasp; it is a mystery we enter into. The liturgy is not a fabrication of the Church's musings upon God, but a gift given to the Church for the glory of God, the good of the Church, and the love of God's people. As a member of the Church — despite there being no earthly equal to him or his authority — the pope is the recipient of liturgy, not its creator or its master.

Thus, the liturgy has a logical priority over the pope, for without the liturgy, the Church has no reason to exist, nor any ability to participate in the divine life of the Holy Trinity. Tradition is the vehicle through which liturgy is transmitted — just as we cannot create a new Calvary, Resurrection, or Pentecost, so too is it impossible to "create" a new liturgy. Its substance, as St. Paul writes, was first "received from the Lord" before being "handed over" (1 Cor 11:23). After all, when Christ commanded His Apostles to "Do this in memory of Me," St. Peter did not dare to suggest "doing that," instead.

It is the pope who serves the Sacred Liturgy as its celebrant, protector, and transmitter — to claim otherwise would reveal a severe misunderstanding not only of liturgy, but also of the papacy.

43

Lapides Clamabunt

ARCHBISHOP CARLO MARIA VIGANÒ

Li{eSiteNews[1]

July 28, 2021

Dico vobis quia si hii tacuerint, lapides clamabunt.
I say to you that if these are silent, the stones will cry out.

LUKE 19:40

"TRADITIONIS CUSTODES": THIS IS THE INCIPIT OF THE document with which Francis imperiously cancels the previous motu proprio *Summorum Pontificum* of Benedict XVI. The almost mocking tone of the bombastic quotation from *Lumen Gentium* will not have escaped notice: just when Bergoglio recognizes the Bishops as guardians of the Tradition, he asks them to obstruct its highest and most sacred expression of prayer. Anyone who tries to find within the folds of the text some *escamotage* to circumvent the text should know that the draft sent to the Congregation for the Doctrine of the Faith for revision was extremely more drastic than the final text: a confirmation, if ever it were needed, that no particular pressure was needed from the historical enemies of the Tridentine Liturgy — beginning with the scholars of Sant'Anselmo — to convince His Holiness to try his hand at what he does best: demolishing. *Ubi solitudinem faciunt, pacem appellant.*[2]

THE MODUS OPERANDI OF FRANCIS

Francis has once again disavowed the pious illusion of the *hermeneutic of continuity*, stating that the coexistence of the *Vetus* and *Novus Ordo* is impossible because they are expressions of two irreconcilable doctrinal and ecclesiological approaches. On the one hand there is the Apostolic Mass, the voice of the Church of Christ; on the other there is the Montinian "Eucharistic celebration," the voice of the conciliar church. And this is not an accusation, however legitimate, made by those who express reservations

---

1 The same essay appeared at numerous sites more or less simultaneously. Translation provided by His Excellency.

2 "They make a wasteland and call it peace" (Tacitus, *Agricola*).

about the reformed rite and Vatican II. Rather it is an admission, indeed a proud affirmation of ideological adherence on the part of Francis himself, the head of the most extremist faction of progressivism. His dual role as pope and liquidator of the Catholic Church allows him on the one hand to demolish it with decrees and acts of governance, and on the other hand to use the prestige that his office entails to establish and spread the *new religion* over the rubble of the old one. It matters little if the ways in which he acts against God, against the Church, and against the Lord's flock are in stark conflict with his appeals to *parrhesia*, to dialogue, to building bridges and not erecting walls: the *church of mercy* and the *field hospital* turn out to be empty rhetorical devices, since it ought to be Catholics who benefit from them and not heretics or fornicators. In reality, each of us is well aware that *Amoris Laetitia's* indulgence towards public concubinage and adulterers would hardly be imaginable towards those "rigid" ones against whom Bergoglio hurls his darts as soon as he has the opportunity.

After years of this pontificate, we have all understood that the reasons given by Bergoglio for declining a meeting with a Prelate, a politician, or a conservative intellectual do not apply to the molester Cardinal, the heretic Bishop, the abortionist politician, or the globalist intellectual. In short, there is a blatant difference in behavior, from which one can grasp the partiality and partisanship of Francis in favor of any ideology, thought, project, scientific, artistic, or literary expression that is not Catholic. Anything that even only vaguely evokes anything Catholic seems to arouse in the tenant of Santa Marta an aversion that is disconcerting to say the least, if only in virtue of the Throne on which he is seated. Many have noted this dissociation, this sort of bipolarity of a pope who does not behave like a Pope and does not speak like a Pope. The problem is that we are faced not with a sort of *inaction* from the Papacy, as could happen with a sick or very old Pontiff; but rather with a constant action that is organized and planned in a sense diametrically opposed to the very essence of the Papacy. Not only does Bergoglio not condemn the errors of the present time by strongly reaffirming the Truth of the Catholic Faith — he has never done this! — but he actively seeks to disseminate these errors, to promote them, to encourage their supporters, to spread them to the greatest possible extent and to host events promoting them in the Vatican, simultaneously silencing those who denounce these same errors. Not only does he not punish fornicating Prelates, but he even promotes and defends them by lying, while he removes conservative Bishops and does not hide his annoyance with the heartfelt appeals of Cardinals not aligned with the new course. Not only does he not condemn abortionist politicians who proclaim themselves Catholics, but he intervenes to prevent the Episcopal Conference from pronouncing on this matter, contradicting that *synodal path* which conversely allows him to use a minority of ultra-progressives to impose his will on the majority of the Synod Fathers.

The one constant of this attitude, noted in its most brazen and arrogant form in *Traditionis Custodes*, is duplicity and lies. A duplicity that is a façade, of course, daily disavowed by positions that are anything but prudent in favor of a very specific group, which for the sake of brevity we can identify with the ideological Left, indeed with its most recent evolution in a globalist, ecologist, transhuman and LGBTQ key. We have come to the point that even simple people with little knowledge of doctrinal issues understand that we have a non-Catholic pope, at least in the strict sense of the term. This poses some problems of a canonical nature that are not inconsiderable, which it is not up to us to solve but which sooner or later will have to be addressed.

IDEOLOGICAL EXTREMISM

Another significant element of this pontificate, taken to its extreme consequences with *Traditionis Custodes*, is Bergoglio's ideological extremism: an extremism that is deplored in words when it concerns others, but which shows itself in its most violent and ruthless expression when it is he himself who puts it into practice against clergy and laity connected to the ancient rite and faithful to Sacred Tradition. Towards the Society of Saint Pius X he shows himself willing to make concessions and to establish a relationship as "good neighbors," but towards the poor priests and faithful who have to endure a thousand humiliations and blackmail in order to beg for a Mass in Latin, he shows no understanding, no humanity. This behavior is not accidental: Archbishop Lefebvre's movement enjoys its own autonomy and economic independence, and for this reason it has no reason to fear retaliation or commissioners from the Holy See. But the Bishops, priests, and clerics incardinated in dioceses or religious Orders know that hanging over them is the sword of Damocles of removal from office, dismissal from the ecclesiastical state, and the deprivation of their very means of subsistence.

THE EXPERIENCE OF THE TRIDENTINE MASS IN PRIESTLY LIFE

Those who have had the opportunity to follow my speeches and declarations know well what my position is on the Council and on the *Novus Ordo*; but they also know what my background is, my *curriculum* in the service of the Holy See and my relatively recent awareness of the apostasy and the crisis in which we find ourselves. For this reason, I would like to reiterate my understanding for the spiritual path of those who, precisely because of this situation, cannot or are not yet able to make a radical choice, such as celebrating or attending exclusively the Mass of St. Pius V. Many priests discover the treasures of the venerable Tridentine Liturgy only when they celebrate it and allow themselves to be permeated by it, and it is not uncommon for an initial curiosity towards the "extraordinary form"— certainly fascinating due to the solemnity of the rite — to change quickly into the awareness of the depth of the words, the clarity of the doctrine, the incomparable spirituality that it gives birth to and nourishes in our souls. There is a perfect harmony that words cannot express, and that the faithful can understand only in part, but which touches the heart of the Priesthood as only God can. This can be confirmed by my confreres who have approached the *usus antiquior* after decades of obedient celebration of the *Novus Ordo*: a world opens up, a cosmos that includes the prayer of the Breviary with the lessons of Matins and the commentaries of the Fathers, the cross-references to the texts of the Mass, the Martyrology in the Hour of Prime... They are sacred words — not because they are expressed in Latin — but rather they are expressed in Latin because the vulgate language would demean them, would profane them, as Dom Guéranger wisely observed. These are the words of the Bride to the divine Bridegroom, words of the soul that lives in intimate union with God, of the soul that lets itself be inhabited by the Most Holy Trinity. Essentially priestly words, in the deepest sense of the term, which implies in the Priesthood not only the power to offer sacrifice, but to unite in self-offering to the pure, holy, and immaculate Victim. It has nothing to do with the ramblings of the reformed rite, which is too intent on pleasing the secularized mentality to turn to the Majesty of God and the Heavenly Court; so preoccupied with making itself understandable that one has to give up on communicating anything but trivial obviousness; so careful not to hurt the feelings of heretics as to allow itself to keep silent about the Truth just at the moment in which the Lord God makes himself present on the altar; so fearful of asking the faithful for the slightest commitment as to trivialize sacred song and any artistic expression linked to worship. The simple fact that Lutheran pastors, modernists, and well-known Freemasons collaborated in the drafting of that rite should make us understand, if not the bad faith and willful misconduct, at least the horizontal mentality, devoid of any supernatural impetus, which motivated the authors of the so-called "liturgical reform"— who, as far as we know, certainly did not shine with the sanctity with which the sacred authors of the texts of the ancient *Missale Romanum* and of the entire liturgical *corpus* shine.

How many of you priests — and certainly also many lay people — in reciting the wonderful verses of the Pentecost sequence were moved to tears, understanding that your initial predilection for the traditional liturgy had nothing to do with a sterile aesthetic satisfaction, but had evolved into a real spiritual necessity, as indispensable as breathing? How can you and how can we explain to those who today would like to deprive you of this priceless good, that that blessed rite has made you discover the true nature of your Priesthood, and that from it and only from it are you able to draw strength and nourishment to face the commitments of your ministry? How can you make it clear that the obligatory return to the Montinian rite represents an impossible sacrifice for you, because in the daily battle against the world, the flesh, and the devil it leaves you disarmed, prostrate, and without strength?

It is evident that only those who have not celebrated the Mass of St. Pius V can consider it as an annoying tinsel of the past, which can be done without. Even many young priests, accustomed to the *Novus Ordo* since their adolescence, have understood that the two forms of the rite have nothing in common, and that one is so superior to the other as to reveal all its limits and criticisms, to the point of making it almost painful to celebrate. It is not a question of nostalgia, of a cult of the past: here we are speaking of the life of the soul, its spiritual growth, ascesis and mysticism. Concepts that those who see their priesthood as a profession cannot even understand, just as they cannot understand the agony that a priestly soul feels in seeing the Eucharistic Species desecrated during the grotesque rites of Communion in the era of the pandemic farce.

THE REDUCTIVE VISION OF THE LIBERALIZATION OF THE MASS

This is why I find it extremely unpleasant to have to read in *Traditionis Custodes* that the reason why Francis believes that the motu proprio *Summorum Pontificum* was promulgated fourteen years ago lay only in the desire to heal the so-called schism of Archbishop Lefebvre. Of course, the "political" calculation may have had its weight, especially at the time of John Paul II, even if at that time the faithful of the Society of Saint Pius X were few in number. But the request to be able to restore citizenship to the Mass which for two millennia nourished the holiness of the faithful and gave the sap of life to Christian civilization cannot be reduced to a contingent fact.

With his motu proprio, Benedict XVI restored the Roman Apostolic Mass to the Church, declaring that it had never been abolished. Indirectly, he admitted that there was an abuse by Paul VI, when in order to give authority to his rite he ruthlessly forbade the celebration of the traditional Liturgy. And even if in that document there may be some incongruent elements, such as the coexistence of two forms of the same rite, we can believe that these have served to allow for the diffusion of the extraordinary form, without affecting the ordinary one. In other times, it would have seemed incomprehensible to let a Mass steeped in misunderstandings and omissions continue to be celebrated, when the authority of the Pontiff could have simply restored the ancient rite. But today, with the heavy burden of Vatican II and with the now widespread secularized mentality, even the mere [recognition of the] liceity of celebrating the Tridentine Mass without permission can be considered an undeniable good — a good that is visible to all due to the abundant fruits it brings to the communities where it is celebrated. And we can also believe that it would have brought even more fruits if only *Summorum Pontificum* had been applied in all its points and with a spirit of true ecclesial communion.

THE ALLEGED "INSTRUMENTAL USE" OF THE ROMAN MISSAL

Francis knows well that the survey taken among Bishops all over the world did not yield negative results, although the formulation of the questions made clear what answers he wanted to receive. That consultation was a pretext, in order to make people believe that the decision he made was inevitable and the fruit of a choral request from the Episcopate. We all know that if Bergoglio wants to obtain a result, he does not hesitate to resort to force, lies, and sleight of hand: the events of the last Synods have demonstrated this beyond all reasonable doubt, with the Post-Synodal Exhortation drafted even before the vote on the *Instrumentum Laboris*. Also in this case, therefore, the pre-established purpose was the abolition of the Tridentine Mass and the *prophasis*, that is, the apparent excuse, had to be the supposed "instrumental use of the Roman Missal of 1962, often characterized by a rejection not only of the liturgical reform, but of Vatican Council II itself." In all honesty, one can perchance accuse the Society of Saint Pius X of this instrumental use, [a Society] which has every right to affirm what each of us knows well: that the Mass of Saint Pius V is incompatible with post-conciliar ecclesiology and doctrine. But the Society is not affected by the motu proprio, and has always celebrated using the 1962 Missal precisely by virtue of that inalienable right which Benedict XVI recognized, which was not created *ex nihilo* in 2007.

The diocesan priest who celebrates Mass in the church assigned to him by the Bishop, and who every week must undergo the third degree through the accusations of zealous progressive Catholics only because he has dared to recite the *Confiteor* prior to administering Communion to the faithful, knows very well that he cannot speak ill of the *Novus Ordo* or Vatican II, because at the first syllable he would already be summoned to the Curia and sent to a parish church lost in the mountains. That silence, always painful and almost always perceived by everyone as more eloquent than many words, is the price he has to pay in order to have the possibility of celebrating the Holy Mass of all time, in order not to deprive the faithful of the graces that it pours down upon the Church and the world. And what is even more absurd is that while we hear it said with impunity that the Tridentine Mass ought to be abolished because it is incompatible with the ecclesiology of Vatican II, as soon as we say the same thing — that is, that the Montinian Mass is incompatible with Catholic ecclesiology — we are immediately made the object of condemnation, and our affirmation is used as evidence against us before the revolutionary tribunal of Santa Marta.

I wonder what sort of spiritual disease could have struck the Shepherds in the last few decades, in order to lead them to become, not loving fathers but ruthless censors of their priests, officials constantly watching and ready to revoke all rights in virtue of a blackmail that they do not even try to conceal. This climate of suspicion does not in the least contribute to the serenity of many good priests, when the good they do is always placed under the lens of functionaries who consider the faithful linked to the Tradition as a danger, as an annoying presence to be tolerated so long as it does not stand out too much. But how can we even conceive of a Church in which the good is systematically hindered and whoever does it is viewed with suspicion and kept under control? I therefore understand the scandal of many Catholics, faithful, and not a few priests in the face of this "shepherd who instead of smelling his sheep, angrily beats them with a stick."[3]

The misunderstanding of being able to enjoy a right as if it were a gracious concession may also be found in public affairs, where the State permits itself to authorize travel, school lessons, the opening of activities and the performance of work, as long as one undergoes inoculation with the experimental genetic serum. Thus, just as the "extraordinary form" is granted on the condition of accepting the Council and the reformed Mass, so also in the civil sphere the rights of citizens are granted on the condition of accepting the pandemic narrative, the vaccination, and tracking

---

3   Quoted from Bishop Schneider; see chapter 33.

systems. It is not surprising that in many cases it is precisely priests and Bishops — and Bergoglio himself — who ask that people be vaccinated in order to access the Sacraments. The perfect synchrony of action on both sides is disturbing to say the least.

But where then is this instrumental use of the *Missale Romanum*? Should we not rather speak of the instrumental use of the Missal of Paul VI, which — to paraphrase Bergoglio's words — is ever more characterized by a growing rejection not only of the pre-conciliar liturgical tradition but of all the Ecumenical Councils prior to Vatican II? On the other hand, is it not precisely Francis who considers as a threat to the Council the simple fact that a Mass may be celebrated which repudiates and condemns all the doctrinal deviations of Vatican II?

OTHER INCONGRUENCES

Never in the history of the Church did a Council or a liturgical reform constitute a point of rupture between what came before and what came after! Never in the course of these two millennia have the Roman Pontiffs deliberately drawn an ideological border between the Church that preceded them and the one they had to govern, cancelling and contradicting the Magisterium of their Predecessors! The *before* and *after*, instead, became an obsession, both of those who prudently insinuated doctrinal errors behind equivocal expressions, as well as of those who — with the boldness of those who believe that they have won, propagated Vatican II as "the 1789 of the Church," as a "prophetic" and "revolutionary" event. Before 7 July 2007, in response to the spread of the traditional rite, a well-known pontifical master of ceremonies replied piquedly: *"There is no going back!"* And yet apparently with Francis one can go back on the promulgation of *Summorum Pontificum* — and how! — if it serves to preserve power and to prevent the good from spreading. It is a slogan which sinisterly echoes the cry of *"Nothing will be as it was before"* of the pandemic farce.

Francis's admission of an alleged division between the faithful linked to the Tridentine liturgy and those who largely out of habit or resignation have adapted to the reformed liturgy is revealing: he does not seek to heal this division by recognizing full rights to a rite that is objectively better with respect to the Montinian rite, but precisely in order to prevent the ontological superiority of the Mass of Saint Pius V from becoming evident, and to prevent the criticisms of the reformed rite and the doctrine it expresses from emerging, he prohibits the old rite, he labels it as divisive, he confines it to Indian reservations, trying to limit its diffusion as much as possible, so that it will disappear completely in the name of the cancel culture of which the conciliar revolution was the unfortunate forerunner. Not being able to tolerate that the Novus Ordo and Vatican II emerge inexorably defeated by their confrontation with the Vetus Ordo and the perennial Catholic Magisterium, the only solution that can be adopted is to cancel every trace of Tradition, relegating it to the nostalgic refuge of some irreducible octogenarian or a clique of eccentrics, or presenting it — as a pretext — as the ideological manifesto of a minority of fundamentalists. On the other hand, constructing a media version consistent with the system, to be repeated *ad nauseam* in order to indoctrinate the masses, is the recurring element not only in the ecclesiastical sphere but also in the political and civil sphere, so that it appears with disconcerting evidence that the deep church and deep state are nothing other than two parallel tracks which run in the same direction and have as their final destination the New World Order, with its religion and its prophet.

The division is there, obviously, but it does not come from good Catholics and clergy who remain faithful to the doctrine of all time, but rather from those who have replaced orthodoxy with heresy and the Holy Sacrifice with a fraternal agape. That division is not new today, but dates back to the Sixties, when the "spirit of the Council," openness to the world, and interreligious dialogue turned two thousand years of Catholicity into straw and revolutionized the entire ecclesial body, persecuting and ostracizing the refractory. Yet that division, accomplished by bringing doctrinal and liturgical confusion into the heart of the Church, did not seem so deplorable then; while today, in full apostasy, they are paradoxically considered divisive who ask, not for the explicit condemnation of Vatican II and the Novus Ordo, but simply for the tolerance of the Mass "in the extraordinary form" in the name of the much-vaunted multifaceted pluralism.

Significantly, even in the civilized world the protection of minorities is valid only when they serve to demolish traditional society, while such protection is ignored when it would guarantee the legitimate rights of honest citizens. And it has become clear that under the pretext of the protection of minorities the only intention was to weaken the majority of the good, while now that the majority is made up of those who are corrupt, the minority of the good can be crushed without mercy: recent history does not lack illuminating precedents in this regard.

THE TYRANNICAL NATURE OF TRADITIONIS CUSTODES

In my opinion, it is not so much this or that point of the motu proprio that is disconcerting, but rather its overall tyrannical nature accompanied by a substantial falsity of the arguments put forward to justify the decisions imposed. Scandal is also given by the abuse of power by an authority that has its own *raison d'être* not in impeding or limiting the graces that are bestowed on its adherents through the Church but rather in promoting those graces; not in taking away glory from the Divine Majesty with a rite that winks at the Protestants but rather in rendering that glory perfectly; not in sowing doctrinal and moral errors but rather in condemning and eradicating them. Here too, the parallel with what takes place in the civil world is all too evident: our rulers abuse their power just as our Prelates do, imposing norms and limitations in violation of the most basic principles of law. Furthermore, it is precisely those who are constituted in authority, on both fronts, who often avail themselves of a mere *de facto* recognition by the rank and file — citizens and faithful — even when the methods by which they have taken power violate, if not the letter, then at least the spirit of the law. The case of Italy — in which a non-elected Government legislates on the obligation to be vaccinated and on the green pass, violating the Italian Constitution and the natural rights of the Italian people — does not seem very dissimilar to the situation in which the Church finds herself, with a resigned Pontiff replaced by Jorge Mario Bergoglio, chosen — or at least appreciated and supported — by the Saint Gallen Mafia and the ultra-progressive Episcopate. It remains obvious that there is a profound crisis of authority, both civil and religious, in which those who exercise power do so contrary to those whom they are supposed to protect, and above all contrary to the purpose for which that authority has been established.

ANALOGIES BETWEEN THE DEEP CHURCH AND THE DEEP STATE

I think that it has been understood that both civil society and the Church suffer from the same cancer that struck the former with the French Revolution and the latter with the Second Vatican Council: in both cases, Masonic thought is at the foundation of the systematic demolition of the institution and its replacement with a simulacrum that maintains its external appearances, hierarchical structure, and coercive force, but with purposes diametrically opposed to those it ought to have.

At this point, citizens on the one hand and the faithful on the other find themselves in the condition of having to disobey earthly authority in order obey divine authority, which governs Nations and the Church. Obviously the "reactionaries" — that is, those who do not accept the perversion of authority and want to remain faithful to the Church of Christ and to their Homeland — constitute an element of dissent that cannot be tolerated in any way, and therefore they must be discredited, delegitimized, threatened, and deprived of their rights in the name of a "public good" that is no longer the *bonum commune* but its contrary. Whether accused of conspiracy theories, traditionalism, or fundamentalism, these few survivors of a world that they want to make disappear constitutes a threat to the accomplishment of the global plan, just at the most crucial moment of its realization. This is why power is reacting in such an open, brazen, and violent way: the evidence of the fraud risks being understood by a greater number of people, bringing them together in an organized resistance, breaking down the wall of silence and ferocious censorship imposed by the mainstream media.

We can therefore understand the violence of the reactions of authority and prepare ourselves for a strong and determined opposition, continuing to avail ourselves of those rights that have been abusively and illicitly denied us. Of course, we may find ourselves having to exercise those rights in an incomplete way when we are denied the opportunity to travel if we do not have our green pass or if the Bishop prohibits us from celebrating the Mass of all time in a church in his Diocese, but our resistance to abuses of authority will still be able to count on the graces that the Lord will not cease to grant us — in particular the virtue of fortitude that is so indispensable in times of tyranny.

THE NORMALITY THAT FRIGHTENS

If on the one hand we can see how the persecution of dissenters is well-organized and planned, on the other hand we cannot fail to recognize the fragmentation of the opposition. Bergoglio knows well that every movement of dissent must be silenced, above all by creating internal division and isolating priests and the faithful. A fruitful and fraternal collaboration between diocesan clergy, religious, and the *Ecclesia Dei* institutes is something he must avert, because it would permit the diffusion of a knowledge of the ancient rite, as well as a precious help in the ministry. But this would mean making the Tridentine Mass a "normality" in the daily life of the faithful, something that is not tolerable for Francis. For this reason, diocesan clergy are left at the mercy of their Ordinaries, while the *Ecclesia Dei* Institutes are placed under the authority of the Congregation of Religious, as a sad prelude to a destiny that has already been sealed. Let us not forget the fate that befell the flourishing religious Orders, guilty of being blessed with numerous vocations born and nurtured precisely thanks to the hated traditional Liturgy and the faithful observance of the Rule. This is why certain forms of insistence on the ceremonial aspect of the celebrations risk legitimizing the provisions of the commissar and play Bergoglio's game.

Even in the civil world, it is precisely by encouraging certain excesses by the dissenters that those in power marginalize them and legitimize repressive measures towards them: just think of the case of the *no-vax* movements and how easy it is to discredit the legitimate protests of citizens by emphasizing the eccentricities and inconsistencies of a few. And it is all too easy to condemn a few agitated people who out of exasperation set fire to a vaccine center, overshadowing millions of honest persons who take to the streets in order not to be branded with the health passport or fired if they do not allow themselves to be vaccinated.

DO NOT STAY ISOLATED AND DISORGANIZED

Another important element for all of us is the necessity of giving visibility to our composed protest and ensuring a form of coordination for public action. With the abolition of *Summorum Pontificum* we find ourselves taken back twenty years. This unhappy decision by Bergoglio to cancel the motu proprio of Pope Benedict is doomed to inexorable failure, because it touches the very soul of the Church, of which the Lord Himself is Pontiff and High Priest. And it is not a given that the entire Episcopate — as we are seeing in the last few days with relief — will be willing to passively submit to forms of authoritarianism that certainly do not contribute to bringing peace to souls. The Code of Canon Law guarantees the Bishops the possibility of dispensing their faithful from particular or universal laws, under certain conditions. Secondly, the people of God have well understood the subversive nature of *Traditionis Custodes* and are instinctively led to want to get to know something that arouses such disapproval among progressives. Let us not be surprised therefore if we soon begin to see the faithful coming from ordinary parish life and even those far from the Church finding their way to the churches where the traditional Mass is celebrated. It will be our duty, whether as ministers of God or as simple faithful, to show firmness and serene resistance to such abuse, walking along the way of our own little Calvary with a supernatural spirit, while the new high priests and scribes of the people mock us and label us as fanatics. It will be our humility, the silent offering of injustices toward us, and the example of a life consistent with the Creed that we profess that will merit the triumph of the Catholic Mass and the conversion of many souls. And let us remember that, since we have received much, much will be demanded of us.

RESTITUTIO IN INTEGRUM

"What father among you, if his son asks him for bread, will give him a stone? Or if he asks for a fish, will give him a serpent instead?" (Lk 11:11–12). Now we can understand the meaning of these words, considering with pain and torment of heart the cynicism of a father who gives us the stones of a soulless liturgy, the serpents of a corrupted doctrine, and the scorpions of an adulterated morality. And who reaches the point of dividing the flock of the Lord between those who accept the *Novus Ordo* and those who want to remain faithful to the Mass of our fathers, exactly as civil rulers are pitting the vaccinated and unvaccinated against one another.

When Our Lord entered Jerusalem seated on a donkey's colt, while the crowd was spreading cloaks as He passed, the Pharisees asked Him: "Master, rebuke your disciples." The Lord answered them: "*I say to you that if these are silent, the stones will cry out*" (Lk 19:28–40). For sixty years the stones of our churches have been crying out, from which the Holy Sacrifice has been twice proscribed. The marble of the altars, the columns of the basilicas, and the soaring vaults of the cathedrals cry out as well, because those stones, consecrated to the worship of the true God, today are abandoned and deserted, or profaned by abhorrent rites, or transformed into parking lots and supermarkets, precisely as a result of that Council that we insist on defending. Let us also cry out: we who are living stones of the temple of God. Let us cry with faith to the Lord, so that he may give a voice to His disciples who today are mute, and so that the intolerable theft for which the administrators of the Lord's Vineyard are responsible may be repaired.

But in order for that theft to be repaired, it is necessary that we show ourselves to be worthy of the treasures that have been stolen from us. Let us try to do this by our holiness of life, by giving example of the virtues, by prayer and the frequent reception of the Sacraments. And let us not forget that there are hundreds of good priests who still know the meaning of the Sacred Unction by which they have been ordained ministers of Christ and dispensers of the Mystery of God. The Lord deigns to descend on our altars even when they are erected in cellars or attics. *Contrariis quibuslibet minime obstantibus* [anything to the contrary notwithstanding].

✠ Carlo Maria Viganò, *Archbishop*
28 July 2021
Ss. Nazarii et Celsi Martyrum,
Victoris I Papae et Martyris ac
Innocentii I Papae et Confessoris

ADDENDUM

August 5, 2021
In Dedicatione B. M. V. ad Nives

DEAR MAIKE [HICKSON],

Regarding your request for clarification, I am sending you some considerations that I hope will make my thoughts more explicit. This is the reference sentence: "It will be our duty, whether as ministers of God or as simple faithful, to show firmness and serene resistance to such abuse, walking along the way of our own little Calvary with a supernatural spirit, while the new high priests and scribes of the people mock us and label us as fanatics. It will be our humility, the silent offering of injustices toward us, and the example of a life consistent with the Creed that we profess that will merit the triumph of the Catholic Mass and the conversion of many souls."

You ask me: "What shall priests and faithful do when the bishop clamps down on them? Shall they go into clandestinity, or shall they cut themselves publicly off, in public disobedience?"

Allow me to say first of all that in continuing to celebrate the Mass of Pope Saint Pius V no priest performs any act of disobedience, but on the contrary he exercises his right sanctioned by God, which not even the Pope can revoke. Whoever has the power to offer the Holy Sacrifice has the right to celebrate it in the ancient rite, as was solemnly proclaimed by Saint Pius V in the Apostolic Constitution Quo Primum, promulgating the Tridentine Liturgy. This has been reiterated by the motu proprio Summorum Pontificum as an indisputable fact. Anyone who contravenes these provisions "should know that he will incur the wrath of Almighty God and of the Blessed Apostles Peter and Paul" (Quo Primum).

The response to any limitation or prohibition of the celebration of the traditional Mass must obviously take into account both the objective elements and the different situations: if a priest has as an Ordinary a sworn enemy of the ancient rite who has no qualms about suspending him a divinis if he were to celebrate the Tridentine Mass, public disobedience could be a way to make the abuse of the Ordinary clear, especially if the news is spread by the media: the Prelates are very afraid of media coverage about their actions, and sometimes they prefer to refrain from canonical measures just to avoid ending up in the newspapers. The priest must therefore consider whether his action will be more effective with a fair and direct confrontation, or by acting with discretion and in hiding. In my opinion, the first option is the most linear and transparent, and the one that responds most to the behavior of the Saints, to which we must comply.

Obviously there may be the case of an understanding Ordinary, who leaves his priest free to celebrate the Tridentine rite; speaking with an open heart to one's Bishop is certainly important, if one knows that he can find in him a father and not an official. Unfortunately, we know well that most of the time it is a question of tolerance, and almost never of encouragement on the path of Tradition. In some cases, however, inviting one's Ordinary to celebrate the Mass of St. Pius V himself can be a way to make him understand, by touching the deepest chords of his heart and his priestly soul, the treasures reserved for the ministers of God who have the opportunity to offer the Holy Sacrifice in the apostolic rite. When this "miracle" happens, the Bishop becomes an ally of his priest, because in addition to the intellectual and rational aspect that makes the traditional Mass preferable, he experiences firsthand its spiritual and supernatural dimension, and how it affects the life of grace of those who celebrate it.

I hope that my words will clarify the points that I had not developed in my previous speech.

44

A Law Must Be Accepted
to Be Valid†

CARDINAL WALTER BRANDMÜLLER

Stilum Curiae
July 29, 2021

WITH HIS MOTU PROPRIO TRADITIONIS CUSTODES, Pope Francis has practically unleashed a hurricane that has upset those Catholics who feel attached to the "Tridentine" rite of Mass revived by Benedict XVI's *Summorum Pontificum*. From now on—according to the essential declaration of *Traditionis Custodes*—Benedict's *Summorum Pontificum* will be in large measure suspended and the celebration of Holy Mass, with some exceptions, will be allowed only according to the Missal of Paul VI. A look at the blogger scene and other media outlets reveals how a global protest has erupted against this document, which is unusual in form and content.

In contrast to the protests relating to the content of *Traditionis Custodes*, it is necessary now to make some reflections that refer to fundamental principles of ecclesiastical legislation. If the discussion about *Traditionis Custodes* has so far concerned the legislative content of the motu proprio, here the text will be considered from a formal point of view as a legal text.

First of all, it should be noted that a law does not require special acceptance by the interested parties to acquire binding force. However, it must be *received* by them. Reception means affirmative acceptance of the law in the sense of "making it your own." Only then does the law acquire confirmation and permanence, as the "father" of canon law, Gratian († 1140), taught in his famous *Decretum*. Here is the original text: "*Leges instituuntur cum promulgantur. Firmantur cum moribus utentium approbantur. Sicut enim moribus utentium in contrariem nonnullae leges hodie abrogatae sunt, ita moribus utentium leges confirmantur*" (c. 3, D. 4). "Laws are established when they are promulgated. They are confirmed when they are approved by the behavior of those who use them. For as due to the behaviors of users in a contrary

---

† The Italian text was translated by Robert Moynihan and published as *Moynihan Letter* #74 (2021); it was cross-posted at *Rorate Caeli* on the same date.

direction, quite a few laws today have been abrogated, so through the behaviors of the users the laws are confirmed."

This means, however, that for a law to be valid and binding, it must be approved by those to whom it is addressed. Thus, on the other hand, some laws today are abolished by non-compliance, just as, on the contrary, the laws are confirmed by the fact that those concerned observe them.

In this context, reference can also be made to the possibility provided for by customary law, according to which a justified objection against a law of the universal Church has, at least initially, a suspensive effect. This means, however, that the law need not be obeyed until the objection has been clarified.

It should also be remembered that, if there is a doubt as to whether a law is binding, it is not binding. Such doubts could be due, for example, to an inadequate wording of the law.

Here it becomes clear that the laws and the community for which the laws are enacted are linked to each other in an almost organic way, to the extent that the community's *bonum commune* [common good] is their goal. Put simply, this means that the validity of a law ultimately depends on the consent of those affected by it. The law must serve the good of the community — and not vice versa, the community (serving) the law. The two things are not opposed to one another, but linked one to the other, neither can exist without or against the other.

If a law is not observed, or is no longer observed, whether from the beginning or after a time, it loses its binding force and becomes obsolete. This — and this must be strongly emphasized — naturally applies only to purely ecclesiastical laws, but in no case to those based on divine or natural law.

As an example of a *lex mere ecclesiastica* [a merely ecclesiastical law], consider the Apostolic Constitution *Veterum Sapientia* of Pope John XXIII of February 22, 1962, in which the Pope prescribed Latin for university teaching, among other things. Young scholar that I was, I reacted only by shaking my head. Well, Latin was the norm at the Gregorian University in Rome, and this made good enough sense given the babel of languages among the students, who came from all continents. But whether Cicero, Virgil, and Lactantius would have understood the lessons is doubtful. And then: the history of the Church, even of modern times, taught in Latin? With all the love professed for the Roman language — how could it work? And so it remained. *Veterum Sapientia* was hardly printed before it was soon forgotten.

But what this inglorious demise of an Apostolic Constitution meant for the prestige of papal authority became evident only six and a half years later, when Paul VI's Encyclical *Humanae Vitae* (1968) was nearly drowned amid protests from the Western world.

The thing is done, therefore, friends, and now, patience. Never has unenlightened zeal served peace or the common good. It was St. John Henry Newman who, quoting the great Augustine, reminded us: "*Securus iudicat orbis terrarum*" [the verdict of the world is conclusive].

In the meantime, let's pay close attention to our language. One might call it "verbal disarmament." In more pious words: no violation of brotherly (and recently sisterly) love! Now — seriously again: what a grotesque idea that the mystery of love itself should become a bone of contention. Again, we quote Saint Augustine, who called the Holy Eucharist the bond of love and peace that unites the head and the members of the Church. No greater triumph of hell could be imagined than if this bond were broken again, as has happened many times in the past. Then the onlooking world would grin: "See how they love one another!"

45

Substance and Form[†]

JUAN MANUEL DE PRADA
ABC
July 30, 2021

A FEW DAYS AFTER BERGOGLIO PRESUMED TO DO AWAY with (or at least relegate to the underground) the traditional Mass, I attended a dinner with a motley crew, in which Catholics and atheists mingled. I found it extremely instructive to discover that this Argentinean decision[1] struck the atheists as a horrendous calamity, as horrendous as decreeing the demolition of the cathedrals; for, although they did not believe in the existence of God (and much less in the sacrificial meaning of the Mass), they recognized the value of a rite that has inspired aesthetic achievements of incalculable value. On the other hand, to the Catholics present at the meeting—all of them party-liners[2]—the Argentinean decision seemed a minor issue, because (as one of them said) "the rite is just a mere question of form." The important thing, for this good gentleman, was "what is celebrated in the Mass—not the verbal finery with which it is celebrated."

That party-line Catholic did nothing more than string together clichés — all of them very hackneyed and foolish — that reminded me of those I have heard other times from inane hipsters[3] in discussions on artistic or literary matters. The party-line Catholic, like the inane hipster, cultivates simplistic dualisms that distinguish between "form" and "substance," like those who distinguish between shell and core. They consider the "form" to be a dispensable piece of litter, a perfectly incidental external envelope which, when removed, makes it possible to distinguish more clearly the

---

† Translated from the Spanish by Gerhard Eger and Peter Kwasniewski for this volume.
1 The author's phrase is *decisión porteña*. *Porteño* refers to someone from Buenos Aires (since it's a port city), but simply translating it as "Argentinean" captures de Prada's desired effect.
2 De Prada uses the term *pompier*, a reference to the nineteenth-century *art pompier* that slavishly followed official academic norms. Here it refers to Catholics who slavishly follow whatever the current pope says, so one might say "party-liners" or "ovine Catholics."
3 The term in Spanish is *gafapasta*, referring to a modern subculture similar to American hipsters.

"substance," where, for the party-line Catholic or the inane hipster, what is truly juicy is to be found. This Manichaean distinction between "substance" and "form" has inevitably produced a praise of "substance" and a contempt for "form" typical of ignorant people who — since they constitute an infinite majority — have imposed their criterion, establishing that "form"— in art as well as in the Mass — is a superfluous garnish, an aestheticist show-off, a rhetorical extravagance that contributes nothing to "substance."

Are the inane hipsters and the party-line Catholics right when they exalt "substance" over "form"? Are we, the defenders of form, frivolous and fussy nitpickers? Nothing could be further from the truth. It happens, however, that we are not functionally illiterate — as they are, besides being submissive slaves of the trends in vogue, even of the most bogus and washed-out; and, because we are not illiterate, we know that the dualism of substance and form is an inconsistent logomachy that hides the true dualism, namely, that between *matter and form*.

Form is not a shell. A writer who, when putting an idea on paper, does not know whether to express it in prose or in verse would seem to us to be a sorry excuse for a writer, since the inspired work is born as a single whole and an idea cannot be perceived without perceiving its realization. Form is not something accidental that is added to the work of art, but something that informs it from within, that configures it and makes it distinctive, that gives it its deepest core. In *Ideas sobre la novela*, Ortega y Gasset points out: "Matter never saves a work of art, and the gold of which it is made never consecrates the statue. . . . Anyone who possesses a delicate aesthetic sensibility will sense a sign of philistinism when, before a painting or a poetic production, someone points to the material as the decisive factor. Of course, without it there is no work of art, just as there is no life without chemical processes. Yet just as life is not reduced to these, but begins to be life when to the chemical law it adds its original complexity of a new order, so the work of art is what it is thanks to the form imposed on the matter or the subject."

Indeed, the term with which form is contrasted is not substance, but *matter*. To think that form is irrelevant, whether in a work of art or in the Mass, is the work of imbeciles, for all things human and divine are vivified through their form. Matter is formless, while form is the principle of determination of matter, the divine seal that allows it to exist in fullness. Form — as Ramon Llull affirmed — is "what gives being to things, as the soul is what gives being to the body." Michelangelo's *David* would not seem more sublime to us if, instead of being sculpted in marble, it had been cast in gold; on the other hand, it could not have existed at all if the genius of Michelangelo had not sculpted it in the form in which he did. The form, the true form, is not accidental, but substantial. It is the creative contact with the form that gives substance to things that, orphaned of it, become mere simulacra, formless shambles, inert matter.

46

The Latin Mass in the Zero-Sum Church

ROSS DOUTHAT

Reactions

July 30, 2021

I PUBLISHED TWO ESSAYS ABOUT THE ROMAN CATH-olic Church in the last few weeks: One an adaptation of the talk I gave at the University of Dallas linking American debates about Catholic politi-cal theory[1] to the harsh facts of American Catholic decline, the other an analysis of Pope Francis's long-awaited, still-unexpectedly-sweeping move against the Tridentine Mass.[2] In this post I want to use a passage from the first essay to illuminate the argument in the second one, and talk briefly about what the trajectory of Catholic decadence might tell us about dec-adence in the Western world writ large.

Here's the passage, which is specifically about the tendency of arguments about a "post-liberal" Catholic politics to turn into a festival of anathemas:

> Ideally, conditions of Catholic decline would forge greater solidar-ity among the Catholics who remain. But quite often the oppo-site happens: The fact of decline makes the stakes of debate seem desperately high. Diminishing institutional spoils are fought over more fiercely. A sense of crisis magnifies differences that in a time of optimism and plenty might be debated in an irenic and frater-nal spirit. And this, of course, only makes the decline more likely to accelerate, because people outside the Church, and the margin-ally attached, look to whether the most fervent Catholics act like Christians, and instead see fratricide — or its Twitter equivalent.

Obviously this rule applies well beyond intellectual debate — and I think it definitely applies to the dynamics that have given us Pope Fran-cis's attempted abrogation of the old Mass, which is intended to provide

---

1 See "Catholic Ideas and Catholic Realities: On Populists, Integralists, Benedictines, and Tradinistas," First Things, August 2021, available online.
2 See chapter 39.

for a slow-motion suffocation of communities connected to the old rite. (Whether it will is, of course, another question.)

From an institutional perspective the move arguably appears perverse: Here you have a Western church conspicuously lacking in public zeal, religious vocations, large families, liturgical seriousness . . . and yet the leaders of the church have decided to act punitively against a small minority that, whatever its highly-debated growth rate,[3] clearly is a locus for intense forms of piety and practice. It's as if a major auto manufacturer whose big brands were all struggling decided to kill off one of its few profitable lines of cars, because it only turned a profit in a niche market and wasn't big enough to subsidize the whole. A strange decision . . .

. . . but under the psychological conditions created by decline also an understandable one. In a general corporate climate of diminishment and disappointment, a small form of success invites resentment: If the small brand isn't capable of subsidizing the whole, then why are its engineers and salesman wasting their talents on its niche market, when they should be contributing to saving the larger company? Shouldn't they be expected to chip in where the need is greatest, in the main brands — by analogy, big, empty diocesan seminaries and struggling Novus Ordo parishes and schools — instead of concentrating their talents serving a more intense but (it's assumed) self-limited market?

And more than that — if you believe that the big brand can survive only if it makes a pretty radical transition, perhaps even to making a completely different kind of car, then the small profits of the niche line are just helping feed a climate of denial about what needs to happen, and encouraging resistance toward the revolution that will (it's imagined[4]) save the company from its otherwise-certain obsolescence and collapse.

Then of course the zero-sum thinking, the mood of crisis-driven mistrust, runs in both directions. The contrast between the niche's success and the institution's larger failures makes the engineers of the niche brand more confident in their own correctness, more apt to criticize the people in charge of the larger company, more inclined to regard the corporation's broad policies as disastrous rather than just mistaken — which in turn gives the corporate hierarchy another reason to regard their success as a danger rather than an opportunity.

They can read the company Slack channel, after all, just as people in the Vatican can scan traditionalist Twitter and YouTube, and the way the

---

3 See "Latin Mass: No Hysteria. A Reply to David Gibson," LMS Chairman, July 27, 2021.
4 See Rita Ferrone, "A Living Catholic Tradition," Commonweal, July 23, 2021.

niche brand's engineers talk about the company's larger mission sounds so hostile and disloyal, so damaging to the corporate leadership's own authority and the wider company's morale, that the case for simply shutting them down and dispersing their talents to other divisions seems that much stronger . . . and if a *few* of them go join the boutique firm[5] that also caters to their niche market, well, no great loss. (I've pushed this analogy far enough that I'm picturing a new sedan called *Gaudium et Spes*, so best to stop there, I think.)

At the height of an earlier Francis-era peak of controversy, over communion for the divorced and remarried, I wrote a post called "Catholicism for the Time Being" that was among other things a partial defense of the uneasy coexistence of different forms of Catholicism, despite their theological and liturgical differences, under the formally conservative pontificates of John Paul II and Benedict XVI.

There is a parallel between that argument and the chapter in *The Decadent Society* where I try to give decadence its due. In both cases the point is that there is still grace to be found living in a time of stagnation and self-contradiction and diminished optimism, and that there are real dangers in policies that try to accelerate things toward a resolution of the tensions, since that resolution might also be a disaster, a great smash.

For the last decade the Francis pontificate has moved back and forth between accelerationism and stalemate, between attempts to bring Catholicism's divisive arguments and deep contradictions up to the surface and decisions that seem to deliberately submerge them once again. My own writing in this era has reflected this up-and-down, back-and-forth movement: In *To Change the Church* I emphasized the possibility that Francis was driving the church toward schism; in *The Decadent Society*, where the book touched on religion and Catholicism, I emphasized the eternal return to 1975, the way that even for a destabilizing pontiff the stalemates and gridlock of the post-Vatican II era have tended to reassert themselves.

But looking at developments in the last couple of years — the push (*clearly* driven by fears of decline and dissolution) by the liberal/German wing of the church for more doctrinal change[6] than Francis can or wants to give, and now the similarly fear-driven crackdown on the TLM — you can see how the dynamics of decline cut against the dynamics of stalemate, pushing a decadent system toward a crisis. The eternal return to 1975 can't actually go on eternally amid conditions of diminishment: Instead with each

---

5   I refer to the Society of St. Pius X (https://fsspx.org/en).
6   "Pope Francis Faces Another German Reformation," *New York Times*, May 11, 2021.

repetition the underlying institutional weaknesses become more important, the returns to stalemate becomes less acceptable, and the competing factions become less inclined to play the long game and more inclined to take truly reckless steps.

Any sustainable decadence depends, by definition, on sustainability: A sense among the factions living with the stalemate that while they may not like each other, *there will be enough to go around*. Thus in Catholicism the muddling-through of the JPII era depended — for liberals who kept their heads down and stuck with the church as much as for conservatives who accepted the very partial restoration of authority — on the sense that things had somewhat stabilized after the shocks of the 1960s, that the condition of the faith was difficult but not exactly dire, and that every group had reasons to be patient, to live with one another and see what happened next. Whereas the pressures of the Francis era increasingly reflect a fear that stability is gone, that the bill is coming due, the money and numbers are drying up, and the only question is which faction will be left standing at the end. Intellectually this feeling can be a spur to creativity — the post-liberal arguments I try to limn in the *First Things* essay are definitely creative — but institutionally it's how you end up with crises, breakage, schism.

In the specific case of traditionalism, it was that sense of relative stability that helped pave the way for the Latin Mass's return from its 1970s exile, for the permissions issued first by John Paul and then more sweepingly by Benedict. And then it's the subsequent weakening of *both* conservative *and* liberal Catholicism — the former pushing more right-wing Catholics tradward, the latter making tradness appear more of a threat to a necessary acceleration of the Vatican II revolution — that's given us the sharpened conflicts between traditionalism and Pope Francis, and now the attempt at outright suppression.

Of course the church is still vast, it still has money and manpower, there are whole Catholic worlds outside the polarized Western debates, and — as we all know — the faith is held together by supernatural as well as normal forces. But the feeling of scarcity still matters — that sense of dwindling resources, not enough parishioners to keep the churches open, not enough money, not enough vocations, not enough to share. That feeling has strengthened since 2010, it's likely to strengthen further by 2030 — and with it, the stresses and zero-sum assumptions that can turn a decadent phase into something more destabilizing, more dissolving, more overtly dire.

Meanwhile this idea of scarcity and its terrors has applications for the potential crack-up of secular forms of decadence as well. One sort of scarcity undergirds Peter Turchin's cyclical theory of civilizational crises,[7] which has various weak spots but predicted our recent turbulence quite well: The idea of overproduction of elites, in which what gets scarce are positions of power or influence, with too many talented or credentialed people chasing too few positions in the ruling class, so that *there isn't enough to go around* becomes the prevailing mood and suddenly every fight is zero-sum.

Another sort of scarcity haunts our economic debates, in which growth has persistently disappointed but Western governments have been able to create more wealth with fiscal and monetary policy; it's why real inflation, the end of that power to simply make abundance happen, would probably be a bigger threat to sustainable decadence than financial crises and the Covid shocks have been.

And of course the anxieties around climate change reflect a fear of ultimate scarcity, of an Earth where uninhabitable zones expand and human spaces contract, where *not enough to go around* applies not just to jobs at law firms or dollars for 401(k) savings but to our crops, our water, the basic stuff of life.

Of late Roman Catholicism seems to be entering into a period of dangerous diminishment at greater speed than our secular ex-Christendom — even if, having the loaves and fishes reading in last Sunday's gospel, we know that God is not bound by the usual laws of scarcity.

But the point applies generally: For all that rising expectations can famously lead to revolution, it's when the course runs the other way, with a society accustomed to stability meeting a future of scarcity and disappointment and decline, that the gods of the copybook heading[8] are most likely to fearfully return.

---

7 Graeme Wood, "The Next Decade Could Be Even Worse," *The Atlantic*, December 2020, available online.

8 Rudyard Kipling, "The Gods of the Copybook Headings," www.kiplingsociety. co.uk/poems_copybook.htm.

47

The Faithful of the "Extraordinary Form" Are the Symptom, Not the Disease[†]

DR. MARTIN GRICHTING

Kath.net

July 30, 2021

AS LONG AS THE CHURCH'S LEADERSHIP IS NOT ABLE to approve a form of liturgy for the whole Church that again truly helps lift the heart to God, it is implausible to make accusations against those who articulate a problem caused by that very Church leadership. The day when people will have the courage to face the real problems of the liturgy will come.

I really became aware that the liturgy created after Vatican II has regrettable shortcomings and leaves the faithful spiritually as well as emotionally starved when I became vicar general in my diocese. Now I was no longer a celebrant as a parish priest, but much more often a concelebrant at episcopal liturgies. Functionally, I was thus not unlike the lay people who participated in the celebration of the Eucharist: fellow worshipers, as the world might say. Spectators and, above all, listeners. It was then that I realized how this form of the liturgy is onesidedly oriented to the intellect. It can be enriched, especially in German-speaking countries, with genuinely spiritual songs. The church building can be majestically built and beautifully decorated. Ideally, the liturgical vestments are also something for the eye. The ear intermittently may get its reward with brilliant organists. But architecture and concert are no substitute for spirituality. And the enjoyment of aesthetics is not to be confused with a living relationship with God. So it remains the case that, during the course of an hour, one is sprinkled in one's mother tongue with words that one understands, but that, with the best will in the world, one can take in intellectually only to a small extent.

[†] Translated from the German by Maike Hickson and published at *LifeSiteNews* on the same date.

In the weekday Masses, the problem is aggravated because it is even more influenced by the word — and this does not mean the Word of God. Even the most diligent, who follow the liturgical texts on their cell phones so as not to be too distracted, must at some point acknowledge that they are reaching their limits.

If you are the celebrant yourself, the situation is different. You must concentrate on the texts, if only to recite them correctly. Moreover, you are always the doer, which alleviates the problem of attention and allows the aspect of feeling to fade into the background. This probably has as its effect that many bishops and priests have so far felt too little understanding for the laity, who are incessantly exposed to a rain of words. This overwhelms them, and not infrequently generates the bad conscience of not having been attentive during the Mass. At the same time, the words of varying weight that are poured over everyone almost non-stop leave the soul dangling in the void. The heart is rarely really reached. It is not warmed, but ignored. Due to all this, awareness and respect for the sacred suffers. And it is only when these things come along with intellectual apprehension that man is kept in the Faith. For otherwise the Faith runs the risk of becoming at best an interesting intellectual occupation — but one that no longer captivates the whole person.

The celebrant, who is turned towards the people and talks to them incessantly, does the rest. Much has already been said about that subject. Even if one expressly withdraws oneself and does not want to act as an entertainer, even if one refrains from putting one's own self in the foreground through political or other philanthropic human interludes... That one represents Jesus Christ as a priest is the theological truth. Yet the reality perceived by the faithful is that one stands far too much in the foreground with one's personality, which is perceived as more or less appealing.

The English writer G. K. Chesterton once said that Protestants believe that God can only be worshipped by way of thinking. Catholics, he said, would do it with all their senses. He said this well before the liturgical reform of Vatican II. Today we have arrived at more or less this Protestant position. This is true even if the liturgy is not pedagogically abused for the propagation of social or environmental concerns or does not serve as a field of experimentation on which liturgists can play out their imaginations.

There would be still much to say, first undoubtedly about the sacrificial character of the Mass, its quality as participation in the divine liturgy rather than as a gathering of "celebrants," and so on. I would like to content myself here with the phenomenological reflection that tries to put itself, above all, in the position of the laity.

One leaves these lay people spiritually hungry. And what do they do? They break away from the flock. They seek their nourishment elsewhere. The longer I watch this after almost 29 years of priesthood, the more convinced I become: despised by the powerful, the faithful who have found a home in the Extraordinary Form of the Roman Rite are the symptom, not the disease. Instead of beating them with the shepherd's crook, one should consider for once that they articulate — perhaps sometimes in an awkward way — a problem. If, as can be seen especially in France and the USA, now relatively many young people (priests and married couples who are still open to children) prefer the Extraordinary Form, it would simply correspond to spiritual prudence, in the sense in which St. Benedict speaks of it, to ask oneself whether the Spirit of God is not also speaking through these young people.

Priests, who are closer to the faithful than liturgical theorists and curial experts of liturgy, feel more and more that many lay people suffer, consciously or unconsciously, precisely from the celebration of the Eucharist. Quite a few, especially older ones, endure liturgically what for them can no longer be changed. They remain faithful to the end and represent the typical worshippers today. Others stay away, disappointed over the course of time. For they have had the experience long enough of not being edified or comforted, of stepping out of the church not supported in being Christian, which is difficult nowadays anyway. Of course, obsolescence and staying away have other reasons, but the liturgy is also one of them. Who wants to deny it?

To repeat: as long as the Church's leadership is not able to approve a form of liturgy for the whole Church that again truly helps lift the heart to God, it is implausible to make accusations against those who articulate a problem caused by that very Church leadership. Instead of harassing these believers, Church leaders should seek to understand what the Spirit of God is saying through these faithful, especially through the many lay people among them. Until this happens, diocesan bishops should exercise reason in the face of a universal disciplinary law that hurts and divides. The easiest way to do this at the diocesan level will be through generous dispensations from the norms of this law.

The day will come when Church's leadership will have the courage to face the real problems of the liturgy. For they continue to exist. They cannot be eliminated with a law. However one judges natural selection according to Darwin, there is a supernatural selection — and it is at work.

48

Mass and Memory[†]

MARTIN MOSEBACH

First Things

July 30, 2021

IN TRADITIONIS CUSTODES, POPE FRANCIS HAS GIVEN a command. He does this at a time when papal authority is unraveling as never before. The Church has long since advanced to an ungovernable stage. But the pope battles on. He abandons his dearest principles—"listening," "tenderness," "mercy"—that refuse to judge or give orders. Pope Francis is roused by something that troubles him: the tradition of the Church.

The limited breathing room that the pope's predecessors granted to liturgical tradition is no longer occupied only by senile nostalgics. The Traditional Latin Mass also attracts young people, who have discovered and learned to love the "buried treasure in the field," as Pope Benedict called the old liturgy. In Pope Francis's eyes, this is so serious that it must be suppressed.

The vehemence of the motu proprio's language suggests that this directive has come too late. The circles that adhere to liturgical tradition have indeed drastically changed in the last decades. The Tridentine Mass is no longer attended only by those who miss the liturgy of their childhood, but also by people who have discovered the liturgy anew and are fascinated by it — including many converts, many who have long been estranged from the Church. The liturgy is their passion and they know its every detail. There are many priestly vocations among them. These young men do not attend only the seminaries maintained by the priestly fraternities of tradition. Many of them undergo the usual training for the priesthood, and are nevertheless convinced that their vocation is strengthened precisely by knowledge of the traditional rite. Curiosity about the suppressed Catholic tradition has grown, even though many had depicted this tradition as obsolete and unsound. Aldous Huxley illustrated this kind of amazement in Brave New World, in which a young man of the modern elite, without a sense of history, discovers the overflowing riches of premodern culture and is enchanted by them.

---

† Translated from the German by Stuart Chessman.

The pope's intervention may impede the growth of the liturgical recovery of tradition for a time. But he will be able to arrest it only for the remainder of his pontificate. For this traditional movement is not a superficial fashion. It demonstrated in the decades of its repression prior to Benedict's motu proprio *Summorum Pontificum* that there persists a serious and enthusiastic devotion to the complete fullness of Catholicism. Pope Francis's prohibition will arouse resistance in those who still have their lives before them and won't allow their futures to be darkened by obsolete ideologies. It was not good, but it was also not wise, to put papal authority to this test.

Pope Francis prohibits Masses in the old rite in parish churches; he requires priests to obtain permission to celebrate the old Mass; he even requires priests that have not yet celebrated in the old rite to obtain this permission not from their bishop, but from the Vatican; and he requires an examination of conscience of participants in the old Mass. But Benedict's motu proprio *Summorum Pontificum* reasons on a totally different level. Pope Benedict did not "allow" the "old Mass," and he granted no privilege to celebrate it. In a word, he did not take a disciplinary measure that a successor can retract. What was new and surprising about *Summorum Pontificum* was that it declares that the celebration of the old Mass does not need any permission. It had never been forbidden because it never could be forbidden. One could conclude that here we find a fixed, insuperable limit to the authority of a pope. Tradition stands above the pope. The old Mass, rooted deep in the first Christian millennium, is as a matter of principle beyond the pope's authority to prohibit. Many provisions of Pope Benedict's motu proprio can be set aside or modified, but this magisterial decision cannot be so easily done away with. Pope Francis does not attempt to do so — he ignores it. It still stands after July 16, 2021, recognizing the authority of tradition that every priest has the moral right to celebrate the never forbidden old rite.

Most of the world's Catholics won't take any interest at all in *Traditionis Custodes*. In view of the small number of traditionalist communities, most will hardly understand what is going on. Indeed, we have to ask ourselves whether the pope had no more urgent task — in the midst of the sex abuse crisis, the Church's financial scandals, schismatic movements like the German synodal path, and the desperate situation of Chinese Catholics — than to suppress this small, devoted community.

But adherents to tradition must grant the pope this: He takes the traditional Mass, which dates back at least to the time of Gregory the Great, as seriously as they do. He, however, judges it to be dangerous. He writes that popes in the past again and again created new liturgies and abolished old ones. But the opposite is true. Rather, the Council of Trent prescribed the ancient missal of the Roman popes — which had arisen in Late Antiquity — for general use, because this was the only one that had not been spoiled by the Reformation.

Perhaps the Mass is not what most concerns the pope. Francis appears to sympathize with the "hermeneutic of rupture" — that theological school that asserts that with the Second Vatican Council the Church broke with her tradition. If that is true, then indeed every celebration of the traditional liturgy must be prevented. For as long as the old Latin Mass is celebrated in any garage, the memory of the previous two thousand years will not have been extinguished.

This memory, however, cannot be rooted out by the blunt exercise of papal legal positivism. It will return again and again, and will be the criterion by which the Church of the future will have to measure itself.

49

The Pope's Boundedness to Tradition as a Legislative Limit

PETER A. KWASNIEWSKI

July 31, 2021[1]

CATHOLIC APOLOGISTS HAVE DONE A LOT OF GREAT work over the last decades. They have refuted many a Protestant, Mormon, Jehovah's Witness, or the like oddity, and have helped Jews, Moslems, atheists, agnostics, neo-pagans, and members of all manner of false religions to find Christ and to enter His Church. For this, we are all grateful, and long may their work in this vein continue.

But the same apologists do not perform so well when they turn their sights to intraecclesial affairs, particularly when it comes to explaining the nature, purpose, and limits of papal infallibility. Even there, the apologists do well when they are justifying wonderful things like *Humanae Vitae*, for its teaching is in accord with natural and divine law and the tradition of the Church, and the pope's job is to uphold all that, regardless of pressures against it. Yet when popes make spectacularly bad decisions or teach that which is ambiguous or *male sonans* (evil-sounding) or materially erroneous, these apologists are caught flat-footed and empty-handed. They are tempted either to ignore the problem as an embarrassing exception or to appeal bravely to an unthinking ultramontanism, as if sheer bluster will somehow paper it over.

We have seen a great deal of the latter problem ever since the release of the motu proprio *Traditionis Custodes*. Most commentators, it is true, fall into two more obvious categories: the progressives who gloat shamelessly over the defeat of the nasty trads, and nearly everyone else who sees Pope Francis's move as unwarranted, malicious, inflammatory, bellicose, unworkable, and — the worst sin after Vatican II — thoroughly unpastoral. But there is a *coetus* of self-styled apologists who have rushed to make podcasts defending the pope's supposed right to create, abolish, and modify liturgy nearly any way he pleases.

---

1 This lecture was given at Our Lady of Mount Carmel Church in Littleton, Colorado, on July 31; the video of it was posted at YouTube the same day; and the transcript was published at *Rorate Caeli* on August 3.

This lecture will not be an extensive critique of *Traditionis Custodes* — that can be found in many other places at this point. Rather, I want to explain how we reached a point of such absurdity that a Roman Pontiff can dare, with the stroke of a pen, to consign to the margins and to eventual oblivion an unbroken liturgical patrimony of millennia and to claim that the new rites created by committee under Paul VI are the "only" (*unica*) *lex orandi* or law of prayer of the Catholic Church — and the even greater absurdity that there are Catholic apologists defending him and his purported "right" to do so.

The fundamental flaw of these apologists is that, like their doppelgänger Protestant opponents, they have fallen for the technique of proof-texting. Instead of *sola scriptura*, it is often *solo papa*; where the Calvinist quotes St. Paul on justification by faith alone, the papalist quotes a conciliar dictum on universal papal jurisdiction. Actually, all controversialists (including rad trads) have a tendency to proof-text, as if it concludes a debate, when, in reality, it only starts it. For one must not only quote a passage from Scripture, the Fathers, the Doctors, or the Magisterium, one must also understand when, where, why, and how it was stated — in other words, its context. Some texts are clear enough that they do the heavy lifting for us, but others are subtle, partial, overstated, understated, etc., and need to be fitted into their place like stones into a wall. It is the wall that we are looking for, not the individual stones torn out of it. [2]

Thus, Catholic apologists love to quote the First Vatican Council's *Pastor Aeternus* (1870) on the pope's jurisdiction:

> Wherefore we teach and declare that, by divine ordinance, the Roman Church possesses a pre-eminence of ordinary power over every other Church, and that this jurisdictional power of the Roman Pontiff is both episcopal and immediate. Both clergy and faithful, of whatever rite and dignity, both singly and collectively, are bound to submit to this power by the duty of hierarchical subordination and true obedience, and this not only in matters concerning faith and morals, but also in those which regard the discipline and government of the Church throughout the world. (*Pastor Aeternus*, ch. 3, n. 2)

They are quick to quote Pius XII's encyclical *Mediator Dei* (1947): "The Sovereign Pontiff alone enjoys the right to recognize and establish any practice touching the worship of God, to introduce and approve new rites,

---

2   For more on the question of context, see my article "Sun, Moon, and Stars: Tradition for the Saints," *OnePeterFive*, February 3, 2021.

as also to modify those he judges to require modification" (n. 58).[3] The *Code of Canon Law* (1983) affirms the pope's "supreme, full, immediate, and universal ordinary power in the Church" (Can. 331). As John Monaco points out: "As the administration of the sacraments falls within Church discipline, it is not surprising that canon law designates the ordering of the liturgy to the pope (Can. 838 §2) and even grants him the power to 'approve or define the requirements for their validity' (Can. 841)."[4]

So far, so good. But to leave them thus is to give texts without context.

First, liturgy cannot be reduced to a matter of discipline alone; it always concerns doctrine of faith and morals as professed by the Church over her entire history, and as expressed in the Magisterium of every age.[5] The pope is not a soloist but a member of an orchestra, and the score he's playing already exists before he comes to office — the more so, the later in history we are.

Second, papal jurisdiction over disciplinary matters does not exist in a vacuum: it is a component of the office of the papacy, which has its own nature, purpose, and duties. The power to introduce, remove, or alter liturgical rites is not a kind of Ockhamist omnipotence with no reference to wisdom, goodness, or rightness: there are conditions inherent in the papacy that delimit and condition the power, that endow its use with authority or a lack thereof.[6]

---

3   It is worth pointing out that the word *ritus* (translated here as "rites") is not at all self-evident; in fact, it is a term of almost notorious vagueness, that can refer to anything from a particular ceremony (the "rite of communion," i.e., how communion is distributed, whether under one or two species) to a full liturgy (the "rite of Mass" or the "rite of baptism," i.e., the entire thing with all its elements) to an entire rite with all its many liturgies ("the Roman rite," "the Byzantine rite") to a particular use within that rite ("the Dominican rite," which would more properly be called "the Dominican use"). Pope Pius XII would not have meant: "I can make up a Pacellian Rite, to stand alongside the Liturgy of St. John Chrysostom and the Roman Mass," but rather something like "the supreme authority of the Church can withdraw the chalice from the non-celebrants." For that matter, would not a patriarch have an analogous power over his ritual church?
4   John A. Monaco, "Was the Sacred Liturgy Made for the Pope, or the Pope for the Sacred Liturgy?," *Catholic World Report*, July 28, 2021 (see above, chapter 42).
5   All authorities recognize that liturgy is a *locus theologicus* unto itself. This implies that it is not simply the product of a handful of theologians on a committee, rubber-stamped by the Church's legislative authority.
6   Fr. John Hunwicke, "A Pontifical Act Lacking *Auctoritas*" (see chapter 7). William of Ockham famously argued that divine omnipotence should be understood as not "limited" in any way by logically prior commitments of what God owes to His own goodness or to the nature of His creatures according to His wise design. For a full exposition, see my article "William of Ockham and the Metaphysical Roots of Natural Law," *The Aquinas Review* (2004):1–84, www.academia.edu/6413044/William_of_Ockham_and_the_Metaphysical_Roots_of_Natural_Law.

This is why historians can make judgments about when popes exercised their power well or badly, prudently or imprudently, justly or unjustly.

Third, just because something is stated in a magisterial document does not mean it is stated in the best possible way, or in a way that does not open it to an erroneous misunderstanding. A telling example is none other than *Mediator Dei*, in which Pius XII at one point inverts the traditional axiom *lex orandi, lex credendi* by saying that the *lex credendi* should determine the *lex orandi*, and that this explains why the pope can modify the liturgy to make it express certain doctrines more clearly.[7] In a way, this is true: what the liturgy already teaches, albeit in a muted or diffuse way, can be crystallized in a new observance, as when Pius XI in 1925 introduced the feast of the kingship of Jesus Christ. That kingship was already long professed by the Church and present throughout the liturgy, but the pope, in response to modern secularism, wished to have the liturgy teach this truth more directly.[8] It would be false, however, to say that a pope has the authority to translate whatever fancy comes into his head, or whatever pet theological project, into some liturgical expression — such as (e.g.) an Anti-Gun Sunday, or the excision of all miracles from the readings in response to modern biblical criticism, or the approval of a rainbow-colored chasuble to symbolize LGBTQ inclusiveness. We might laugh at such examples and say "it could never happen," but the only reason we think so is that we implicitly recognize that the pope is not the one who principally or ultimately defines either the *lex credendi* or the *lex orandi*.[9]

---

7   For a critique of the Pian formulation, see Fr. Christopher Smith, "Liturgical Formation and Catholic Identity," in *Liturgy in the Twenty-First Century: Contemporary Issues and Perspectives*, ed. Alcuin Reid (London/New York: Bloomsbury, 2016), 260–86. Fr. Smith quotes Aidan Kavanaugh: "To reverse the maxim, subordinating the standard of worship to the standard of belief, makes a shambles of the dialectic of revelation. . . . The law of belief does *not* constitute the law of worship. Thus the creeds and the reasoning which produced them are not the forces which produced baptism. Baptism gave rise to the Trinitarian creeds. So too the Eucharist produced, but was not produced by, a scriptural text, the Eucharistic prayer, or all the various scholarly theories concerning the Eucharistic presence. Influenced by, yes. Constituted or produced by, no" (261–62).
8   And in fact, the potential falsehood in Pius XII's reformulation ends up being actualized by Paul VI's deconstruction and reconstruction of the feast of Christ the King: see Michael P. Foley, "A Reflection on the Fate of the Feast of Christ the King," *New Liturgical Movement*, October 21, 2020; idem, "The Orations of the Feast of Christ the King," *New Liturgical Movement*, October 23, 2020; Peter Kwasniewski, "Should the Feast of Christ the King Be Celebrated in October or November?," *Rorate Caeli*, October 22, 2014; idem, "Between Christ the King and 'We Have No King But Caesar,'" *OnePeterFive*, October 25, 2020.
9   If one objects that the pope couldn't make such changes because he couldn't teach the doctrines behind them, I would note that my three examples need not be taken as

In order to grasp the relationship between the papacy and liturgical leg-islation, we must start with the fundamental question: what is the pope's obligation to tradition? An exemplary answer to this question may be found in an early medieval source: the Pontiff's Attestation of Faith, or "Papal Oath," contained in the *Liber Diurnus Romanorum Pontificum*, a handbook of formularies used by the pontifical chancellery, some of which date back as far as St. Gregory the Great.[10] While there is debate about the exact use of this oath in the rite by which a pope was invested with his office, there can be no doubt that it reflects the mind of Christendom, in the sense that it summed up what was expected of a pope, as well as how the popes viewed themselves, how they spoke and acted. It is thus a valuable testi-mony of what our forefathers from the end of the first millennium to the start of the second saw as the limits of papal power. "The main obligation and the most distinguished quality of a new pope," as Bishop Athanasius Schneider summarizes, was "his unshakeable faithfulness to the Tradition as it was handed down to him by all his predecessors." The oath "named, in concrete terms, fidelity to the *lex credendi* (the Rule of Faith) and to the *lex orandi* (the Rule of Prayer)."

---

actually *asserting* heresies: to be against possession of weapons is not to say self-defense is immoral; to remove miracles from the readings is not, in itself, a denial of their truth or of divine inspiration; to suggest certain sinners should be permitted to attend Mass is not necessarily an endorsement of their lifestyle — although all three would *imply* errors and promote their flourishing. The absurdity of such papal innovations would not be exclusively doctrinal, but simultaneously liturgical, theological, and moral.

10   Contrary to what some have claimed, this Papal Oath is certainly authentic, although many spurious versions of it circulate on the internet. There are two modern critical editions of the *Liber Diurnus*, the one published in 1869 by Marie Louis Thomas Eugène de Rozière, and another published in 1889 by Theodor E. von Sickel. According to Sickel, the three versions that survive to-day (the Vatican, Clermont, and Milan MSS; in 1958 Hans Foerster published diplomatic editions of all three) represents its state of develop-ment during the reign of Hadrian I (late eighth to early ninth centuries). The papal oath is formula 83, and although Gottfried Buschbell argued in 1896 that it stopped being used after 787, in his 1948 book on the Photian schism Francis Dvornik makes an excel-lent case for its continued use in the eleventh century, when Cardinal Deusdedit wrote a compilation of canon law and included the papal oath therein. It appears that the papal oath ceased to be used sometime after the eleventh century; it is tempting to connect its fall into desuetude with the expansive views of papal power held by St. Gregory VII and his reformist successors. N. B. I must reiterate that I quote the oath simply because it splendidly exhibits the ecclesiology prevalent in the Church for many centuries, in which the pope is seen as a member of the Church placed within a synchronic and diachronic community of faith — specially equipped for his office, to be sure, but not one who towers over the Church as if separated from it and authorized to modify it *ad libitum*.

According to the Oath, the pope swears:

I, (name), by the mercy of God deacon, elect and future bishop, by the grace of God, of this Apostolic See, swear to you, blessed Peter, prince of the Apostles ... and to your Holy Church, which today I have taken up to rule under your protection, that I shall guard with all my strength, even unto giving up the ghost or shedding my blood, the right and true faith which, having been handed down by Christ its author and transmitted by your successors and disciples unto my smallness, I found in your Holy Church; and with your help I shall patiently bear the difficulties of the times; I shall preserve the mystery of the holy and individual Trinity which is one God, as well as the dispensation according to the flesh of the only-begotten Son of God, Our Lord Jesus Christ, and the other dogmas of God's Church, just as they are deposited by the universal councils and constitutions of the apostolic pontiffs and the writings of the most approved doctors of the Church, that is, all that concerns the rightness of your and our orthodox faith handed down by you; I, too, shall guard unaltered even by a tittle the holy and universal councils ... and I shall preach whatsoever they preached and condemn in heart and word whatsoever they condemned; I shall moreover diligently and heartily confirm and safeguard undiminished all the decrees of the apostolic pontiffs my predecessors, and whatever they promulgated and confirmed in synod and individually, and maintain them in unwavering vigor just as my predecessors established them, and condemn with a sentence of equal authority whatever things and persons they condemned and rejected; I shall keep inviolate the discipline and ritual of the Church just as I found and received it handed down by my predecessors [*disciplinam et ritum Ecclesiae, sicut inueni et a sanctis predecessoribus meis traditum repperi, inlibatum custodire*], and I shall preserve the Church's property undiminished and take care it is kept undiminished; I shall neither subtract nor change anything from the tradition my most esteemed predecessors have safeguarded and I have received, nor shall I admit any novelty, but shall fervently keep and venerate with all my strength all that I find handed down as verily my predecessors' disciple and follower; but if anything should come about contrary to canonical discipline, I shall correct it, and guard the sacred canons and constitutions of our pontiffs as divine and heavenly mandates, knowing that at the divine Judgment I shall render a strict account of all that I profess to you whose place I occupy by divine condescension and whose role I fulfill by the aid of your intercession.[11]

Similarly, the fifteenth-century Council of Constance (1414 – 1418) "pronounced about the pope as the first person in the Church who is bound by the Faith and who must scrupulously guard the integrity of the Faith":[12]

> Since the Roman Pontiff exercises such great power among mortals, it is right that he be bound all the more by the incontrovertible bonds of the faith and by the rites that are to be observed regarding the Church's Sacraments.

According to this thirty-ninth session of Constance, the newly elected pope was to make an oath of faith that included this passage:

> I, N., elected pope, with both heart and mouth confess and profess to almighty God, whose Church I undertake with his assistance to govern, and to blessed Peter, prince of the apostles, that as long as I am in this fragile life I will firmly believe and hold the Catholic Faith, according to the traditions of the apostles, of the general councils, and of other holy fathers... and I will preserve this Faith unchanged to the last dot and will confirm, defend, and preach it to the point of death and the shedding of my blood, and likewise I will follow and observe in every way the handed-down rite of the ecclesiastical sacraments of the Catholic Church.[13]

---

11 Translated by Gerhard Eger and Zachary Thomas, from the Vatican MS text as edited by Hans Foerster (1958, pp. 145–48). For the full Latin text and additional notes, see "'I Shall Keep Inviolate the Discipline and Ritual of the Church': The Early Mediæval Papal Oath," *Canticum Salomonis*, July 31, 2021.

12 See Bishop Athanasius Schneider, "On the Question of a Heretical Pope," *Gloria Dei*, March 28, 2019.

13 This and the preceding text are from the thirty-ninth session of Constance, held October 9, 1417, and subsequently ratified by Pope Martin V and Pope Eugene IV, with the implicit or explicit caveat (to quote the words of the latter) "absque tamen præjudicio juris dignitatis et præeminentiæ Sedis Apostolicæ" (see "The Council of Constance," https://www.ewtn.com/catholicism/library/council-of-constance-1459; cf. T. Shahan, s.v. Council of Constance, in *The Catholic Encyclopedia* [New York: Robert Appleton Company, 1908]). Although the text of this oath was copied from a forged oath attributed to Boniface VIII, it nevertheless expresses a properly Catholic attitude toward the papacy at a time when many were scandalized by an office that was failing, in practice, to secure unity of faith and governance. See Phillip H. Stump, *The Reforms of the Council of Constance* (1414–1418) (Leiden: Brill, 1994), 115 (https://bit.ly/3Co6Ug3). My citing of approved passages of Constance should not be taken as an endorsement of conciliarism or Gallicanism, as some hotheads have claimed.

Such texts are not bizarre outliers but reflect a common consensus of the pope's *boundedness to tradition*, so much so that eminent canonists and theologians could maintain that a pope deserves to be resisted if he is guilty of injuring either tradition or the Christian people who rely on it. Cardinal Juan de Torquemada (1388 – 1468) states that if a pope fails to observe "the universal rite of ecclesiastical worship" and "divides himself with pertinacity from the observance of the universal church," he is "able to fall into schism" and is neither to be obeyed nor "put up with" (*non est sustinendus*).[14] The well-known commentator on St. Thomas, Cardinal Cajetan (1469 – 1534), counsels: "You must resist, to his face, a pope who is openly tearing the Church apart — for example, by refusing to confer ecclesiastical benefices except for money, or in exchange for services... A case of simony, even committed by a pope, must be denounced."[15] Cajetan is talking about simony, the buying or selling of ecclesiastical offices, which was obviously a massive problem in centuries past; but it is far from being the worst sin or the greatest problem. Objectively speaking, the imposition of harmful discipline such as the promulgation of a valid but inadequate and inauthentic liturgy, or an assault on the integrity of doctrine, is certainly worse than simony. Francisco Suárez (1548 – 1617) declares: "If the Pope lays down an order contrary to right customs, one does not have to obey him; if he tries to do something manifestly opposed to justice and to the common good, it would be licit to resist him; if he attacks by force, he could be repelled by force, with the moderation characteristic of a good defense."[16] Suárez moreover claims that the pope could be schismatic "if he wanted to overturn

---

Conciliarism is to be rejected quite as much as hyperpapalism. In a healthy ecosystem, every organism depends on every other one doing its own thing in its proper place. When one species takes over, or a foreign species is introduced, the whole ecosystem suffers harm.

14   *Summa de ecclesia*, lib. IV, pars Ia, cap. xi, § Secundo sic (fol. 196v of the 1489 Roman edition, p. 552 of the 1560 Salamanca edition, and p. 369v of the 1561 Venice edition). For the full text, see my lecture "Beyond *Summorum Pontificum*: The Work of Retrieving the Tridentine Heritage," *Rorate Caeli*, July 14, 2021, note 13.

15   Cajetan, *De Comparatione Auctoritatis Papae et Concilii*. For a remarkable example of opposition to a papal command, see the account of what was done by Robert Grosseteste, recounted in Paul Casey, "Can a Catholic Ever Disobey a Pope?," *OnePeterFive*, July 17, 2020.

16   Suárez, *De Fide*, disp. X, sect. VI, n. 16. Compare a statement by the SSPX on July 19, 2021: "The traditional Mass belongs to the most intimate part of the common good in the Church. Restricting it, pushing it into ghettos, and ultimately planning its demise, can have no legitimacy. This law is not a law of the Church, because, as St. Thomas says, a law against the common good is no valid law" ("From *Summorum Pontificum* to *Traditionis Custodes*, or From the Reserve to the Zoo," published at fsspx.news).

all the ecclesiastical ceremonies resting on apostolic tradition."[17] (Note he says "resting on," *apostolica traditione firmatas*: he's talking about the whole structure that has been raised upon apostolic origins. That would mean something like the 1570 *Missale Romanum*.) The Dominican Sylvester Prierias (1456 – 1523), a leading figure in the initial response to Martin Luther, explains that if the pope is destroying the Church by evil actions,

> he would certainly sin; he should neither be permitted to act in such fashion, nor should he be obeyed in what was evil; but he should be resisted with a courteous reprehension. . . . He does not have the power to destroy; therefore, if there is evidence that he is doing it, it is licit to resist him. The result of all this is that if the Pope destroys the Church by his orders and acts, he can be resisted and the execution of his mandate prevented. The right of open resistance to prelates' abuse of authority stems also from natural law.[18]

Francisco de Vitoria (1483 – 1546) likewise says: "If the Pope by his orders and his acts destroys the Church, one can resist him and impede the execution of his commands." St. Robert Bellarmine (1542 – 1621) concurs:

> As it is lawful to resist the pope, if he assaulted a man's person, so it is lawful to resist him, if he assaulted souls, or troubled the state, and much more if he strove to destroy the Church. It is lawful, I say, to resist him, by not doing what he commands, and hindering the execution of his will; still, it is not lawful to judge or punish or even depose him, because he is nothing other than a superior.[19]

---

17   De *Caritate*, disp. XII, sect. 1: "si nollet tenere cum toto Ecclesiae corpore unionem et conjunctionem quam debet, ut si tentaret totam Ecclesiam excommunicare, aut si vellet omnes ecclesiasticas caeremonias apostolica traditione firmatas evertere." It is important to note here that, when it comes to the oldest elements of liturgical rites, we very often don't have any way to know (and may never have the ability to know) which of these are of merely ecclesiastical institution and which are dominical, apostolic, or subapostolic, which makes it all the more crucial not to eliminate them.

18   Prierias, *Dialogus de Potestate Papae*, cited by Francisco de Vitoria, *Obras*, pp. 486 – 87. For a good discussion of this point of Catholic doctrine, see José Antonio Ureta, "The Faithful Are Fully Entitled to Defend Themselves Against Liturgical Aggression" (see above, chapter 37). See also the superb Appendix II, "The Right to Resist an Abuse of Power," in Michael Davies, *Apologia pro Marcel Lefebvre* (Kansas City: Angelus Press, 1979, repr. 2020), 379 – 419.

19   Bellarmine, *De Romano Pontifice*, Bk. 2, ch. 29, seventh reply. "Judge" here means "bring to judgment" or issue a formal judicial sentence; it obviously does not exclude making a judgment of his words or acts.

Note — and this is a crucial point — that all of these authorities *assume we are capable of recognizing* that the pope is assaulting souls or destroying the Church at a given moment or with a given policy. In other words, the pope is not the sole judge of whether or not he is helping or harming the Church, as if we are waiting for him to announce: "Brothers and Sisters, I am now helping the Church, so you must needs obey me perfectly" or "Woe is me, I am now harming the Church, so you are permitted to resist me." There is some role for our informed reason and faith to play in evaluating his words and actions. The faithful of Christ are not simply in a passive stance to papal commands, decrees, or actions; their obedience is intelligent, free, and conscientious.

Of course, the "default position" for a Catholic is to assume the best, to wish to obey and follow; so that one would have to be, as it were, compelled into a different posture, especially a posture of resistance; but even to say this much is to admit that it is possible for a pope to act so wrongly that he can be seen to be harming the Church and to be deserving of resistance. In short: the right to resist an abuse of power logically implies the right to judge that something is an abuse of power.[20] This capacity to recognize abuse is inseparable from the laudable and normative adherence of the faithful to immemorial custom and venerable tradition. For the Church's "immune system" to be functional in a time of crisis, there must be Catholics who are not so cowed by authority, whether secular or ecclesiastical, that they will cease to hold fast to that which they have received. This, indeed, is exactly what the first generation of traditionalists did in the wake of the postconciliar liturgical reform.[21]

To see that the position I am defending here is not extravagant, we should consider a famous proponent of it in recent times: none other than Joseph Ratzinger. In *The Spirit of the Liturgy* (2000), Ratzinger writes:

---

20   Nor can this be excluded as Protestant "private judgement." Private judgement is, rather, the claim to be the final arbiter about what is contained in the Word of God. A pope does not lay claim to be such a final arbiter unless he makes an *ex cathedra* declaration and anathematizes those who refuse to embrace it as part of the deposit of faith, or unless there is a teaching on a matter of faith and morals that is part of the universal ordinary Magisterium. With papal disciplinary decisions and policies, we are in the realm of practical and prudential matters that can be evaluated by all who are involved, and where the pope's own mind and will enjoy no guarantee of inerrancy or even of probity.

21   See my article "It's Time to Imitate Our Forefathers: Never Give Up!," *OnePeterFive*, July 28, 2021.

After the Second Vatican Council, the impression arose that the pope really could do anything in liturgical matters, especially if he were acting on the mandate of an ecumenical council. Eventually, the idea of the givenness of the liturgy, the fact that one cannot do with it what one will, faded from the public consciousness of the West. In fact, the First Vatican Council had in no way defined the pope as an absolute monarch. On the contrary, it presented him as the guarantor of obedience to the revealed Word. The pope's authority is bound to the Tradition of faith, and that also applies to the liturgy. It is not "manufactured" by the authorities. Even the pope can only be a humble servant of its lawful development and abiding integrity and identity. . . . The authority of the pope is not unlimited; it is at the service of Sacred Tradition.[22]

Benedict XVI takes up the same theme in 2005, in his first papal homily at St. John Lateran:

The power that Christ conferred upon Peter and his Successors is, in an absolute sense, a mandate to serve. The power of teaching in the Church involves a commitment to the service of obedience to the Faith. The pope is not an absolute monarch whose thoughts and desires are law. On the contrary: the pope's ministry is a guarantee of obedience to Christ and to his Word. He must not proclaim his own ideas, but rather constantly bind himself and the Church to obedience to God's Word, in the face of every attempt to adapt it or water it down, and every form of opportunism. . . . The pope knows that in his important decisions, he is bound to the great community of faith of all times, to the binding interpretations that have developed throughout the Church's pilgrimage. Thus, his power is not being above the Word of God, but at the service of it. It is incumbent upon him to ensure that this Word continues to be present in its greatness and to resound in its purity, so that it is not torn to pieces by continuous changes in usage.[23]

Note that Ratzinger acknowledges the pope's freedom to act or *not* act in accord with his boundedness; he is not an automaton who will never fail to do the right thing, but one who has received a solemn duty that he must fulfill, lest he injure the Church.

---

22   Joseph Ratzinger, The Spirit of the Liturgy [2000], trans. John Saward, commemorative edition with Romano Guardini's The Spirit of the Liturgy [1918], trans. Ada Lane (San Francisco: Ignatius Press, 2018), 179–80.

23   Homily for the Mass of Installation as the Bishop of Rome, May 7, 2005.

If we have this truly Catholic understanding of the papacy — which sees it as an office in service of a sacred heritage to be received, safeguarded, defended, expounded, and handed on — it follows that abolition of immemorial liturgical rites is absolutely beyond its reach. As Joseph Ratzinger noted in a speech in 1998: "It is good to recall here what Cardinal Newman observed, that the Church, throughout her history, has never abolished nor forbidden orthodox liturgical forms, which would be quite alien to the Spirit of the Church."[24] We can see already the germ of his well-known statement in the letter to bishops that went out with *Summorum Pontificum*: "What earlier generations held as sacred, remains sacred and great for us too, and it cannot be all of a sudden entirely forbidden or even considered harmful. It behooves all of us to preserve the riches which have developed in the Church's faith and prayer, and to give them their proper place." Recall the striking statement Cardinal Ratzinger made in an interview in 1996: "A community is calling its very being into question when it suddenly declares that what until now was its holiest and highest possession is strictly forbidden, and when it makes the longing for it seem downright indecent. Can it be trusted any more about anything else? Won't it proscribe tomorrow what it prescribes today?"[25]

As we saw a moment ago, Ratzinger refers to Cardinal Newman as a witness. Let's have a look at the pertinent passage in the great Oxford don. In a sermon called "Ceremonies of the Church," St. John Henry Newman explains that so great is the reverence we must have towards inherited liturgical forms that even Our Lord Himself and His Apostles, instead of creating the Christian liturgy *de novo*, continued to follow the Jewish rites of worship, which were elaborated and transformed by them into the apostolic rites of the Mass, the sacraments, the Divine Office, blessings and consecrations:

> Matters of faith, indeed, He reveals to us by inspiration, because they are supernatural: but matters of moral duty, through our own conscience and divinely-guided reason; and matters of form [i.e., ways of praying], by tradition and long usage, which bind us to the observance of them, though they are not enjoined in Scripture.... The forms of devotion are parts of devotion. Who can in practice separate his view of body and spirit? for example,

---

24 Cardinal Joseph Ratzinger, "Ten Years of the Motu Proprio *Ecclesia Dei*," a lecture given at the Ergife Palace Hotel, Rome, October 24, 1998, https://adoremus.org/2007/12/ten-years-of-the-motu-proprio-quotecclesia-deiquot/.
25 Joseph Ratzinger, *Salt of the Earth: The Church at the End of the Millennium* (San Francisco: Ignatius Press, 1996), 176–77.

what a friend would he be to us who should treat us ill, or deny us food, or imprison us; and say, after all, that it was our body he ill-treated, and not our soul? Even so, no one can really respect religion, and insult its forms. Granting that the forms are not immediately from God, still long use has made them divine to us; for the spirit of religion has so penetrated and quickened them, that to destroy them is, in respect to the multitude of men, to unsettle and dislodge the religious principle itself. In most minds usage has so identified them with the notion of religion, that the one cannot be extirpated without the other. . . .

The services and ordinances of the Church are the outward form in which religion has been for ages represented to the world, and has ever been known to us. Places consecrated to God's honor, clergy carefully set apart for His service, the Lord's-day piously observed, the public forms of prayer, the decencies of worship, these things, viewed as a whole, are sacred relatively to us, even if they were not, as they are, divinely sanctioned. Rites which the Church has appointed, and with reason, — for the Church's authority is from Christ, — being long used, cannot be disused without harm to our souls. [26]

Wolfram Schrems comments on this passage:

The Church never abolishes customary prayers sanctified through long use. . . . It is always a sacrilege and severely damaging to the Faith when an ancient, sanctified custom of prayer is abolished. Pope St. Pius V, whose Tridentine reform of the missal was anything but revolutionary, declared that from thenceforward all rites in the Latin church were prohibited except those that were more than 200 years old. Pius V knew the limits of papal power. [27]

When Ratzinger furnishes a definition of "rite," he ties it immediately to tradition, the content of the faith, and the act of handing-on (in Latin, *traditio*; in Greek, *paradosis*):

---

26 Someone may object that Newman spoke these words as an Anglican. However, the truth they express is not specifically tied to Anglicanism but is part of that common Catholic inheritance that Newman first recognized and then later consistently followed back to its root and home in the Catholic Church, whose traditional liturgy he so eloquently praised. See my articles "St. John Henry Newman, the Traditionalist" parts 1 and 2, published at *New Liturgical Movement* on October 14 and 21, 2019.

27 Wolfram Schrems, "The Council's Constitution on the Liturgy: Reform or Revolution?," *Rorate Caeli*, May 3, 2018.

The "rite," that form of celebration and prayer which has ripened in the faith and the life of the Church, is a condensed form of living Tradition in which the sphere using that rite expresses the whole of its faith and its prayer, and thus at the same time the fellowship of generations one with another becomes something we can experience, fellowship with the people who pray before us and after us. Thus the rite is something of benefit that is given to the Church, a living form of *paradosis*, the handing-on of Tradition.[28]

In other words, once again: *lex orandi, lex credendi, lex vivendi.* The rite develops over time in the bosom of the Church as the expression of who she is, what she believes, how she prays, and it is therefore always *given* to the Church in successive ages. The pope may not and must not interrupt this transmission or cause it to deviate but rather be that "servant of the servants of God" who assists in its faithful realization.

This is why Cardinal Ratzinger was able to write these powerful words about what went wrong in the period after the Council:

The liturgical reform, in its concrete realization, has distanced itself even more from its origin. The result has not been a reanimation, but devastation. In place of the liturgy, fruit of a continual development, they have placed a fabricated liturgy. They have deserted a vital process of growth and becoming in order to substitute a fabrication. They did not want to continue the development, the organic maturing of something living through the centuries, and they replaced it, in the manner of technical production, by a fabrication, a banal product of the moment.[29]

Ratzinger favored a gradual and conservative liturgical reform. Even though he always acknowledged the sacramental validity of the Novus Ordo, he understood the break that had taken place owing to a pope who, unlike hundreds of his predecessors, had failed to act as a gardener and chose rather to act as a mechanic or fabricator, resulting in a form of the Roman liturgy so different from its preceding tradition that it had to be seen as a

---

28   Reid, *Organic Development of the Liturgy*, 11.

29   The original quotation is from an article in the German publication *Theologisches* 20.2 (February 1990): 103–4, referring to Ratzinger's contribution to the book *Simandron — Der Wachklopfer. Gedenkschrift für Klaus Gamber* (1919–1989), www.theologisches.net/files/20_Nr.2.pdf. It has been quoted many times in many languages and forms: for a full history, see Sharon Kabel, "Catholic Fact Check: Cardinal Joseph Ratzinger and the Fabricated Liturgy," June 19, 2021, https://sharonkabel.com/post/ratzinger-fabricated-liturgy/.

year zero, the start of a new "tradition" and not the continuation of the old tradition. That is why Benedict XVI could call them two "forms" and propose their coexistence; he could not think of a *papally responsible* way out of the impasse except to allow what he considered the strengths of each "form" to rub off on the other, for their "mutual enrichment." However convoluted his solution may have been, we must note that it was chosen (ironically, perhaps) because it best cohered with a traditional vision of the papacy: the pope, concerned above all to transmit what he had received — even if some of what he had received was problematic! — fosters gradual, organic processes rather than imposing sudden "fixes" that threaten further chaos.[30]

I think we are now in a better position to see why the first and most basic mistake the papal apologists make is to assume that liturgy is merely "disciplinary,"[31] and that the pope's "universal, immediate" jurisdiction endows him with the power to change *anything* other than the "substance of the sacraments" consisting of their "matter and form."[32] They can cite proof-texts to this effect, but in so doing they remove them from *the context of living tradition*, at once diachronic and synchronic, that establishes the boundaries for the exercise of such power. Sebastian Morello expresses this point extremely well:

> Government exists per se for the protection of society and its way of life, so that society may achieve the ends for which human communities are formed; government is not the *creator* of society. So too, the pope and bishops are mandated to guard and pass on the tradition that has been handed down to them (2 Thess. 2:15), and are not to repudiate or abrogate it, or concoct their own novel version. The Church's tradition, both belief and practice, is not

30   As *Traditionis Custodes* makes manifest, Pope Francis does not have the same vision of the papacy, the same patience, or the same trust in the capacity of the "holy people of God" to be drawn toward that which is sacred and great, that which is traditional. For a more critical take on *Summorum Pontificum*, see my lecture "Beyond *Summorum Pontificum*" mentioned earlier.

31   The quotation from Cardinal Burke, below, will make the point most explicitly: a liturgical act is a profession of faith and an exercise of the virtue of religion, so liturgical legislation cannot be divorced from the Church's dogmatic teaching or her customary (and anthropologically grounded) exercise of justice toward God.

32   A more fundamental problem, as Tracey Rowland has pointed out, is that neither then nor now has the Church developed an adequate theological language to talk about "culture." There is *law* (we can talk about liturgy as a "discipline") and sacramentology (we can talk about *its* validity, etc.), but for some reason we haven't cognized what all the canonists and theologians of earlier ages took for granted, which is *the sanctity of inherited custom* as constitutive of the Catholic way of life.

theirs, with which they may do as they wish. The Church's tradition belongs to the whole faithful. Of this tradition, the bishops (including the pope) are the guardians and servants. They can never be the creators nor the owners of the Church's doctrine, practice or liturgical life, but are charged with protecting and promulgating the common religious inheritance of the whole faithful. For popes and bishops to behave as if the Church's tradition is their belonging, with which they may do as they please, with the rest of the faithful just having to accept it, marks the crudest form of clericalism.[33]

As John Henry Newman recognized, papal authority makes sense precisely within the context of communal tradition: it serves an obvious purpose of preventing corruption and resolving difficulties that may arise. It is not a free-floating abstraction but a service to a certain deposit, which primarily is the revealed deposit of faith, but also a deposit of ecclesiastical traditions and customs that have grown up with it, expressive and protective of it. This sum total is entrusted to the pope for safekeeping and transmission. Yes, we all know that small additions or modifications are possible and at times desirable, but the general *agreement* among canonists and theologians is that these should be of a nature as to remain in harmony with, and respectful of, what is already there.

To say that *the pope alone* gets to determine when and how he exercises his disciplinary authority is to say that there is no possible way the pope can ever abuse it — or abuse anyone or anything. It is to say he has rights, but no duties; power, but no limits — natural, divine, ecclesiastical — to his power. Those who maintain that the pope has the authority to abrogate or abolish an immemorial liturgical rite and replace it with a new construction show that they have abandoned historic confessional Catholicism in favor of a caricature. It is a *reductio ad absurdum* of the papacy, which plays into the hands of Protestant and Orthodox controversialists who would be entirely right to object to it.[34]

---

33   Sebastian Morello, "Revolution and Repudiation: Governance Gone Awry" (above, chapter 23).

34   For the sake of strict accuracy we would have to distinguish between the act of creating and imposing on nearly everyone a different rite than the patrimonial one (which would be an act of violence and bad enough) and the act of abolishing or abrogating an immemorial liturgical rite (which is very much worse). Paul VI did the former but not the latter, whatever his practical intentions may have been; St. Pius V, St. John Henry Newman, and Joseph Ratzinger all suggest that it wouldn't be easy to abrogate an immemorial liturgical tradition and that the Church has never actually

To manifest more fully the absurdity to which Catholicism would necessarily be reduced by following out the logical consequences of the hyperpapalist line, let us consider four sets of questions that might be posed.[35]

1. Can the pope remove entire portions of the Mass — e.g., decree that Mass is just the Mass of the Faithful or Liturgy of the Eucharist, and not it together with the Mass of the Catechumens or Liturgy of the Word?

2. What discretion does the pope have for changing feast dates and liturgical seasons? Can he change the date of Christmas? Could he remove Christmas or Easter from the liturgical calendar altogether? Could he remove Lent and Advent from the calendar?

3. Can the pope change the Byzantine rite, mandating that it be offered only in Latin (or in Esperanto)? Can he completely suppress the Byzantine rite? Can he force a Byzantine rite *sui juris* Church to use the Armenian rite?

4. Can the pope create an entirely new liturgical rite, based on no precedent? Could he create an Amazonian rite that has no resemblance to the Roman rite? Could he change the rite of the Latin Church to the Amazonian rite or, for that matter, the Byzantine rite? Would that adoption then make the Byzantine rite the Roman rite in that it is literally the rite of the Church in Rome?

To all these questions, a papalist of strict observance would have to answer "yes." The point at stake is not whether the pope *will* do such a thing, but whether he *can*, and whether he *may*. And there are two possibilities alone. Either he has the *power* to do it — he could issue a decree with the force of law — but he lacks the (moral) authority to do it; *or* he has, in fact, no such power at all: he can make a procedurally valid decree that would fail to be legally valid because of its content (as natural lawyers say is possible). In the former scenario he makes a procedurally valid and legally binding decree that was morally wrong to make; in the latter scenario he makes an act that is null and void, not having the *ratio* of law.[36] In either case, the resulting law or appearance of law would bring grave harm to the Church

---

done so — not even *Traditionis Custodes* directly attempts to do this. May we draw the conclusion that it is impossible in principle? I think we may.

35 These questions were inspired by John A. Monaco's "Some Questions on *Traditionis Custodes*," OnePeterFive, July 20, 2021.

36 See St. Thomas, *Summa theologiae* I-II, q. 96, a. 4: "The like [unjust laws] are acts of violence rather than laws; because, as Augustine says (*De Lib. Arb.* i, 5), 'a law that is not just, seems to be no law at all.' Wherefore such laws do not bind in conscience . . ."

and the legislator himself would be guilty of grave sin.[37] If it is bad law, we would be right to work and pray for its repeal or modification and to seek to mitigate its effects as much as possible; if it is an unjust law and therefore no law at all, we could rightfully ignore it and freely act contrary to its provisions.

Such questions as the four sets mentioned above help us to see the implicit or explicit boundaries that exist before a pope ever comes to power and that surround the exercise of his office. Liturgical realities are concrete and definite; they are genuine *regula* or rules for the Church. This is why Massimo Viglione is surely right to say:

> The *lex orandi* of the Church, in fact, is not a "precept" of positive law voted on by a parliament or prescribed by a sovereign, which can always be retracted, changed, replaced, improved, or worsened. The *lex orandi* of the Church, furthermore, is not a specific and determined "thing" in time and space, as much as it is the collective whole of theological and spiritual norms and liturgical and pastoral practices of the entire history of the Church, from evangelical times — and specifically from Pentecost — up to today. Although it obviously lives in the present, it is rooted in the entire past of

---

37   As Fr. Zuhlsdorf recently reminded us, Karl Rahner (*Studies in Modern Theology* [Herder, 1965], 394–95) discussed exactly this scenario: "Imagine that the Pope, as supreme pastor of the Church, issued a decree today requiring all the uniate churches of the Near East to give up their Oriental liturgy and adopt the Latin rite. . . . The Pope would not exceed the competence of his jurisdictional primacy by such a decree, but the decree would be legally valid. But we can also pose an entirely different question. Would it be morally licit for the Pope to issue such a decree? Any reasonable man and any true Christian would have to answer 'no.' Any confessor of the Pope would have to tell him that in the concrete situation of the Church today such a decree, despite its legal validity, would be subjectively and objectively an extremely grave moral offense against charity, against the unity of the Church rightly understood (which does not demand uniformity), against possible reunion of the Orthodox with the Roman Catholic Church, etc., a mortal sin from which the Pope could be absolved only if he revoked the decree.

"From this example one can readily gather the heart of the matter. It can, of course, be worked out more fundamentally and abstractly in a theological demonstration:

"1. The exercise of papal jurisdictional primacy remains — even when it is legal — subject to moral norms, which are not necessarily satisfied merely because a given act of jurisdiction is legal. Even an act of jurisdiction which legally binds its subjects can offend against moral principles.

"2. To point out and protest against the possible infringement against moral norms of an act which must respect these norms is not to deny or question the legal competence of the man possessing the jurisdiction."

the Church. Therefore, we are not talking here about something human — exclusively human — that the latest boss can change at his pleasure. The *lex orandi* comprises all twenty centuries of the history of the Church, and there is no man or group of men in the world who can change this twenty-century-old deposit. There is no pope, council, or episcopate that can change the Gospel, the *Depositum Fidei*, or the universal Magisterium of the Church. Nor can the Liturgy of all time be [decisively] changed.[38]

Recall a fact that seems astonishing to us today, but would have surprised no one for most of the Church's history: the liturgy of the Western or Latin-rite Church existed in its many varieties for 1,500 years — for fully fifteen centuries — before any pope wielded papal authority to codify or define a liturgical book. In response to the Protestant Revolt, St. Pius V took the grave step of establishing a definitive edition or *editio typica* of a rite that had been used for century after century as an authoritative *custom*. So far from "creating his own missal" (as some people ignorantly continue to say), Pius V took the most conservative action possible in the circumstances: he acted precisely to *conserve tradition* in the face of a massive heretical onslaught with its innumerable innovations.

Cardinal Raymond Leo Burke, one of the most eminent canonists in the Catholic Church and for years the chief canonist of the Vatican, takes the same stance, in a passage that summarizes all of our considerations to this point.

> Can the Roman Pontiff juridically abrogate the *usus antiquior*? The fullness of power (*plenitudo potestatis*) of the Roman Pontiff is the power necessary to defend and promote the doctrine and discipline of the Church. It is not "absolute power" which would include the power to change doctrine or to eradicate a liturgical discipline which has been alive in the Church since the time of Pope Gregory the Great and even earlier.... Our Lord Who gave the wonderful gift of the *usus antiquior* will not permit it to be eradicated from the life of the Church.
>
> It must be remembered that, from a theological point of view, every valid celebration of a sacrament, by the very fact that it is a sacrament, is also, beyond any ecclesiastical legislation, an act of worship and, therefore, also a profession of faith. In that sense, it is not possible to exclude the Roman Missal, according to the

---

38 "'They Will Throw You out of the Synagogues' (Jn 16:2): The Hermeneutic of Cain's Envy against Abel" (above, chapter 25).

usus antiquior, as a valid expression of the *lex orandi* and, therefore, of the *lex credendi* of the Church. It is a question of an objective reality of divine grace which cannot be changed by a mere act of the will of even the highest ecclesiastical authority.[39]

Thus, when apologists blithely say: "The pope can change the liturgy as he pleases," we might interrupt to express our polite disagreement. The pope, or others in the hierarchy, can legislate *for* the liturgy, in the sense of the conditions surrounding it, the printed editions of it, the qualifications of ministers for it, etc., but they do not legislate *liturgy per se*. Fullness of power means power to do anything that can (lawfully) be done, not power to do whatever the wielder of it wants.[40] If the statement "the pope can change the liturgy as he pleases" is accepted without qualification, then *tradition means essentially nothing*. And this is not a Catholic view (and never has been), but a nominalistic and voluntaristic one.[41] The Catholic standard is formulated resoundingly by Fr. John Hunwicke:

---

39 "The Wonderful Gift of the *Usus Antiquior*" (above, chapter 27). In a similar vein, Martin Mosebach writes ("Mass and Memory," above, chapter 48): "Pope Benedict did not 'allow' the 'old Mass,' and he granted no privilege to celebrate it. In a word, he did not take a disciplinary measure that a successor can retract. What was new and surprising about *Summorum Pontificum* was that it declares that the celebration of the old Mass does not need any permission. It had never been forbidden because it never could be forbidden. One could conclude that here we find a fixed, insuperable limit to the authority of a pope. Tradition stands above the pope. The old Mass, rooted deep in the first Christian millennium, is as a matter of principle beyond the pope's authority to prohibit. Many provisions of Pope Benedict's motu proprio can be set aside or modified, but this magisterial decision cannot be so easily done away with. Pope Francis does not attempt to do so — he ignores it. It still stands after July 16, 2021, recognizing the authority of tradition that every priest has the moral right to celebrate the never forbidden old rite."

40 "[A]t the [first] Vatican Council the idea that the Pope could govern the Church arbitrarily was dismissed as an absurdity by the majority of Fathers. Fr. Cuthbert Butler, the historian of Vatican I, relates that when Bishop Verot of Savanna (USA) proposed a canon to this effect: 'If anyone says that the authority of the Pope in the Church is so full that he may dispose of everything by his mere whim, let him be anathema,' the response was that the Council Fathers had not assembled in Rome 'to hear buffooneries'" (Geoffrey Hull, *The Banished Heart: Origins of Heteropraxis in the Catholic Church* [London: T&T Clark, 2010], 148).

41 For a full exposition of why it is not and cannot be a Catholic view but is, in fact, anti-Catholic, see Fr. Chad Ripperger, *The Binding Force of Tradition* (n.p.: Sensus Traditionis Press, 2013) and *Topics on Tradition* (n.p.: Sensus Traditionis Press, 2013); Roberto de Mattei, *Apologia for Tradition. A Defense of Tradition Grounded in the Historical Context of the Faith* (Kansas City, MO: Angelus Press, 2019).

Holy Tradition, which, of course, has Holy Scripture as one of its ruling structures. Holy Tradition, the foremost manifestation of which, day by day, is in the Liturgy. Holy Tradition is our truest Mistress. Holy Tradition is the ultimate and over-ruling *auctoritas* in the life of the Household of God. No *auctoritas* can subsist in enactments which manifestly subvert Holy Tradition.[42]

* * *

In this lecture I haven't explored in depth the specific provisions of *Traditionis Custodes* or the account Pope Francis gives of his decision in the accompanying letter.[43] But this is on everyone's mind and so it seems fitting to address it more directly.

On July 29, 2021, Cardinal Walter Brandmüller released a short article in which he pointed out that a law that is not "received" or "approved," that is, a law set aside in practice and not complied with, is recognized in the canonical tradition as lacking the full nature of law. He says, moreover, that there are situations in which customary law can suspend the obligatoriness of a new law contrary to it; canon law envisions customs that override contrary legislation. Lastly, His Eminence reminds us that a doubtful law does not bind — that is, if the law's relevance, applicability, or compatibility with other laws is unclear or problematic, it lacks the full force of law.[44] And that is certainly true of this error-ridden and canonically slipshod motu proprio. I would go further and assert that the motu proprio lacks juridical standing — in other words, it is illicit or illegitimate because it is founded on multiple demonstrable falsehoods and contains contradictions and ambiguities that would make its application arbitrary and uncertain.[45]

Even if for the sake of argument we were to grant that the document has legal force (at least to the extent that it is intelligible) and that its provisions fall within what the pope *can* do, we would still have the right and the duty to strive for its repeal and to resist it in every way open to us. For it would still be a tyrannical use of power by which a hierarch lords it over his subjects and strips them of what belongs to them, and, in fact, seeks ultimately the liquidation of a minority in the Church, much as the Chinese Communist Party, with whom the Vatican has a secret alliance, rounds up

---

42   See chapter 7.
43   See my interview at *The Remnant* (chapter 22) and my video interview with Cameron O'Hearn (https://youtu.be/GsywBhpSDGI).
44   See chapter 44.
45   See my article "Does *Traditionis Custodes* Lack Juridical Standing?": chapter 19.

ethnic and religious minorities and puts them in "reeducation camps" where they can learn how to be model Chinese citizens.

How did we reach this point, where instead of a pope who receives, guards, promotes, and hands on tradition, we have a pope who has attempted to unleash a global war against Catholics, against priests, religious, and laity, who are doing what he is supposed to be doing? That is a huge question for which another lecture would be needed, but let me give an outline of an answer. There are two primary causes.

The first cause is what I have called "the spirit of Vatican I"— Vatican I, mind you. That council gave a narrow definition of papal infallibility together with a broad description of the pope's unique position as vicar of Christ in the visible body of the Church on earth. Tragically, instead of being accepted in its modesty and received in continuity with the fuller understanding of the papacy's relationship with tradition that I have summarized in this talk, the constitution *Pastor Aeternus* was taken by many as an endorsement of a hyperpapalism that concentrates all authority, all truth, all law, and the sum total of "Catholic identity" in the papal office and in the very person of the pope, as if it then emanates from him to every other authority.

Although the most flamboyant ultramontanes lost at the council, their *cultus* of the Roman Pontiff not only survived but thrived, leading over time to the phenomenon of the superstar pope whose every word and action is transmitted instantly across the globe to a palpitating audience awaiting guidance. This has tended to weaken the Catholic instinct for receiving the truth of the Faith from a rich network of sources by which it comes to us: Sacred Scripture, Sacred Tradition, the monuments of ecclesiastical tradition (the greatest of which is the Sacred Liturgy), the Fathers and Doctors of the Church, the great mystical and ascetical saints, popular devotions and customs. It has, moreover, substituted a new kind of epistemology or theory of knowledge in which our access to the truth is had not so much by the exercise of the virtue of faith and the power of reason on their proper objects as by the subjugation of one's intellect and will to a hierarchical superior's intellect and will, taken as a sole and sufficient measure of truth. Obedience is then reinterpreted as evacuating oneself of one's own knowledge and judgment in order to be filled with whatever content is filled in, with no questions asked about how it is or is not in harmony with any other content from any other source.

Now, Catholicism is inherently about hierarchical submission, and the virtue of obedience is precious to us; but as we know, *corruptio optimi pessima*, the corruption of the best is the worst: there is a rightful and a wrongful submission, a true and a false obedience, and the difference can be dramatic. Such distinctions are seldom made because we are all under the influence of an exaggeratedly Jesuit notion of blind obedience (which I will not blame on St. Ignatius of Loyola whose birthday into eternal life we celebrate today, but rather on his successors[46]), and, consequently, we have lost a richer *sensus Catholicus* of the norms that govern Christian life and thought.

Returning then to ultramontanism, we see in it a confluence of several factors: a growing tendency for the Church to imitate the absolutism of the modern State, together with the breakdown of intermediate, subsidiary legal structures and cultural centers of gravity that acted as "checks and balances," so to speak, on centralized authority and monopolizing ideas;[47] a kind of clericalism and triumphalism that are not at all the same as celebrating the dignity of the priesthood and the reign of Christ the King; and, as I mentioned, a Jesuit notion of blind obedience to religious authority. If you put all these things together, you end up with the view that the Church is ruled by an absolute monarch[48] whose ideas are right, whose will is law, whose power unlimitedly surpasses all history, custom, tradition, or even prior magisterial teaching. He is a Delphic oracle, a mortal god, an image of divine omnipotence, a concentration of all of Catholicism. This, needless to say, is not and cannot be what the papacy is.[49]

The second cause of our crisis is Modernism, which emerged in the latter half of the nineteenth century, reaching its first apogee during the reign of Pius X, and then, having gone underground, reemerged with greater force during the pontificate of Pius XII, after which it flowed into the Second Vatican Council and exercised an unquestionable influence on the formulation of the documents as well as their implementation. The entire program of "modernization" was given not only a pastoral or practical dimension, which *might* arguably have been innocent, but also a theological one, which became ideological: a conforming of the Church to the ideals and values of the liberal world produced by the age of revolutions, in perfect

---

46   See John Lamont, "Tyranny and Sexual Abuse in the Catholic Church: A Jesuit Tragedy," *Rorate Caeli*, October 27, 2018.

47   See Bronwen McShea, "Bishops Unbound," *First Things*, January 2019, available online.

48   Contrary to the interpretation of Vatican I that Pius IX himself confirmed to a number of concerned parties.

49   For more, see "My Journey from Ultramontanism to Catholicism," *Catholic Family News* online, February 4, 2021.

contradiction to the condemnations in Pius IX's *Syllabus of Errors*.[50] Until John XXIII, the popes had been more or less resolutely anti-modernist. After John XXIII, the situation becomes more ambiguous, confusing, and anarchic, with the popes seeming to speak out of both sides of their mouths: sometimes they reaffirm traditional teaching, while at other times they appear to contradict it, or mingle it with foreign ideas, or simply avoid it, condemning it to silence.

With Pope Francis, however, we have moved into a new phase, where modernism, to one degree or another, is mingled in with nearly everything he says and does; nor is this difficult to prove. So, in the pontificate of Francis the two streams have joined together: he unites in one person the spirit of Vatican I and the spirit of Vatican II, an ultramontanist vision of papal leadership and a modernist theological orientation.[51] Truly a monstrous combination, and the greatest trial the Church has ever faced, even though most Catholics are so besotted with modernity and so star-struck at papal authority that they tend to think it would be worse for the pope to have a mistress or to practice simony. As I like to remind people, Pope Alexander VI — a Borgia who had at least seven children by means of two mistresses who were also married women, and who freely lavished offices on his relatives — did not resist his appetites of lust and ambition, but he never *dared* to touch the liturgy of the Catholic Church, her doctrine, or

---

50   Recall Joseph Ratzinger's comment that *Gaudium et Spes* represents a "counter-syllabus," as well as his claim, in the Christmas 2005 speech on the hermeneutic of reform-in-continuity, that the Church must sometimes repudiate certain teachings in order to remain faithful to others that are more fundamental.

51   I say a "theological orientation" because it is difficult to think of Francis as a theologian; he is rather a product of the great modernists who came much earlier, and inconsistently parrots their views. He also may seem to lack a Pio Nono conception of the papacy, since he refuses to wear pontifical vestments, goes on about synodality, and in general presents himself as a manager rather than a ruler (so that *Traditionis Custodes* stands out starkly for its sweeping use of papal prerogatives); and yet he is treated like an absolute monarch by the people for whom this is useful, and he knows it. It is, in the end, his view of things that synodality is supposed to endorse, which makes him still the "be-all and end-all." It's a more confusing version of ultramontanism than the straight-up one seen in earlier pontificates, but the later version would be unimaginable without the earlier, and its capacity for damage is proportionate to the continuing hold of this false view of papal authority. Something similar was true about Paul VI as well: he wouldn't discipline dissidents against *Humanae Vitae* and wouldn't say the magic words even to attempt to abrogate the Old Mass, but he was treated as an absolute monarch by ultramontanists around him and the liturgy was the one area in which he wielded his power atypically and to devastating effect.

even her moral teaching that he himself violated. [52] He did not, for example, suppress liturgical texts that speak of sin, judgment, death, and the reality of hell, [53] or of the need to despise earthly goods and long for heavenly ones. [54] He did not declare that capital punishment was wrong or that divorced and civilly remarried Catholics could receive the sacraments without repentance and sexual continence. Such egregious acts against the nature, purpose, and limits of the papacy were left for Paul VI and Francis to commit.

Having opened up these enormous vistas, I must bring this lecture to a close. What should be our response as Catholics to a truly catastrophic situation in the Church? The answer is as simple as it is ancient: *ora et labora*, pray and work. That is how the Benedictine monks and nuns kept the light of Faith burning in the Dark Ages and laid the foundations for the glorious era that followed, Christendom at its zenith. We have fallen into a new Dark Ages, but our tools must be the same as theirs. Part of our labor must be the labor of study: we need to be reading books — not just spiritual books — that will help us to understand, to think clearly, to act well, and to give good explanations to others. Not everyone is called to be a scholar, but everyone can set aside daily time for ten or twenty pages. I want to recommend four books in particular that relate to my theme.

1. Bishop Athanasius Schneider's *Christus Vincit: Christ's Triumph Over the Darkness of the Age* (Angelico, 2019). When people ask me: "What should I read to understand the current crisis in the Church, how we got here, and how we get out of it?," I always recommend this book, which is written with the clarity, fortitude, kindness, and orthodoxy for which Bishop Schneider is famous.

2. Roberto de Mattei's *Love for the Papacy and Filial Resistance to the Pope in the History of the Church* (Angelico, 2019). We need to know about times in history where popes have messed up, doctrinally or prudentially, and were legitimately resisted by members of the Church. It is comforting — in both the current meaning of the word (consoling, reassuring) and its old-fashioned sense (strengthening, galvanizing) — to know that there are precedents for such

---

52   It seems Alexander VI had quite a few more mistresses and children than the ones mentioned here, but historians cannot pinpoint all the details.

53   As does the Novus Ordo; see the work of (*inter alia*) Lauren Pristas, Anthony Cekada, Lorenzo Bianchi, and Michael Fiedrowicz.

54   See Daniel van Slyke, "*Despicere mundum et terrena*: A Spiritual and Liturgical Motif in the *Missale Romanum*," *Usus Antiquior: A Journal Dedicated to the Sacred Liturgy*, 1.1 (2010): 59 – 81, https://doi.org/10.1179/175789409X12519068630063.

resistance, and to know what they looked like. Divine Providence raises the right people at the right moment.

3. *Defending the Faith Against Present Heresies* (Arouca, 2021), edited by John Lamont and Claudio Pierantoni. The best one-volume critique of Pope Francis's theology and Church governance. As I said before, context is very important for achieving understanding, and this book provides a rich and full context for grasping the significance and function of *Traditionis Custodes*. You may have to acquire this book from Barnes & Noble online.

4. Lastly, *Are Canonizations Infallible? Revisiting a Disputed Question* (Arouca, 2021). Many traditional Catholics have been bothered by the rapid-fire canonization of the trio of popes of the Second Vatican Council, namely, John XXIII, Paul VI, and John Paul II. This collection offers an excellent introduction to the history of canonization, the changes made to the process at various points, the nature and objects of papal infallibility, and, finally, reasons for questioning the infallibility of canonizations — in other words, that some canonizations may be in error, and that this is a stance Catholics are permitted to take.

What, then, do we do? I'd like to echo a recent statement of Dr. Joseph Shaw: "The best way to respond to *Traditionis Custodes* is to carry on with the work of restoring Tradition," in whatever ways are available to us. (Shaw goes on to talk about altar server training and mending vestments.) Now and always, hold to the Faith. Teach the Faith. Live the Faith with love and zeal. God will take care of the rest.

50

Peace-Builder or Pacifier?[†]

RUBÉN PERETÓ RIVAS

Caminante Wanderer

July 31, 2021

POLITICAL THEORY IN THE ANGLO-SAXON WORLD makes an interesting distinction between the concepts of "peace-building" and "pacification." The first, "the building of peace," refers to a process by which peace is sought through dialog between the parties in a conflict. In the second, on the other hand, peace is achieved by coercive military action which forces the parties to keep silent about their complaints under pain of violent reprisals.

This schema can also be applied to the reading of what has happened in the Church in the last several years in regard to the traditional Mass. The conflict which dragged on from the very moment of the promulgation of the new Missal by Paul VI was previously almost resolved with Benedict XVI's motu proprio *Summorum Pontificum*, who in this way became a "builder of peace." With the sudden appearance a few weeks ago of *Traditionis Custodes*, Pope Francis has not only dynamited the dialog and peace reached in liturgical matters, but has also established himself as a "pacifier" in the Anglo-Saxon sense of the term: one who imposes peace by force, while threatening the punishment of those who do not accept his designs.

This is the reading which the majority of analysts of the ecclesiastical and liturgy situation have made, such as Cardinal Müller, Cardinal Burke, Mons. Rob Mutsaerts and Fr. Guillaume de Tanoüarn,[1] reaching the conclusion that *Traditionis Custodes* (TC) is, fundamentally, a profoundly anti-pastoral document, one which generates division and reopens a painful conflict, causing enormous damage to many of the faithful. Undoubtedly, this is the most important characteristic of the most recent motu proprio, but it may not be the most grave, since from the theological point of view, it

---

† Translated from the Spanish by Gregory DiPippo and published at *New Liturgical Movement* on August 3.

1 For the first three, see chapters 16, 27, and 30; for the last-named, see "It is Francis who contradicts communion. We are witnessing a rare case where the pope destroys communion," *Rorate Caeli*, July 27, 2021.

dismantles the construction which Benedict XVI had achieved, and creates a thorny problem which becomes unresolvable.

Pope Francis bases part of what little argumentation he provides to justify his draconian measures in regard to the traditional Mass on the assertion that it was permitted by Pope John Paul II, and afterwards regulated by Pope Benedict XVI, with the "desire to favor the healing of the schism with the movement of Mons. Lefebvre." Although it is certainly true that both Popes wished to resolve the problem posed by the SSPX, as all good Catholics should want to do, they also wanted to maintain continuity with the traditional liturgy. In the book *The Last Testament: In His Own Words*, Pope Benedict responded to the claim that the reauthorization of the Tridentine Mass was a concession to the Society of St. Pius X, with these clear and conclusive words. "That is absolutely false! For me, what is important is the unity of the Church with itself, in its interior, with its past; that that which was holy for her before should not be in any way an evil now."[2]

And there are many other witnesses who can be cited in support of this. Cardinal Antonio Cañizares, as prefect of the Congregation for Divine Worship, one with privileged knowledge of the thought and intention of Pope Benedict in *Summorum Pontificum*, wrote: "The will of the Pope was not only to satisfy the followers of Mons. Lefebvre, nor to limit himself to answering the just wishes of the faithful who feel attached, for various reasons, to the liturgical inheritance represented by the Roman Rite, but also and especially to open the Church's liturgical riches to all the faithful, making possible in this way the discovery of the treasures of the Church's liturgical patrimony by those who still do not know them."[3]

The website of the now-defunct Pontifical Commission *Ecclesia Dei*, which can still be visited, and which, according to the introduction by Cardinal Darío Castrillón Hoyos, then president of the Commission, is not an opinion site, but a site that includes "information and material in absolute fidelity to the thought of the Holy Father," affirms that "the legitimacy of the Church's liturgy resides in continuity with tradition." Therefore, the *usus antiquior* certainly has legitimacy; it has hundreds of years of history behind it, and the other rites both eastern and western recognized by the Church alongside it. It has the Tradition to defend it. The idea that brought Pope Benedict to hold this position is that a rite which was a sure path to

---

2 Pope Benedict XVI with Peter Seewald, *The Last Testament* (London: Bloomsbury, 2016), 201–2.
3 Prologue to the book *The Reform of Benedict XVI*, by Nicola Bux.

sanctity over the ages cannot suddenly become a threat, "if the Faith which is expressed in it is still considered valid," says one of the documents on the aforementioned site. To present an opposition of missals — one good and one bad, and therefore prohibited — as Pope Francis does in TC, although it may on the practical level redound to the detriment of the old one, on the level of principles reveals the weak foundation of the new one.

In this theological perspective, what is left weakened is the Missal of Paul VI, since it is clearly a construction hastily put together in a laboratory by a group of specialists, as the protagonists of its creation bear witness in their memoirs (e.g., those of Louis Bouyer, Bernard Botte, or Annibale Bugnini).

Joseph Ratzinger, while he was still a priest, wrote in 1976 to Prof. Wolfgang Waldstein: "The problem of the new Missal lies in its abandonment of a historical process that was always continual, before and after St. Pius V, and in the creation of a completely new book, although it was compiled of old material, the publication of which was accompanied by a prohibition of all that came before it, which, besides, is unheard of in the history of both law and liturgy. And I can say with certainty, based on my knowledge of the conciliar debates and my repeated reading of the speeches made by the Council Fathers, that this does not correspond to the intentions of the Second Vatican Council."[4]

This worry has accompanied Pope Benedict all his life — how to theologically save the Missal of Paul VI, which lacks the continuity with tradition that always existed in the Church's liturgy. Since it was impossible to demonstrate this continuity as a matter of history, the only way to do so was, and is, through an act of the will, without further proof that this continuity existed. And this is precisely what he did in *Summorum Pontificum*. Pope Francis has just dynamited this theological assemblage, which saved the two missals and re-established the *pax liturgica*, thereby not only rekindling the conflicts of the '70s and '80s, but also, and more importantly, aborting the solution which was found in the theological field to justify the liturgical reform of the late '60s.

Certainly, the theology which is hidden behind TC is not an original creation of Pope Francis. It is in fact no more than a by-product of the rupturist position developed by the School of Bologna, and curiously, coincides with the theories which one of the lesser representatives of that school, Andrea Grillo, has published in recent years.

---

4 Wolfgang Waldstein, "Zum motu proprio *Summorum Pontificum*," in *Una Voce Korrespondenz* 38/3 (2008): 201–14, at 203.

TC also shows the concepts of authority and obedience to which Pope Francis holds, nearer to *perinde ac cadaver*[5] than to the tradition and theology of the Church. His authoritarian and absolutist reflections bring to my mind a passage of Lewis Carroll's *Through the Looking-Glass*:

> "When I use a word," Humpty Dumpty said in rather a scornful tone, "it means just what I choose it to mean — neither more nor less."
>
> "The question is," said Alice, "whether you can make words mean so many different things."
>
> "The question is," said Humpty Dumpty, "which is to be master — that's all."

With TC, Pope Francis seeks to impose on the Church the mentality of Humpty Dumpty, and govern it as a despot: the question is, which is to be master?

We must recognize one success of the motu proprio, its title: the opening words which give the document its name, *Traditionis Custodes*, are perfectly true, since the bishops are the "guardians of the tradition," which is to say, they are obliged to know it, contemplate it, and protect it. And for this reason, it is the tradition as something objective which ought to determine their actions as bishops. However, we must here note a certain nuance: the motu proprio seems to understand the expression in the sense that the tradition is what the bishops — and especially the bishop of Rome — decide it is: *La tradition, c'est moi.*

---

5   The Latin words *perinde ac cadaver*, "just like a corpse," are often used to describe a notion of religious obedience introduced by the Jesuits. A trenchant essay by John Lamont, published at *Rorate Caeli* in 2018, describes it very well as one open to a "tyrannical understanding of authority in general as based on the arbitrary will of the possessor of power, rather than on law." Law here may also be replaced by "tradition" or "custom."

51

Does *Traditionis Custodes* Pass Liturgical History 101?

DOM ALCUIN REID

Catholic World Report

August 6, 2021

IN THE BROUHAHA FOLLOWING THE PROMULGATION of the motu proprio *Traditionis Custodes* on July 16th we have been treated to a torrent of commentary from the victors that betrays such a distortion of liturgical history as to be comparable to the most unprincipled secular journalists crowing with their revisionist by-lines on the morning after "their" candidate gains power in whatever election. Let us not now pretend that this is anything other than a political ecclesiastical war, howsoever disturbing that reality may be—even more so given that a liturgical tolerance if not peace had been taking root, growing and bearing fruit in many if not most dioceses, until July 16th.

The Pope has gone back "strongly to what Vatican II said and upheld it," we have been told. "Some of what Pope Benedict did was contrary to the Second Vatican Council," it is said. "The entire church" will be "returning to the 1970 Mass," it is trumpeted. "The 1970 missal" is blithely said "in a sense to be superior, more faithful to the will of the Lord as understood by the Second Vatican Council." "Active participation" in the liturgy and the liturgy of Vatican II "are synonymous," it is asserted. We are to be relieved that corrupt "medieval" elements of the liturgy have been discarded once and for all.

So too, the very first article of the motu proprio itself, which seeks to establish the modern liturgical books as the "unique expression of the *lex orandi* of the Roman rite," betrays a fundamentally defective understanding of the history of the liturgy, of the relationship of the *lex orandi* and the *lex credendi*, and of the power of those whose ministry in the Church is indeed that of guarding her living Tradition. One shudders with embarrassment that those behind this document managed to entice the Holy Father to place his signature under such a statement. In this they have not served him well at all.

A recapitulation of some basics of liturgical history is thus in order.[1] Let's start with the supposed medieval "corruption" of the liturgy — a theory quite fashionable amongst mid-twentieth-century liturgists and propagated widely by their doyen, Joseph A. Jungmann, S. J. According to this theory the "pure" liturgy of the early Church was corrupted in the medieval period and overlaid with inappropriate elements. Based on this assumption, twentieth century reformers eagerly sought to remove the illegitimate accretions and to return to the liturgy before it was thus corrupted, which they made available anew through the liturgical reform of St. Paul VI.

This theory, sometimes called "antiquarianism," denigrates all liturgical forms growing up in the life of the Church from the fall of the Roman Empire through to the Renaissance — approximately 1,000 years — denying the possibility that the Holy Spirit could inspire legitimate developments in the liturgy in this period. It is staggering in its arrogance, but truly useful as a political tool. In the end even Paul VI resisted its harshest implications, refusing liturgists' demands to abolish the Roman Canon, the Confiteor, the Orate fratres, etc. (One may argue that more often than not, in practice, they were abolished nevertheless by becoming mere options, or by being maltranslated, but that is another issue.)

If Jungmann's corruption theory was the fundamental error underpinning the work of mid-twentieth-century reformers, the "new clothes" of the liturgical Emperors of our own times are stitched together with the assumption that active participation in the liturgy and the liturgy of Vatican II (read: the liturgical books promulgated by Paul VI) are coterminous. Well, no, they are not. Let's return to our tutorial.

Firstly, that the liturgy is "the primary and indispensable source from which the faithful are to derive the true Christian spirit" and that true participation in it was essential for all was asserted by St. Pius X in 1903 and reiterated by his successors up to the Council. Furthermore, his 1903 assertion gave rise to what became known as the twentieth-century liturgical movement dedicated to promoting actual participation in the liturgy as it then was (that is, what is now seen as the older form of the Roman rite — the "usus antiquior"). Decades of work followed wherein pastors and scholars diligently led people to discover and drink deeply from that primary and indispensable source of the Christian spirit as the basis of their daily life.

---

1   For more detailed examinations of these questions and relevant bibliographical references, see my works The Organic Development of the Liturgy (Ignatius, 2005) and the T&T Clark Companion to Liturgy (Bloomsbury, 2015).

It is true that in so doing some came to believe that this true participation could be facilitated by liturgical reform — a partial introduction of the vernacular, for example. Accordingly, some reforms were enacted, beginning in the 1950s. It is in this context that the Second Vatican Council — an unquestionably legitimate ecumenical Council of the Church — authoritatively judged it apposite to call for an organic development of the Roman rite, a modest reform so as to achieve the noble pastoral ends the Constitution on the Sacred Liturgy sets out in its first paragraph.

It is also true that some voices at the time, and in the 1950s, betrayed a misunderstanding of the nature of the liturgy, seeking to adapt it almost completely to the image and likeness and supposed needs of "modern man," thereby evacuating its very content and turning it into something more akin to Protestant worship. Some liturgists, numerous over-enthusiastic younger clergy, religious, and laity, and even one or two Council Fathers rode this wave of liturgical "creativity." Such theories and practical "abuses" are less frequent today, but they did incalculable damage.

In the midst of this, the official group entrusted with the implementation of the Council's reform (the "*Consilium*") whether through enthusiasm, sheer opportunity, or sincere conviction that it was for the good of the Church (or a combination of these factors), went well beyond the reform envisaged by the Council and produced rites that owed more to the desires of key players on the *Consilium* than they did to the principles of the Council's own *Constitution on the Sacred Liturgy*. Where did the Council call for new Eucharistic Prayers? Where did it authorize the 100% vernacularization of the liturgical rites? One could enumerate further examples. The *Consilium's* Secretary, Father Bugnini himself, boasts in his memoirs of exceeding the Council's mandate.

What is crucial here is that a legitimate distinction can be made between the Council and the reform implemented in its name. Questioning the continuity of the modern liturgical books with liturgical tradition, and with the sound principles laid down by the Council *is not* denying the Council or its authority. It is, rather, to seek to defend the Council from those who distorted its stated intentions.

Nevertheless, as is evident from his public discourses at the time, Paul VI was personally convinced in 1969/1970 that these further steps in producing the reformed rites he promulgated — all of which he personally and authoritatively approved in their specific detail — were worth the sacrifice of the venerable liturgical rites. He sincerely believed that they would bring about a new springtime in the life of the Church in his day. The liturgical books he promulgated are unquestionably authoritative. The sacraments celebrated according to the rites in them are valid. But, given that they went beyond the Council's mandate, it is historically and liturgically true to say that they are the liturgical books of Paul VI, not of the Second Vatican Council. And on this basis it is legitimate to question their continuity with liturgical tradition.

The new, more recent use of the Roman rite (the "*usus recentior*") is an innovation, judged apposite by the supreme authority. His competence to do this is another question, particularly in the light of the teaching of the *Catechism of the Catholic Church* that: "No sacramental rite may be modified or manipulated at the will of the minister or the community. Even the supreme authority in the Church may not change the liturgy arbitrarily, but only in the obedience of faith and with religious respect for the mystery of the liturgy" (n. 1125).

Later in his pontificate Paul VI had misgivings. His 1975 summary dismissal of the key architect of the reform (by then Archbishop) Bugnini, and his severe treatment of those who opposed the reform may be seen as symptoms of this. The expected new springtime in the life of the Church had not materialized, as statistics demonstrate only too well. To be sure, many sociological factors contributed to the gravity of the crisis, but the fact remains that the much-hailed "new" liturgy did not produce the results its architects had promised. Participation in the liturgical rites rapidly diminished for the very simply reason that the first and most necessary participation is physical presence at them. As the statistics demonstrate all too clearly, increasingly the people no longer came at all.

St. John Paul II's election in 1978 sought a stricter implementation of the reformed liturgical books — abuses were strongly denounced — and in 1984 a limited permission was given for the *usus antiquior* as a means of healing divisions that had hardened under Paul VI. This permission was widened in 1988 in response to Archbishop Lefebvre's unlawful consecration of bishops, and, significantly, because the Pope recognized the "rightful aspirations" of those attached to the previous liturgical reforms. This recognition facilitated the formation of Institutes and personal parishes and other communities of which the *usus antiquior* was (and is) the lifeblood. The full, conscious, and actual participation in the liturgical rites witnessed in these communities to this day — something of which the Council Fathers would be proud — has borne significant fruit ever since, particularly in attracting the young and in generating vocations to the priesthood and religious life.

Recognizing this reality and understanding the larger question of the need to address the rupture in the Church's liturgical tradition, John Paul II's right-hand man for two decades, Joseph Cardinal Ratzinger, undertook two initiatives. As a Cardinal and in the capacity of a private theologian he wrote and spoke often about the need for a new liturgical movement to recapture the true spirit of the liturgy. And he spoke about the desirability of a "reform of the liturgical reform," to correct the liturgical books of Paul VI, as it were. The former was general enough to cause no concern amongst the partisans of the missal of Paul VI, but the concrete proposal to retouch and improve the *usus recentior* was too much for them. Even after his election to the papacy, talk of a possible "reform of the reform" was forbidden within the walls of his own Congregation for Divine Worship, effectively blocking its progress. The opportunity lost by the rigid insistence that the liturgical books of Paul VI are irreformable may not be judged well by history.

As pope, Benedict XVI acted on his convictions and in 2007 exhorted the Church to a more worthy celebration of the *usus recentior* in continuity with liturgical tradition (*Sacramentum Caritatis*). Some months later he established that the *usus antiquior* had its rightful place in the liturgical life of the Church and freed it from the parsimonious grip of the bishops who had, in too many places, sought to strangle it (*Summorum Pontificum*).

As a result, the growth stimulated by John Paul II accelerated. Peaceful liturgical coexistence augmented the life of many dioceses. Some mutual enrichment between the uses began to grow. Visiting bishops encountered young, vibrant, apostolic communities — sometimes in stark contrast to others in their diocese.

Were these acts of Benedict XVI contrary to the Council? For those of us too young to have been there it is difficult to say. We did not work daily with its Fathers, nor did we help draft its documents. Benedict XVI did. And he has dedicated his theological and episcopal ministry to its interpretation in a hermeneutic of continuity, not of rupture — which is surely the only valid way to interpret its reforms. So too, the discourses and documents of Benedict XVI reference the Council constantly, far more than those of his successor. That is not to criticize the Holy Father, who has his own approach, but simply to observe that Pope Benedict's teaching was thoroughly Conciliar, even though by no means warped by the ideological belief that the Church (or a new Church) started at Vatican II. If Benedict XVI's acts are seen as contrary to the Council, it is because they challenged and corrected this ideological "Council" and its progeny that is so dear to many with historical and theological reality.

What is significant — and this was unexpected by many — is that the pontificate of Benedict XVI revealed him to be a gentle and fatherly professor, quite generous to those of differing views. He did not harshly sanction those with whom he disagreed. Rather, he sought to teach them, often by example. Liturgically, whilst himself celebrating the *usus recentior* well, he recognized and respected the importance of the *usus antiquior* in the life of the Church of the 21st century, and in particular its attraction to the young. The riches of diversity in unity were a reality in many dioceses and were valued.

At Pope Benedict's resignation it was unimaginable that any successor could rescind *Summorum Pontificum*. And yet that has now happened. Why?

The stated motivation is urgently to protect the unity of the Church which is threatened by Council-denying traditionalists' attitudes and utterances. It is true that there are loud self-styled "rad trads" whose pontificating on any aspect of the faith and on the sacred liturgy in particular at times takes one's breath away for its presumption, arrogance, or ignorance. And yes, there are the professional traditionalists who have never had an unpublished or unmonetized thought and who presume to dictate the media narrative, or even dispense from liturgical law, based on their own private judgement. And there are the laptop liturgists who should otherwise be in seminaries or monasteries but who, through their own or through others' fault, find themselves able only to talk about the liturgy rather than to live it, and who end up living in a liturgical world of their own based on their personal and often quite eccentric preferences.

If there is division or denial fomented by these people, it is virtual — which is not to say that it is not serious, particularly given the capacity of virtual reality to influence minds. But, as many bishops worldwide have attested in recent weeks, this is not the on-the-ground reality in the communities who live a tangible liturgical and apostolic life centered on the fruitful participation in the riches of the *usus antiquior*. What is needed is not an edict ordering these peoples' extermination, but the provision of centers of integral liturgical life that can draw people from the fringes back into the heart of the communion of the Church, with mercy, charity, and yes, when necessary, with correction. To overreact to this problem simply demonstrates one's insecurity in the face of it. It also goes some way towards proving the point of the critics, and further fuels their narrative.

Many bishops, including some who are no real friends of the *usus antiquior*, have been prompt to take a pastoral stance in respect of the measures enacted by *Traditionis Custodes*. This may simply be because its provisions are untenable, or unworkable, in the judgement of diocesan bishops with real problems with which to deal. It has also often been because they know that the problem motivating this legislation does not exist in their dioceses. The widespread "non-reception" of this motu proprio by the episcopate may itself turn out to be an important event in liturgical and papal history.

Seemingly, though, there are those in the Roman Curia who sincerely believe that *Traditionis Custodes* will result in the disappearance of the *usus antiquior* from the Church. With all due respect to their Eminent, Most Reverend, and Right Reverend persons, they are as out of touch with reality as they are with historical fact. Blind suicidal obedience is a thing of the past. They may rekindle liturgical wars and drive people underground or outside the ordinary ecclesiastical structures, they may well frustrate and even destroy Christian lives and vocations, they may increase division in the Church in the name of purportedly protecting its unity (and for all of that they shall have to answer to Almighty God), but this will only serve to underline the importance and crucial value of the *usus antiquior* in the life of the Church of today and of tomorrow. So too, the perceived need to resort to such drastic measures to "protect" the *usus recentior* some fifty years after its promulgation is, perhaps, its greatest indictment.

Some prelates might take comfort in repeating the mantra that the Missal of Paul VI is "a witness to unchanging faith and uninterrupted tradition," as an article of faith. But that is not actually true. The need to employ such language to assert continuity where it is so patently absent belies the propaganda such a statement in fact is. That the Missal of Paul VI contains theological and liturgical differences to that of St. John XXIII which are substantial and intentional is something on which the post-conciliar reformers themselves, honest and intelligent protagonists of the *usus recentior* today, and its critics, all agree. *Traditionis Custodes* itself, in its assumption that the *usus antiquior* has no place in the post-conciliar Church, implicitly affirms this.

If it is true that the new Prefect of the Congregation for Divine Worship was a key player (or pawn?) in the production of this motu proprio, and if it is true that he boasted that his clique would succeed in annihilating *Summorum Pontificum*, then it is clear that this is part of an orchestrated campaign. Has the Holy Father been misled or even abused by some zealots, or does he labor under a profound historical misconception in respect of these questions? We must redouble our prayers for him, and for the Church. The votive Mass for the Unity of the Church should not be ignored in these days.

As I have said many times, I am not a traditionalist. I am a Catholic. And as a Catholic I hold that the bitterness, fear, alienation, and growing division directly brought about by *Traditionis Custodes* is a situation of the utmost grave concern. It is a source of scandal well beyond those whom it targeted and, pastorally speaking, is already a disaster — particularly amongst the young.

In the face of this, as a liturgical historian, I cannot remain silent. Legislation cannot change historical facts. Nor can an act of legal positivism determine what is or is not part of the *lex orandi* of the Church, for as the Catechism teaches, "the law of prayer is the law of faith: the Church believes as she prays. Liturgy is a constitutive element of the holy and living Tradition" (par. 1124) — of which the bishops, and first amongst them, the Bishop of Rome, are guardians — *not* the proprietors. For as one humble Pope taught when taking possession of his cathedral in Rome: "The Pope is not an absolute monarch whose thoughts and desires are law. On the contrary: the Pope's ministry is a guarantee of obedience to Christ and to his Word. He must not proclaim his own ideas, but rather constantly bind himself and the Church to obedience to God's Word, in the face of every attempt to adapt it or water it down, and every form of opportunism" (Homily, 7 May 2005).

The same pope was a diligent student of theology and of liturgical history. This led him to conclude that: "What earlier generations held as sacred, remains sacred and great for us too, and it cannot be all of a sudden entirely forbidden or even considered harmful." He insisted that "It behooves all of us to preserve the riches which have developed in the Church's faith and prayer, and to give them their proper place." Any other conclusions fail Liturgical History 101. They wouldn't pass the theology or pastoral care courses either.

52

Is the Missal of Paul VI the Unum Necessarium?[†]

JOSEPH SHAW

Iota Unum Lecture

August 6, 2021

THE ANCIENT LATIN MASS, OFTEN IDENTIFIED WITH the Missal of 1962 but substantially unchanged since the twelfth century and going back to the time of the Fathers of the Church, is a precious spiritual possession, the birthright of Latin Rite Catholics, and a fundamental monument of world culture. By its origin as the Mass of the Papal court, it unites the worshipper to that centre of unity, the Office of the Papacy.

That, at least, is my view. It was the view, essentially, of the cultural figures, including Agatha Christie, who signed a petition in 1971 to preserve the Traditional Mass. It was also the view expressed over many years by Cardinal Ratzinger, later Pope Benedict XVI.

On the face of it, it does not imply anything bad about the Second Vatican Council, or the authority of the Pope. But the ancient Mass is not theologically inert. It exerts a centripetal force on the Catholics attending it, drawing them back to the centre of orthodoxy. Catholics attending it reveal to researchers that they accept the hard teachings, on divorce and sexuality, as well as on the Real Presence, to a far greater extent than do those who attend the reformed Mass. Those attached to the Old Mass often experience this, in themselves and in others. This Mass has the power to draw in non-believers and the lapsed, as well as to inspire the fervent. In a time when the moral authority of the Church is at a low ebb, and people will not accept the truth of things just because the Pope or Bishops say so, it is a valuable spiritual means of drawing people into the truths entrusted to the Church by Christ.

If what I have said is true, many will find the Traditional Mass helpful in growing in holiness. Since there are many kinds of people in the world, others may not find it particularly helpful, just as they may not be particularly interested in a specific devotion. If both the Traditional Mass and the

---

[†] This lecture was given as a podcast under the title "After Traditionis Custodes."

reformed Mass are available, what objection could there be? Why would anyone with the interests of the Church at heart, let alone a Pope, want to see this Mass disappear?

In this podcast I want offer some explanation of *Traditionis Custodes*: of how it could be that this document has been promulgated, with the stated aim of the eventual elimination of the ancient Mass. I will go on to discuss the effect it is having on different groups of Catholics. Finally, I will give some indication of where we go from here.

I. IS THE VALUE OF THE OLD MASS OFFICIALLY RECOGNIZED?

Has the value of the ancient liturgical Tradition has ever been officially recognised, in the post-Conciliar magisterium? The answer is yes.

Pope Paul VI, contrary to what one might imagine, refused to say some harsh things about the old Mass to justify his liturgical reform. The reform was in earnest preparation, and the Mass was already being celebrated in the vernacular, when he said this about the ancient Latin Office, in 1966, in an Apostolic Letter addressed to religious superiors, *Sacrificium Laudis*.

> Your founders and teachers, the holy ones who are as it were so many lights within your religious families, have transmitted this to you. The traditions of the elders, your glory throughout long ages, must not be belittled. Indeed, your manner of celebrating the choral office has been one of the chief reasons why these families of yours have lasted so long, and happily increased. It is thus most surprising that under the influence of a sudden agitation, some now think that it should be given up.
>
> In present conditions, what words or melodies could replace the forms of Catholic devotion which you have used until now? You should reflect and carefully consider whether things would not be worse, should this fine inheritance be discarded. It is to be feared that the choral office would turn into a mere bland recitation, suffering from poverty and begetting weariness, as you yourselves would perhaps be the first to experience. One can also wonder whether men would come in such numbers to your churches in quest of the sacred prayer, if its ancient and native tongue, joined to a chant full of grave beauty, resounded no more within your walls.

When the time came to announce the launch of the Novus Ordo itself, November 19, 1969, he was inspired to even greater rhetorical extravagance. Referring to the reform, he said:

This is something that affects our hereditary religious patrimony, which seemed to enjoy the privilege of being untouchable and settled. It seemed to bring the prayer of our forefathers and our saints to our lips and to give us the comfort of feeling faithful to our spiritual past, which we kept alive to pass it on to the generations ahead...

The introduction of the vernacular will certainly be a great sacrifice for those who know the beauty, the power and the expressive sacrality of Latin. We are parting with the speech of the Christian centuries; we are becoming like profane intruders in the literary preserve of sacred utterance. We will lose a great part of that stupendous and incomparable artistic and spiritual thing, the Gregorian chant.

We have reason indeed for regret, reason almost for bewilderment. What can we put in the place of that language of the angels? We are giving up something of priceless worth. But why? What is more precious than these loftiest of our Church's values?

The answer he gave, naturally, is that there was more to be gained by the reform than to be lost. What is important to note is that this was an exchange of the good for the better, not the replacement of something in itself bad.

Pope John Paul II did not have occasion to speak at such length, but he did refer to the old liturgy in an early encyclical, Dominicae Cenae (1980). Noting the advantages conferred by the reform, he went on:

Nevertheless, there are also those people who, having been educated on the basis of the old liturgy in Latin, experience the lack of this "one language," which in all the world was an expression of the unity of the Church and through its dignified character elicited a profound sense of the Eucharistic Mystery.

Twenty years later, he returned to the old Mass in a Message to the Congregation for Divine Worship in 2001:

In the Roman Missal, called "of St. Pius V," as in various Eastern Liturgies, there are beautiful prayers with which the priest expresses the deepest sense of humility and reverence before the holy mysteries: they reveal the very substance of any liturgy.[1]

---

1   Message to Participants in the Plenary Assembly of the Congregation for Divine Worship and the Discipline of the Sacraments, September 21, 2001.

It will be no surprise to hear that Pope Benedict XVI wrote in praise of the Traditional Mass. In his Letter to Bishops accompanying his Apostolic Letter *Summorum Pontificum*, he declared that

> it has clearly been demonstrated that young persons too have discovered this liturgical form, felt its attraction and found in it a form of encounter with the Mystery of the Most Holy Eucharist, particularly suited to them.

Again, he referred to "the sacrality which attracts many people to the former usage."

Finally, Pope Francis, in 2013, early in his pontificate, responded to a journalist who asked him about the Eastern Rites, as follows:

> In the Orthodox Churches, they have retained that pristine liturgy, which is so beautiful. We have lost some of the sense of adoration. The Orthodox preserved it; they praise God, they adore God, they sing, time does not matter. God is at the centre, and I would like to say, as you ask me this question, that this is a richness.

He goes on to repeat his regret that this is something the West has lost.

Naturally all these Popes were officially committed to the superiority of the reformed Mass and the overall fruitfulness of the reform. Similarly, all were acutely aware of the problem of liturgical abuses, upon which they blame any shortcomings of the reform. None of them undertook any significant changes to the new Missal after 1970, contrary to the expectations of its architect, Archbishop Annibale Bugnini, who wanted his reformed texts to be the beginning, and not the end, of a process of perpetual adaptation. Instead, the official position seems to be that *in itself* the reformed liturgy is more or less perfect, and that it replaced something that was good.

Bugnini was frustrated in his efforts to get some kind of official abrogation of the 1962 Missal, and ascribed his failure to an official attitude concerned not to "cast odium on the liturgical tradition." That is one way of expressing the situation illustrated by the quotations I have given. For these four Popes, the older liturgy is the liturgy they grew up with. It could not be vilified without vilifying their own formative spiritual experiences.

Although in these quotations, Pope John Paul II and Pope Benedict both refer explicitly to Catholics who continue to be attached to the older liturgy, these Catholics, though parties to continuing discussions and negotiations, and subject to various official documents over the decades, are almost never referred to in magisterial texts. With the Indults, the permissions, of Pope Paul VI in 1971, for England and Wales, and of Pope John Paul II, in 1984 and 1988, for the whole world, the Church began the experiment of having the old and the new side by side in public celebrations, but until 2007 this was never the subject of any official comment, good or bad. Indeed, after 1988, the only time Pope John Paul II referred to the fact that this was going on was an address to the monks of Le Barroux, a Traditional French Benedictine community who were granted an audience with him in 1990. I managed to find this on the Vatican website. It is only a few lines long, and hardly mentions the liturgy.

2. RATZINGER AND LITURGICAL COHABITATION

Pope Benedict's frankness, in his Letter to Bishops, about the two Forms existing side by side and perhaps even influencing each other, was in this way revolutionary. It broke through a barrier of official embarrassment at the possibility that, at least for some people in some circumstances, the older Mass might actually be more spiritually helpful than the newer one. Like a particular school of spirituality or devotion, it should in that case become a permanent part of the Church's toolkit.

The idea of cohabitation, one might assume, was implicit in the 1988 deal. If there are to be religious communities and priestly institutes attached to the ancient Mass, it would not make sense to say that the permission was only temporary, a matter of easing the transition to everyone attending the new one again. What would happen to these communities and institutes when the transition period elapsed? But there were those in Rome who clung to the transitional theory. In 1999 Cardinal Angelo Felici of the Pontifical Commission Ecclesia Dei wrote to the then Superior of the Fraternity of St. Peter, Fr. Josef Bisig, setting out his conception of the role of the Commission, which would be that of "integrating the traditionalist faithful into the reality of the Church." This turned out to mean, not unity under the bishops in a single faith, but adopting, as a first step, the changes made to the Roman Missal in 1965. It was thus apparently a cause of concern to Cardinal Felici that the people had not sung the Pater Noster in Masses celebrated during the Chartres Pilgrimage. It was only an almighty row — not only with the FSSP but also with the Una Voce Federation — that brought it about that the 1962 edition of the Missal was re-established as a baseline for permissions relating to the Traditional Mass.

Even Pope Benedict has been understood to be referring to a transitional theory in his Letter to Bishops, on the basis that his famous remarks about mutual enrichment indicate a pathway to an eventual merger of the two Missals. Thus, Cardinal Raymond Burke remarked in 2011: "It seems to me that what he [Pope Benedict] has in mind is that this mutual enrichment would seem to naturally produce a new form of the Roman rite — the 'reform of the reform,' if we may [so call it] — all of which I would welcome and look forward to its advent." Cardinal Robert Sarah repeated the idea in 2017: "It is a priority that, with the help of the Holy Spirit, we can examine through prayer and study, how to return to a common reformed rite always with this goal of a reconciliation inside the Church."

DIGRESSION: MERGED MISSALS

I would like to take few moments out of the main argument of this podcast to note that this project of creating a merged Missal is utterly doomed, for a great many reasons.

One is that, with a very few exceptions mostly dating to the early 1990s, there is absolutely no enthusiasm among priests who celebrate the old Mass for adopting practices introduced after 1962, and even less enthusiasm among the laity. If the merging Missals idea depends on priests adopting these practices voluntarily, with the support of their congregations, it is a forlorn one.

Another point is that the transitional liturgical practices of the years between 1962 and 1969 were not conceived of as a coherent and stable liturgical settlement. The documents promulgating them make this quite clear. The so-called Missal of 1965 is in fact just a list of changes mandated by the Instruction *Inter Oecumenici*, applied by priests to their old Missals with felt-tip pens, since it was mostly a matter of crossing things out. I mean this quite literally: I own a Missal to which this was done. The Instruction says about itself that it "authorises or mandates that those measures that are practicable before revision of the liturgical books go into effect immediately." These are not necessarily the measures most useful or most fundamental or closest to what Vatican II called for. On the last point, indeed, few if any of the 1965 changes, which include the abolition of the Last Gospel and the Preparatory Prayers, can claim direct support from Council documents. Other things which were mandated by the Council, such as the multi-year lectionary and the revision of the prayers, had to wait until 1969 simply because they were so complicated to prepare.

A third problem is illustrated by Cardinal Sarah's specific idea, to impose the reformed Lectionary on the unreformed Missal. His advisors had apparently not tumbled to the fact that the 1969 Lectionary doesn't make provision for the Season of Septuagesima, or that there is a web of cross-references between the propers and the lections throughout the old Missal. Liturgy is not like Lego, which can be broken down into pieces, combined with pieces from other sets, and rebuilt.

But the really big obstacle to this project is the idea, introduced by Pope Benedict's reference to *mutual* enrichment, that it would involve the Novus Ordo making some concessions to the 1962 Missal: the convergence would come from both directions. This idea had lots of Reform of the Reform enthusiasts sharpening their pencils with excitement, but it is utterly baffling to liturgical moderates, and absolutely emetic to progressives.

With that opposition, this idea is going nowhere. Pope Francis has made the rejection of the Reform of the Reform a keynote of his papacy, saying in 2016, "to speak of a 'reform of the reform' is a mistake." He seems to think of the Reform of the Reform as a matter of high-handed clergy imposing things on the unwilling laity. There is just enough truth in this, in fact, to make this route out of the liturgical crisis impassable.

The alternative method Pope Francis seems to have adopted for bringing Catholics attached to the ancient Mass back to participation in the Novus Ordo, is not tinkering with either Missal, but simply restricting the celebration of the older one. (End of digression.)

To return to the main point, what I have been describing can be summarised as follows. First, the post-Conciliar Popes can all be quoted as praising the Traditional Mass, and even noting in specific ways the loss that accompanied the gain achieved by the liturgical reform, notably the sense of the sacred in the ancient Mass, and the contemplative engagement with the liturgy it elicited.

In conceding the use of the older Missal, there is, however, a strong tendency among observers, including curial officials, to see any concession as necessarily temporary. The initial assumption, under Paul VI, was that the older generation who wanted it would simply die off; when it became clear that new generations were taking it up, the idea took hold after 1988 that incremental changes to the older Missal might bridge the gap. With this collapse of this possibility, then restricting celebrations might seem the way forward.

I believe Pope Benedict was an exception to this tendency. The examples of mutual enrichment he gives in the Letter to Bishops do not suggest, at least to me, the idea of a merged Missal, but on the contrary he appears to look forward to a future in which both Missals would continue to exist side by side fruitfully. Enrichment of the 1962 Missal with the possibility of celebrating new saints suggests that the distinctive calendar is here

to stay: why change a calendar which is to be abolished? The enrichment of the 1970 Missal consists simply of its being celebrated with more
decorum: that, at any rate, is the only example he gives in the Letter to
Bishops. Hopes, or fears, that Pope Benedict would introduce changes to
the reformed Missal, such as allowing a silent Canon or the old Offertory
Prayers, were not fulfilled.

What is interesting is the level of apparently instinctive resistance to
the idea of the coexistence of the two Missals. On the interpretation of
his views just set out, Pope Benedict's vision seems quite reasonable. After
all, why not?

For fifty years Traditional Catholics have sought a peaceful coexistence.
They have quoted the documents of Vatican II praising liturgical diversity.
They have pointed out that there are actually quite a few different Missals in
use in the West, to say nothing of all the Eastern ones. They have affirmed
that in many cases they received their own formation in the reformed
rites, were baptised using them, and have no hesitation about their sacramental validity. This is true of me: I was baptised and confirmed with the
reformed rites, made my confessions and attended Mass according to them
for the first thirty years of my life. These arguments, however, have found
surprisingly little foothold, even when suggested by Pope Benedict himself.

Immediately after *Summorum Pontificum* I recall an Italian bishop lament-
ing "the reform is cancelled!" A strange outburst, but a heartfelt one. The
problem is that the older Missal is seen as an *affront* to the reform. Saying
you'd like to attend the version of Mass which has *not* been reformed, implies
that you don't *like* the reform. Even, that the reform failed.

3. ARE TRADITIONALISTS BAD PEOPLE?

This is the key to understanding the hostility now being revived against
Catholics attached to the old Missal. It certainly needs some explanation.
The accusations made against them in Pope Francis's *Letter to Bishops* seem
strangely without context or proportion. He writes:

> ever more plain in the words and attitudes of many is the close
> connection between the choice of celebrations according to the
> liturgical books prior to Vatican Council II and the rejection of the
> Church and her institutions in the name of what is called the "true
> Church." One is dealing here with comportment that contradicts
> communion and nurtures the divisive tendency — "I belong to
> Paul; I belong instead to Apollo; I belong to Cephas; I belong to
> Christ" — against which the Apostle Paul so vigorously reacted.

This injustice of this characterisation of the faithful who have benefitted from the provisions made for the older Mass by Pope Benedict is shocking. One gets the impression that some adviser to Pope Francis has got his browser stuck on a sedevacantist website, or on one of the more fevered threads of an online discussion forum. It should be obvious that people who reject "the Church and her institutions" will also reject the celebrations of Mass that have the permission of the local bishop. Indeed, I have encountered people who regard members of the Latin Mass Society as no better than liberal apostates, and Masses celebrated with the permission of the local bishop as so tainted by this that, regardless of the holiness of the celebrant or the Rite used, they would refuse to attend. At least, I used to encounter such individuals, particularly before 2007.

Like the poor, the crazies will always be with us, but Pope Benedict's magnanimity made a profound impression even on people hard to reach with reasoned arguments, and also brought into celebrations of the older Missal many new attendees who did not feel the need to adopt extreme theories in order to justify assisting at this Mass. They simply went along because it was a legitimate option, and it fed their souls.

It is clear to all fair-minded observers that the problem of extremism among those attending the old Mass was always primarily found outside the structures of the Church, at celebrations of the SSPX, "independent" priests, and sedevacantists, and in any case has vastly decreased in scale since 2007. As the *Catholic Herald's* US Editor, David Mills, wrote, after saying that he didn't attend the old Mass himself:

> The apologists for suppression claim that the people who want the old Mass are divisive. If that is true, and it is sometimes, the obvious answer is to remove the reason for their alienation. Extend to them the care, and the concessions, you extend to other marginal groups. Some will remain cranky and disgruntled, but the Church has room for the cranky and disgruntled.

Let us hope she does have room, because there are many such at the Novus Ordo. One might point out, indeed, that certain kinds of Novus Ordo celebration have a close connection with the rejection of the Church and her institutions in the name of some imagined "true Church." I am thinking here of progressive liturgies larded with liturgical abuses, whose regular attendees reliably believe that the hierarchical Church is an empty shell obscuring the true Church, where there would be women priests, gay marriage, contraception, and all the rest of it.

Are Pope Francis's advisers and apologists really so out of touch that they think that theological dissent and a schismatic mindset are more closely associated with, for example, the Sunday afternoon Extraordinary Form option in some conservative parish, than they are with the pro-LBGT New Ways Ministry, the women who claim to have been ordained in boats on the Danube, the Dutch churches where lay women invent their own Eucharistic prayers with which to lead services, the Australian parishes where invalid baptismal formulas were used for years on end, the American priest who filmed himself performing pornography on the altar of his church with two prostitutes, or syncretist Masses in India where Our Lord Jesus Christ must compete for attention with Shiva?

Those advisors and apologists are not ignorant of these problems. The US bishops have forbidden the New Ways Ministry to call itself Catholic. The lady would-be ordinands and the Australian priest with the invalid baptisms were excommunicated. The Dutch group were eventually forced to move out of the parish church. The American pornographer was suspended. Most of these things happened under Pope Francis. Nor is Pope Francis's circle unconcerned with the really large-scale schismatic potential of liberal developments such as the German synodal path. The concern about the Traditional Mass, which seems objectively so completely disproportionate, is not to do with how many Traditional Catholics have made immature remarks on Facebook: as far as that kind of thing goes, Traddies are completely outclassed by liberal Catholics, and we should stop beating ourselves up about it. It is fundamentally about the use of the earlier Missal *in itself*. This fundamental worry serves to magnify the problems of annoying Traditional Catholics, which are real but, in themselves, on an utterly insignificant scale.

The clue is given in the text of the Letter, where it says that the reformed Missal is the "unica," not the "unique" but the *only* expression of the *lex orandi*, the "law of prayer," of the Roman Missal. This is a puzzling statement, since the document itself allows the celebration of the older Missal, and what can it be but at least *an* expression of the Church's *lex orandi*? And what about all the other Missals, like the reformed Carthusian Missal, or the unreformed Dominican one, which are also still in use in the Latin Church? I think the answer would have to be: never mind all that, in some vague but important sense the Missal of Pope Paul VI is the *unum necessarium*, the one thing necessary. Pope Francis goes on:

> I am nonetheless saddened that the instrumental use of the *Missale Romanum* of 1962 is often characterized by a rejection not only of

the liturgical reform, but of the Vatican Council II itself, claiming, with unfounded and unsustainable assertions, that it betrayed the Tradition and the "true Church.". . .

To doubt the Council is to doubt the intentions of those very Fathers who exercised their collegial power in a solemn manner *cum Petro et sub Petro* in an ecumenical council, and, in the final analysis, to doubt the Holy Spirit himself who guides the Church.

To understand this passage we need to take a little step back. Anyone with experience of the liberal Catholic mindset will know that Vatican II is not regarded as a set of documents, so much as a direction of travel. For such Catholics it is a matter of indifference if they contradict the words of the Council, if they think that they are travelling in the direction set by the Council. Thus the Council told religious to simplify their habits but not to discard them. According to the liberal way of thinking, the religious who did discard them were following the *direction* of the Council, which moved *away from* traditional habits, and *towards* not having habits at all, even if it did not go all the way. The bit forbidding religious to get rid of their habits has no force, on this view, despite being in the Council text, because it sets an arbitrary limit to the *direction* set by the Holy Spirit.

Something similar seems to be going on with the Letter to Bishops. Oceans of ink have been spilt on the meaning of the Council texts. Libraries of books have been written on the problems of its implementation. And yet, the desire to attend the unreformed Mass is here the first of a series of falling dominos: to reject the reform, to reject the Council, to reject the intentions of the Council Fathers, to reject the Holy Spirit. Logically, one could stop this sequence at any point: one could like the old Mass without rejecting the reform in itself; one could criticise the reform that actually took place but not the Council; one could criticise the Council documents without impugning the intentions of the Fathers; one could question the Fathers' intentions without rejecting the Holy Spirit. But in the Letter the sequence is rolled into one appalling rejection of the *direction of travel* the Council set in motion: at the prompting, so it is claimed, of the Holy Spirit. To question what has been done in the name of the Council implies a sin against the Holy Ghost.

4. SOME QUALIFICATIONS

What I have suggested needs a bit of qualification. One thing I should emphasise is that it is very difficult to discern the different influences on Pope Francis's documents in relation to ecclesial politics. I am not going to attempt to do so, but it is clear that not everyone in the Curia, or among the Italian bishops, or among those close to Pope Francis, has exactly the same views. There was nothing inevitable about the emergence of these documents. It happened because of a no doubt complex interplay of factors. Pope Benedict had established a position which seemed reasonable and was increasingly widely accepted by the bishops of the world, writing in his Letter to Bishops: "Many people who clearly accepted the binding character of the Second Vatican Council, and were faithful to the Pope and the Bishops, nonetheless also desired to recover the form of the sacred liturgy that was dear to them."

This was for fourteen years the hermeneutical key for many people considering the relationship between the Traditional movement and Vatican II. Again, back in 1988 Cardinal Ratzinger had derided the idea that the Second Vatican Council was a "super dogma" which rendered everything else irrelevant, [2] and on another occasion expressed his outrage about how some in the Church made even the *desire* for the old Mass seem somehow *indecent*. [3]

For reasons which we may not know till all secrets are revealed at Doomsday, an anti-Ratzingerian group have, perhaps only momentarily, gained the upper hand in Pope Francis's inner circle. It was not *naïve* of us all to be shocked by *Traditionis Custodes*. Indeed, it is hard to know if it is this *new* direction which represents the real Francis, or the former policy. For Pope Francis himself had given little indication of such a move; he had previously been very *laissez faire* about the old liturgy. There is quite a long list of achievements in its favour which could be ascribed quite directly to him: the continued access of the *Summorum Pontificum* Pilgrimage to St. Peter's Basilica and other churches in Rome; the multiplying concessions to pre-1962 practices by the Congregation for the Doctrine of the Faith; the granting of faculties to the SSPX for hearing confessions; the giving, only last year, of a basilica a stone's throw from the Ponte Sant'Angelo in Rome for the use of the traditionalist Institute of Christ the King Sovereign Priest, and many others. The mere fact that Pope Francis gave us all eight years of his pontificate before reversing course, eight years of ordinations in the Traditional Institutes, of the multiplication of Traditional Mass-centres and apostolates, of the softening of bishops towards the Old Mass, of the turn-over of the generations in all kinds of offices to men not embittered

---

2   Address to the Bishops of Chile, July 13, 1988; text available at *Views from the Choirloft* of Corpus Christi Watershed, November 7, 2019.

3   *Salt of the Earth: The Church at the End of the Millennium* (San Francisco: Ignatius Press, 1996), 176.

by personal experience of the liturgical reform, of the increasingly evident imbalance of conservative seminarians over liberal ones, of the development of the lay movement in support of *Summorum Pontificum*: this may, in the end, prove his most lasting achievement. *Summorum Pontificum* worked its work not for a mere five years or so, until shortly after Pope Benedict's resignation, which might have happened, but for almost exactly *fourteen years*. After fourteen years, it is going to be pretty difficult to get the genie back into the bottle.

5. AN OBJECTION TO LITURGICAL COHABITATION

An objection may be raised at this point. I have described two ways of looking at the continuing use of the ancient Missal: the first, that this by itself calls into question the "legitimacy," in Pope Francis's expression, of the liturgical reform, and therefore of Vatican II; the second, that of Pope Benedict, that it is simply part of the Church's legitimate diversity. The objection is simply that Pope Francis is correct and Pope Benedict was wrong, because there is a fundamental dissonance between the two forms of Mass.

This view has been expressed in the mainstream by liberal Catholics, for example in *Commonweal*; sometimes, though less often, something like it is heard from Catholics attached to the old Mass. In the latter case, it takes its start from a radical critique of the liturgical reform. I can't give an assessment of that critique, but it should be pointed out that, before his election as Pope, Cardinal Ratzinger himself made some very serious criticisms of the reform, especially in his great book, *The Spirit of the Liturgy*. These are not part of Church teaching, of course, but he published this book during his very long stint as Prefect of the Congregation for the Faith, and it would be ridiculous to suggest that making such criticisms implies a rejection of the Council, or puts one outside the Church. There is room for serious discussion about the pros and cons of the reform as it was carried out, and the theological and liturgical principles underlying it.

Alternative liturgical traditions can co-exist in the Church even if they contrast quite strongly, but there is of course a limit to how much they can differ in their fundamental principles before we have a real problem. However, the problem doesn't arise from some "conflict between the Missals." The problem, if there is one, would be a matter of a liturgy conflicting, not with another liturgy, but with the teaching of the Church.

Every now and then the Church has to judge whether some Missal or specific text or practice can be used liturgically. Examples include former

Lutherans wanting to receive from the Chalice in the sixteenth century; Chinese Catholics wanting to honour their ancestors with traditional Confucian ceremonies in the seventeenth century; and former Anglicans wanting to use Cranmer's Prayer of Humble Access today. There are limits to the Church's flexibility, but they are surprisingly wide, and in each of these examples the Church's judgement was positive, if not unqualifiedly so.

Evidently, the Church's judgement of the ancient Roman Missal, in use practically unchanged from the *Missale Romano-Seraphicum* of the thirteenth century up to 1964, has been a positive one. In the case of the Novus Ordo, it was promulgated with the authority of Pope Paul VI, which gives it both legal validity and also the benefit of the doubt, in terms of how it should be understood in relation to the Church's perennial teaching. If there are problems with it, such as those identified by Cardinal Ratzinger, they must be faced, but they wouldn't go away even if the unreformed Mass were never celebrated again.

Indeed, I have a shelf-full of books criticising the Novus Ordo by liturgical conservatives who believed that the widespread restoration of the Traditional Mass was a non-starter: they include the work of Fr. Jonathan Robinson, Laszlo Dobszay, Mgr. Andrew Burnham, Fr. Aidan Nichols, and Fr. Michael Lang. The stream of such work on the Reform of the Reform has dried up since 2007. Why? *Summorum Pontificum* released a pressure valve on the Novus Ordo. Those who were worried about it have turned their attention to the Traditional Mass, and conflict about the Novus Ordo has subsided as a result.

If the 1962 option is blocked again, the liturgical pressure within the Novus Ordo will start rising once more. Some people have suggested that this would actually be a good thing: stay with the reformed Mass, they say, and make it better! But this ignores the extreme bitterness of the internal Novus Ordo conflicts and the very limited progress the Reform of the Reform movement had been making. In any case, as already noted, this is not what Pope Francis wants to see.

6. CONSERVATIVES AND TRADITIONALISTS

Having attempted an explanation of how *Traditionis Custodes* could have happened, I want now to consider its consequences. To do this I need to consider, first, the evolution of the attitude of what we call conservative Catholics: those who regard themselves as orthodox, but do not go in for the Old Mass. Then I'll briefly note the situation of liberal Catholics, and turn to the bishops.

Rewinding the tape to 1969, the implementation of the Vatican II reform of the liturgy was resisted fiercely by some. But it must be conceded that those who made a public stand against it were a tiny group of people.

The reason for this was only partly the exaggerated conception of obedience which characterised the conservative Catholics of that era. This was certainly a factor, but thoughtful Catholics had the option of playing up to this or playing it down, and they had two important reasons, as they thought, for playing up to it.

One was liturgical. Pope Paul made the point, introducing the Novus Ordo in one of his General Audiences in November 1969: "this reform puts an end to uncertainties, to discussions, to arbitrary abuses."[4] He was not alone in hoping this would be true. Liturgical abuses and experimentation had reached epidemic proportions during the time of successive changes in the 1960s. It was natural for people concerned about this to seize on the new Missal as a rock of stability, something guaranteed by the highest authority of the Church, and which could be legally enforced.

The other was doctrinal. In the previous year, 1968, Pope Paul had promulgated Humanae Vitae, reiterating the Church's teaching on contraception. It was preceded and followed by a massive and well-organised campaign of dissent.

At this moment of crisis, it is not surprising that many conservative Catholics considered that this was not the moment to be quibbling about the extent of papal authority. Insofar as the hyper-papalism of the pre-Conciliar era still had traction with the faithful, it could come in very handy.

For many years these two considerations continued to push conservative Catholics towards unquestioning obedience to the Holy Father. The 1970 Missale Romanum continued to be a reference point against liturgical abuses which were, in anyone's book, vastly worse than the Novus Ordo in itself. And a steady stream of papal documents sought to combat doctrinal dissent. For conservative Catholics, explaining away Pope John Paul's equivocations on the death penalty, and working up some enthusiasm for the Luminous Mysteries of the Rosary, seemed far preferable to giving away the obedience card which could be used against the liberals.

In this context, it wasn't just that Traditional Catholics weren't obeying the Pope's wishes in liturgical matters. More fundamentally, conservatives could not forgive them for questioning their own very wide conception of obedience as a principle. Without papal authority and obedience, how was anyone to oppose the liberal agenda, when the liberals seemed to have

4   November 17, 1969.

the arguments, the professors of theology, and the younger generation on their side?

Gradually, of course, things changed. Today liberal Catholics no longer have anything of intellectual interest or academic credibility to say. They can no longer claim to represent the rising generation, and even freely admit this.

Then, with Pope Benedict, the direction of papal liturgical policy suddenly changed. Those determined to follow every whim of the reigning Pope had to find nice things to say about the Traditional Mass. For many this acted like the removal in confession of the obex of sin which stops the flow of grace. The ancient Mass suddenly gained a big new following, both lay and clerical. These new trads had to confront the fact that until five minutes earlier papal policy had been not only misguided, but unjust and even theologically problematic, according to the reigning Pope himself. As Pope Benedict put it, the liturgical discontinuity represented by the complete obliteration of the older Missal created a hole in the heart of the Church, between the present and the past, which "called her very being into question." This insight of Pope Benedict's is absolutely critical, and having argued it before his election, he refers to it again in the Letter to Bishops which accompanied *Summorum Pontificum*, and cites it as his key motivation for that document, in his post-abdication book-interview *Last Testament*.

Although just as eager to obey Pope Benedict as they had been to obey Pope John Paul II, this admission of Pope Benedict's fatally weakened the classical conservative position. It has forced the more thoughtful conservatives to find a new way of defending the Church's doctrines: not merely because the Pope says so, and Jesus Christ gave the Pope authority, but because they are established by the Traditions of the Church, hang together, and make sense: in short, a Traditionalist approach. This way of going about apologetics puts the ancient liturgy on the inside of the set of things which should be defended, not out in the cold: it becomes a limb of the baby, not part of the bath-water. For the liturgy is also the product of tradition, and not only coheres with doctrine, but as Pope Benedict also reminded us, it is a theological source: a proper basis for arguments to theological conclusions.

It has been into this fatally weakened hyperpapalism that Pope Francis collided. With the Family Synods and *Amoris Laetitia* he overturned the expectation that the Pope would always exercise his authority in a conservative direction on the hot-button issues of doctrine and discipline:

contraception, same-sex attraction, and divorce. Long-term proponents of the conservative position like George Weigel, the late Germain Grisez, and Fr. Thomas Weinandy, and conservative institutions like First Things and EWTN, at first struggled to accommodate Pope Francis's eccentricities into their outlook, and then redefined themselves as the Loyal Opposition. It might look as though their papalism was only ever of instrumental importance to them, but to be fair one could say that the combination of Benedict and Francis has shown that the position was simply untenable. As this point one either turns into an unabashed papal positivist without any fixed theological beliefs at all, like the hard-core Francis fanatics on Twitter, or one maintains some modicum of intellectual self-respect.

In this context, it is not surprising that Traditionis Custodes has been greeted by a chorus of criticism from across the spectrum of opinion. Again and again I have read people say: I don't regularly attend the Traditional Mass, but..., or I have only recently starting attending, and... People, that is, who have not drunk very deeply, or at all, of any Traditional Catholic critique of Vatican II or of the Liturgical Reform, have been thrown into opposition to Pope Francis.

Conservative Catholicism as a way of interpreting the world can no longer insist on obedience to every word which falls from the Papal lips. And the ancient Mass itself is no longer completely outside their experience as a live liturgical option: they can in many cases see the effect it has had on friends and family members, and even on themselves.

It is interesting to note that at the same time liberal Catholics have also been put in a difficult position by Traditionis Custodes. Their hopes for Pope Francis as the man to deliver their agenda have already largely been dashed. That might sound odd, given the consternation of conservatives over Amoris Laetitia, but liberals wanted a clear green light for remarriage after divorce, female ordination, contraception, and their other favourite things. They have not had it, and it no longer looks to anyone as though they are going to get it from Pope Francis.

The most they have had is an emphasis on pastoral concern in preference to rules. But this, vague as it is, seems in complete contradiction to the tone and content of Traditionis Custodes. Where, one may ask, is the accompaniment? Where is the hagan lío, the mess-making? Instead we are offered regimentation and uniformity, to be enforced with sweeping Papal commands. Thus we find even liberal Catholics, like Catherine Pepinster, the former editor of The Tablet, expressing grave misgivings about Pope Francis's apparently arbitrary use of papal power.

7. TRADITIONIS CUSTODES AND THE BISHOPS

The Apostolic Letter also causes a problem for the bishops of the world. Some, of course, will be pleased to be given the moral authority to clamp down on celebrations of the old Mass, and presumably it is these whose views are reflected in the document. These, however, are very few. They include the handful of bishops whose predecessors had been significantly more friendly to the Traditional Mass than they are themselves. For nearly every other bishop in the world, however, the situation of the Traditional Mass in their dioceses, whether completely absent, plentifully present, or somewhere in between, is more or less what they already want it to be.

Summorum Pontificum made a big difference, but the difference it made was not a matter of bishops being forced to allow celebrations. Occasionally they may have been shamed into allowing them, but no bishop was ever removed from office for refusing to comply. It gave a psychological boost to the cause for the Traditional Mass, which meant that as the years passed there were more and more places in which the bishop's diminishing aversion to it ceased to outweigh increasing demands for it from priests and people. It helped that there were more and more priests available to celebrate it, whether from the Traditional Priestly Institutes or the younger generation of diocesan priests, and, in the context of the accelerating decline of the Church in the developed world, an ever-increasing number of redundant church buildings.

This meant that by negotiation, experimentation, and taking the opportunities of manpower and real estate which presented themselves in the course of time, establishing or allowing celebrations of the Old Mass solved problems for the bishops: what to do with an historic church, how to get a group of Traditional Catholics off his back, how to satisfy the desires of certain priests. Once that had happened, bishops would often begin to appreciate the fruits of the apostolates which emerged: the marriages and baptisms, the feeling of being treated like a real old-fashioned bishop when visiting the parish, the outsized financial contributions, and above all the vocations, many of them coming into the diocesan seminary.

Sometimes the path of least resistance is also the right thing to do. There are now scores of bishops who have experienced this around the world. *Traditionis Custodes* has given them, not the power to solve a problem they had, but a new problem that they did not want.

What the path of least resistance now means for these bishops, the ones not strongly motivated by ideology, today depends on a complex calculation. Some may feel that they should make a show of implementing the Apostolic

Letter to avoid blotting their copy-books with the Nuncio. How important that is may depend on the Nuncio, the attitude of neighbouring bishops, and the bishop's personal ambitions. Others will repeat a form of words about complying but find canonical and pastoral arguments for doing precisely nothing. These arguments, indeed, are perfectly respectable ones, and the Latin Mass Society has contributed to their development.

The overall effect will certainly be a fall in the number of celebrations and traditional apostolates, but it is already becoming manifest that passive resistance to the Apostolic Letter among bishops is going to be extremely widespread. Having accepted, in some measure at least, Pope Benedict's policy over the last fourteen years, it is difficult for them to see why they should suddenly go into reverse gear.

8. AFTER TRADITIONIS CUSTODES

Where does that leave us, lay Catholics attached to the ancient Mass?

The Latin Mass Society and Una Voce groups around the world have been making the case for bishops to allow celebrations of the Old Mass for fifty years. In most places, until 2007, it was like getting blood out of a stone. In a lot of places it carried on being like that. I could cite many cases in Africa, Latin America, Asia, and southern Europe, where *Summorum Pontificum* had yet to arrive when *Traditionis Custodes* was published.

Traditionis Custodes does not change the task of the Latin Mass movement. Pope Francis allows the old Mass to continue where the good of souls requires it, and we will continue to explain to bishops that for the good of souls this or that Traditional Mass centre should be maintained, or that this or that Traditional Pilgrimage or Retreat should be allowed, in accordance with the law of the Church and in union of faith and charity with the bishop and the Holy Father. The more sympathetic bishops will listen to our arguments, and the less sympathetic ones will not. We will continue to do the work of preparing music, training altar servers, mending vestments, teaching Latin, encouraging priests to learn the old Mass, organising events, and maintaining a network of mutual encouragement and support.

We will not be returning to the situation of 1969, however, because the balance of forces in the Church has changed radically since then. Pope Francis's power to make things happen, either by moral leadership or by legislation, is low by historical standards. He can no longer count on slavish obedience from conservative hyperpapalists, or from liberals hoping for concessions. He has consistently and deliberately played down the office of the Papacy, its prerogatives and prestige, and the place of rules in the

Church. He has shown little interest in the Roman Curia, except to criticise its staff. To cap it all, his recent major operation has reminded the ambitious of his mortality.

Bishops are not going to ignore *Traditionis Custodes*, but it would hardly be the first time for them that implementing a missive from the Vatican has had to be balanced against other considerations.

In this interesting situation, the movement for the Latin Mass may not flourish, but it will certainly survive. In the medium term it doesn't seem too fanciful to imagine an incoming Pope surveying the scene and deciding that more problems can be solved by lifting restrictions on the celebration of the ancient Mass than by keeping them in place. The reality of cohabitation between the two forms of Mass, which in many places will still be in place from before *Traditionis Custodes*, will then be officially confirmed once more.

In that case, the movement for the Traditional Mass will bounce back. Things will not be the same again, however, because after such a series of policy reversals Papal prestige will be seriously weakened. In the future, the fate of the new and old Masses will not be determined by the fancies of the reigning Pope, but on the basis of their pastoral and theological merits, worked out in practice, locally. This may be a bit chaotic, but the ancient Mass will be able to reach more and more people. To return to a point I made at the beginning of this presentation, we will see its power to draw people in, not to a private experience which they happen to prefer, but to the centre of the Church's spirituality and teaching.

53

Three Rhetorical Questions about Vatican II and Tradition

PHIL LAWLER

CatholicCulture.org

August 11, 2021

THE PROMULGATION OF TRADITIONIS CUSTODES HAS given new urgency to an old debate about interpretation of the Second Vatican Council. Pope Francis believes that Catholics who prefer the traditional Latin Mass are likely to reject the Council's teachings. Traditionalists counter that the Council's teachings—in particular, those on the reform of the liturgy—have been regularly ignored. And so we return yet again to the question of whether the "spirit of Vatican II," so frequently invoked by liberal Catholics, is at odds with the Council's actual work.

It is odd, isn't it, that fifty years after the Council, there is no settled consensus on what the Council fathers taught? Disagreement about nuances of theology would be understandable, but in this case, competent theologians hold utterly incompatible views, and cite the Council to support them. There is precedent for fierce disputes in the wake of Church councils; one recalls that the Oriental Orthodox churches split with Rome over the Christological definitions of the Council of Chalcedon. But has there ever before been such a profound division of opinion about what the Council said?

With very little hope of resolving that old argument — since the opposing sides have been digging into their fortified positions for several decades now — let me ask a few rhetorical questions, which might at least help clarify the situation we now face.

1. *Should we interpret the teachings of Vatican II in the light of tradition, or interpret tradition in the light of Vatican II?*

This is essentially the question that Pope Benedict XVI raised, when he decried the "hermeneutic of rupture" that has led many theologians to suggest that the Second Vatican Council marked a radical break with previous Church teachings.

In *Traditionis,* Pope Francis argues rightly that a believing Catholic cannot reject the work of an ecumenical council without calling into question the doctrinal tenet that the Holy Spirit guides the work of the Church. But by the same logic, a faithful Catholic cannot accept the notion that the Church was misguided for centuries; the Holy Spirit was at work *before* Vatican II as well. The "hermeneutic of continuity" — the understanding that the Council *could not* fundamentally change Church teaching, but only clarify and develop what was already taught — is the only option available to a faithful Catholic. So the Council must be properly understood through the perspective of the Church's constant tradition. If there are passages in the Council documents that appear to conflict with that tradition, then further clarification, further development, or even perhaps simple correction is necessary.

2. *Did the Council wish for the Church to engage with the modern world, or to be guided by the modern world?*

The eras of the Reformation, the Enlightenment, and the French Revolution had driven the Church into a defensive posture vis-à-vis modernity. Pope John XXIII saw a need to sally forth from the ecclesiastical fortress, to open fresh lines of communication with the secular world. But did he, or did the Council fathers, intend that the Church should judge her successes and failures according to the standards of that secular world? Certainly not. On the contrary, the Council exhorted lay Christians to transform the secular world through the power of the Gospel.

Today, unfortunately, that exhortation is too often reduced to a suggestion that Christians should concentrate on the "good works" that our secular society recognizes — to the detriment of the prophetic witness that the Church offers when Christians condemn the evils of a society that tramples on the dignity of human life.

Which brings me to my third and final rhetorical question.

3. *Did the Council proclaim the universal call to holiness, or the universal call of holiness?*

That is, did the Council fathers teach that all Christians are called to sanctify themselves and the world around them? Or did they teach that all Christians are *already* sanctified, and should be encouraged and praised in every action they undertake? Were we Catholics enjoined to make the world holy, or to recognize the world as already holy?

The quest for holiness is an arduous campaign, whereas a complacent Church would be satisfied to set lower standards, to accept personal failings, to wink at minor transgressions. The reader can judge for himself whether, for instance, the "synodal path" of the German hierarchy will lead to holiness or to complacency.

There may indeed be some traditionalist Catholics who reject all the teachings of Vatican II. But there are far more, I submit, who recognize that something has gone seriously awry within the Church in the past few generations. And if the problems of Catholicism cannot be blamed on the Council — because those problems were in evidence before the Council fathers gathered — it is also sadly evident that the Council did not *solve* all the problems. So earnest Catholics look further back into the traditions of the Church to find a sure foundation on which to build.

54

Pope Francis Is Tearing the Catholic Church Apart[†]

MICHAEL BRENDAN DOUGHERTY

New York Times

August 12, 2021

IN THE SUMMER OF 2001, I DROVE UP TO POUGHKEEP-sie, N.Y., to find what we called "the traditional Latin Mass," the form of Roman Catholic worship that stretched back centuries and was last authorized in 1962, before the Second Vatican Council changed everything. Back then, conservative Catholics called people who sought it out "schismatics" and "Rad Trads."

The Mass-goers there weren't exactly a community; we were a clandestine network of romantics, haters of Pope John Paul II, people who had been jilted by the mainstream church and — I believe — some saints.

There I learned that the Latin language was not the only distinguishing feature of this form of worship. The entire ritual was different from the post-Vatican II Mass. It wasn't a mere translation into the modern vernacular; less than twenty percent of the Latin Mass survived into the new.

It took me a month to adapt to its rhythm. But in that thick August air, the long silence before the consecration of the host fell upon my heart, like sunshine landing on the bud of prayer for the very first time.

Years later, Pope Benedict allowed devotees of this Mass to flourish in the mainstream of Catholic life, a gesture that began to drain away the traditional movement's radicalism and reconcile us with our bishops. Today, it is celebrated in thriving parishes, full of young families.

Yet this Mass and the modestly growing contingent of Catholics who attend it are seen by Pope Francis as a grave problem. He recently released a document, *Traditionis Custodes*, accusing Catholics like us of being subversives. To protect the "unity" of the church, he abolished the permissions Pope Benedict XVI gave us in 2007 to celebrate a liturgy, the heart of which remains unchanged since the seventh century.

For those of us who travel long distances to participate in it, its perseverance is a religious duty. For the pope, its suppression is a religious priority. The ferocity of his campaign will push these young families and communities toward the radicalism I imbibed years ago in Poughkeepsie, before Benedict. It will push them toward the belief that the new Mass represents a new religion, one dedicated to the unity of man on earth rather than the love of Christ.

In the Latin Mass, the priest faces the altar with the people. It never has oddities, as you sometimes encounter in a modern Mass, like balloons, guitar music or applause. The gabby religious talk-show host style of priest is gone. In his place, a priest who does his business quietly, a workmanlike sculptor. By directing the priest toward the drama at the altar, the old Mass opens up space for our own prayer and contemplation.

In the years after Pope Benedict liberalized the old rite, parishes began to bring back the mystical tones of Gregorian chant, the sacred polyphony written by long-dead composers like Orlando Lassus and Thomas Tallis as well as contemporary composers like Nicholas Wilton and David Hughes.

These cultural offshoots of the Latin Mass are why, after Vatican II, the English novelists Agatha Christie and Nancy Mitford and other British cultural luminaries sent a letter to Pope Paul VI asking that it continue. Their letter doesn't even pretend to be from believing Christians. "The rite in question, in its magnificent Latin text, has also inspired a host of priceless achievements in the arts — not only mystical works, but works by poets, philosophers, musicians, architects, painters and sculptors in all countries and epochs. Thus, it belongs to universal culture as well as to churchmen and formal Christians."

But the Vatican Council had called for a revision of every aspect of the central act of worship, so the altar rails, tabernacles and baldachins were torn up in countless parishes. This ferment was accompanied by radical new theologies around the Mass.[1] A freshman religious studies major would know that revising all the vocal and physical aspects of a ceremony and changing the rationale for it constitutes a true change of religion. Only overconfident Catholic bishops could imagine otherwise.

The most candid progressives agreed with the radical traditionalists that the council constituted a break with the past. They called Vatican II "a new Pentecost" — an "Event" — that had given the church a new self-understanding. They believed their revolution had been stalled in 1968 when Pope Paul VI issued Humanae Vitae, affirming the church's opposition

---

1   Like those of Schillebeeckx, Rahner, and Küng.

to artificial contraception, and then put on ice in 1978 with the election of Pope John Paul II.

To stamp out the old Latin Mass, Pope Francis is using the papacy in precisely the way that progressives once claimed to deplore: He centralizes power in Rome, usurps the local bishop's prerogatives and institutes a micromanaging style that is motivated by paranoia of disloyalty and heresy. Perhaps it's to protect his deepest beliefs.

Pope Francis envisions that we will return to the new Mass. My children cannot return to it; it is not their religious formation. Frankly, the new Mass is not their religion. In countless alterations, the belief that the Mass was a real sacrifice and that the bread and wine, once consecrated, became the body and blood of our Lord was downplayed or replaced in it. With the priest facing the people, the altar was severed from the tabernacle. The prescribed prayers of the new Mass tended never even to refer to that structure anymore as an altar but as the Lord's table. The prayers that pointed to the Lord's real presence in the sacrament were conspicuously replaced with ones emphasizing the Lord's spiritual presence in the assembled congregation. [2]

The prayers of the traditional Mass emphasized that the priest was representing the same sacrifice Christ made at Calvary, one that propitiated God's wrath at sin and reconciled humanity to God. The new Mass portrayed itself as a narrative and historical remembrance of the events recalled in Scripture, and the offering and sacrifice was not of Christ, but of the assembled people, as the most commonly used Eucharistic prayer in the new Mass says: "from age to age you gather a people to yourself, in order that from east to west a perfect offering may be made." [3]

For Catholics, how we pray shapes what we believe. The old ritual physically aims us toward an altar and tabernacle. In that way it points us to the cross and to heaven as the ultimate horizon of man's existence. By doing so, it shows that God graciously loves us and redeems us despite our sins. And the proof is in the culture this ritual produces. Think of Mozart's great rendition of faith in the Eucharist: *Ave Verum Corpus* (Hail, True Body).

The new ritual points us toward a bare table, and it consistently posits

---

2 See Alfredo Cardinal Ottaviani and Antonio Cardinal Bacci, *The Ottaviani Intervention: Short Critical Study of the New Order of Mass*, trans. Anthony Cekada (West Chester, OH: Philothea Press, 2010).

3 In a new edition of the new missal in 2011, this was replaced with the following more accurate translation: "You never cease to gather a people to yourself, so that from the rising of the sun to its setting a pure sacrifice may be offered to your name."

the unity of humankind as the ultimate horizon of our existence. In the new Mass, God owes man salvation, because of the innate dignity of humanity. Where there was faith, now presumption. Where there was love, now mere affirmation, which is indistinguishable from indifference. It inspires weightless ditties like "Gather Us In." Let's sing about us!

I believe the practice of the new Mass forms people to a new faith: To become truly Christian, one must cease to be Christian at all. Where the new faith is practiced with a zealous spirit — as in Germany now — bishops and priests want to conform the religion's teaching to the moral norms of the nonbelieving society around them. When the new faith was young, after the council, it expressed itself in tearing up the statues, the ceremonies and religious devotions that existed before.

I don't know if bishops will adopt Francis's zeal to crush the Latin Mass. I don't know how painful they are willing to make our religious life. If they do, they will create — or reveal — more division in the church. The old slogan of the traditional Latin Mass movement comes to mind: We resist you to the face.

I have faith that one day, even secular historians will look upon what was wrought after Vatican II and see it for what it was: the worst spasm of iconoclasm in the church's history — dwarfing the Byzantine iconoclasm of the ninth century and the Protestant Reformation.

Pope Benedict had temporarily allowed us to begin repairing the damage. What Pope Francis proposes with his crackdown is a new cover-up.

55

Why Restricting the TLM Harms Every Parish Mass

PETER A. KWASNIEWSKI

Crisis Magazine

August 13, 2021

THANKS TO THE INSPIRATION OF JOSEPH RATZINGER'S writings on liturgy, and especially the "rising tide" effect of *Summorum Pontificum*, a grass-roots movement to restore sacredness to the modern rite of Paul VI was in full swing. It was not Vatican decrees or diocesan reforms that yielded better Masses, but rather the influence of priests who were either trained in the traditional Latin Mass or picked up the "vibe" by reading articles, watching videos, and observing their brethren.

Clergy carried over traditional habits and rubrics into the new Mass. Soon one saw the old vestments returning. The finger and thumb were held together from consecration to ablution. Laity were encouraged to receive Communion kneeling and on the tongue. Some daring clergy started to face eastward as they offered the Holy Sacrifice, making use of the long-neglected Roman Canon and sometimes speaking in a more subdued tone. Latin and Gregorian chant migrated from the *Missa cantata* to the main parish Mass; at times, even the amice, maniple, and biretta came across the divide. Such gentle, unthreatening reinforcements from an older piety were expressions of that "mutual enrichment" Benedict had hoped would occur, although we have to say the enrichment was going mostly in a single direction: it was the young, half-dressed waif who needed the clothing, not the regally-attired monarch.

Nor is this phenomenon surprising. The Tridentine Mass is like the great old tree on which — in the most optimistic interpretation — the branch of the Novus Ordo has been grafted and from which it lives. The roots bring it water and nutrients; cut off from the roots, it withers and dies. If you take away the Roman template, you take away the knowledge of how a Catholic liturgy looks, sounds, and functions.

Over the decades, many have complained about the glaring lack of rubrical detail and of normative structure in the rite of Paul VI: so many options, so many possible realizations, so little that is set in stone and inflexibly followed. This is why Msgr. Peter J. Elliott had to write his own series of manuals — not only to resolve tiny details, as had been the case with preconciliar rubrical guides, but to provide an entire *ars celebrandi* that the missal and its general instruction lack. All of this was "reverse engineered" from the Tridentine rite. Now that Pope Francis is attempting to cut off that rite as no longer the *lex orandi* or even the *lex credendi* of the Latin-rite Church, the Novus Ordo has been set adrift more than ever, orphaned from its own family.

In addition to the already considerable obstacles faced by proponents of a "reform of the reform,"[1] *Traditionis Custodes* now adds the supreme obstacle of an ideological skepticism directed at the millennial tradition of the Catholic Church. What was sacred and great in the liturgy of the past — including, for example, the Latin language, Gregorian chant, a prominent place for silence, certain kinds of vestments and altar vessels, the regular use of incense — now falls under a cloud of suspicion, an implicit disapproval for its "Tridentinism." "For many," writes Shawn Tribe of *Liturgical Arts Journal*, "it is about breaking with everything that has shaped the liturgical and ecclesiastical patrimony."[2]

That this interpretation will indeed be given to the motu proprio is already obvious from the way certain bishops and groups of bishops are "reading between the lines" by outlawing not only the Latin Mass but also anything supposedly derived from it or influenced by it. The bishops of Costa Rica wrote in their decree of implementation:

> In particular today we must remember that our liturgy, celebrated according to the books promulgated by Saints Paul VI and John Paul II, must be preserved from any element coming from ancient

---

1   See my article "Why the 'Reform of the Reform' Is Doomed," *OnePeterFive*, April 22, 2020.

2   Note, in this regard, that the Vatican's publisher, Libreria Editrice Vaticana, has made it clear that it has no plans to reprint the reformed breviary (*Liturgia Horarum*) in Latin (see Fr. John Zuhlsdorf, "Can't get 'Liturgy of the Hours' in Latin," Fr. Z's *Blog*, September 6, 2017; a search in September 2021 of the LEV website confirms it). Moreover, the last time a Latin edition of the new lectionary was published was 1972; the four-volume *Missale Romanum cum lectionibus* (1977) has also never been republished. Neither of these lectionaries use the current neo-Vulgate text from 1986, which means there is no current edition of the *Lectionarium* that can be used in Novus Ordo Masses. While conducting the entire service in Latin is not likely to be a high-demand option outside of a rare monastery, this lack of availability indicates a salient and symbolic point: there is presently no way to do the reformed "Latin-rite" liturgy in Latin, and apparently no interest in making it possible.

forms. The prayers, vestments, or rites that were characteristic of the liturgy prior to the 1970s reform should not be introduced into our celebrations.

After altogether prohibiting the older form of the liturgy in his diocese in Puerto Rico, Bishop Ángel Luis Ríos-Matos added, for good effect:

> I also make provision that in our Eucharistic celebrations, with or without the people present, the Gothic chasuble shall be worn, avoiding the use of the Roman chasuble, biretta, copes, linen tablecloths, humeral veils, burses, maniples, and other ornaments appropriate to such a rite.

Since most of these items have always been allowed in the context of the Novus Ordo, the list of contraband reveals the hierarch's profound liturgical ignorance; but try to tell a bishop that he is ignorant and see how far you get.

Bishop Anthony Taylor of Little Rock, one of the first and swiftest to cancel diocesan Latin Masses, reminded his people that "elements of the Traditional Latin Mass are not to be grafted onto the Novus Ordo Mass." Bishop Taylor might simply be referring to a clumsy mingling of the two different forms, but such language welcomes a broad interpretation.

In past years, I myself was accused more than once of trying to "Tridentinize" the Novus Ordo — for example, if I had the schola sing the Gradual chant instead of the usual responsorial psalm, even though the *General Instruction of the Roman Missal* allows for that option. It is not so easy to overcome fifty years of bad or shallow liturgical habits. It will be even more difficult when the younger generation's burgeoning love for Catholic tradition is stigmatized as harmful and quasi-schismatic.

If "acceptance of Vatican II" (in all the manipulable and open-ended vagueness of that expression) is now the litmus test that will separate Catholics who belong to the Church from those who do not belong, and if the liturgical reform *exactly as it played out in the late sixties* is to be equated with the will of the Council and of "the popes of the Council," then it follows that the Novus Ordo as it is celebrated today and forever must be as greatly *novus* and as little *vetus* as possible. That is why Pope Francis's statement that the new liturgy should be celebrated with "decorum and fidelity to the new liturgical books . . . without eccentricities and abuses" is, in fact, cold comfort; for all the popes have said similar things over the past half-century, and little had actually changed for the better — except on account of the *Summorum Pontificum* knock-on effect.

The next time you're hankering for a bit of Gregorian chant or a prayer in Latin or the common turning to the east (*ad orientem*), remember that such "preconciliar" things are *verboten*: they are old, they have been superseded by the momentum of the liturgical reform. If you try to point out that Vatican II said nothing about getting rid of such things and even spoke appreciatively of them, you will be silenced in the name of the "Living Magisterium," which claims to be the sole correct interpreter and implementer of Vatican II. [3]

In other words, your literacy, your education, your *sensus fidei*, your love of tradition, your desire to be faithful to what the Council actually said — all of this is *irrelevant*. Worse, it is *irreverent*. You are not allowed to question the rupture masquerading as fidelity.

How much this contrasts with the teaching — not just the policy — of Benedict XVI is not difficult to see. In his Letter to Bishops on March 10, 2009, that pope wrote:

> Some of those who put themselves forward as great defenders of the Council also need to be reminded that Vatican II embraces the entire doctrinal history of the Church. Anyone who wishes to be obedient to the Council has to accept the faith professed over the centuries, and cannot sever the roots from which the tree draws its life.

Where, pray tell, has the faith been more "professed over the centuries" than in the venerable Roman liturgy itself?

One of the salutary effects of Francis's act of *traditio* — a word that can also mean betrayal: the betrayal of his living predecessor and of many of the faithful — may be to deliver modern "conservative" and "traditionalist" Catholics from their false ideas about papal authority, which has tempted them to be morally slothful and intellectually suicidal. Drawing on a broader and deeper tradition than the often-simplistic reception (or

---

3   It bears recalling that it was never Paul VI's intention that the Novus Ordo be celebrated in Latin with Gregorian chant, apart from in a few monasteries with no pastoral care. Rather, he said the Church must bid farewell to these treasures for the sake of apostolic outreach to the modern world. (As to how well this evangelistic strategy has worked, we need only consider the initial exodus of Catholics from the Mass during the period of volatile change, and then the plummeting Mass attendance rates every decade since the Council.) For full documentation of Paul VI's repudiation of the liturgical "hermeneutic of continuity" prized by the Reform of the Reform, see my lecture "A Half-Century of Novelty: Revisiting Paul VI's *Apologia* for the New Mass," *Rorate Caeli*, April 2, 2019.

rather, extrapolation) of Vatican I, we need to arrive at a truer idea of papal authority, one that does not require us to abdicate our reason or put the demands of faith aside in service of the papal agenda *du jour*.

An attack on the elder brother is an attack on the whole family. The sooner today's conservatives realize this, the more quickly they will join forces with their traditionalist brethren in refusing to accept *Traditionis Custodes* and resisting its implementation in every possible way. If they throw their traditional brethren under the bus in the hopes of currying favor and improving their fortunes, they will quickly discover that the revolution consumes moderates as much as it does the standard-bearers of the *ancien régime*. The drive to impose the spirit of Vatican II will flatten the loyal defenders of the sixteen documents ("but we're only trying to follow *Sacrosanctum Concilium!*") as much as it will the Council's fiercest critics.

Make no mistake: rejecting a whispered low Mass today will mean the rejection of an *ad orientem* parish Mass tomorrow; rejecting a biretta and maniple today will mean the rejection of the entire ensemble of smells and bells tomorrow. The movement of *Adoremus* depends on the immobility of *Quo Primum*. This will seem like a paradox only to one who does not understand that tradition is not a flowing river, always in flux, but a foundation of rock on which the Church's life can be safely built. Any time the Novus Ordo rises above its 1970s minimalism or mediocrity to the heights of magnificence and mystery, it is owing to the magnetism of a tradition that stands above and beyond it.

56

Tradition Devoured by the Magisterium[†]

RUBÉN PERETÓ RIVAS

Caminante Wanderer

August 14, 2021

I WOULD LIKE TO PROPOSE A THESIS: IN THE COURSE of the centuries, and especially after the Council of Trent, there has been a shift from an objective notion of Tradition as a revealed deposit to a subjective notion, which insists above all on the organ that proposes the truth—that is, the Magisterium. In scholastic terms, there has been a transition from *quod* to *quo*.

Whoever studies the *Summa theologiae* will see that the theological method St. Thomas applies is not the one that, according to modern manuals, must be followed to prove a theological proposition. This would consist rather of proof by the Magisterium, proof by Scripture, and proof by Tradition. In St. Thomas, however, there is no proof by the Magisterium; for him the *auctoritates* are Scripture and the Fathers. Quotations from popes or councils are scarce.

If we take up Denzinger, we will see that the first thirteen centuries of the Church — that is, up to the death of St. Thomas — account for only *one-fifth* of the total interventions of the Magisterium. And we could continue to add significant data: the word "magisterium" does not appear at the Council of Trent, but the notion begins to take shape from Stapleton at the end of the sixteenth century, and especially in the theological treatises of the eighteenth century such as those of Mayr, Gotti, and Billuart.

All this does not mean — and it is important to clarify this — that the primacy of the Roman See is in doubt; it is simply to note that before modern times this See did not exercise the active magisterium of dogmatic definitions and constant formulation of Catholic doctrine that it has exercised since the pontificates of Gregory XVI and, above all, of Pius IX. In antiquity, the Roman See functioned more like a supreme court of last

† Translated from the Spanish by Peter Kwasniewski and published at *Rorate Caeli* on September 1, 2021.

appeal, acting only once the question under dispute had been studied and broken down by doctors, theological schools, universities, and local councils.

We can say roughly that in the first centuries and until well into the second millennium, the *regula fidei* was objective, that is, it was the same doctrine received from the Apostles, and that the popes, councils, and bishops fulfilled a function of conservation and of testifying to the fact that a doctrine had always been maintained — that it went back to the origins and therefore belonged to the aforesaid *regula fidei*.

What can be observed is that a kind of reduction of Tradition to the Magisterium has been slowly taking place since the beginning of the second millennium and more rapidly in the last few centuries. There was a transition from conceiving Tradition as the content of the Apostolic Deposit to conceiving Tradition from the vantage of the transmitting organ, considered as residing in the Church's Magisterium. The next step was to speak, probably beginning in the nineteenth century, of Tradition and Scripture as "remote rules" of faith, while the Magisterium would be the "proximate rule." Theologians of the early twentieth century already speak of the Magisterium as having a formal function in relation to the objective deposit. Finally, the notion of remote rule is criticized, and the conclusion is reached of attributing the quality of rule of faith exclusively to the "living Magisterium." With this process, the Magisterium has been introduced into the very definition of Tradition. To put it in an exaggerated way, Catholics today believe in Tradition because the Magisterium commands it. And for this reason, the faithful today wait for the Pope to pronounce on this or that matter, in order to know what to believe. And they obey slavishly in absolutely everything that the pope of the day comes up with, even his gestures or personal tastes.

This is not what happened during the first fifteen centuries of the Church. When a pope (or a council with the pope) spoke, it was because the situation was truly critical — for example, the Arian crisis, or Nestorianism, Monophysitism, Protestantism, Jansenism, Modernism, etc.

The most ultramontane positions could argue that the First Vatican Council defined, as a matter *de fide*, that the Roman Pontiff possesses universal, supreme, and immediate power even in jurisdictional and disciplinary matters, and whoever does not wish to accept it, *anathema sit* (Denzinger 1821–1831); therefore, the foregoing thesis could be seen as an attack against this dogma of faith.

It is definitely not so, because what is questioned is not the pope's universal power but the papal absolutism of the second millennium. Supreme power is not equivalent to absolutism, which is the same power taken to excess.

On the other hand, it is necessary to be precise about what is understood by "supreme and universal power," since many consider that it empowers the Roman Pontiff to do whatever he wants. This is not so. There are many things the pope cannot do. He cannot suppress institutions of divine right. He cannot suppress the episcopal order. He cannot abrogate sacraments. He cannot modify or annul the commandments. He cannot admit someone in mortal sin to sacramental communion. He cannot bless morally evil acts.

And above all, there is a general principle of natural law that applies to any authority: commands must be rational. If a command is not ordered by reason, it is not law but force and violence. And while the pope cannot be judged by anyone on earth, his manifestly irrational laws or commands can be resisted. For example, even if the pope did not like people of color, he could not suppress the African dioceses; nor could he ordain all the males of his family bishops to give luster to the Bergoglios. If he does not like kibbeh and sfiha, he could not suppress the Maronite rite; and we could give other examples of irrationalities that a pope could not do — in regard to which, were he to do them, it would be licit, if not obligatory, to resist him.

Finally, an argument from authority. When Benedict XVI took office as Bishop of Rome in the Basilica of St. John Lateran, he said in his homily: "The pope is not an absolute monarch whose thoughts and desires are law." And while still prefect of the Congregation for the Doctrine of the Faith, he wrote: "The pope is not an absolute monarch whose will is law; rather, he is the guardian of the authentic Tradition and, thereby, the premier guarantor of obedience. He cannot do as he likes, and he is thereby able to oppose those people who, for their part, want to do whatever comes into their head. His rule is not that of arbitrary power, but that of obedience in faith." [1]

In light of the above thesis and the words of Pope Benedict XVI, it is worth asking, once again, to what extent the despotic act with which Francis has suffocated the traditional liturgy through *Traditionis Custodes* should be obeyed — thus ceasing to be the "guardian of authentic tradition" and becoming its executioner.

---

1   Reid, *Organic Development of the Liturgy*, 10–11.

57

On the Credibility of the Catholic Church[†]

CARDINAL ROBERT SARAH

Le Figaro
August 14, 2021

DOUBT HAS TAKEN HOLD OF WESTERN THOUGHT. Intellectuals and politicians alike describe the same impression of collapse. Faced with the breakdown of solidarity and the disintegration of identities, some turn to the Catholic Church. They ask her to give a reason to live together to individuals who have forgotten what unites them as one people. They beg her to provide a little more soul to make the cold harshness of consumer society bearable. When a priest is murdered, everyone is touched and many feel stricken to the core.

But is the Church capable of responding to these calls? Certainly, she has already played this role of guardian and transmitter of civilization. At the twilight of the Roman Empire, she knew how to pass on the flame that the barbarians were threatening to extinguish. But does she still have the means and the will to do so today?

At the foundation of a civilization, there can only be one reality that surpasses it: a sacred invariant. Malraux noted this with realism: "The nature of a civilization is what gathers around a religion. Our civilization is incapable of building a temple or a tomb. It will either be forced to find its fundamental value, or it will decay."

Without a sacred foundation, protective and insuperable boundaries are abolished. An entirely profane world becomes a vast expanse of quicksand. Everything is sadly open to the winds of arbitrariness. In the absence of the stability of a foundation that escapes man, peace and joy — the signs of a long-lasting civilization — are constantly swallowed up by a sense of precariousness. The anguish of imminent danger is the seal of barbaric times. Without a sacred foundation, every bond becomes fragile and fickle.

[†] Originally in French; the *National Catholic Register* published on the same date a translation provided by the author. © 2021 EWTN News, Inc. Reprinted with permission from the *National Catholic Register*–www.ncregister.com.

Some ask the Catholic Church to play this solid foundation role. They would like to see her assume a social function, namely to be a coherent system of values, a cultural and aesthetic matrix. But the Church has no other sacred reality to offer than her faith in Jesus, God made man. Her sole goal is to make possible the encounter of men with the person of Jesus. Moral and dogmatic teaching, as well as mystical and liturgical patrimony, are the setting and the means of this fundamental and sacred encounter. Christian civilization is born of this encounter. Beauty and culture are its fruits.

In order to respond to the world's expectations, the Church must therefore find the way back to herself and take up the words of Saint Paul: "For I resolved to know nothing while I was with you except Jesus Christ, and Jesus crucified." She must stop thinking of herself as a substitute for humanism or ecology. These realities, although good and just, are for her but consequences of her unique treasure: faith in Jesus Christ.

What is sacred for the Church, then, is the unbroken chain that links her with certainty to Jesus. A chain of faith without rupture or contradiction, a chain of prayer and liturgy without breakage or disavowal. Without this radical continuity, what credibility could the Church still claim? In her, there is no turning back, but an organic and continuous development that we call the living tradition. The sacred cannot be decreed, it is received from God and passed on.

This is undoubtedly the reason for which Benedict XVI could authoritatively affirm: "In the history of the liturgy there is growth and progress, but no rupture. What earlier generations held as sacred, remains sacred and great for us too, and it cannot be all of a sudden entirely forbidden or even considered harmful. It behooves all of us to preserve the riches which have developed in the Church's faith and prayer, and to give them their proper place."

At a time when some theologians are seeking to reopen the liturgy wars by pitting the missal revised by the Council of Trent against the one in use since 1970, it is urgent to recall this. If the Church is not capable of preserving the peaceful continuity of her link with Christ, she will be unable to offer the world "the sacred which unites souls," according to the words of Goethe.

Beyond the quarrel over rites, the credibility of the Church is at stake. If she affirms the continuity between what is commonly called the Mass of St. Pius V and the Mass of Paul VI, then the Church must be able to organize their peaceful cohabitation and their mutual enrichment. If one were to radically exclude one in favor of the other, if one were to declare them irreconcilable, one would implicitly recognize a rupture and a change of orientation. But then the Church could no longer offer the world that sacred continuity, which alone can give her peace. By keeping alive a liturgical war within herself, the Church loses her credibility and becomes deaf to the call of men. Liturgical peace is the sign of the peace that the Church can bring to the world.

What is at stake is therefore much more serious than a simple question of discipline. If she were to claim a reversal of her faith or of her liturgy, in what name would the Church dare address the world? Her only legitimacy is her consistency in her continuity.

Moreover, if the bishops, who are in charge of the cohabitation and mutual enrichment of the two liturgical forms, do not exercise their authority to this effect, they run the risk of no longer appearing as shepherds, guardians of the faith they have received and of the sheep entrusted to them, but as political leaders: commissars of the ideology of the moment rather than guardians of the perennial tradition. They risk losing the trust of men of good will.

A father cannot introduce mistrust and division among his faithful children. He cannot humiliate some by setting them against others. He cannot ostracize some of his priests. The peace and unity that the Church claims to offer to the world must first be lived within the Church.

In liturgical matters, neither pastoral violence nor partisan ideology has ever produced fruits of unity. The suffering of the faithful and the expectations of the world are too great to engage in these dead-end paths. Everyone has a place in the Church of God!

58

We Will Persevere, and with God's Help We Will Prevail[†]

JOSEPH SHAW

Latin Mass Society Annual General Meeting

August 14, 2021

I AM SURE WE ALL FEEL A BIT SHELL-SHOCKED SINCE the publication of Pope Francis's Apostolic Letter *Traditionis Custodes* and the *Letter to Bishops* which accompanied it. I certainly am. I am pleased that the Latin Mass Society was able to respond quickly, and in the light of careful advice, with a document of Canonical Guidance, as well as statements to the press and a formal statement.

Since we got those I have been writing quite a lot which you can find on my blog, and insomniacs will be interested to hear that last week we released an hour-long podcast talk by me, part of our Iota Unum series, trying to make sense of *Traditionis Custodes* in its historical context.[1] Today I will try to approach the issue in a complementary way, by saying what it means, in itself and in practice.

I. WHAT DOES TRADITIONIS CUSTODES MEAN? THE LETTER OF THE LAW

Somewhere among his talks and writings, the late Michael Davies gave us some sound advice for reading documents emanating from the Holy See. Ask yourself, he said, what it allows that was not previously allowed, and what it forbids that was not previously forbidden. The rest, he suggested, is just padding. He had in mind documents such as those allowing Communion in the Hand, under Pope Paul VI, and the service of the altar by females, under Pope John Paul II, which surrounded these permissions with pious wishes that, in effect, people would not use them. Davies was correct, inasmuch as the expressions of theological principles and heartfelt aspirations in these documents made no difference to their legal force. Once

---

† Dr. Shaw delivered this address as the Chairman of the Latin Mass Society of England & Wales.

1 See chapter 52.

something the liberals wanted was allowed, it would be all but impossible for bishops and priests opposed to it to resist, and it would become the norm.

The same was true when the boot was on the other foot, in relation to various permissions for the Traditional Mass: the English Indult of 1971, the world-wide Indults of 1984 and 1988, and *Summorum Pontificum* in 2007. Some people were upset that these documents made reference to the theological views of Catholics attending the Traditional Mass, as if they were a permanent source of suspicion. For example, in the 1984 Indult, a condition is imposed on those who are attached to the Traditional Mass: "that it be made publicly clear beyond all ambiguity that such priests and their respective faithful in no way share the positions of those who call in question the legitimacy and doctrinal exactitude of the Roman Missal promulgated by Pope Paul VI in 1970."

Yes, this was upsetting, and unjust and a bit weird in all sorts of ways, but we should keep it in perspective. It was just a way of clawing back a little from the permission which was being given. This clawing back was a matter of pure rhetoric: the idea that anyone could or should try to test the theological purity of Mass-goers at the door before letting them attend the Traditional Mass was obviously impractical and, indeed, ludicrous, even if it was actually occasionally attempted. It gave the documents the appearance of balance, in the sense that it gave something to each side of the debate, but what it gave to Catholics attached to the Traditional Mass was of actual practical value, and what it gave to their opponents was just warm words.

It is somewhat reassuring to apply Michael Davies' analysis to *Traditionis Custodes*. I won't go into the details of the legislation, since we have done that elsewhere, but the long and the short of it is that no bishop is obliged by this document to close down any celebrations of the Traditional Mass. In a small number of cases a bishop might feel he should move a celebration from a parish church to a place of worship which is not a parish church — I note that Bishop Mark Davies has done this in the city of Shrewsbury. But this applies only to those celebrations which serve a formalised "group" of faithful, and should it prove impractical the obligation can be set aside for the good of souls, under the general principle expressed in the *Code of Canon Law*, in Canon 87 § 1.

While not forbidding anything previously allowed, or allowing anything previously forbidden, the document does give bishops and the Holy See powers they did not previously have, and transfers oversight of the Traditional Mass around the Curia. The key power given to the bishop is to permit, or not, his priests to celebrate the Traditional Mass. We have made the argument that, as *Traditionis Custodes* does not abrogate the 1962 Missal — and it does not claim to do so — then priests have a right to celebrate it, as asserted by *Summorum Pontificum*. In this context, this power of the bishop must be understood to apply only to public celebrations: any priest of the Latin Church retains the right to celebrate the ancient Mass in private. As far as public celebrations go, bishops may find this new power convenient, but they were already the moderators of the liturgy in their diocese, as Pope Benedict's Letter to Bishops accompanying *Summorum Pontificum* emphasised. As we all know, if a bishop doesn't like what a priest is doing, he has many ways of stopping him doing it, ranging from having a quiet word with him to assigning him to an exciting new role on the moon. Bishops hostile to public celebrations of the Traditional Mass rarely found it difficult to ensure that they did not take place. In other words, while some bishops may feel greater confidence than before in closing down celebrations which they had never liked very much, the practical difference this power makes is small.

Even smaller is the difference made by the new power of the Holy See. At first glance *Traditionis Custodes* gives the Holy See the power to veto newly ordained priests being allowed to celebrate the Traditional Mass. On closer inspection, however, *Traditionis Custodes* Article 4 only asks bishops to *consult* the Holy See about giving newly ordained priests permission. We are given a clue what the word "consult" means by the fact that, as the accompanying *Letter to Bishops* explains, *Traditionis Custodes* was composed following a "detailed consultation" of bishops around the world, some of whom, it now transpires, never even received the questionnaire.

2. THE SPIRIT OF THE LAW

Listeners may be thinking, however, that some departure from Michael Davies' approach is necessary in dealing with this document. Although in terms of what it allows and forbids, it arguably makes very little difference, there is something about the spirit of the document which is significant, and will make a difference.

For example, it transfers responsibility for the oversight of the Traditional Mass away from the Congregation for the Doctrine of the Faith, to the Congregation for Divine Worship, and of the communities and priestly Institutes attached to the Traditional Mass to the Congregation for Religious. Such purely administrative changes can make a big difference because of the difference between officials in the different dicasteries. I am not going to speculate about what difference this may make in practice. Not only do we not know what the officials currently in post there will do, but there is no telling how long they will remain in post and who will succeed them. I will only recall that during the period when Traditional Mass matters were dealt with by an independent curial entity, the Pontifical Commission Ecclesia Dei, the Una Voce Federation twice found itself faced with Cardinal-Presidents who took the view that their job was to close down the Traditional Mass as diplomatically as possible. This precipitated major rows, with Cardinal Antonio Innocenti in 1992 and with his successor Cardinal Angelo Felici in 1999. The point being that it wasn't all roses back then.

Another way the document can make a difference beyond its precise legal implications is in giving the general impression of approval or non-approval with regard to the Traditional Mass. This, after all, was the main way that *Summorum Pontificum* made a difference. Bishops and priests and lay Catholics alike became aware, thanks to this document, that the value of the Traditional Mass was officially recognised, and that there was no disloyalty in getting involved with it. It is an interesting fact that the Indults of 1971, 1984, and 1988 did not have this effect.

Many factors influenced this outcome, but a key one was the difference between the generation of bishops and senior clergy who received the earlier Indults, and the more open-minded generation who received *Summorum Pontificum*, and continued to implement it over the succeeding years. Another factor is that there was an important constituency of bishops and clergy who saw loyalty to the Pope as absolutely crucial to staving off liturgical and doctrinal chaos. Those bishops and priests needed a really clear signal from the Pope that this Mass was legitimate, before they would permit or celebrate it, and that is exactly what they received.

What exciting times they were, the immediate aftermath of *Summorum Pontificum*! The Latin Mass Society's Priest Training Conferences were huge, and the number of celebrations rocketed. It was clear we were dealing with pent-up demand: a whole group of priests who were ready to begin celebrating the Traditional Mass as soon as they heard the starting pistol.

Will the spirit of *Traditionis Custodes* have a similar effect, in the opposite direction? Will a large body of priests and bishops, who have been celebrating the Traditional Mass, or simply witnessing its effects, read that the official favour of the Holy See for it has been withdrawn, after fourteen years, for reasons that are somewhat opaque, and decide that they should have nothing to do with it from now on? Is there a parallel pent-up demand to stop celebrating, and indeed attending, the Mass, today, as there had been to celebrate and attend it, then? Is there a parallel attitude among an influential body of clergy and bishops that they should put aside their personal feelings because only obedience to the Holy Father can stave off chaos and confusion about all sorts of issues of discipline and doctrine?

Well, no. There is no such thing as pent-up demand not to do something no one is forcing you to do. Again, the idea that adhesion to the personal projects of whoever happens to be pope is the key to keeping the Church out of trouble doesn't have the same attraction in 2021 as it did in 2007. Pope Francis's downplaying of papal prerogatives and prestige over the eight years of his pontificate has not been entirely in vain.

3. TRADITIONIS CUSTODES IN PRACTICE: MASS PROVISION

I don't want to suggest that the document will have no effect. Indeed, it already has, and looking at its brief period of implementation up to now gives us some clues about the longer term. It has had immediate and practical effects, in terms of Masses being celebrated or not, and it has also had effects on the way discussion about the Traditional Mass is being played out within the Church.

On the celebration of Masses, there are some bishops, so far a very small number, who have felt inspired by the Pope's documents to order the complete cessation of celebrations of the Traditional Mass in their dioceses. A few more have reduced the number of Masses. Both groups will certainly grow as bishops consider how to implement it on their return from their summer breaks and after consultations. This will cause spiritual distress to many Catholics directly affected by these decisions, and we all feel this. There is nevertheless reason to hope that the great majority of regular celebrations will continue, in this country and around the world, and that occasional celebrations such as pilgrimages and weddings will also be possible in most places.

The Latin Mass Society has spent the whole of its history negotiating with bishops and assisting priests in politically delicate situations, and this work will continue. It is worth emphasising that this aspect of our work never came to an end, as some naively imagined it would with *Summorum Pontificum*. As a Local Representative I have been involved in such negotiations throughout the *Summorum Pontificum* era in my own patch, in Oxford, and as Chairman of the LMS and Secretary of Una Voce International I have helped other people around England and Wales and around the world involved in the same work. Sometimes we have gained our objective, but more often we did not. I have personally seen a number of appeals, under the terms of *Summorum Pontificum*, through priest, bishop, and all the way to Rome. None were immediately successful: indeed, none of those letters to Rome even received an acknowledgement. It has often felt as though all we were achieving was the creation of a paper-trail for the melancholy enjoyment of the historians of the future. Nevertheless, as the years went by we did make progress, sometimes in unexpected ways. We were chipping away at the resolution of various office-holders to keep the ancient Mass in its little box. Our polite but insistent letters pointing out the obvious were like drops of water wearing away at a stone. The key thing in this situation is not to get discouraged and give up. Try a different request. Try a different parish. Try again when there's a new priest or a new bishop. Keep it polite, keep it simple, and keep going. This is part of the vocation of an activist for the Traditional Mass.

Some listeners might doubt the efficacy of this work. They might say that any change in attitude on the part of priests and bishops which happened during this time derived from other factors, and that our requests served only to annoy people. However, this is not the case. The Traditional Mass would not have survived in the decades after 1970 if no lay people had asked for it. The priests who loved it would have said it privately until they died and that would have been that. The English Indult, we all know, was a response to a petition by lay people, and the later indults, and *Summorum Pontificum*, address the question of how priests and bishops should handle requests from lay people. These requests showed that there was an ongoing pastoral problem in refusing the Traditional Mass, and which needed to be addressed somehow. It is the needs of the lay faithful which justify the existence of the Traditional Priestly Institutes, and the donations of the lay faithful which sustain them. It is the continuing spiritual needs of lay people which justify the continuing usage of the 1962 Missal in *Traditionis Custodes* itself.

We may compare our work to letter-writing campaigns in favour of prisoners of conscience. I used to participate in these when I was at school, when Amnesty International was still about political prisoners and not its own political agenda. What possible use, one might ask, was writing to the leaders of the Soviet Union, or to the military dictators of Burma? Why should they care about a few letters from foreign countries, written by people they had never heard of? Well, those letter-writing campaigns did not solve all the world's problems, but they had their successes, because they made it clear that those prisoners were not being forgotten. The slight discomfort the various leaders felt about how their actions looked was amplified, and extended through time. At least in some cases, this was enough to make them change their minds.

Even in the darkest days of the movement, our priests and bishops were more sympathetic to Catholics' spiritual needs than the apparatchiks of the Communist bloc — even if it didn't always look like it — but they still needed to be reminded, as time passed, that we hadn't simply gone away. If we had gone away, that would have been the end of the movement and the end of the Mass. When we couldn't get weekly Masses, we established annual Masses; when we couldn't get Sunday Masses, we established Masses on First Fridays. We clung on, even with the famous weekday afternoon quarterly Masses in churches in the middle of nowhere with no loo and no parking. It was ridiculous, but we persevered, and we were vindicated.

In the time of *Traditionis Custodes*, whether this turns out to be long or short, the odds against us are increased. Nevertheless, for several reasons we are not going back to the situation of the 1970s and 1980s. The movement is in an immeasurably stronger position now than it was then. We are better resourced and better connected. It is clear today that demand for the Traditional Mass is coming predominantly from the young, and not only from the old. And a new generation of priests, and also of bishops, has discovered that the Traditional Mass is not something sterile and oppressive, appealing only to the nostalgic, but theologically rich and spiritually powerful.

4. THE LITURGICAL DEBATE BEFORE TRADITIONIS CUSTODES

This takes me to the question of how the liturgical issue will be debated from now on. Up to now the challenge has been to show that the ancient Mass is not incompatible with Vatican II. Back in 2011, I began work on a series of short Position Papers for the Una Voce Federation, as the chief writer and editor of a panel of people with much greater expertise than I had myself. This rather dominated my life until the collection of thirty-six papers was published as a book in 2019.[2] The point of these papers is to vindicate, or at least render comprehensible, specific aspects of the Traditional Mass in terms of the post-conciliar magisterium, as well as in terms of the history of the liturgy and wider theological and pastoral considerations. I spent a great deal of time reading official documents about the liturgy, and the papers are larded with references to those documents.

Thus, I list about twenty distinct liturgical abuses, condemned by official documents, which don't arise if Holy Communion is not given under the species of wine. I quote Pope John Paul II and the *Catechism of the Catholic Church* saying that we should engage with the liturgy not in a purely intellectual way but contemplatively, with our whole person. I quote Pope Paul VI

---

2 Joseph Shaw, ed., *The Case for Liturgical Restoration* (Brooklyn, NY: Angelico Press, 2019).

praising Gregorian Chant as the key to vocations to the religious life, John Paul II on the need to rediscover silence in the liturgy, the Congregation for Catholic Education warning sternly of the pastoral consequences of the disappearance of Latin, and the Congregation for the Eastern Churches condemning the usual polemic used against the celebration of Mass facing east. The endnotes in the book take up 78 pages.

Justifying the Traditional Mass in terms of the modern magisterium has always been a difficult argument to make, however, because there is evidently an important difference between the old Order of Mass and the new, and the new often seems to be regarded as the crystallisation of the thinking of the Council. Any difference between the two Missals is bound to be regarded with suspicion, according to this mindset.

5. THE LITURGICAL DEBATE IN TRADITIONIS CUSTODES

If things were difficult before *Traditionis Custodes*, now they are more so. On the one hand, it reiterates the idea that the *Novus Ordo Missae* is the ultimate reference point for the liturgy, saying in Article 1 that it is "the only expression of the *lex orandi* of the Roman Missal." On the other hand, the accompanying *Letter to Bishops* links Catholics who attend the Traditional Mass to the "rejection of the Church and her institutions."

Both of these points are very puzzling. The claim that the reformed Mass is the only *lex orandi* of the Roman Rite seems at first glance like a technical, legal point. However, it doesn't make sense as that, and I think it must really function as more of a rhetorical gesture, to the effect that the old Mass is not of any real account. It doesn't have any theological weight.

One way of trying to understand it is to look at the published works of the man widely regarded as the author, or ghost writer, of *Traditionis Custodes*, the Italian lay liturgist Andrea Grillo.[3] I have not been following his work very closely up to now, but I find in a review of his book, *Beyond Pius V* (2014) an interesting idea — and here I quote directly from the book: "the reform of the books and rites, of the texts and gestures, is a necessary condition . . . for an authentic experience of the liturgy as *fons*" (p. 53). *Fons* being the Latin for source or fount, as in the famous phrase of Vatican II, that the liturgy is the *fons* of the Christian life. As the reviewer, Dom Alcuin Reid, writing in the *New Liturgical Movement* blog, expresses it, Grillo's view seems to be that (and I quote Dom Alcuin): "one cannot truly draw from the Sacred Liturgy as the source and summit of Christian

---

3   See Peter Kwasniewski, "Andrea Grillo: The Mind Behind the Motu Proprio," *OnePeterFive*, August 18, 2021.

life other than through these particular ritual reforms. Where that leaves non-Western Catholics or the centuries of worshippers who lived before the 1970s one can only wonder."[4]

Grillo certainly seems a plausible source for the claim in *Traditionis Custodes* that the reformed Mass is the only expression of the Roman Rite's *lex orandi*, but this context doesn't help us understand it as much as we might wish. This is for two reasons. First, we must understand an official text in the context of other official texts and the magisterium as a whole, not in the context of the personal ideas of the humble scribe who drafted it (if, indeed, he did). Secondly, Grillo's ideas are themselves incomprehensible for the reasons Dom Alcuin adduces. There is simply no sense to be made of the idea that the liturgical reform of the 1960s created the one and only authentic form of the Mass. Such an idea makes Luther's claim that the Church had been in a Babylonish captivity from the time of the Church Fathers up to the sixteenth century look modest by comparison. Grillo apparently thinks the Church never had a proper liturgy until 1969.

On the theological deficiencies of the people who attend the Traditional Mass, the characterization of Traditional Catholics found in the *Letter to Bishops* seems to be based on the views of sedevacantists: at least, that is the obvious meaning of the idea of rejecting the Church and her institutions. Could someone please tell Pope Francis that people who reject the Church and her institutions don't come to Masses celebrated in union with the Pope, which take place with the permission of the local bishop?

One could try to understand the phrase in a wider sense, to suggest not literal rejection but criticism or the like, but the strength of its condemnation would be accordingly weakened. Certainly, Traditional Catholics have criticisms to make of decisions made in the Church since 1962, but then so do liberal Catholics. We are all permitted to present our own interpretations and objections to non-binding statements coming from Rome: that is what it means to say that they are non-binding. I have books at home criticising the liturgical reform for being too conservative, for failing to release the creative potential of the People of God, and for failing to allow sufficient opportunities for inculturation. Some writers go so far as to talk of a betrayal of the Second Vatican Council by conservative bishops and curial officials. Some of Pope Francis's strongest supporters are associated with such views. If they are allowed to examine the Novus Ordo critically, then so are we.

---

4   See "*Beyond Pius V*, by Andrea Grillo — Review by Dom Alcuin Reid," *New Liturgical Movement*, January 21, 2014.

Again, one can try to get behind the official text to understand what the concern might be. One idea which has floated past me is that the Traditional Mass has become associated in the curial mind with criticisms of Pope Francis by the likes of Archbishop Carlo Maria Viganò. I don't want to get involved in Viganò's views, or his reception by elements of the online Catholic world, but I will just point out that he has no strong connection with the Traditional Mass. He only began to celebrate it in recent times, and until very recently he seemed to have no particular interest in liturgical matters.

Something similar is true of many of the most powerful critics of Pope Francis over the years. It was of much greater significance that *Amoris Laetitia* was criticised by the late Professor Germain Grisez and by Fr. Thomas Weinandy than by any number of Traditional Catholics, because those two men were deeply embedded in the Catholic establishment in the USA, whereas the traddies are relatively marginal figures. The biggest bombshell affecting Pope Francis's reputation, in my view, came when Cardinal Sean O'Malley intervened on the issue of the Chilean Bishop Barros in 2018. None of these three men had or have the smallest commitment to the Traditional Mass.

Again, the most powerful voices at the 2014 Family Synod, opposing what most people assumed was Pope Francis's preferred direction of travel, were Cardinal George Pell and Cardinal Robert Sarah. As far as I have been able to find out, each of these Cardinals has celebrated the Traditional Mass in public only once: Cardinal Pell in 2014 in Rome, and Cardinal Sarah in Chartres in 2018. There may have been other occasions, but their Eminences are hardly closely integrated into the movement for the Traditional Mass. Cardinal Sarah seems just as happy leading a charismatic celebration in Medjugorje, as he was doing earlier this month.

These observations do not exclude the possibility that due to some unfortunate association of ideas Traditional Catholics are being punished for the actions of other people, those who could possibly be described, from a partisan point of view, as acting (in the language of the *Letter to Bishops*) "to widen the gaps, reinforce the divergences, and encourage disagreements that injure the Church, block her path, and expose her to the peril of division."

However, I am sceptical about this. As I have argued at greater length in the Iota Unum podcast mentioned earlier,[5] I incline to the view that the key motivation of *Traditionis Custodes* is not ecclesial politics, but the liturgy. It is the rejection of Pope Benedict's idea, which had been fiercely attacked

---

5 See chapter 52.

by Andrea Grillo among others, that we should consider the new and the old Masses as able to coexist as two expressions of the Roman Rite. The exaltation of the reformed Mass as something which excludes everything else is characteristic of a strain of thought among progressive liturgists, and it is this which for some reason has, for the moment, gained the upper hand in the corridors of power. The fact that some people attached to the Old Mass have been a bit annoying, whether it be on Twitter, or in defending the Church's immemorial discipline on the reception of Holy Communion by the divorced and remarried, is a side issue. If *Traditionis Custodes* Article 1 is correct, then the Traditional Mass has got to go, however docile its defenders might be.

6. THE LITURGICAL DEBATE AFTER TRADITIONIS CUSTODES

How do we defend ourselves against the accusation that we like attending a Mass which is not the Mass of 1970? This accusation is today being made by people who are convinced that the 1970 Mass is the only liturgical form which gives proper expression to the Church's teaching and spirituality.

Anyone who is facing an opponent whose mind is entirely made up has the option of addressing, not him, but the audience. It seems unlikely that we will make a convert of Andrea Grillo — though you never know — but we can make arguments and carry on our work for the Traditional Mass in such a way that less ideologically committed people will see us as more reasonable than him.

This, indeed, is the approach we have been taking since our foundation in 1965, and this is what we will continue to do. It is interesting to see the publicity work of the founding generation of Latin Mass Society activists, such as Professor Alexandra Zaina, who wrote in the *Catholic Herald* in 1969 that since Catholics' spiritual needs differed, it was reasonable to allow different liturgical options. The 1971 petition organised by Alfred Marnau for the Society, which was signed by cultural figures, including Agatha Christi, made another argument, that the ancient Mass should be considered a monument of world culture, as the inspiration for so much art, literature, and music. Such arguments were not going to move the likes of Annibale Bugnini, but they made many reasonable people feel uncomfortable about the suppression of this form of the liturgy. Because they point to something obviously true: this Mass has value, in itself and for at least some people. This being so, its deliberate destruction seems harsh and unreasonable.

There are, indeed, many good arguments to be made for the preservation of the Traditional Mass in itself, and for the specific celebrations which we help to organise. At this moment of crisis we take account of the way the debate has developed, and of the people who are open or less open to persuasion, but the fundamental task has not changed. We must continue to make the case for the Traditional Mass in public as politely and insistently as we make it in private to our priests and bishops.

One advantage we have today over our predecessors is in the number of celebrations of the Traditional Mass and the vigour of the movement. In a couple of weeks our walking pilgrimage to Walsingham will take place with the largest number of pilgrims ever: it looks as though it will be well over a hundred.[6] While parishes are being closed all around us, and one after another Catholic retreat centres and seminaries and Catholic newspapers disappear from the scene, we can see that the Traditional Mass is here to stay. The Latin Mass Society has this message for its members and supporters: we will persevere, and with God's help we will prevail.

---

6   In the event, 120 walking pilgrims were supported by 12 non-walking volunteers. — Ed.

59

Is the Novus Ordo
the Only Law of Prayer?

JOSEPH SHAW

OnePeterFive

August 16, 2021

THE PRACTICAL FALL-OUT FROM TRADITIONIS CUSTO-
des will be making itself felt for some time to come. In some places it has
already been devastating; in others, it appears it will be minimal. The
theological fall-out, however, threatens a profound problem on a different
plane. This arises from the claim made in Article 1 of the document, and
repeated in the accompanying Letter to Bishops, that "the liturgical books
promulgated by Saint Paul VI and Saint John Paul II, in conformity with
the decrees of Vatican Council II, are the unique expression of the *lex orandi*
of the Roman Rite."

The official English translation which I have quoted is actually a poor rendering of the Italian expression, "l'unica espressione," which means the *only*
expression. The document is claiming that the *only* Missal which expresses
the Roman Rite's *lex orandi*, its "law of prayer," is the reformed Missal.

The Church's law of prayer, her *lex orandi*, must correspond to, and indeed
determine, her law of belief *(lex credendi)*: that was the claim of Prosper of
Aquitaine when he coined the phrase in the 5th century. Prosper was making the point that if you want to know what people believe, then look at
how they express themselves in prayer. If they genuflect at the reference to
the Incarnation in the Creed, of if they kneel to receive Holy Communion,
this tells you something: Arians will refuse to do the first, and Evangelical
Protestants the second. A Missal is a "law of prayer" in the sense that it sets
out a way for people to pray, and we would expect Catholic Missals to give
a theologically correct law of prayer and Arian and Evangelicals ones to
give theologically erroneous ones. What, then, can it mean to say that the
Roman Rite has only one law of prayer, and that this is the one expressed
in a particular Missal, and not in another, in a document which allows both
to be used in the Church?

I have not been alone in struggling to understand what this means. I recently took part in a collaborative blog-post[1] with Fr. Anthony Ruff, the founder of the Pray Tell blog. On this issue Fr. Ruff responded:

> [Pope Francis] did not say that the 1962 Missal has no lex orandi, or is opposed to the Church's lex orandi. The 1962 Missal reflects the Roman rite's lex orandi to the extent that it reflects the Church's liturgy as found in the 1970 Missal. There is continuity between 1962 and 1970 in the sense that the core features of the reformed liturgy, which oftentimes derive from Catholic tradition of earliest centuries, are found in the 1962 Missal but in an occluded and obscure manner which needed to be made more apparent.

Fr. Ruff appears to be saying that the 1962 Missal has validity on loan, as it were, from the 1970 Missal: insofar as it agrees with the later Missal, it can be said to express the Roman Rite's lex orandi. I'm not sure whether this can be squared with the wording of Traditionis Custodes or not, but it doesn't matter because Fr. Ruff's sympathetic interpretation does nothing to fend off the real problem with Article 1, which can be expressed as the simple question: what was the Church's lex orandi up to 1962?

This question is addressed by Dr. Richard H. Bulzacchelli, Lecturer in Theology at Catholic Studies Academy and Senior Fellow with the St. Paul Center for Biblical Theology, in a video talk.[2] On the hypothetical supposition that Traditionis Custodes should be understood literally, Dr. Bulzacchelli explains (from about the 19-minute mark):

> If the Novus Ordo is the unique expression of the lex orandi of the Roman Rite then by definition no other liturgical form can express that lex orandi. The logical implications of this assertion are staggering. If the Usus Antiquior cannot express the lex orandi of the Roman Rite, then what we call the Roman Rite today . . . isn't the same thing as what we called the Roman Rite in 1962. Yet that attitude is exactly what Francis says he wants to correct. The only way that's not a contradiction is if the decision flowing from his own defined will is what determines what the truth is in the objective order of reality. . . . Did the Roman Rite exist for fifteen centuries without an authentic expression of its lex orandi? This would be impossible . . .

What Dr. Bulzacchelli is saying is that, if it is absurd to suggest (as surely it is) that the Roman Rite had no lex orandi of any kind in 1962, then it

---

1 See "Two Views on Liturgical Reform: Joseph Shaw (Latin Mass Society) and Anthony Ruff (Pray Tell)," Rorate Caeli, August 2, 2021.
2 www.youtube.com/watch?v=cZLlkYeloq8.

appears that Article 1 is claiming that the Roman Rite's *lex orandi* changed in 1970 from the one expressed by the older Missal to that expressed by the newer Missal. Now, in 1970 the Church adopted a new Missal, and by doing so adopted a new law of prayer, just in the sense that we had a new way of celebrating Mass. This is clearly true. But what does it mean that there is (now) only *one* expression of the Roman Rite's law of prayer? The only reason for rejecting a Missal as a *lex orandi* is if it is theologically problematic, as we would reject the *lex orandi* of the Anglican *Book of Common Prayer*: it does not correspond faithfully to the Church's *lex credendi*. So is *that* the claim? That the 1962 Missal is theologically defective? But this implies after all that there was no authentic law of prayer for the Roman Rite in 1962. Unless it *became* theologically defective in 1970, or later, by a *legislative act*: as Bulzacchelli puts it, "the decision flowing from his own defined will is what determines what the truth is in the objective order of reality."

Now possibly someone might say this: a statement might become theologically defective with the passage of time because of the way the Church's Magisterium has developed. Thus we find that before the Definition of the Marian Dogmas, the Divine Praises did not include the lines "Blessed be her Holy and Immaculate Conception. Blessed be her Glorious Assumption." Looking for the text online to create a booklet for Benediction, I once found a version which excluded those lines and I realized I had stumbled on a website maintained by one of the splinter groups deriving from the "Old Catholic" schism of 1870. Their *lex orandi* is defective, we might say, not because of something they had *changed*, but something they had *refused to change*.

However, this is not really right. The older version of the Divine Praises is not theologically defective: it is in no way incompatible with the Catholic Faith. Certainly the Old Catholic schismatics are motivated to keep it because they reject the dogmas, but liturgical texts which are merely silent about particular theological issues are not for that reason unusable: to say so would be absurd. Were it to become an issue in the context of the reconciliation of a body of schismatics to the Holy See, historical precedent would suggest that they would be allowed to make a statement of Faith and carry on with the older texts, if it meant so much to them.

And the parallel with the 1962 Missal is hard to make out. Could someone please show me the dogmatic definitions which are reflected in the reformed Missal, and whose absence from the older Missal gives an opportunity, for those attached to it, to display their rejection of them? There are of course no such definitions. The closest anyone has come to making the case for this is in relation to the Prayer for the Jews in the Good Friday Liturgy. I have examined this argument elsewhere[3] but briefly it doesn't survive the observation that the 1974 *Liturgy of the Hours* calls for the Jews to accept Jesus as their Messiah, and does so *several times*.[4]

Nevertheless something like this reasoning may be behind Article 1. In the accompanying Letter to Bishops, Pope Francis criticizes the "rejection not only of the liturgical reform, but of the Vatican Council II itself, claiming, with unfounded and unsustainable assertions, that it betrayed the Tradition and the 'true Church.'" Instead, he stresses continuity, calling Vatican II "a recent stage of this dynamic," the "dynamic of Tradition."

The problem is, if the 1962 Missal does *not* express the Church's *lex orandi*, or does so (as Fr. Ruff imagines) only in an inadequate way and by reference to a later "stage of the dynamic"— in short, if it has no validity *in and of itself*— then it does look as though whatever the content of the tradition up to 1962 was, it was altered in its substance —"betrayed," a partisan of that tradition might say — by the 1970 Missal.

This is why Dr. Bulzacchelli is concerned that *Traditionis Custodes* appears to be *making true* the very criticism of the Novus Ordo which it condemns, and which had hitherto seemed, not least to me, to be extreme and unwarranted. Either we say, with Pope Benedict XVI, that the old and the new are both legitimate expressions of the Church's *lex orandi* (alongside all the other rites and usages), or we say that they conflict, and that the historical transition from old to new marked the moment at which the Church did not just develop its expression of existing doctrines, in which case the older expressions would remain valid, but adopted a new law of belief. Which of course is impossible.

My own view is that Pope Benedict was correct and that this part of *Traditionis Custodes*, as it stands and in the context of the Letter to Bishops, fails to express anything: it is incomprehensible because it is self-contradictory. This may seem a drastic option, but it is better than to swallow the logical implications Dr. Bulzacchelli draws out. Readers may derive some comfort from the thought that until the document appears, perhaps in Latin, in the *Acta Apostolicae Sedis* (as we have been promised it will), the text can still be tweaked, as actually happened, for far less serious reasons, with the text of *Summorum Pontificum*.[5] However, I won't be holding my breath.

---

3 See "The Good Friday Prayer for the Jews," in *The Case for Liturgical Restoration*, 275–91.
4 See "The Other Prayers for the Jews," *LMS Chairman*, March 12, 2016.
5 See "More Letters in the *Catholic Herald*," *LMS Chairman*, September 12, 2010.

60

After the Shock, the Analysis†

CHRISTOPHE GEFFROY

AND ABBÉ CHRISTIAN GOUYAUD

La Nef

August 19, 2021

THE PUBLICATION OF THE MOTU PROPRIO TRADITIONIS *Custodes* on July 16, in the middle of summer, was a shock for many.¹ After the surprise and emotion, it is now time to step back and reflect on what the Pope is asking for. Indeed, it is an act of government by the supreme authority that cannot be rejected, filial obedience being the rule for every Catholic. But in order to obey, as Dom Jean Pateau, Abbot of Fontgombault, reminded us, "one must want to listen, hear, and understand."² In the Church, in fact, obedience must not be blind, but must be joined with the assent of an intellect enlightened by reflection and advice. It can therefore leave room for legitimate questions and requests formulated with respect for authority.

First of all, let us note that this motu proprio does not prohibit the celebration of Mass according to the missal of St. John XXIII. It returns us to a situation prior to the motu proprio *Ecclesia Dei* of 1988, although more favorable than the indult of 1984. It is a return to the regime of concession. The bishops have regained control, which is logical, but with limited room to maneuver, since the creation of any new group is forbidden, as is the celebration of Mass in parishes, and they will have to consult the Apostolic See to grant any authorization to a priest ordained after *Traditionis Custodes* who wishes to celebrate with the 1962 missal. There is a clear desire to do away eventually with this liturgy, as Francis clearly explains in his letter to the bishops accompanying the motu proprio; the liturgy is there for "those who are rooted in the previous form of celebration and who need time to return to the Roman rite promulgated by Saints Paul VI and John Paul II."

These measures, expressed with harshness, without compassion, are of a rare severity and seem unjust to those who were peacefully following the Tridentine liturgy without any spirit of contestation of the Novus Ordo and

† Translated from the French by Zachary Thomas and Peter Kwasniewski for this volume.
1 See Christophe Geffroy, "An Incomplete Argument and False Information" (chapter 6).
2 Interview on the *Famille chrétienne* website, July 19, 2021.

the Second Vatican Council. They create a deep wound in many of the faithful who do not understand why our common Father is so relentless against them, at the risk of breaking a movement in the Church that displays a real dynamism, with many large families and just as many young people, giving rise to more vocations than anywhere else. Who, from now on, will want to enter a traditional seminary knowing that no ministry will be offered to him on leaving? Francis, usually so concerned with building bridges, is erecting a wall here to isolate the traditionalists and make them gradually disappear.

AN OPPORTUNITY TO ASK QUESTIONS

The ordeal is certainly heavy, but the situation is not set in stone and depends on the bishops — in France, the first reactions were paternal and understanding, suggesting that things would not change much at first[3] — as well as on the behavior of traditionalist circles. For the latter, isn't the Pope's motu proprio a providential opportunity to ask themselves what the Holy Father expects of them? For, finally, if Francis's description of the followers of the old "extraordinary form" is not representative of the whole of that world, it is not totally foreign to it either. Who can deny that some traditionalists have taken advantage of Benedict XVI's generosity to refuse systematically the celebration of the "ordinary form" and to retreat into more or less open opposition to the Council? Let us recall that all those who benefited from the motu proprio *Ecclesia Dei* of 1988 undertook to respect the protocol of agreement of May 5, 1988, signed between Archbishop Lefebvre and Cardinal Ratzinger, which specified: "With regard to certain points taught by the Second Vatican Council or concerning subsequent reforms of the liturgy and law, and which seem to us difficult to reconcile with Tradition, we commit ourselves to a positive attitude of study and communication with the Apostolic See, avoiding all polemics" (n. 3). Have all of them kept this commitment?

The difficulty is that Pope Francis presents the traditional movement as homogeneous and altogether hostile to the Mass reformed by Paul VI and to Vatican II, whereas the reality is much more diverse. To simplify, we can distinguish three groups within this movement.

1. Those who love the Tridentine liturgy and who recognize the full legitimacy of the Novus Ordo and Vatican II. Among the faithful, this group is certainly in the majority, and many move easily from one Mass to the other — this is especially true among young people who do not have

---

3   Canon 87 § 1 of the *Code of Canon Law* allows the diocesan bishop to exempt the faithful from the disciplinary laws erected by Rome whenever he deems it beneficial.

the rigidities and wounds of their elders. Without a doubt, it is less of a majority among priests, but we can still mention, without being exhaustive, Fontgombault and its three French foundations, Le Barroux, Lagrasse, the Missionaries of Divine Mercy, without forgetting, of course, diocesan priests who habitually or occasionally use the "extraordinary form," all of whom agree to celebrate the "ordinary form" and who support the Second Vatican Council, including by means of substantial theological works, such as those of Father Basile Valuet (Le Barroux) on religious freedom.

2. Those who question neither the Novus Ordo nor Vatican II as such, but who do not refrain from criticism and, in the case of priests, who refuse to celebrate the "ordinary form" while still attending and receiving communion at this Mass. One can assume that this refusal to celebrate the current Mass, especially at the Chrism Mass — a fact deplored by many bishops — is at least partly responsible for the severity of this motu proprio, with many paying for this indefensible rigidity. All the more indefensible because this request from Rome is old and the priests concerned have always circumvented it, now reaping the fruit of this unecclesial spirit. All the way back in 1999, on the occasion of the crisis in the Priestly Fraternity of St. Peter and the *Responsa* published the same year by the Congregation for Divine Worship,[4] no step had been taken towards the requested opening to the ordinary form. Similarly, in 2007, on the occasion of *Summorum Pontificum*, the requirement of Benedict XVI, very clearly formulated in his letter to the bishops, was superbly ignored. This practical refusal to concelebrate even the Chrism Mass reveals a certain disloyalty to Benedict XVI who, in his 2007 letter to the bishops, asked them to recognize "the value and sanctity" of the new missal; therefore, "in order to live full communion, priests of communities that adhere to the old usage cannot, as a matter of principle, exclude the celebration according to the new books." There are other signs of communion than concelebration, argue the refractory. Of course, but that is not the problem! If the legitimate authority requires this sign — which has become customary — there is no reason to refuse it. By wanting to keep their "hands clean" liturgically, these priests thereby discredit the reformed Mass, which, for them, is not "celebrable." If all the institutes that refuse to celebrate the Novus Ordo were to receive this motu proprio from Francis and revise their position on this central question, it would be a strong asset in hoping for a change of heart...

---

4 These *Responsa* confirm the impossibility of a superior of an institute forbidding his priests to celebrate the ordinary form, which is the common law in the Church of the Roman Rite.

In fact, many of these traditionalists have refused to accept what Cardinal Ratzinger asked for, especially in 1998 during his conference in Rome for the tenth anniversary of *Ecclesia Dei*,[5] namely, that the essential principles of the Constitution *Sacrosanctum Concilium* be taken into consideration: unity of the liturgical action, access to the Word of God, and the participation of the congregation, even when celebrating according to the old *Ordo Missae*. Similarly, when Benedict XVI called for a "reciprocal enrichment" between the two forms of the Roman Rite, few adhered to this project, both on the part of the ecclesiastical authorities and on the part of those traditionalists who felt that there could only be a unilateral contribution and that they had no enrichment to receive from the ordinary form. On the contrary, in certain institutes, one observes a fussy rubricism and a "Baroque" approach that is akin to the liturgical archaeology denounced by Pius XII; here one thinks of the return to the pre-1955 Holy Week. It is true that the Ecclesia Dei Commission did not follow a very clear line, not supporting the most open traditionalists,[6] while the Roman instruction of 2011 [*Universae Ecclesiae*] laid down a strict requirement of sticking to the 1962 edition of the Roman Missal for the celebration of the extraordinary form, even though that of 1965, keeping the essential structure of the Mass codified by St. Pius V, already took into account what the Conciliar Fathers of Vatican II wanted.

Another aspect to be mentioned here is the rejection by certain traditional institutes of the *nouvelle théologie*, exemplified by a De Lubac or a Ratzinger, and the fixation on a state of theology, that of the neo-scholasticism of the 1930s or 1940s, whose model of reference remains Father Garrigou-Lagrange, an undisputed authority in certain seminaries and houses of Ecclesia Dei formation. If this author is not mediocre, his work nevertheless corresponds to a rationalist Thomism of manuals, essentially deductive, and is drafted into the fight against Modernism; this makes it difficult to apprehend, even positively, contemporary problems. It is to this *forma mentis* that we can undoubtedly attribute the difficulty of entering into the designs of a Council aimed at establishing a dialogue, perforce ambivalent, with the "world of this time."

---

5   Conference in Rome, October 24, 1998, published in full in *La Nef* n°89 of December 1998.

6   A reference to those who (like Lefebvre himself initially, and the Solesmes Congregation) were/are open to accepting the 1965 missal that incorporates some of the Council's desiderata. To the author's mind, the Ecclesia Dei Commission was never supportive of this type of "open-minded" traditionalist, and tended to side more with the supposedly backward-looking traditionalist (who wishes, e.g., to recover the old Holy Week, or who looks to the Baroque for ceremony). — Ed.

3. Finally, the third group are those who correspond, strictly speaking, to the description given by the Pope in his letter to the bishops, namely the movement "which is increasingly characterized by a growing rejection not only of the liturgical reform, but of the Second Vatican Council, with the unfounded and untenable claim that it betrayed Tradition and the 'true Church.'" Among them are, first and foremost, the members of the Society of St. Pius X, who fit this portrait very precisely, but having already broken off ecclesial communion, they cannot be the ones Francis is referring to. To stick to France, it cannot be denied that there are people in the "trad" movement who have officially remained in full communion with Rome and yet who correspond to this profile. Abbé Claude Barthe, an affable and courteous man, who has surprisingly become a spokesman of this traditional movement to the point of being a columnist in many magazines and a participant in broadcasts, holds — and congratulates himself on holding — that the celebration of Mass according to the old *Ordo Missae* has been and remains a "driving force behind the non-acceptance of Vatican II."[7] From publication to publication, he denies the magisterial character — and therefore the binding nature, according to the level of authority of its texts — of Vatican II and resolutely adheres to a hermeneutic of rupture. He considers, moreover, that the motu proprio *Traditionis Custodes* is a "paradoxically providential affair"[8] because it puts forward the doctrinal opposition between Vatican II, whose *lex orandi* is represented by the "conciliar Mass," and the antecedent Magisterium, whose *lex orandi* is expressed in the preceding missal. That is to say, Father Barthe recognizes himself exactly in that with which Francis reproaches the followers of the old rite — and assumes it!

TWO OPPOSING APPROACHES

Fundamentally, the most serious aspect of this affair is that Francis's motu proprio seems to bury Benedict XVI's approach, which envisaged the new missal and the Second Vatican Council from the point of view of "the hermeneutics of reform, of renewal in the continuity of the single subject-Church."[9] If there is a rupture between *Summorum Pontificum* and *Traditionis Custodes*, it is right there. This is manifested by the fact that Francis has abolished the approach of his predecessor who, in order to get out of the imbroglio of the juridical status of the Mass known as the Mass of St. Pius V, had explained that there were two "forms" of the same Roman rite, the

---

7   Claude Barthe, *La messe de Vatican II* (Le Chesnay: Via Romana, 2018), 258.
8   Interview in *Présent*, July 20, 2021, p. 2.
9   Speech to the Roman Curia, December 22, 2005.

"ordinary" of the new missal and the "extraordinary" of the old. The latter now finds itself in fact in a juridical vacuum, as if it did not exist, "the only expression of the *lex orandi* of the Roman Rite" being "the liturgical books promulgated by the Holy Pontiffs Paul VI and John Paul II in accordance with the decrees of the Second Vatican Council" (art. 1 of *Traditionis Custodes*).

The rupture is obvious if one considers that John Paul II and Benedict XVI acted, through their motu proprios, not only out of compassion for the segment of the People of God attached to the ancient liturgical forms, not only to try to contain a hemorrhage towards the Society of St. Pius X in rupture of communion, but also to protect the "Extraordinary Form" *as such*, independently of those who follow it, because it represents an ancient treasure of more than a thousand years and therefore belongs to the liturgical patrimony of the universal Church. In *Summorum Pontificum*, Benedict XVI wrote that the Roman Missal of St. Pius V should "be honored because of its venerable and ancient usage" (art. 1) and, in his letter to the bishops, he added: "There is no contradiction between the two editions of the *Missale Romanum*. The history of the liturgy is one of growth and progress, never of rupture. What was sacred for previous generations remains great and sacred for us, and cannot all of a sudden be totally forbidden, or even be considered harmful. It is good for all of us to preserve the riches that have grown in the faith and prayer of the Church, and to give them their rightful place."

The Pope Emeritus's design was to bring about an internal reconciliation in the Church, with its liturgy, but also with its past. This noble ambition is forgotten in Francis's document, which shows no interest in the Tridentine Mass itself.[10]

The pope justifies his measures by pleading for the unity of the Roman rite, which is obviously desirable in theory. Benedict XVI believed that this unity was preserved by declining the single Roman rite into two forms; and in fact, unity is not synonymous with uniformity, even though it is well understood that this is an unusual and transitory historical situation, awaiting a reunification of the two "forms" when minds and times would have been conducive to a "reform of the reform." In our fragmented world, is it shocking that the faithful can live their faith in two "forms" of the Roman Rite, each with a different spiritual ethos? Are there too many Christians such that we can afford to lose some along the way in the name of a closed vision of liturgical unity, when John Paul II praised "this diversity [which]

10 Some see in this the influence of the Roman liturgists of Sant'Anselmo, Prof. Andrea Grillo in particular.

also constitutes the beauty of unity in variety"?[11] Francis believes that "those who wish to celebrate devoutly according to the previous liturgical form will have no difficulty in finding in the Roman missal, reformed in the spirit of the Second Vatican Council, all the elements of the Roman rite." This is a very authoritarian and clerical way of dealing with the problem, and even if the Pope calls for praiseworthy efforts to celebrate the reformed Mass better, it is clear that for the past fifty years the celebration of this Mass in an eastward-oriented way, in Latin, and sung in Gregorian chant — things possible according to the reformed books — remains marginal, confined essentially to the Saint-Martin Community or to abbeys such as Solesmes, at least for that which concerns Latin and Gregorian chant.

FAILURE OF SUMMORUM PONTIFICUM?

In conclusion, can we say that *Summorum Pontificum* was a failure? No doubt it was, if, like Francis, one fails to remark the diversity of the traditionalist world. This 2007 motu proprio has, however, led to a "calmer situation," according to the French bishops themselves; it has also allowed the Tridentine Mass to be decompartmentalized, to be known by many young priests who testify that it has helped them to celebrate the Ordinary Form better. Benedict XVI's objective was to disconnect this ancient liturgy from the "trad" world, so that it would no longer be its exclusivity or its "property": in this respect, the results are mixed, but it is true that few efforts have been made in this direction and that not enough time has been given to this promising experiment.

Benedict XVI was also concerned with resolving the Lefebvrist rupture: the liberalization of the old Mass was a prerequisite posed at the time by Bishop Fellay, then Superior General of the Society of St. Pius X. From this point of view, the failure is obvious, since no agreement of reconciliation was obtained, despite the meritorious efforts of the pope. Nevertheless, the motu proprios of John Paul II and Benedict XVI have been successful in stemming the number of defectors to the Society of St. Pius X, since the Ecclesia Dei movement has grown from almost nothing in 1988 to many more faithful today. It is to be feared that, from this point of view, *Traditionis Custodes* will lead to the opposite result.

In this regard, Rome's credibility in ecumenical matters may not emerge unscathed, and the Society of St. Pius X is now at liberty to say that Rome cannot be trusted. If what has been conceded widely (*Ecclesia Dei*) and then recognized as a right (*Summorum Pontificum*) can be forbidden going forward,

---

11   Motu proprio *Ecclesia Dei*, n. 5a.

what will happen, for example, to the personal ordinariates established by Benedict XVI to accommodate groups of Anglicans who have been granted the faculty to celebrate the sacraments according to the books proper to their tradition?

Finally, we remain convinced that the only way to resolve the complex issues related to liturgical reform and the Second Vatican Council is to consider them within the effective approach developed by Benedict XVI of the "hermeneutics of reform, of renewal in the continuity of the one subject-Church."

61

A Regrettable Step Backwards[†]

ARCHBISHOP HÉCTOR AGUER

InfoCatólica

August 24, 2021

I WAS ORDAINED A PRIEST FOR THE ARCHDIOCESE OF Buenos Aires on November 25, 1972; I celebrated my first Mass the following day in the parish of San Isidro Labrador (Saavedra neighborhood), where I had resided all that year, exercising the diaconate. Obviously I celebrated according to the Novus Ordo promulgated in 1970. I have never celebrated "the ancient Mass," not even after the motu proprio *Summorum Pontificum*; I would have to study the rite, of which I have distant memories, having served as an altar boy. Recently, while attending the Divine Liturgy of the Syrian Orthodox Church, I seemed to notice a certain resemblance to the Latin Solemn Mass with deacon and subdeacon, in which I often assisted, especially at funerals, which in my parish were often celebrated with special solemnity.

I insist: I have always celebrated, with the greatest devotion I can muster, the rite in force in the Universal Church. When I was Archbishop of La Plata, I used to sing the Eucharistic prayer in Latin every Saturday at the "St. Joseph" Major Seminary, using the precious Missal published by the Holy See. We had formed, according to the recommendation of the Second Vatican Council in the Constitution *Sacrosanctum Concilium* n. 114, a *schola cantorum*, which was eliminated at my retirement. *Traditionis Custodes* (Art. 3 §4) speaks of a priest delegated by the bishop to be in charge of the celebrations of the Mass and the pastoral care of the faithful of the groups authorized to use the Missal prior to the reform of 1970. It states that he "should have a knowledge of the Latin language." It should be remembered that it is possible to celebrate in Latin the Mass currently in force in the whole Church. The Council affirmed in *Sacrosanctum Concilium* 36 §1, "Particular law remaining in force, the use of the Latin language is to be preserved in the Latin rites." Unfortunately, the "particular law" seems to be to prohibit Latin, as in fact is done (this is not a *boutade*). If someone dares to propose celebrating in Latin, he is looked upon as a misguided, unforgivable troglodyte.

† Translated from the Spanish by E. F. and published at *Rorate Caeli* on August 25.

Latin was for centuries the bond of unity and communication in the Western Church. Today it is not only abandoned, but hated. In the seminaries its study is neglected, precisely because it is not useful. They do not realize that this closes off direct access to the Fathers of the Western Church, who are very important for theological studies: I am thinking, for example, of St. Augustine and St. Leo the Great, and of medieval authors such as St. Anselm and St. Bernard. This situation seems to me to be a sign of cultural poverty and willful ignorance.

I wrote down those stories about my beginnings in the ministry to show that in my priestly life I have never nourished nostalgia for not being able to use the previous rite, which so many priests and saints celebrated for centuries. However, my theological studies and many readings and constant reflection on the Church's liturgy allow me to judge and maintain that instead of creating a new Mass, the previous one could have been updated in a discreet reform that strongly emphasized continuity. In this regard, I recall an eloquent anecdote. The eminent theologian Louis Bouyer relates that the secretary of the *Consilium ad exsequendam Constitutionem de Sacra Liturgia*, Bishop Annibale Bugnini (frequently and widely reputed to be a Freemason), required certain members of that Commission to present as an exercise drafts of Eucharistic prayers. Bouyer relates that he, with the Benedictine liturgist Dom Botte, composed, in a trattoria in Trastevere, a text that to his astonishment was included in the new Missal as Eucharistic Prayer II! It is the one chosen by most priests, because its brevity gives them the impression of shortening the Mass by a few seconds. It seems to me a very beautiful text; I only regret that the word *sacrificium* does not appear in it, but rather the notion of memorial, since after the consecration is said *memores*; the faithful cannot identify the memorial with the sacrifice that is offered.

What has been written so far is a kind of prologue, by way of justification, to the rapid critical commentary that follows on the motu proprio *Traditionis Custodes*, dated July 16 of this year, which establishes new dispositions for the use of the Missal edited in 1962 by St. John XXIII. It is recognized that St. John Paul II and Benedict XVI wished to promote concord and unity in the Church, and that they proceeded with paternal solicitude towards those who adhered to the liturgical forms prior to Vatican II. The current Pontiff declares that he wishes to pursue still further the constant search for ecclesial communion (Prologue of *Traditionis Custodes*) and, in order to make this purpose effective, he eliminates the work of his predecessors by placing arbitrary limits and obstacles to what they established with intra-ecclesial ecumenical intention and respect for the freedom of priests and faithful! It promotes ecclesial communion in reverse. The new measures imply a regrettable step backwards.

The basis of this intervention — the prologue says — is a consultation of the Congregation for the Doctrine of the Faith addressed to the bishops in 2020 on the application of Benedict XVI's motu proprio *Summorum Pontificum*, the results of which (it says) have been carefully considered. It would be interesting to know what were the auspices formulated by the Episcopate.

Thus, in the first article, the extraordinary form of the Roman Rite is eliminated. The purpose of Benedict XVI in making official the free use of the 1962 Missal was — as I understand it — to attract or maintain within the unity of the Church those who, scandalized by the universal liturgical devastation, had turned away or risked turning away because they did not wish to accept this *de facto* situation. An affection for ecclesial communion determined the opening of a reasonable way for liturgical living. It is now in the hands of the diocesan bishops to grant authorization for the use of the previous missal. Everything begins anew, and it is to be feared that the bishops will be miserly in granting permissions. Many bishops are not *traditionis custodes*, but *traditionis ignari* (ignorant), *obliviosi* (forgetful), and even worse, *traditionis evertores* (destroyers).

I think it is very good to require [of the faithful who assist at the old rite] that they not exclude the validity and legitimacy of the decrees of Vatican II, of the liturgical reform, and of the magisterium of the Supreme Pontiffs. For those who already made use of the extraordinary form of the Roman Rite, was the ordinary vigilance of the bishops and the eventual correction of offenders not sufficient? It would be necessary to use charity and patience with the rebels; there is no lack of good arguments. This approach would complete the just requirement expressed in Article 3 §1.

The limitation of places and days for celebrating according to the 1962 Missal (Art 3 §2 and §3) presents unjust and undesirable restrictions. Every priest should be able to use the extraordinary form of the Roman Rite (this means backtracking on the prohibition) in the first place when celebrating alone, and also in public wherever the faithful are already celebrating it if the priest has explained that he would use that Ordo, highlighting its venerable antiquity and religious value. The bishop's vigilance would suffice to ensure that this faculty is not exercised against the pastoral benefit of the faithful.

Article 3 §6 is an unjust and painful restriction by preventing other groups of the faithful from enjoying participation in the Mass celebrated according to the 1962 Missal. It is curious that while officially promoting a "polyhedral" structure of the Church, with the ease that this attitude implies for the spread of dissent and errors against the Catholic Tradition, a liturgical uniformity is imposed that seems to have been chosen solely against that Tradition. I know that many young people in our parishes are fed up with the liturgical abuses that the hierarchy allows without correcting them; they desire a Eucharistic celebration that guarantees a serious and profoundly religious participation. There is nothing ideological in this aspiration.

I also find it unpleasant that the priest who already has the permission and has exercised it correctly should have to apply for it again (Art. 5 §1). Is this not a ploy to take the permission away from him? It occurs to me that perhaps there are more than a few bishops (new bishops, for example) who are reluctant to grant it.

All the provisions of *Traditionis Custodes* would be gladly acceptable if the Holy See would attend to what I call the devastation of the liturgy, which occurs in many cases. I can speak of what happens in Argentina. In general, it is quite common that the Eucharistic celebration assumes a tone of banality, as if it were a conversation the priest has with the faithful, and in which the congeniality of the priest is fundamental; in certain places it becomes a kind of show presided over by the "entertainer" who is the celebrant, and the children's Mass becomes a little party like the kind held for birthdays. Among us there has been an event that I hope is exceptional; I have no news that something similar has happened in other parts of the world. A bishop celebrated Mass on the beach, dressed in a beach habit on which he wore a stole; a small tablecloth on the sand (or a corporal), and instead of the chalice a *mate*. (Clarification for foreigners: *mate* is a dried and emptied gourd used to drink an infusion of *yerba mate*, and the act of drinking the infusion through a *bombilla* is also called *mate*; it is usually a community exercise: the *mate* is circulated among those present and someone is in charge of priming it.) Other cases that have become known show the celebration as the closing of a meeting. Papers, glasses, soft drinks are left on the table; the faithful help themselves to communion. In general, it can be said from this geographical angle of vision that each priest has "his" Mass; the faithful can choose: "I go to Father N's Mass."

The bishops are not concerned with these realities, but they are quick to react against a priest who with utmost piety celebrates in Latin: "it" is forbidden. Could this prohibition be the "particular law" referred to in the Constitution *Sacrosanctum Concilium* 36 § 1, in the passage where it speaks of the preservation of Latin? By virtue of this criterion, Latin chants that were commonly sung by the simple faithful in parishes, such as the *Tantum ergo* at the Eucharistic Benediction, have disappeared from use. The lack of correction of abuses leads to the persuasion that "this is how the liturgy is now." It would suffice simply to enforce what the Council determined, with prophetic wisdom: "that no one, even a priest, should add, subtract or change anything in the liturgy on his own initiative" (*Sacrosanctum Concilium* 22 § 3). It cannot be denied that the Eucharistic celebration has lost accuracy, solemnity, and beauty. And silence has disappeared in many cases. Sacred music (*sacred?*), according to *Sacrosanctum Concilium*, deserved a separate chapter. [1] I insist: Rome should concern itself with and pronounce itself on these disorders.

To conclude, I seem to notice a relationship in the tone of this decisive decree and the speech given by the Holy Father last June 7, addressed to the community of priests of St. Louis des Français in Rome. I perceive in both texts (I could be wrong, of course) a lack of affection, despite certain appearances. It is true that the motu proprio, by the nature of its genre, does not allow for pastoral effusions; however, in its conciseness it could have been presented as a sign of pastoral love. The comparison does not seem arbitrary to me. In both cases it would be desirable to notice that merciful attitude so celebrated in the current Pontiff. It would seem that the judgment of the course of ecclesial life that the Church renders in its highest court proceeds according to two weights and two measures at variance with each other: on the one hand, tolerance and even appreciation and identification with heterogeneous positions with respect to the great Tradition ("progressive," as they have been called), and, on the other hand, distance or dislike with respect to persons or groups that cultivate a "traditional" position. I am reminded of the resolution brutally enunciated by a famous Argentine politician [Juan Domingo Perón]: "To the friend, everything; to the enemy, not even justice." I say this with the utmost respect and love, but with immense sorrow.

---

1   That is, the subject was deemed so important it was made chapter 6 of the conciliar Constitution.

62

When a Bishop Outlaws Private Traditional Masses

PETER A. KWASNIEWSKI

OnePeterFive

August 24, 2021

IN A THREE-PAGE LETTER DATED AUGUST 20, 2021, AND addressed to "Dear Brothers in Christ," Most Reverend David A. Zubik, Bishop of Pittsburgh—apparently in an effort to show that he is more Bergoglian than Bergoglio—takes a hearty step beyond what is demanded by a strict interpretation of Pope Francis's motu proprio *Traditionis Custodes* [TC]. In spite of the fact that Pittsburgh is one of the United States' most depressed and collapsing dioceses—as can be seen from relentless parish closures that have left the city pockmarked with churches converted into restaurants, bars, penthouses, and other secular venues—the infusion of spiritual energy from the wellsprings of tradition is evidently too risky to allow. Better a dead church than a traditional one.

The bishop's letter is a disturbing sign of how bishops who lack understanding of or sympathy with Catholic tradition and who fail to grasp the pastoral advisability of invoking Canon 87 might end up "applying" TC within their dioceses. Zubik declares that there will be only one "full-service" TLM parish in the entire city, namely, The Most Precious Blood of Jesus, run by the Institute of Christ the King Sovereign Priest. At two other named parishes, Masses will be allowed occasionally, but expressly *not* on Christmas, Easter, and Pentecost. The other sacraments (Baptism, Confirmation, Confession, Marriage, Extreme Unction) are permitted *only* for registered parishioners of the Institute's apostolate; any other use is forbidden.

Worst of all, diocesan priests are forbidden to offer private Masses in the traditional Roman Rite. The bishop writes:

> With the promulgation of *Traditionis Custodes* on July 16, priests no longer have general permission or faculties to celebrate the Eucharist or the other sacraments according to the Roman Missal of 1962, not even in private. Instead, they must be expressly given the faculty to do so by their local diocesan bishop (or his delegate).

> Furthermore, the Holy Father has made it clear that permission for
> the celebration of the Eucharist according to the Roman Missal of
> 1962 is not meant to be for the personal devotion of any particular
> priest; rather, it is only to be given for the benefit of groups of
> the faithful. . . . Once again, this faculty will not be granted to
> priests who request permission to celebrate privately according to
> the Roman Missal of 1962.

Let us think for a moment about the implications of this step.

The Latin Mass of the Roman Rite that has never ceased to be offered,
at whatever stage of its development, from the fourth century until today
(even after 1969 there was never a total break in the celebration of the *usus
antiquior*): this is now deemed so harmful to Church unity, so dangerous
to souls, that even a priest who, on a given day, has no other pastoral
responsibility is to be forbidden its use? Even the priest who finds great
spiritual nourishment in the rich *lex orandi* of the traditional Mass, who
knows from experience that it unites him in a special way to the Holy
Sacrifice of the Cross and helps him to pray fervently for the intention of
the Mass — he must be deprived of this food, this more profound union,
this more intense grace of devotion, which (as we know from St. Thomas
Aquinas) wins greater fruits from the Mass?

Over the years, I've heard from many priests whose discovery of the
Latin Mass has transformed their priesthood and their entire spiritual life,
renewing their youth like the eagle's. Typically, they start by saying the
usus antiquior once in a while; then it moves up to once a week on their
day off, an oasis in the midst of the heat; then they find a way to get it
into the parish schedule, even adding a Sunday Mass.[1] In his book *Cor Iesu
Sacratissimum*, Roger Buck quotes from a letter sent to him by just such a
priest, who readily celebrates the reformed Mass but especially values his
contact with the old rite:

> These [traditional] Masses are special to me, and so great a priv-
> ilege to be united with Christ as His Priest, and offer with Him

---

1 Do we ever hear about a priest starting with the traditional Latin Mass and then
"discovering" the greatness of the Novus Ordo and moving over more and more to
it, until he offers it exclusively? Until he has a longing in his heart and his hands to
offer just the Novus Ordo, even to the point of suffering for it, and possibly losing
everything? No, we do not. Once in a blue moon we hear of a traditional priest who
goes diocesan and alternates between the two rites for pastoral reasons — but the
spiritually transformative experience that I described is a grace that flows from the
springs of tradition. To me, this says more about the realities we are dealing with than
a thousand documents from the Vatican, or from diocesan chanceries, could ever tell us.

the sacrifice of Calvary, for the living and the dead. It is through using the Tridentine form that I have come to appreciate something of the great significance of what I am doing each morning. Can there be anything more important than this?

Archbishop Carlo Maria Viganò movingly testifies:

> Many priests discover the treasures of the venerable Tridentine liturgy only when they celebrate it and allow themselves to be permeated by it, and it is not uncommon for an initial curiosity towards the "extraordinary form" — certainly fascinating due to the solemnity of the rite — to change quickly into the awareness of the depth of the words, the clarity of the doctrine, the incomparable spirituality that it gives birth to and nourishes in our souls.
>
> There is a perfect harmony that words cannot express, and that the faithful can understand only in part, but which touches the heart of the Priesthood as only God can. This can be confirmed by my confreres who have approached the *usus antiquior* after decades of obedient celebration of the *Novus Ordo*: a world opens up, a cosmos that includes the prayer of the Breviary with the lessons of Matins and the commentaries of the Fathers, the cross-references to the texts of the Mass, the Martyrology in the Hour of Prime…
>
> They are sacred words — not because they are expressed in Latin, but rather they are expressed in Latin because the vulgar language would demean them, would profane them, as Dom Guéranger wisely observed. These are the words of the Bride to the divine Bridegroom, words of the soul that lives in intimate union with God, of the soul that lets itself be inhabited by the Most Holy Trinity. Essentially priestly words, in the deepest sense of the term, which implies in the Priesthood not only the power to offer sacrifice, but to unite in self-offering to the pure, holy, and immaculate Victim. [2]

Abolishing the private traditional Mass is something so evil one can hardly fathom it. That's what an enemy of Christ and His Church would do. No one but an enemy would seek to outlaw this consolidator of priestly identity, this font of fervent prayer, this haven of spiritual refreshment and copious graces.

Priests would be entirely within their rights before God and Holy Mother Church to refuse to comply with such restrictions or prohibitions

---

2 See chapter 43.

(as previous "disobedience" to unjust liturgical commands has been twice exonerated by the Holy See itself).[3] Priests in the diocese of Pittsburgh or any other diocese that implements a similarly cruel and anticlerical policy should continue to celebrate the Latin Mass and to utilize the other traditional sacramental rites whenever it is possible to do so, e.g., if they go somewhere on retreat, or are visiting trustworthy family and friends.

Yet this watershed might also be a priest's moment of realization. Could this be a call from the Lord to continue calmly doing what he was doing before, in defiance of a manifestly unjust prohibition? Such a course of action is almost certain to result in his being sacrificed ("cancelled") like a lamb led to the slaughter. The priest will likely be called on the carpet, stripped of faculties, hung out to dry — because, don't you know, we have so many extra clergy that we can just afford to retire them early if they don't fit the mold!

Perhaps it is time for many priestly grains of wheat to fall into the ground and die, so that they may bear a greater fruit of holiness than collaboration with abusive chanceries would allow. They will quickly find laity who will support them in their needs. More home chapels than ever are being built; the lay faithful are busy preparing for this next phase of resistance to wayward pastors' attacks on the Church's common good.

Let us recall that traditional Catholic worship and the way of life it sustains was saved in the late sixties and seventies by priests and laity willing to do exactly this, and nothing less, to remain true to what they knew to be true.[4] It was initially a tiny minority who kept the flame burning and who spread it, one person at a time, across the world. Very often they had to do so outside of the official structures of the Church, or rather, outside of the self-endorsing legal fictions of churchmen and their self-destructive "renewal." They were, for a time, "pastors out in the cold,"[5] but they would

---

3 See "Why the Term 'Extraordinary Form' is Wrong," *The Meaning of Catholic*, August 9, 2019. It is crucial to understand that, in the Catholic tradition, obedience has precise requirements and limits. For more on this point, see Peter Kwasniewski, *The Holy Bread of Eternal Life: Restoring Eucharistic Reverence in an Age of Impiety* (Manchester, NH: Sophia Institute Press, 2020), 257–71. As St. Thomas Aquinas teaches, an unjust law does not have the rationale of law and therefore should not be followed. In this case, the one who does not follow it is not guilty of the sin of disobedience but rather is to be praised for obedience to a higher law. On the question of whether TC possesses the wherewithal to be legitimate, see chapter 19, above.

4 See my article "It's Time to Imitate Our Forefathers: Never Give Up!," *OnePeterFive*, July 28, 2021.

5 See Jean-Claude Dupuis, "A Tribute to Father Normandin (1925–2020)," *Rorate Caeli*, February 7, 2021.

never exchange their clean conscience, Catholic integrity, pastoral fruitfulness, and spiritual consolation for any emoluments from a corrupt and corrosive system.

Stuart Chessman of the Society of St. Hugh of Cluny analyzed the transition from cold war to hot war:

> Everywhere there's a sense that a boundary has been crossed, that the Church has moved into new and uncharted waters. War does have the advantage of clarifying issues and power relationships, of advancing from mystification to reality.
>
> However, the "fortunes of war" are inherently unpredictable. A nation, like France in 1870, may enter into war, as its prime minister at that time, Émile Ollivier, said, "with a light heart." So did all Europe in 1914, Germany in Russia in 1941, Japan at Pearl Harbor later that same year, and the United States subsequently in Vietnam, Iraq, and Afghanistan. In all these cases, the confrontation that emerged was unimaginably different from the assumptions governing at the beginning. The Roman Catholic Church will shortly be experiencing the same.
>
> Moreover, Pope Francis has declared his intent to conduct that most difficult of martial undertakings, an aggressive war of annihilation. As Martin van Creveld points out, such a war, by leaving the enemy only two outcomes: victory or extinction, dramatically solidifies the enemy's will to resist regardless of what his previous political or military weakness may have been. In this respect, TC is the "Operation Barbarossa" of the Church.[6]

"Operation Barbarossa" was the code name for Hitler's invasion of Russia in 1941. It commenced with the German Reich at a high tide of power and confidence, with wave after wave of soldiers and fearsome military equipment. Surely this campaign could not fail. But fail it did, and rapidly. The fortunes of war turned against the Reich's hunger for hegemony.

For its part, *Traditionis Custodes* marks a similar attempt on the part of the progressive faction that holds most of the Church's offices. They have gambled everything on a final assault against the last outposts withstanding their wintry "new Pentecost." Those who comply with unjust decrees will place themselves by that very fact on the side of the would-be extinguishers of Catholic tradition. Those who find ways to resist, be it secretly or openly, will have the merit and glory of fighting for the faith of our fathers, which,

---

6 See "*Traditionis Custodes*: Dispatches from the Front," *The Society of St. Hugh of Cluny*, August 18, 2021.

so far from being our possession to treat as if it were raw material for exploitation, is to be gratefully received as a fully-formed gift, which we humbly benefit from, and faithfully hand on.

This is the true Spirit of Pentecost, which those who have been touched by the Pentecost Octave (abolished in the Novus Ordo),[7] who have savored each day the honeysweet words of the *Veni, Sancte Spiritus*, have come to know as their source of unconquerable fortitude in the midst of a conflict for which all human forces are inadequate.

To quote once more Archbishop Viganò:

> How many of you priests — and certainly also many lay people — in reciting the wonderful verses of the Pentecost Sequence were moved to tears, understanding that your initial predilection for the traditional liturgy had nothing to do with a sterile aesthetic satisfaction, but had evolved into a real spiritual necessity, as indispensable as breathing? How can you and how can we explain to those who today would like to deprive you of this priceless good, that that blessed rite has made you discover the true nature of your priesthood, and that from it and only from it are you able to draw strength and nourishment to face the commitments of your ministry? How can you make it clear that the obligatory return to [exclusively] the Montinian rite represents an impossible sacrifice for you, because in the daily battle against the world, the flesh, and the devil it leaves you disarmed, prostrate, and without strength?... It is not a question of nostalgia, of a cult of the past: here we are speaking of the life of the soul, its spiritual growth, ascesis and mysticism. Concepts that those who see their priesthood as a profession cannot even understand . . .[8]

---

7   See my article "What's the Big Deal with the Pentecost Octave?," *The Remnant*, May 22, 2021.
8   See chapter 43.

63

Traditionis Custodes: Divide and Conquer?†

JEAN-PIERRE MAUGENDRE

Renaissance Catholique

August 25, 2021

THE ANTHILL IS IN TURMOIL. WITH THE MOTU PRO-
prio *Traditionis Custodes*, which aims to do away with the traditional Latin Mass by affirming that "the [reformed] liturgical books are the only expression of the *lex orandi* of the Roman rite," Pope Francis has given a masterly kick to the anthill of the traditional world, which was developing peacefully under the more or less benevolent eye of the ecclesiastical authorities.

Reactions and analyses have been numerous. Charlotte d'Ornellas (in *Valeurs actuelles*, "Who wants the trads to die?") pitted the "good trads" of the Ecclesia Dei communities against the evil "fundamentalists" of the Society of Saint Pius X, while Christophe Geffroy and Father Christian Gouyaud (in *La Nef*) divided the traditional world into three categories: the "good guys" who accept the Council and the new Mass, the "rigid" who do not refrain from criticism of the Council and the liturgical reform, and finally the "contestants," those through whom all evil comes, who reject the Council and the liturgical reform, and in particular the members of the Society of Saint Pius X.[1]

First of all, it is hardly good policy, when the teacher has just raised her voice in the classroom, to commence one's defense with, "It wasn't me, it was the boy next to me!" Christophe Geffroy's approach is, in fact, akin to denouncing those who do not play the game of accepting the Council and the liturgical reform without reservation. In fact, if the "good guys" — and it is not clear on what authority he affirms that they are in the majority — are called out by name, then the "bad guys," to varying degrees, are perfectly identifiable. We are here involved in the search for a scapegoat, very Girardian, which hardly seems to serve the common good of the Church and its Tradition.

---

† Translated from the French by Zachary Thomas and Peter Kwasniewski for this volume.
1 See chapter 60.

WHAT COMMUNION?

Basically, the expression "full communion with Rome" is regularly used by these authors to deplore the behavior of Charlotte d'Ornellas' "fundamentalists" who are also Christophe Geffroy's "rigid" and "schismatic" category. This formula is completely new and constitutes an unidentified theological object. Communion with the Church is manifested by adherence to the whole Creed and recognition of the authority of the pope and the bishops. The Society of Saint Pius X has never questioned a single dogma of faith and manifests its recognition of the authority of the pope and the bishops when the priests, at Mass, pray for the intentions of the Sovereign Pontiff and the local bishop. Similarly, during solemn Benediction with the Blessed Sacrament, the "Tu es Petrus" is sung publicly for the intentions of Pope Francis.

On August 8, the television program Le Jour du Seigneur (The Lord's Day) broadcast the Mass and the sermon of Brother Gabriel Nissim. In his homily, Brother Gabriel said: "The Mass is above all a meal, the Lord's Supper." Children for whom catechism was not limited to filling in coloring books and singing "Jesus, Come Back!" are able to respond to this grown-up priest that these words seem hardly reconcilable with the teaching of the Catechism of St. Pius X: "The Holy Mass is the sacrifice of the Body and Blood of Jesus Christ, offered on our altars under the species of bread and wine in commemoration of the Sacrifice of the Cross." Who, among those who preach "full communion with the Church," has publicly questioned the real communion of this preacher with the Tradition of the Church, on the basis of remarks that, in former times, would have earned him the wrath of the Holy Office? No one, to our knowledge. It so happens, moreover, that the devotees of "full communion" are often also fervent believers in the "hermeneutic of continuity." We await with interest the "homogeneous development" that would transform the Mass from a sacrifice to a meal, as well as the coherence between Traditionis Custodes and the conciliar teaching of Sacrosanctum Concilium art. 4: "The Holy Council declares that the Holy Church considers all legitimately recognized rites to be equal in right and dignity, and that she wishes to preserve and favor them in the future in every way." Nor should we forget, on this subject, what Cardinal Ratzinger had recalled in his Principles of Catholic Theology: "This text [Gaudium et Spes] plays the role of a 'counter-syllabus' [to Pius IX's Syllabus of Errors of December 8, 1864] insofar as it represents an attempt for an official reconciliation of the Church with the world as it had developed since 1789." Let's just say that none of this asks to be taken very seriously.

In the face of this authoritarianism, one bishop, Msgr. Mutsaerts, auxiliary bishop of Bois-le-Duc in the Netherlands, declared: "The liturgy is not a toy of the popes but the heritage of the Church."[2]

Many observers also frequently return to the "schismatic act" of the episcopal consecrations of 1988. On that date, Archbishop Lefebvre, at the age of 83, proceeded with what he called "Operation Survival of Tradition," by consecrating four bishops, without any jurisdiction, but also without a pontifical mandate. In fact, the Holy See had agreed in principle to the consecration of a bishop, but its repeated procrastination about the date led him to fear that Rome was trying to gain time until his death. It should be noted that the 330-member Fraternity of Saint Peter, founded by former priests of the Fraternity of Saint Pius X, has still not seen one of its priests become a bishop, more than thirty years after its foundation.

WHAT ARE THE MOTIVES?

In fact, the so-called "good guys" are those who seem to have no real and objective reason to make the choices they have made. They have chosen the traditional liturgy "and what goes with it" (Mgr. Brouwet), but we don't really know *why*, since they are supposed to have nothing to say in reproach of that which they have left. Call the psychiatrist! Spare us the argument that the Mass we find in parishes is not the Mass of the Council. Everyone knows that the "conciliar authorities" have never condemned these parish practices as they have the traditional Mass. The fact that, almost sixty years after its conclusion, the Council has still not been properly "received" leads one to question, at the very least, its clarity.

Finally, to oppose the evil "integralists" of the Society of Saint Pius X or the disciples of Abbé Barthe to the good trads of certain Ecclesia Dei communities is a dialectical vision of the life of the Church already denounced in his day by Jean Madiran: "The terms 'integralists' and 'integralism' were born and spread as polemical sobriquets" (*L'intégrisme: Histoire d'une histoire*). They live by the same faith, receive the same sacraments, are confronted with the same difficulties in the education of their children, and often attend the same places for Mass. This is undoubtedly what too many observers forget: the crisis of the Church persists, and is even growing. Generally speaking, participants in the traditional Mass are only looking to pray in a ceremony that is not a "self-celebration of the community" (J. Ratzinger) but a true liturgy, transcendent and leading them to God. The priorities of these lay people could be enumerated as follows:

---

2   See chapter 30.

first the faith and the sacraments, then the hierarchy, then canon law.

They love and respect the priests who preach to them the Catholic faith in its integrity. Such priests remind them that the Mass is a sacrifice, that the Blessed Virgin Mary is the Immaculate Conception, that hell exists and is not empty, etc. How many parishes preach these truths? Too few! The priority in most homilies is rather the obligation to get vaccinated or to welcome migrants.

Traditionalist laymen are, of course, not much concerned with the con-celebration of priests and generally have little interest in the Acts of the Second Vatican Council, a dated *pensum*[3] of 800 pages. They have no inten-tion, however, of "returning in due course to the Roman rite promulgated by Saints Paul VI and John Paul II." They know what they have left and why. All they really ask is to pray in peace and to live, quietly, in the faith of their fathers. What harm is there in that?

---

3   A *pensum* is a task assigned in school, often as a punishment.

64

Defense of the Motu Proprio Collapsing in Contradictions

JOSEPH SHAW

OnePeterFive

August 25, 2021

POPE FRANCIS HAS OFFERED TWO REASONS FOR WISHING to bring celebrations of the Traditional Mass to an end: attitudes of some of the faithful which have become associated with this form of the Mass, and the idea that the unity of the Church requires a unity of liturgical rite. Accordingly, some of his defenders have focused on one of these points, and some on the other. Both are having difficulty explaining and justifying Pope Francis's action.

TARGETING THE INNOCENT TO PUNISH THE GUILTY?

I recently fisked an article by Michael Sean Winters which laid the blame for *Traditionis Custodes* (TC) on the people who like the Latin Mass, singling out the journalist Michael Brendan Dougherty.[1] There is much wrong with Winters' argument, but supposing he was right about Dougherty being a dangerous schismatic, what would be the significance of this? To be crass about it, who cares what some journalist thinks? If Dougherty were the head of an organization, clerical or lay, with serious popular support, which was closely associated with the TLM, that might indicate a wider problem, but as it is, it proves nothing at all.

As if realizing that he needed to widen his evidence base, towards the end of his article Winters brings in Martin Mosebach, accusing him of rejecting Vatican II without being able to quote him doing so, and the views of George Weigel, apparently unaware that Weigel has a long and distinguished history of gratuitously insulting Catholics attached to the Traditional Mass.[2] As a

---

1 Michael Brendan Dougherty, "Pope Francis Is Tearing the Catholic Church Apart," *New York Times*, August 12, 2021 (see chapter 54); Michael Sean Winters, "Traditional Latin Mass advocates prove Pope Francis was right to suppress the old rite," *National Catholic Reporter*, August 16, 2021; Joseph Shaw, "Michael Sean Winters attacks Michael Brendan Dougherty," LMS *Chairman*, August 17, 2021.
2 See my article "Response to George Weigel in *The Tablet*," *Joseph Shaw's Philosophy Blog*, July 16, 2017.

representative of the movement, he doesn't really fit the bill. Nevertheless, that's the best Winters can come up with.

Another problem with this approach is identified by Terrence Sweeney on the *Where Peter Is* blog, and in fact is acknowledged even by Winters himself: in Sweeney's words, "Even if many are acting schismatically, this does not justify a restriction that affects those who attend the Tridentine rite but remain faithful." [3]

It is not just that Pope Francis seems to be punishing the innocent along with the guilty. If deprivation of the Traditional Mass is indeed a punishment, it is not going to affect at all those ministered to by the SSPX, "independent" priests, and sedevacantists. I think I can say, without insulting anyone or risking contradiction, that if there are any people attending the TLM who say the Vatican II institutions are not (in the words of Pope Francis) the "true Church," you're a lot more likely to find them in those congregations than in the ones meekly obeying their bishops. But the only way they are going to be affected by TC is if they are crowded out of their own chapels by refugees from diocesan celebrations which have been closed down.

DEFENDING VATICAN II BY CONTRADICTING VATICAN II

So Winters takes the view that the real problem lies not in the views of the traddies (despite what Pope Francis says) but in the mere fact of two Missals being celebrated side by side. Fr. Anthony Ruff takes the same view, [4] and it conforms with the ideas of Andrea Grillo, widely regarded as responsible for drafting TC. The three of them have all come up with variations on the idea that liturgical diversity puts the unity of the Church at risk.

This does indeed seem to be implied by TC, but it presents the difficulty that Vatican II was in favor of liturgical diversity, not against it. Allow me to be the thousandth person to quote *Sacrosanctum Concilium* 37: "even in the liturgy, the Church has no wish to impose a rigid uniformity." And again, *Orientalium Ecclesiarum* 2: "variety [sc. of Rites] within the Church in no way harms its unity; rather it manifests it." It is a puzzle that in order to manifest the truths of Vatican II, one must contradict Vatican II.

This awkward fact means that these authors have to come up with a reason why the diversity of the old and new forms of the Roman Rite is bad, while other kinds of diversity are acceptable, and even good. Accordingly, they claim that the reformed Mass is superior, a better and more complete expression of the theology of the Church as developed by Vatican II. This is

---

3   "Pope Francis: Guardian of Tradition," *Where Peter Is*, August 18, 2021.
4   Fr. Anthony Ruff and Joseph Shaw, "Two Views on Liturgical Reform," *Rorate Caeli*, August 2, 2021.

a natural claim for them to make, but in itself it doesn't really help. Suppose we say that one liturgical form or rite is superior to another, it surely doesn't follow that the inferior one needs to be utterly obliterated. That has never been the Church's principle of liturgical development. Indeed, given how views about what makes for a good liturgy vary, between people and over time, it has the potential to be a very destructive principle indeed.

DEFENDING ECUMENISM BY DESTROYING ECUMENISM

More problems arise when we look at the features of the liturgy which they think show that it is superior to the Traditional Mass. It uses a vernacular language. It has a multi-year lectionary. It allows the people to hear the liturgy clearly, and make responses.

There are also more vague claims, such as that it includes the people, "activates" the laity, and militates against "clericalism" (though Sweeney has the grace to admit that the Novus Ordo has its own form of clericalism), but presumably these are consequences of the concrete features already mentioned.

The problem is that if they were trying to avoid the conclusion that the diversity represented by Eastern and Western Rites is okay, but not the diversity between the old and new Missals of the West, they have come up with precisely the wrong features to pick out. If the TLM must be annihilated because it lacks these features, if liturgical diversity between a liturgical form which has these features and one which does not is intolerable because the latter is an implicit rejection of Vatican II, then it follows that the Church's Eastern Rites will need to be wiped off the face of the earth as well. Indeed, even those with a limited knowledge of these rites will realize that some of these features are more strongly present in them than they are in the traditional Roman Rite. Use of a sacred language? Check. One year lectionary? Check. Liturgical rites difficult to hear (or, indeed, see)? Check.

Indeed, what of the Iconostasis, which prevents the people from seeing what is going on in much of the Mass in the major Eastern Churches? If the Roman Rite of the Medieval period was bad, with the Rood Screen and silent Canon, this is presumably worse. And on this admittedly ridiculous way of judging a liturgy, the Roman Rite as celebrated today is better than the Roman Rite as celebrated in the Middle Ages, because Rood Screens went out of fashion several centuries ago and very few churches still have them.

The richest aspect of the hole these writers have dug themselves into is the fact that one of the things those bad people attached to the Traditional Mass are supposed to be against is ecumenism (a claim made by Fr. Thomas

Reese).[5] What kind of ecumenism, we might ask, is based on the denigration of the ancient and beautiful liturgical traditions of our dialogue partners the Eastern Churches, liturgies which date from long before the tragedy of 1054, and which are the glory of these Churches? Which made the ambassadors of Vladimir the Great of Russia return from Constantinople and report, with awe, that they knew not whether they had been in heaven or on earth? Which evangelized vast regions of Central and Eastern Europe and Asia, and which sustained the Faith of hundreds of millions of Christians, under centuries of Islamic rule, and the horrors of Communist persecution?

I would say, politely, that these writers have not thought this one through. The truth is that they are afflicted with an extraordinary parochialism, both of place and in time. The problem of the Eastern Rites has been pointed out to them, and they sometimes even acknowledge it, as with the amusing Footnote 2 of Sweeney's article: "Nothing I am saying here is meant to indicate any disunity between the Rites nor is it meant to indicate any inferiority of the other Catholic Rites." All the same, they can't bring themselves to take it seriously. Oh that's just some silly marginal phenomenon, they seem to say, don't distract us from the main issue. But it's not marginal at all, it is a crucial matter of principle with giddying implications for world-wide ecclesial politics.

They are even more immune to the point that the Western Church itself has several Rites, some reformed after the Council, and some still used as they were before it. Okay, so most Catholics don't attend these, particularly if one's experience is solely of the USA, but then they keep reminding us that only a tiny percentage of Catholics attend the Traditional Roman Rite: it is present in "less than of 4% of all Mass venues in the United States," and 6.5% of Mass venues in the United Kingdom, according to The Pillar.[6] In nearly all of these places it would be a matter of one Traditional Mass being celebrated on a Sunday or indeed on a weekday, alongside, say, eight Novus Ordo celebrations over the week. If we don't need to worry about small-scale anomalies like the reformed Ambrosian Rite or the unreformed Dominican Rite, tell us again why the attendance of Catholics at the Traditional Roman Rite represents some cosmic contradiction of Vatican II which must be expurgated from the Church lest some terrible consequence arise?

It seems to me that the defenders of TC need to come up with some better arguments.

---

5   See my article "Pope's Latin Mass Edict Not Only Attacks Catholics, but Harms Interreligious Dialogue," LifeSiteNews, July 26, 2021.
6   Brendan Hodge, "How Extraordinary is the Extraordinary Form? The Frequency of the 'Usus Antiquior,'" The Pillar, July 19, 2021.

65

The "Hermeneutic of Rupture" Cancels Pope Benedict— and the Council

A CATHOLIC PRIEST[1]

Rorate Caeli
August 27, 2021

PROFESSOR MARTIN MADAR HAS WRITTEN IN LA CROIX (August 9, 2021) a revealing article concerning the larger project represented by *Traditionis Custodes*. It bears the title "Pope Francis should correct his predecessor on another point." The project here is one to which all Catholics, especially bishops, should pay close attention because it reveals what is really at stake in the current debates about the future of the traditional Mass. It is not so much the individual author who matters: he stands in for an ecclesiastical party that is very prominent today; were it otherwise, Catholics outside the ivory tower could just ignore this article and others like it.

Here we have yet another rearguard attempt to achieve the permanent institutionalization of the "hermeneutic of rupture" which Benedict XVI had dedicated his pontificate to combating. We are told in this article that with his motu proprio, "Francis defended both the liturgical reform of Vatican II and the council's ecclesiology," but that "to be more thorough . . . Francis should correct a document of the Congregation for the Doctrine of the Faith (CDF) from 2007, which asserts that Vatican II did not change the doctrine on the church." In the rest of the article we can easily see the point: the author seems to bang his fist on the table and insist, *But, yes! Vatican II really did change everything! Nothing can be the same anymore! You can't believe like they did before the Council and you can't worship like they did the before the Council!* Although the author slams those he calls "Lefebvrists," it seems not to occur to him that he shares their basic thesis that "Vatican II changed everything," disagreeing only on whether the change was good or bad.

---

1 The author belongs to a traditional institute whose existence is threatened by *Traditionis Custodes*.

We shall return later to the attention paid by the author to the clarification made by the Congregation for the Doctrine of the Faith in 2007 and why he opines that it must be overturned. But first, some general considerations. In Catholicism today there are essentially three ways to grapple with the implications of the Second Vatican Council for the life of the Church going forward.

First, there is the more extreme (which does not necessarily mean false) traditionalist "rupturist" view which identifies outright contradictions between the teaching of Vatican II and that of earlier councils or popes, and which sees this rupture as a bad thing whose possibility can only be explained by the fact that the Council did not define dogmas or invoke the charism of infallibility for its teachings[2] and was thus theoretically capable of falling into error. In such a thesis, the resulting situation presses hard upon but does not destroy the indefectibility of the Church, which necessarily presupposes continuity in the Church's (infallible) teachings.

Second, there is the progressivist "rupturist" view, which also sees an essential difference between pre- and post-Vatican II Catholicism, viewing this as a *good* thing and going so far as to see the Council as a New Pentecost or even, as one might say today, a Great Reset. The putative contradiction between pre-conciliar and post-conciliar teaching on things like ecumenism or religious liberty is not a problem to be solved but a rupture to be celebrated, since it portends the hoped-for change in other doctrinal spheres such as those of sexual morality or women's ordination. For them, Vatican II opened the door to a new Church and we need to walk right through it and push back hard when anyone tries to shut the door.

---

2   In a doctrinal note preceding the conciliar constitution *Lumen Gentium*, an interpretive key is provided by this declaration already given by the Theological Commission of the Council on March 6, 1964: "Taking conciliar custom into consideration and also the pastoral purpose of the present Council, *the sacred Council defines as binding on the Church only those things in matters of faith and morals which it shall openly declare to be binding*. The rest of the things which the sacred Council sets forth, inasmuch as they are the teaching of the Church's supreme magisterium, ought to be accepted and embraced by each and every one of Christ's faithful according to the mind of the sacred Council. The mind of the Council becomes known either from the matter treated or from its manner of speaking, in accordance with the norms of theological interpretation" (emphasis added). At his general audience on January 12, 1966, after the Council had been closed, Pope Paul VI reiterated this proviso: "There are those who ask what authority, what theological qualification, the Council intended to give to its teachings, knowing that it avoided issuing solemn dogmatic definitions backed by the Church's infallible teaching authority. The answer is known by those who remember the conciliar declaration of March 6, 1964, repeated on November 16, 1964. In view of the pastoral nature of the Council, it avoided proclaiming in an extraordinary manner any dogmas carrying the mark of infallibility."

Then there is a third view, which emphasizes the fundamental continuity in the Church before and after Vatican II.[3] It takes as its premise the notion that there *cannot* be a "new" Church; to suggest otherwise is to destroy the very foundations of Catholicism.

The overriding project of the Ratzinger pontificate was to combat "rupturist" ecclesiology. Pope Benedict's liturgical initiatives — especially *Summorum Pontificum* — must be seen in this light. Yes, like John Paul II before him, he was also interested in finding the most just pastoral accommodation for the "rightful aspirations" of the "Catholic faithful who feel attached to some previous liturgical and disciplinary forms of the Latin tradition"[4] and in establishing this pastoral solution on a firm legal basis; yes, he was keenly interested in the question of the liturgy in its own right and saw that the new liturgy itself was not likely to be celebrated reverently, in visible continuity with the historic Roman Rite, unless it were to be infused with the ethos of the old.[5] But even more than that, Benedict XVI

---

3 This view covers something of a spectrum, depending on just how sanguine one is about the contributions of Vatican II or how concerned one is about its "points of doctrine which, *perhaps because they are new*, have not yet been well understood by some sections of the Church" (John Paul II, *Ecclesia Dei Adflicta* [July 2, 1988], 5b, emphasis added). On the one hand, the fact that the teachings of Vatican II are not *infallible* should not cause one to leap automatically to the conclusion that they are necessarily *erroneous*. On the other hand, the sheer verbosity of this Council compared to every other Council in history, combined with the fact that it did not define any dogmas or issue any anathemas, with the precise language that both dogmatic definitions and anathemas require, opens the possibility that the Council could here and there contain ambiguities, even quite serious ones — all the more reason to apply to this Council a hermeneutic of continuity (or better yet, a hermeneutic of continuity by means of correction from Tradition), rather than a hermeneutic of rupture. When one encounters an ambiguity without having already absorbed the Tradition, in practice that ambiguity is likely to lead one into error.

4 *Ecclesia Dei Adflicta*, 5c.

5 The meaning of the expression "Roman Rite" is very different for Pope Benedict and for Pope Francis. For Benedict, it is a *descriptive* term: the Roman Rite as it slowly developed in history and became something that was passed down before being codified at the time of Pope Pius V after the Council of Trent. For Pope Francis, the Roman Rite is a purely *juridical* reality — something popes can simply create or discard as they see fit. Ratzinger's view is this: "The Pope is not an absolute monarch whose will is law, but is the guardian of the authentic Tradition, and thereby the premier guarantor of obedience. . . That is why, with respect to the Liturgy, he has the task of a gardener, not that of a technician who builds new machines and throws the old ones on the junk-pile" ("The Organic Development of the Liturgy," 30 Days, 2004, no. 12), whereas Pope Francis feels able to make the mind-blowing statement that after a continuous usage of centuries, the historic Roman Rite is, in 2021, quite simply not part of the Church's *lex credendi*. This statement, like others in *Traditionis Custodes*, is contradicted explicitly by a claim of Ratzinger/Benedict in 2001 which is much more grounded in reality: "There is no doubt, on the one hand, that a venerable rite such as the Roman rite in use up to 1969 *is a rite of the Church*, it belongs to the Church, is

wanted concretely to oppose a widespread notion which has become such an unacknowledged assumption of Catholic life over the last half century. As he said in one of his papal audiences: "After the Second Vatican Council some were convinced that everything was new, that there was a different Church, that the pre-conciliar Church was finished and that we had another, totally 'other' Church — an anarchic utopianism!"[6]

Even from his time as cardinal-prefect of the Congregation for the Doctrine of the Faith, Ratzinger saw clearly that opposition to the pre-Vatican II liturgy was more about opposition to the pre-Vatican II Church than it was about aesthetics or liturgy as such. He put his finger on the problem when he said:

> A sizable party of Catholic liturgists seems to have practically arrived at the conclusion that Luther, rather than Trent, was substantially right in the sixteenth century debate. . . . It is only against this background of the *effective denial of the authority of Trent*, that the bitterness of the struggle against allowing the celebration of Mass according to the 1962 Missal, after the liturgical reform, can be understood. The possibility of so celebrating constitutes the strongest, and thus (for them) the most intolerable contradiction of the opinion of *those who believe that the faith in the Eucharist formulated by Trent has lost its value.*[7]

---

one of the treasures of the Church, and ought therefore to be preserved in the Church" (*Looking Again at the Question of the Liturgy with Cardinal Ratzinger: Proceedings of the July 2001 Fontgombault Liturgical Conference*, ed. Alcuin Reid, O. S. B. [Farnborough, UK: St. Michael's Abbey Press, 2003], 149, emphasis added). Since Pope Benedict clearly stated that the old rite "was never juridically abrogated and, consequently, in principle, was always permitted" (letter *Con Grande Fiducia*, July 7, 2007), this means that Pope Francis is being disingenuous when he speaks of "the decision to suspend the *faculty granted by my Predecessors*" (emphasis added); in fact, *Summorum Pontificum* did not simply "grant a faculty" so much as it acknowledged a reality! The ecclesiological — and even ecumenical — implications of the differences between the views of Ratzinger and Bergoglio are striking, because Pope Francis has an absolutist view of the papacy in which the pope has the power to change even reality and questions of fact. The repugnance with which Orthodox Christians and Protestant "fellow travelers" must regard such a parodied display of papal absolutism is not difficult to imagine. The Vatican II decree on ecumenism states: "All in the Church must preserve unity in essentials. But let all, according to the gifts they have received enjoy a proper freedom, in their various forms of spiritual life and discipline, in their different liturgical rites, and even in their theological elaborations of revealed truth" (*Unitatis Redintegratio*, 4).

6 General Audience, March 10, 2010.

7 *Looking Again at the Question of the Liturgy*, 20, emphasis added. Luther objected especially to the prayers of the Offertory and the Canon of the Roman Mass, as these prayers unmistakably express Catholic doctrine concerning the sacrificial nature of the Mass. The excision of these prayers in the liturgical reform raises uncomfortable questions.

This is why Ratzinger promoted the practical solution he did: "in order to emphasize that *there is no essential break, that there is continuity in the Church, which retains its identity*, it seems to me indispensable to continue to offer the opportunity to celebrate according to the old Missal, *as a sign of the enduring identity of the Church*."[8] That is what was, and is, really at stake: the enduring identity of the Church.

This is not to say that those who prefer the New Mass call into question the Church's defined (and thus irrevocable) Eucharistic doctrines; but it is to say that *those who ideologically oppose the traditional Mass* do tend to call into question the Church's defined doctrines. What the new rite expresses obscurely, the old rite expresses limpidly and unmistakably, which is why no one who rejects the dogmas of Trent can feel at home in the old Mass. It must be stamped out if the revolution is to succeed. Those who may prefer the new forms, all the while continuing to adhere to the perennial Catholic religion (unlike the committed neo-modernists), need to understand that the war against the traditional Mass is also a war against the Catholic faith itself.

The "post-conciliar Church" does not have to be a new religion, but the crisis is that its most ardent partisans make it into one, and claim that theirs is the only plausible interpretation. Benedict, again, fought against this tendency, since it undermines the Church's own self-identity. As he once wrote to the world's bishops: "Some of those who put themselves forward as great defenders of the Council also need to be reminded that Vatican II embraces the entire doctrinal history of the Church. Anyone who wishes to be obedient to the Council has to accept the faith professed over the centuries, and cannot sever the roots from which the tree draws its life."[9] Any truly Catholic hermeneutic (rule of interpretation) necessarily has to take this defined principle as its working premise: "That meaning of the sacred dogmas is ever to be maintained which has once been declared by Holy Mother Church, and there must never be any abandonment of this sense under the pretext or in the name of a more profound understanding."[10] *That* is a dogma of an ecumenical council.

The pressing problem in the Church today, then, is not: Do traditionalists accept Vatican II, but rather: Do the anti-traditionalists accept everything that came before Vatican II?[11] The common lot of people attending Latin

---

8   Ibid., 149, emphasis added.
9   *Letter to the Bishops of the Catholic Church*, March 10, 2009.
10   Vatican Council I, *Dei Filius*, cap. 4, 14.
11   One of the tragic ironies of *Traditionis Custodes* is that Pope Francis, in his quest for unity, focuses on supposed breaches in unity caused by those attached to the

Masses today do "accept Vatican II," inasmuch as it was legitimately convened and concluded by legitimate popes; yet they are not willing to let
"accepting Vatican II" be a pretext or an occasion for rejecting or neglecting
what came before Vatican II. And this is the real reason for the rage of the
anti-traditionalists.

When Pope Francis states in his letter accompanying Traditionis Custodes that the decision of Pope Benedict to issue Summorum Pontificum "was
above all motivated by the desire to foster the healing of the schism with
the movement of Mons. Lefebvre," he is notoriously misrepresenting the
truth. A pope can do many things, but changing history is not one of
them. The still-living (!) legislator of Summorum Pontificum has contradicted
Francis's claim. Just a few short years ago, Benedict stated explicitly: "The
reauthorization of the Tridentine Mass is often interpreted primarily as a
concession to the Society of Saint Pius X. This is just absolutely false! It
was important for me that the Church is one with herself inwardly, with
her own past; that what was previously holy to her is not somehow wrong
now." [12] Only one of these two popes can be right about his claim, and basic

---

traditional Mass but passes over in complete silence the very real disunity coming from
the growing schism in Germany, the diversity of pastoral practices occasioned by his
own Amoris Laetitia, the scandal of celebrity priests and even some bishops who promote
LGBT ideology in rejection of Church teaching, etc. Pope Francis has tolerated or even
actively abetted these offenses against unity, something everybody knows, even if many
bishops are afraid to acknowledge this publicly. Even if some caustic traditionalists
occasionally fall into faults against charity which are unfortunately encouraged by
social media, it is not a bad tone which undermines the unity of the Church, but error,
since all Catholics are bound to be united in the profession of the same (immutable)
faith. To the extent that doctrinal error goes unchecked, to that extent the unity of
the Church is undermined.

12 Last Testament in His Own Words (London: Bloomsbury, 2016), 201–2, emphasis
added. Already in 2001, Cardinal Ratzinger had stated: "Personally, I was from the
beginning in favour of the freedom to continue using the old Missal, for a very simple
reason: people were already beginning to talk about making a break with the pre-
conciliar Church, and of developing various models of Church — a preconciliar and
obsolete type of Church, and a new and conciliar type of Church. This is at any rate
nowadays the slogan of the Lefebvrists, insisting that there are two Churches, and
for them the great rupture becomes visible in the existence of two Missals, which
are said to be irreconcilable with each other. It seems to me essential, the basic step,
to recognise that both Missals are Missals of the Church, and belong to the Church
which remains the same as ever" (Looking Again at the Question of the Liturgy, 148–49).
If anything, Pope Benedict's decision to liberate the traditional Mass in Summorum
Pontificum was, far from being a "concession" to the Society of Saint Pius X, rather a
challenge to their way of thinking, which emphasizes the rupture effected at Vatican
II and through the reforms subsequently carried on in its name. One of the ironies
of Traditionis Custodes is that, in qualifying the Novus Ordo as the "unique [i.e., only]
expression of the lex orandi of the Roman Rite," Pope Francis is implying that the

human logic indicates that the one who issued Summorum knows what his own motives actually were.

This is the whole crux of the matter: *the Church is one with herself inwardly.*

Traditionis Custodes, therefore, does not merely call into question Pope Benedict XVI's entire theological legacy, but — what is far more serious — calls into question the Church's own self-understanding. If the premises of *Traditionis Custodes* are true, then Catholicism loses the inner coherence and historical continuity which are a consequence of the principle of non-contradiction and which are essential to the plausibility of the Church's claims to be the authorized teacher of divine revelation.

Now, back to that article in *La Croix*. How does it privilege the hermeneutic of rupture?

The year 2007 must have been a bad year for people like Dr. Madar, because not only was *Summorum Pontificum* published, but also the lamented document from the Congregation for the Doctrine of the Faith. This is the double sin which Pope Francis must efface if he is to be the dutiful servant of the cause of rupture. Here is how Madar characterizes Benedict's double sin:

> It is hardly an accident that these two documents were issued within days of each other. Rather, they indicate that Pope Benedict was aware of a close connection between the council's reform of the liturgy and its ecclesiology. Perhaps he was even responding to those who argued that the liturgy had to change because the ecclesiology had changed. What we hear from Benedict via CDF, however, is that the ecclesiology did not really change. Between the lines, the message seems to be that it would not be correct to restrict the use of the unreformed rite on the account that it is incompatible with the council's ecclesiology and that its use severs the link between the *lex orandi* (the rule of prayer) and the *lex credendi* (the rule of belief).

The 2007 responsum from the CDF is noteworthy in several respects. First of all, the document in question is a response to *dubia* received by the Holy See about some questionable teachings arising in some quarters

reformed liturgy expresses a *different theology* than that expressed by the liturgy which the Church had used for many centuries — and which the Church had defended against the accusations of heretics. Whereas Pope Benedict made a noble attempt at demonstrating the basic continuity of the Church before and after Vatican II, Pope Francis is implicitly lending comfort to the theses of the more "extreme" traditionalists. If there really is such a rupture, then Pope Francis has perhaps made a very damning admission.

on the basis of appeals to certain texts of the Council. The Holy Office, acting in concert with the pope, whose duty it is to "confirm thy brethren" in the faith (Luke 22:32), thus showed itself solicitous to fulfil its role of preserving the unity of the faith. That is why "the Congregation wishes to respond to these questions by clarifying the authentic meaning of some ecclesiological expressions used by the magisterium which are open to misunderstanding in the theological debate."[13] This approach is obviously a marked contrast to Pope Francis's persistent refusal even to concede an audience to the Eminent authors of the *dubia* they submitted concerning the interpretation of *Amoris Laetitia*, and *its* "expressions . . . which are open to misunderstanding."

Second of all, the responsum contains five articles (*dubia* and responses), whereas Madar only addresses the first one, which rather generically states that the "Second Vatican Council neither changed nor intended to change this doctrine [concerning the Church]." The *dubium* had asked, "Did the Second Vatican Council change the Catholic doctrine on the Church?" Because he is mostly concerned with the "close connection between the liturgical reform of Vatican II and its ecclesiology," Madar focuses in his article on the "People of God" ecclesiology promoted by Vatican II, supposedly in rupture with the different ecclesiology attributed to the medieval and Tridentine periods.

In fact, however, as the other four articles of the responsum show, the CDF document is not so much concerned with this internal ecclesiological question that so interests Madar (and certainly at different moments in history one aspect or the other of the Church's doctrine concerning herself may have been emphasized), as it is with reasserting the Church's understanding of her own identity, in contradistinction with non-Catholic bodies, since many people have understood Vatican II as renouncing the traditional idea that the Catholic Church is the "one true Church" founded by Jesus Christ. Though of less concern for the article in *La Croix*, because the liturgical implications are not as obvious, the question of whether Catholic dogma about the identity of the true Church has changed is obviously essential for addressing the "rupturist" project overall.

The pre-Vatican II doctrine was very clear: as recently as 1950 a pope could teach plainly, "the Mystical Body of Christ and the Roman Catholic Church are one and the same thing,"[14] and recent books like those by Ralph

---

13   *Responses to Questions Regarding Certain Aspects of the Doctrine on the Church* (June 29, 2007), Introduction.
14   Pius XII, *Humani Generis*, 27.

Martin[15] and Eric Sammons[16] have shown that the eclipsing of this truth in the minds of Catholics since Vatican II (whether intended or not) has crippled evangelizing efforts. The responsum is trying to address the question of why the Council (in *Lumen Gentium* 8) used the expression "subsists in," rather than the more readily understandable "is," when speaking of the identity of the Catholic Church concretely existing now with the Church founded 2000 years ago by Jesus Christ. (Actually, though, we should not forget that the Council *did* also use the more conventional word "is" when defining the Church in another document: "The Holy Catholic Church, *which is the Mystical Body of Christ*, is made up of the faithful who are organically united in the Holy Spirit by the same faith, the same sacraments and the same government."[17])

The responsum makes clear that the Council's intention was to find one handy verb which would *both* reaffirm the identity of the Catholic Church as the Church founded by Christ *and* teach that certain "elements of sanctification and truth" can be found in communities outside the visible confines of the Church — elements which belong by right to the Catholic Church but which can nonetheless be occasions of grace for those who are non-Catholics in good faith. Without wishing to reopen debates here about whether the phrase *subsistit in* really was the most opportune way to express these truths (and without judging the success of the CDF's attempt to justify this change of expression as having "developed, deepened and more fully explained" Catholic teaching), a correct understanding of the point *Lumen Gentium* is trying to make can be assisted by this insight from Cardinal Newman:

> We do not think it necessary to carp at every instance of super-
> natural excellence among Protestants when it comes before us, or
> to explain it away; all we know is, that the grace given them is
> intended ultimately to bring them into the Church, and *if it is not
> tending to do so, it will not ultimately profit them*; but we as little deny

---

15   *Will Many Be Saved? What Vatican II Actually Teaches and Its Implications for the New Evangelization* (Grand Rapids, MI: William B. Eerdmans, 2012).

16   *Deadly Indifference: How the Church Lost Her Mission and How We Can Reclaim It* (Manchester, NH: Crisis Publications, 2021).

17   *Orientalium Ecclesiarum*, 2. The external bonds of unity which are constitutive of the true Church mentioned here are globally the same as those specified by Pius XII in his great encyclical on the Church: "Actually only those are to be included as members of the Church who have been baptized and profess the true faith, and who have not been so unfortunate as to separate themselves from the unity of the Body, or been excluded by legitimate authority for grave faults committed" (*Mystici Corporis*, 22).

its presence in their souls as they do themselves; and as the fact is
no perplexity to us, it is no triumph to them.[18]

In other words, on this point, as on others, the optimism of Vatican II can
benefit by being tempered by a dose of realism.

What frustrates Madar most about the corrective provided by the CDF
in 2007 is the very assertion that Vatican II did not change any doctrine.
For him it is important to assert that "the council's ecclesiology represents
a micro-rupture with the preconciliar ecclesiology." To bolster his desire
to overturn forever the supposedly clericalist ecclesiology of the Tridentine
era in favor of a more democratic ecclesiology, he appeals to a well-known
Notre Dame dissident:

> The council's renewal of liturgy was a logical and necessary follow-
> up to its renewal of ecclesiology. It could not have been otherwise.
> As Richard McBrien observes, "How could the council have spoken
> of the whole Church as the People of God, and then have allowed
> the Church's central act of worship to remain a clerical rite, in an
> unintelligible language, with little or no meaningful role for the
> rest of the faithful?"

Latin Mass-going Catholics do not object to a theology of the Church
drawing on the concept of the People of God, with its traditional biblical
resonances. There is no contradiction between an ecclesiology that draws
attention to the Church as the People of God and the celebration of the
old Mass, which Madar denounces as "clericalist," even though Vatican II
emphasizes that "the common priesthood of the faithful and the minis-
terial or hierarchical priesthood . . . differ from one another *in essence and
not only in degree.*"[19] The Old Testament antecedent of the People of God
was clearly hierarchical, and this too sheds light on the New Testament
Church, as we see in the rich typology of the traditional rites of ordination.
So, Latin Mass-going Catholics do not object to the contributions that
Vatican II can make to the theology of the Church; what they do object
to, as all Catholics must, is the desire of the "rupturists" to banish the
ecclesiology of Trent and Vatican I and Leo XIII and Pius XII in order to
push a Marxist and overly horizontal interpretation of the People of God,

---

18 *Certain Difficulties Felt by Anglicans in Catholic Teaching*, Lecture 3, 5, emphasis added.
John Henry Newman has been canonized by Pope Francis himself and is often hailed
as a precursor of Vatican II, although many scholars, like Stanley Jaki, dispute this
overly facile association.
19 *Lumen Gentium*, 10, emphasis added.

and then on that basis to preclude the celebration of the inherited liturgy. As one would expect, when Vatican II speaks of the Church as the "new People of God,"[20] it cites a well-known line from the New Testament: "those who believe in Christ . . . are finally established as 'a chosen race, a royal priesthood, a holy nation, a purchased people . . . who in times past were not a people, but are now the people of God' (1 Pet 2:9 – 10)." Protestants had already falsified the import of this verse by overlooking the fact that when God constituted His People under the former alliance, He used almost identical words: "you shall be to me a priestly kingdom, and a holy nation" (Ex 19:6). When the Lord God constituted the people of Israel, He also gave them their sacred hierarchy, their Temple cult, and their minute and fastidious ritual — a liturgy which *La Croix* would certainly denounce as "a clerical rite . . . with little or no meaningful role for the rest of the faithful." However, the People of God does not exist in *opposition* to an inherited and carefully articulated liturgy; it is *constituted* by the possession of such a liturgy!

Even under the New Covenant, priests are also part of the People of God, and Vatican II states, "older [priests] should likewise endeavor to understand the mentality of younger priests, even though it be different from their own."[21] The sledgehammer approach of *Traditionis Custodes* seems to indicate that many members of the geriatric Vatican II generation have not made peace with this teaching and that they still recoil unsympathetically in horror from the cassocks and Latin Masses which are part of the natural habitat of the younger clergy today.

The People of God surely also includes the "young persons" referred to by Benedict XVI, who "have discovered this liturgical form, felt its attraction and found in it a form of encounter with the Mystery of the Most Holy Eucharist, particularly suited to them."[22] Oddly enough, those who most vociferously promote a democratic view of the Church are often the ones most inclined to defend the clericalist power structure of the Bergoglio Vatican, in which a narrow court of fawning sycophants disregards the sentiments of the "little people" and imposes rigid norms from on high.

Ideologues who have latched onto their own idea of Vatican II are pathologically incapable of responding to Vatican II's prophetic invitation to read "the signs of the times."[23] One of those signs is that fact that, since

---

20 *Lumen Gentium*, 9.

21 *Presbyterorum Ordinis*, 8.

22 Letter accompanying *Summorum Pontificum*, July 7, 2007.

23 *Gaudium et Spes*, 4. The Council refers on multiple occasions to the necessity of discerning the "signs of the times." It is interesting that the Holy See, in a highly clericalist vein, sent its heavily skewed survey about the Latin Mass in 2020 only to

the imposition of the liturgical reform, the overwhelming majority of the "People of God" who were supposed to be the beneficiaries of this new user-friendly liturgy glowingly described in Dr. Madar's article have in fact stopped coming to Mass at all, and of those who do come, most do not believe in the Real Presence or that the Mass is a true propitiatory sacrifice. On the other hand, another sign of the times is the attraction felt by people born in the 1980s, '90s and 2000s for a liturgy that connects them to their Catholic past. Does their voice not matter? Is there a prejudice against smelling like certain kinds of sheep?

Far from being a threat to the legacy of Vatican II properly understood, the restoration of the traditional Latin Mass provides the visible reaffirmation that the Church is at peace with herself, and it is only in the context of such a *pax ecclesiastica* — a necessary self-confidence — that any Council can be properly received. The establishment of this peace was the life's work of Benedict XVI; and far from serving the interests of Vatican II, the hermeneutic of rupture in fact makes its reception untenable. By asking Pope Francis to push this hermeneutic even further, Madar and his ilk are showing their hand and exposing the entire conciliar experiment to failure.

Whether Madar and others of his ilk who are trying to push the waning Bergoglio pontificate in an even more explicitly rupturist direction like it or not, any renewal in the Church today is going to have to accept as a given not only the "legitimacy" of Vatican II as a validly convened Council, but also the immutability of Catholic doctrine. How precisely the authority

the world's bishops (many of whom said they did not even receive it), as opposed to consulting the People of God in general. (For that matter, while paying lip service to the authority of bishops, Pope Francis in fact ties their hands, as he did in 2016 when taking away their discretion in the erection of clerical and religious societies of diocesan right, in a way that treats bishops more as branch managers of Catholic Church, Inc., than as successors of the Apostles with true jurisdiction over their dioceses.) This strange lacuna goes directly against the teaching of Vatican II: "They [the clergy] must willingly listen to the laity, consider their wants in a fraternal spirit, recognize their experience and competence in the different areas of human activity, so that together with them they will be able to recognize *the signs of the times*" (*Presbyterorum Ordinis*, 9). Many lay intellectuals, musicians, architects, students, and parents in the traditional movement have plenty of insights they can share with the hierarchy, in keeping with this invitation extended by Vatican II. The traditional laity would be delighted if Pope Francis and his Curia would "consider their wants in a fraternal spirit." Whereas *Summorum Pontificum* made provisions for the faithful to contact their priest, then their bishop, then the Holy See itself in order to find practical ways to facilitate their aspirations, *Traditionis Custodes* harshly closes the door on the People of God and even orders bishops to see to it that "groups" of such faithful are not even allowed to form!

of Vatican II fits into this picture is and will be for the foreseeable future a subject of debate among orthodox bishops and theologians. Vatican II was a "real" Council, but was it not in some ways also a "different" type of Council, as both enthusiasts and critics suggest? Since Catholic doctrine precludes that this difference could create a "new" Church (or recover a putatively pure pre-Constantinian Church that had been lost for centuries), it is impossible to appeal to Vatican II to legitimize a rupture with what came immediately before. If there *were* such a rupture, that would speak against the Council and not in favor of the rupture!

Although Ratzinger himself certainly wanted on the whole to "save" Vatican II with his "hermeneutic of continuity," [24] he also hinted at the possibility that the only way to integrate Vatican II might be, in a way, to relativize it, in the sense of receiving it only *in relation* to the Tradition that came before and not the other way around. As he pointed out already in 1988:

> There are many accounts of it which give the impression that, from Vatican II onward, everything has been changed, and that what preceded it has no value or, at best, has value only in the light of Vatican II. The Second Vatican Council has not been treated as a part of the entire living Tradition of the Church, but as an end of Tradition, a new start from zero. The truth is that this particular Council defined no dogma at all, and deliberately chose to remain on a modest level, as a merely pastoral council; and yet many treat it as though it had made itself into a sort of "super-dogma" which takes away the importance of all the rest. [25]

Evaluations will differ as to how effective Pope Benedict's solution was ever likely to be. By trying to save the conciliar "project," perhaps he was ultimately trying to fix a gaping wound with a band-aid. Maybe the providential fallout over *Traditionis Custodes* is that the bishops of the Church, who on the whole are as startled and disoriented as everyone else by Pope Francis's rigid and unpastoral motu proprio, will start to ask questions that for decades have been preemptively disqualified before the discussion

---

24   In the famous Address to the Curia on December 22, 2005, Benedict uses the expression "'hermeneutic of reform,' of renewal in the continuity of the one subject-Church which the Lord has given to us," adding that the Church "is a subject which increases in time and develops, yet *always remaining the same*, the one subject of the journeying People of God" (emphasis added), but in 2007 he did also adopt the expression "hermeneutic of continuity" (*Sacramentum Caritatis*, 3, n. 6).
25   Address to the Bishops of Chile, July 13, 1988.

could even begin. Is Vatican II, very much a product of its times, really the most solid basis for renewal in the Church of the twenty-first century? Does its juridical legitimacy as a Council really mean that all its pastoral orientations are effective or that none of its doctrinal formulations may be tainted with ambiguity? Given the catastrophic collapse of every single Catholic indicator over the last fifty years, are we not permitted to ask if there may be some causal relationship between the tree and the fruits? As one American bishop recently observed: "I'd like to point out that there is a difference between accepting the validity of the Second Vatican Council and believing that it has failed in its objectives."[26]

No Catholic — be he layman, theologian, or bishop — should even start to absorb Vatican II until he has, for example, digested the *Catechism of the Council of Trent* and the great encyclicals of popes like Leo XIII, Pius X, and Pius XII, and maybe even spent time with the much-maligned classic pre-Vatican II theology manuals.[27] When Vatican II itself tells us that the Council "leaves untouched (*integram*) traditional Catholic doctrine,"[28] it stands to reason that no one can adequately receive the Council to whom that "traditional Catholic doctrine" is not already second nature. One reason that the "hermeneutic of rupture" has enjoyed so much success and has been undergoing such a quasi-official recrudescence under Pope Francis is that so many of those whose reflexes are soundly Catholic but who simply

---

26   Bishop Thomas Paprocki of Springfield, Illinois, interview with *Catholic World Report*, July 27, 2021. [The bishop must mean: there is a difference between accepting the validity of a council and believing it has *succeeded* in its objectives.] On this question of whether an ecumenical council can fail to achieve its goals, Joseph Ratzinger once stated, speaking specifically of Lateran Council V, which preceded the outbreak of the Protestant Reformation by a few years: "Not every valid council in the history of the Church has been a fruitful one; in the last analysis, many of them have been a waste of time," and the Council he refers to carried on its work "without doing anything effective to prevent the crisis that was happening" (*Principles of Catholic Theology: Building Stones for a Fundamental Theology*, trans. Sister Mary Frances McCarthy [San Francisco: Ignatius Press, 1987], 378).

27   Rusty Reno, in his article "Theology after the Revolution," *First Things*, May 2007, notes that "*Ressourcement* does not work if students have neither context nor framework in which to place the richness and depth of the tradition . . . without a standard theology, the Church will lack precisely the sort of internally coherent and widespread theological culture that is necessary for understanding and employing bold new experiments and fruitful recoveries of past traditions."

28   *Dignitatis Humanae*, 1; the word *integram* has the sense of whole and entire, undiminished. The context here is Catholic teaching on religious liberty: "Therefore it leaves untouched traditional Catholic doctrine on the moral duty of men and societies toward the true religion and toward the one Church of Christ." See, for example, the writings of Professor Thomas Pink for one interpretation plausibly seeking continuity between pre-conciliar teaching on religious liberty and the teaching of *Dignitatis Humanae*.

accept Vatican II as a "given" do not have the solid foundation provided by the anterior doctrinal Tradition of the Church, which would be necessary for them to contextualize Vatican II and to oppose the errors of this hermeneutic of rupture.

Unwittingly, even many of the orthodox have accepted as if by osmosis the idea that Vatican II, unlike any earlier council, really does represent a "new beginning." Regardless of how sanguine one is about the pastoral reforms of Vatican II or how hesitant one is about the occasional ambiguities in its wordy documents, *that* is one idea that must absolutely be exorcised if the Church is to survive. There can be no new beginning!

The article in *La Croix* tells us: "To retire the experiment of *Summorum Pontificum* more thoroughly, Pope Francis should revisit the question of whether Vatican II changed the doctrine of the church." But *Summorum Pontificum* is not the experiment that needs retiring. Articles like Madar's — and, fundamentally, *Traditionis Custodes* itself — do more to discredit Vatican II in the eyes of Catholics than even the most strident traditionalist critique, because their premise is one that the Catholic conscience can never accept: the idea that the Church can contradict herself and still *be* herself.

Madar's title suggests that one pope should "correct" his predecessor, and this premise is perhaps more correct than he knows. If the Catholic Church is to survive at all — which is a foregone conclusion, given the divine promises — then it is certain that a future pope will have to correct Pope Francis and put to rest forever the progressivist hermeneutic of rupture. For, when a pope needs correction, it is not because he has *maintained* Tradition but because he has *departed* from it. That was the criterion employed in the seventh century by Pope Leo II when he condemned his predecessor Pope Honorius, "who did not purify this Apostolic Church by the doctrine of the apostolic tradition, but rather attempted to subvert the immaculate faith by profane treason" and because he "allowed the immaculate rule of the *apostolic tradition that he had received from his predecessors* to be stained."[29]

The fact that even relatively feeble reaffirmations of the immutability of Catholic dogma under the Ratzinger pontificate — like in the 2007 CDF document we have been considering or the earlier *Dominus Jesus* of 2000 — still provoke such a state of panic in the "rupturist" class shows that they feel their revolution is in jeopardy as long as there are still reminders of the old religion. They have to change ideas and wipe out everything that

---

29 Quoted by Claudio Pierantoni in J. Lamont and C. Pierantoni, eds., *Defending the Faith Against Present Heresies* (Waterloo, ON: Arouca Press, 2021), 237–38, emphasis added.

reminds people of the old ones, because that is how revolutions work. What every orthodox Catholic needs to understand — even if he personally does not prefer to worship according to the old rite — is that in the bloody civil war tearing apart the Church today, the defense of the traditional liturgy is now the battle line in the defense of the Catholic faith itself, since the traditional liturgy is the visible reminder of the "before" time — the visible reminder that the Church did not begin in 1962.

66

They Do Not Even Know What Has Been Taken from Them†

MICHAEL FIEDROWICZ

CNA-*Deutsch*

August 30, 2021

LEX ORANDI—LEX CREDENDI

On July 16, 2021, the feast day of Our Lady of Mount Carmel, the Apostolic Letter in the form of a motu proprio *Traditionis Custodes* on the use of the Roman Liturgy before the 1970 reform was promulgated. Article 1 reads, "The liturgical books promulgated by Popes St. Paul VI and St. John Paul II in conformity with the decrees of the Second Vatican Council are the sole expression (*l'unica espressione*) of the *lex orandi* of the Roman Rite."

To appreciate the full implications of this provision, it is necessary to know that the term *lex orandi* — the law or rule of prayer — is part of a broader formula coined in the 5th century. The Gallic monk Prosper of Aquitaine, between 435 and 442, formulated the principle: "so that the rule of prayer may determine the rule of faith" (*ut legem credendi lex statuat supplicandi*). In the background was a theological controversy about grace. The question was whether the first beginning of faith (*initium fidei*) also proceeded from the grace of God or from the decision of man. Prosper referred to the Church's prayer of intercession and thanksgiving, which is significant for the doctrine of grace: "But let us also take into account the mysteries of the priestly prayers, which, handed down by the apostles, are solemnly offered uniformly throughout the world and throughout the entire Catholic Church, so that the rule of prayer may determine the rule of faith" (*Indiculus* 8). Prosper then enumerated various requests made by the Church in her official prayers and deduced from them the necessity of divine grace, since otherwise the Church's petition and thanksgiving would be useless and meaningless. For Prosper, then, the faith of the Church manifested itself in the prayer of the Church, so that the Church's official prayer is the standard by which the Church's faith is to be read.

† Translated from the German by Peter Kwasniewski and published at *Rorate Caeli* on the same date.

Already Prosper's teacher Augustine had developed the idea that the prayer of the Church testifies to its faith and makes it recognizable. The principle *lex orandi–lex credendi* was henceforth part of the basic understanding of Catholic doctrine. The liturgy, like the Scriptures and Tradition, is a *locus theologicus*, a place of discovery, a source of knowledge and a witness to what the Church believes. Pope Pius XII called the liturgy "a faithful reflection of the doctrine handed down by our ancestors and believed by the Christian people" (Encyclical Letter *Ad Coeli Reginam*, 1954). Likewise, he emphasized, "The liturgy as a whole, therefore, contains the Catholic faith insofar as it publicly testifies to the faith of the Church" (Encyclical *Mediator Dei*, 1947).

THE SOLE EXPRESSION OF ALL THE ELEMENTS OF THE ROMAN RITE?

Pope Francis, however, now defines, or rather reduces, the liturgy of the Roman Rite to that which is expressed in the liturgical books promulgated by Paul VI and John Paul II. These books are "the sole expression of the *lex orandi* of the Roman Rite." If one assumes the original [i.e., face-value] meaning of the terminology used here, then the *lex credendi* — what is to be believed — would also have to be taken from those books alone. But is this true? Are these books really the only ones that suffice to be able to read the Catholic faith from them?

Certainly, the papal letter accompanying the motu proprio suggests that all the essentials of the Roman Rite before the liturgical reform can also be found in Paul VI's missal: "Those who wish to celebrate with devotion the earlier liturgical form will not find it difficult to find in the Roman Missal, reformed according to the spirit of the Second Vatican Council, all the elements of the Roman Rite, especially the Roman Canon, which is one of the most characteristic elements." Leaving aside the experience of liturgical practice, where the Roman Canon is almost never used in the Novus Ordo — either in parish services, in episcopal churches, or at papal liturgies — the question must be asked whether indeed "*all* the elements of the Roman Rite" are to be found in the new liturgical books. This question can be answered in the affirmative only by someone who considers obsolete much of what has characterized the Roman Rite for centuries and constituted its theological-spiritual richness, as is evidently the case with Pope Francis.

LITURGICAL REFORM: DAMNATIO MEMORIAE

This would include everything that was eradicated by the driving forces of the liturgical reform, whether to accommodate Protestants in a misguided ecumenical effort or to meet the supposed mentality of "modern man."

To name just a few examples: Feasts of the saints were abolished or degraded in the liturgical hierarchy. The Offertory prayers with the clear and unambiguous idea of sacrifice were replaced by a Jewish table prayer. The *Dies irae*, the poignant depiction of the Last Judgment, was no longer tolerated in the Requiem Mass. The Apostle Paul's warning in the Maundy Thursday epistle that he who communicates unworthily eats and drinks condemnation (1 Cor 11:27) was omitted. The Orations: those "most beautiful jewels of the Church's liturgical treasure" (Dom Gérard Calvet, O. S. B.), which are among the most ancient components of her spiritual heritage and are completely imbued with dogma, constitute virtually a *"summa theologica"* in nuce, expressing the Catholic faith unabridged and concisely... The Orations of the Classical Rite alone, of which only a very small part was incorporated unchanged into the Missal of Paul VI, contain and preserve numerous ideas that have been weakened or have disappeared altogether in the later modified versions, but which belong indissolubly to the Catholic faith: detachment from earthly goods and the longing for the eternal; the struggle against heresy and schism; the conversion of unbelievers; the necessity of returning to the Catholic Church and to unadulterated truth; merits, miracles, apparitions of the saints; God's wrath against sin and the possibility of eternal damnation. All of these aspects are deeply rooted in the biblical message and have unmistakably shaped Catholic piety for nearly two millennia.

In addition to these direct modifications to the Roman Rite itself, however, we must not forget the other concomitants that reveal a profoundly changed basic understanding of the Holy Mass: precious high altars destroyed, with meal tables taking their place; valuable paraments burned or sold off; "Tinnef and Trevira" (M. Mosebach) made their entrance,[1] Gregorian chant and the Latin sacral language were banished from the liturgy. The approach of the liturgical reform is partly reminiscent of the *damnatio memoriae* in ancient Rome, the erasure of the memory of disliked rulers. Names on triumphal arches were erased, coins with their images melted down. Nothing should remind us of them anymore. All the changes that actually took place in the course of the liturgical reforms unmistakably resemble a *damnatio memoriae*, a deliberate erasure of the memory of the traditional Catholic liturgy.

PARALLELS IN THE FOURTH CENTURY

The history of the Church presents similar situations again and again. In the middle of the fourth century, the divinity of Christ and that of the Holy Spirit were denied: Son and Spirit were only creatures of God. Bishoprics

---

1 "Tinnef" means items made out of recycled plastics. "Trevira" is a type of polyester fabric.

and churches were widely in the hands of the Arian heretics. Those who remained orthodox gathered in remote places to worship. In 372, Bishop Basil of Caesarea gave a moving description of the situation:

> The teachings of the fathers are despised, the apostolic traditions are ignored, and the churches are filled with the inventions of innovators. The shepherds have been driven out, and in their place they bring in ravening wolves to tear apart the flock of Christ. The places of prayer are deserted by those who gathered there, the wastelands are filled with wailing people. The elderly lament as they compare the former time with the present; the young are even more pitiful because they do not even know what has been taken from them. (*Epistula* 9:2)

These words from the fourth century undoubtedly also apply to the generations born after the Second Vatican Council: for a long time they did not even know what had been taken from them, knowing only the present appearance of the Church.

TWO EXPRESSIONS OR ONE?

Pope Benedict XVI, with the motu proprio *Summorum Pontificum* of July 7, 2007, made the treasures of the Church's undiminished deposit of faith accessible again, so that younger generations could now know again and witness from their own experience what had been taken from them. The then-pontiff spoke of there being "two expressions of the *lex orandi* of the Church," the ordinary expression (*ordinaria expressio*) found in the Missal promulgated by Paul VI, and the extraordinary expression (*extraordinaria expressio*) found in the Roman Missal reissued by St. Pius V and John XXIII (SP, art. 1). In his most recent motu proprio, Pope Francis refers directly to this passage (*espressione della 'lex orandi'*) in his choice of words and sentence structure, but places himself in diametrical opposition to it by now determining only a "single form of expression" (*l'unica espressione*) of the *lex orandi* as valid (TC, art. 1).

But what significance can the traditional form of the liturgy still claim for the Church's consciousness of faith? If the recent motu proprio and the accompanying letter make readily apparent that the real goal in the middle or long-term is the total destruction of the traditional liturgy, and that for the time being it is still being granted a grace period with drastic restrictions that are intended rigorously to prevent any possibility of its further expansion, then — should decisive resistance fail to materialize — St. Basil the Great's lament about the fate of the younger generation of his time will once again obtain with renewed force: "For they do not even know what has been taken from them."

SAVING THE BRIDE OF CHRIST FROM AMNESIA

The newly enacted regulations are frighteningly reminiscent of what the author George Orwell described as a bleak vision of the future in his 1948 novel *1984*. There is the dictatorship of a Party, which rules in a totalitarian surveillance state: "Big Brother is watching you." In this state there are different ministries. The Ministry of Peace prepares the wars. The Ministry of Abundance manages the socialist economy of scarcity. There is no mention of a Ministry of Health, but there is a Ministry of Truth, which spreads the official propaganda of lies: the Party is always right. For this to be so, every memory of the past must be erased. No more comparisons must be possible; everything must appear to have no alternative. The Ministry of Truth is busy changing everything that could remind one of the past and make such a comparison possible. Orwell writes:

> Already we know almost literally nothing about the Revolution and the years before the Revolution. Every record has been destroyed or falsified, every book has been rewritten, every picture has been repainted, every statue and street and building has been renamed, every date has been altered. [2]

To associate Orwell's words with the recent Council does not seem illegitimate, since Vatican II was widely celebrated as a "revolution of the Church from above." Thus the paradoxical situation arises: in order that the Bride of Christ, the Church, may be preserved from amnesia, from a loss of memory, Catholics faithful to tradition will now have to prove themselves as counter-revolutionaries, conservative faithful will have to assume the role of rebels, in order that they themselves might ultimately be found to be, before the judgment of history and above all in the eyes of God, the true and only *traditionis custodes*, guardians of tradition, who really deserve this name.

---

2 *1984* (New York: Signet Classics, 1961), 155.

67

The Council's Last Stand?[†]

ABBÉ CLAUDE BARTHE

Res Novae

September 1, 2021

THE NON-RECEPTION OF THE SECOND VATICAN COUN-
cil is focused in a concrete way on the refusal of the liturgical reform, even
though a number of practitioners of the ancient Mass affirm their adherence
to the conciliar intuitions if "correctly interpreted." In any case, the existence
of the traditional liturgy is a persistent and growing instance of non-reception.
Marginal? Pope Bergoglio, who wants to be the pope responsible for the full
realization of Vatican II, has come to be convinced that the phenomenon is
sufficiently important that he must work to eradicate it. As a consequence,
the possibly marginal has certainly become central: the Tridentine Mass is
avowed as the evil to be destroyed; the seminaries training priests to say it,
as cankers to be eliminated. And all this has to happen at once.

A RETURN TO THE ORIGINAL VIOLENCE OF THE LITURGICAL REFORM
So it is outlawed once again, as it was under Paul VI. The letter that
accompanies Traditionis Custodes explains unambiguously the ultimate goal
of the pontifical text: to ensure "a return to a unitary form of celebration,"
the new liturgy. The decision is brutal and peremptory: the pope has decided
to end both the traditional Mass and the whole traditional world, whom he
accuses — and only them! — of attacking the unity of the Church.

Vatican II — whose grand design was an opening to the modern world
in its modernity in order to be better understood by the men of this time —
is a kind of "in-between" between traditional orthodoxy and heterodoxy
(in this case, a neo-modernist relativism). For example, its use of several
ambiguous propositions allows one to affirm that a separated Christian can,
as such, be in a certain communion with the Church: according to Unitatis

---

† Translated for this anthology by Zachary Thomas and Peter Kwasniewski. The title
in French, "Traditionis Custodes: les dernières cartouches conciliaires?," alludes to an
1873 painting by the French artist Alphonse de Neuville, depicting the French soldiers
of Bazeilles who fought to the last cartridge during the 1870 Battle of Sedan in the
Franco-Prussian War.

362

Redintegratio, Luther, who thought he had broken with the Church of the pope, remained in reality an "imperfect" Catholic (UR 3).

Since his election, Pope Francis has skirted along this apparent ridge as far as possible: he transmutes collegiality into synodality, and goes beyond *Nostra Aetate* and the Day of Assisi with the Abu Dhabi declaration, but he is careful not to cross the threshold beyond which one would fall — or fall faster — into that nothingness into which the most daring of progressive theologies are already tipping. Like Paul VI, he remains faithful to ecclesiastical celibacy and the male priesthood, but bypasses traditional discipline by way of the lay ministries created by Pope Montini (the institution of ministers who hold clerical roles without being clerics, with the probable ultimate goal of creating the ministry of deaconess or even president of a non-formal Eucharist) and by entrusting to lay men and women quasi-jurisdictional offices (ever higher positions in the Roman dicasteries).

In other words, Francis is keeping enough of the institution, but continuing to empty it of its doctrinal substance. In his words, he is tearing down the walls:

– *Humanae Vitae* and a set of texts following this encyclical had preserved conjugal morality from the liberalization that the Council had brought to bear on ecclesiology. *Amoris Laetitia* has overturned this dam: people living in public adultery can remain in it without committing a serious sin (AL 301).

– *Summorum Pontificum* had recognized a right to that conservatory of the Church of yesterday, the ancient liturgy, with its associated catechesis and clergy who are attached to it. *Traditionis Custodes* swept away this attempt at a "return": the new liturgical books are the "sole expression of the *lex orandi* of the Roman rite" (TC, art. 1).

The fact remains that the pope and his advisors took great risks in adopting these hastily drafted and violent measures. Stunned commentators speak of the Latin American pope's lack of knowledge of the Western ecclesial terrain; they point to the stinging disavowal of the major work of Benedict XVI; they point to the contradictions of a chaotic government that crushes the traditionalist "insiders" while granting the traditionalist "outsiders," those of the SSPX, faculties that amount to a semi-recognition; they are surprised, finally, when the fire of schism is burning in Germany and quiet heresy is everywhere, that one would attack a liturgical practice that is innocent of either schism or heresy.

But one can imagine that the pope and his entourage only shrug their shoulders at such criticism. The justification for the repressive assault they have unleashed is decisive for them: the Tridentine Mass crystallizes the existence of a Church within the Church because it represents a *lex orandi ante* and therefore *anti*-conciliar. One can compromise with the drifts of the German Church, which are at worst too conciliar; one cannot tolerate the ancient liturgy which is anti-conciliar.

There is nothing debatable about Vatican II or anything that is in it! In a very characteristic way, the letter that accompanies *Traditionis Custodes* infallibilizes the Council. The liturgical reform stems from Vatican II; this Council was an "exercise of collegial power in a solemn way"; to doubt that the Council is inserted in the dynamism of Tradition is therefore "to doubt the Holy Spirit himself who guides the Church."

A REPRESSION THAT COMES TOO LATE

But we are in 2021, no longer in 1969, the time of the fresh and joyous promulgation of the new missal, nor in 1985, when *The Ratzinger Report* and the Synod assembly made an already uneasy assessment of the fruits of Vatican II, nor even in 2005, when the appearance of the expression "hermeneutics of reform in continuity" sounded like a laborious attempt to recompose a reality that was increasingly disintegrating. Today, it is too late.

The Church's institutional reality is enervated, the mission is abandoned, and, in the West at least, the visibility of priests and faithful has vanished. Andrea Riccardi, the principal member of the Community of Sant'Egidio, the opposite of a conservative, in his last book, *A Church in Flames: The Crisis and Future of Christianity*,[1] considers the burning of Notre Dame in Paris as a parable of the situation of Catholicism, and analyzes its collapse in Europe, country by country. His language is characteristic of the disappointed Bergoglians, who have become disappointed conciliars.

Can we be surprised when authors much less engaged than he is with the ecclesiastical apparatus sound the alarm and do not hesitate to say where the evil comes from? The academician Jean-Marie Rouart in *This Country of Godless Men*,[2] thinks that Western society's battle against Islam is already lost, whereas only a "Christian leap," that is to say a radical reversal, could save us: the Church, he writes, "must initiate the equivalent of a Counter-Reformation, a return to that Christian reform which allowed it to confront and defeat the challenge of Protestantism in the seventeenth century."[3] Or Patrick Buisson in *The End of a World*,[4] who devotes two parts of his long

---

1   *La Chiesa brucia: Crise e futuro del cristianesimo* (Rome: Editori Laterza, 2021).
2   *Ce pays des hommes sans Dieu* (Paris: Éditions Bouquins, 2021).
3   Ibid., 64.
4   *La fin d'un monde: Une histoire de la révolution petite-bourgeoise* (Paris: Éditions Albin Michel, 2021).

book to the situation of Catholicism: "The Crash of the Faith" and "The Massacre of the Sacred." "In a way that is both disconcerting and brutal," he writes, "the Tridentine rite, which had been the official rite of the Latin Church for four centuries, was, overnight, decreed undesirable, its celebration proscribed, and its faithful hunted down."[5] We have left Catholicism behind for a "conciliar religion."

Moreover, in 2021, the balance of power between those who "made the Council" and those who were subjected to it is very different from what it was in the 1970s. Andrea Riccardi, like everyone else, makes this realistic observation: "Traditionalism is a reality of some importance in the Church, both in organization and in means." The traditional world, although a minority (in France, 8 to 10% of churchgoers), is growing everywhere, especially in the United States. It is young, fertile in vocations (at least in comparison with the fertility of Catholicism in mainstream parishes), capable of ensuring the transmission of catechetics, attractive to young clergy and diocesan seminarians.

This is what Pope Bergoglio, arriving from Argentina, took a long time to understand, until the Italian bishops and the prelates of the Curia pointed out to him the unbearable growth of the traditional world, all the more visible because it was taking place in the midst of the general collapse. It was therefore necessary to apply the appropriate "remedies," the same ones that were administered to the flourishing seminary of San Rafael in Argentina, to the Franciscan congregation of the Immaculate, to the diocese of Albenga in Italy, to the diocese of San Luis in Argentina, etc.[6]

FOR A "FORWARD" EXIT FROM THE CRISIS

For all that, the conciliar Church has not been revitalized and the mission has continued to wither. A battery of documents have dealt with mission: *Ad Gentes*, the conciliar decree of 1965; the exhortation *Evangelii Nuntiandi* of 1975; the encyclical *Redemptoris Missio* of 1990; the document *Dialogue and Proclamation* of 1991; the apostolic exhortations which tirelessly take up the theme of the "new evangelization": *Ecclesia in Africa*, 1995, *Ecclesia in America*, 1999, *Ecclesia in Asia*, 1999, *Ecclesia in Oceania*, 2001, *Ecclesia in Europa*, 2003. A Pontifical Council for the Promotion of the New Evangelization was created. Numerous colloquia have asserted that mission must be carried out as dialogue, that evangelization must not be proselytism, etc. Never has there been so much talk about mission. Never has there been so little conversion.

---

5 Ibid., 124.
6 All effectively suppressed or crippled. — Ed.

François Mitterrand used to say about the reduction of unemployment, "we have tried everything." The same goes for saving the post-Vatican II Church: the attempt to maximize the Council, represented by the election of Pope Bergoglio, was a failure, just as the attempt to soften the Council, represented by the election of Pope Ratzinger, was (we must admit) a failure. So, is it time for a return to the past? Yes, but in the manner of a "forward" exit.

There are many, even among yesterday's supporters of Pope Bergoglio, who consider the brutal repression of the traditional world indefensible, for the sole reason that it is too alive. Can we imagine, with a future pontificate, a bracketing of *Traditionis Custodes*? Certainly, and something even better, we think: a freedom granted to the "living forces" in the Church. Since this essential force represents a tradition of many centuries, it is reasonable to envisage the negotiation of a compromise that would be more favorable to the Church than the compromise represented by *Summorum Pontificum*. The aim should be to remove all special supervision — in other words, to give the ancient liturgy and all that goes with it complete freedom. And this in the name of common sense. Just as a certain number of bishops in the world have allowed all those "living forces," communities, foundations, and works that bear missionary fruit to develop in their dioceses, so, at the level of the universal Church, the time must come for freedom to be given to everything that works.

Summorum Pontificum can be analyzed as an attempt to allow Catholics who do not receive the liturgy of Vatican II to coexist with a moderate conciliar world. A new attempt could be established with a conciliar world apparently more "liberal" than that of Benedict XVI, but which is now aware of the irremediable failure of the utopia embraced fifty years ago.

68

Where Is Peter?

MICHAEL BRENDAN DOUGHERTY
National Review
September 15, 2021

THE ROMAN CATHOLIC ARCHBISHOP OF LIVERPOOL,
the Most Reverend Malcolm McMahon, made a very curious intervention
into the debate about the church's traditional Latin liturgy, which Pope
Francis has recently tried to suppress in a document titled "Guardians of
Tradition." In a very brief letter to his diocese, Archbishop McMahon wrote
something on the matter worth pondering at length:

> One thing that annoyed many Catholics is that those devoted to
> the old ways of worship often describe themselves as "traditional."
> I think they have hijacked the word for their own use. Pope Fran-
> cis has reclaimed the world "tradition" by clearly stating that the
> bishops are the guardians of the tradition. Tradition has a particular
> meaning in theology, it refers to St. Paul when he says that he
> passes on to us what he has received. In other words, tradition is
> a living concept not something stuck in the past. The Mass which
> I celebrate daily is the one which I received from Pope St. Paul VI
> and Pope St. John Paul II and is therefore the "traditional" Mass.
> The point I am making is more than simple semantics; it is about
> the very life of the Church itself.

In fact, I think the archbishop has unwittingly demonstrated a subtle
truth about the modern Catholic Church, that the church's self-conception
is now a snake swallowing its own tail. Old catechisms used to say that there
were three sources of religious authority in Catholicism: the scriptures,
tradition, and the magisterium of the church. And together, these preserve
for us the deposit of faith given to the apostles by our Lord. But in the
archbishop's telling, the church exists not for the Gospel, but for itself. Its
authority is to teach that it has authority to teach. I propose that this error
could only have crept into the church because of the liturgical reform.

In August, I wrote two short essays about the Latin Mass and Pope Francis's attempt to withdraw permission for priests to say it. One appeared in

the New York Times, and the other here at National Review. Both came out while I was away, and I haven't been able to respond to criticism of these essays, of which there was plenty. Some of these criticisms can be dismissed easily. One accuses me of committing the perennial sin of mistaking the constant reform of the church with corruption, and the search for a "pure" Christianity. All I can do is point back to the ressourcement theologians, and to the liturgical antiquarians who promoted the new Mass in precisely these same terms, as a way of recovering the noble simplicity of the early church from Tridentine corruption.

One criticism can be answered relatively easily. In an essay at the blog Where Peter Is, Rachel Amiri and Mike Lewis note that I was advancing the argument made by Archbishop Marcel Lefebvre and other traditionalists that the reforms of the Second Vatican Council aimed at rupture with the tradition and were taken on to detach Catholics from certain beliefs about the Mass itself. I also argued that Pope Francis's attempt at suppressing the Mass would push traditionalists toward this belief. "How can Francis push anyone to believe something they already believe?" they ask.

Well, what perhaps did not come through in that essay is that my view — the Lefebvrite reading of recent history — was made into the minority view in the traditionalist movement by Pope Benedict's gesture of goodwill in 2007. I described my views as a radicalism I imbibed before Summorum Pontificum. After 2007, the parishes that brought in the traditional Mass tended to be filled with people who took Pope Benedict's view that there was no contradiction between the modern Ordinary Form of the Roman Rite and the traditional "Extraordinary Form" of it. The experience of peace between these rites tended to bolster that view. The vast majority of priests who took up Benedict's permission in 2007 also say the new Mass; no clearer demonstration can be made of their commitment to Benedict's idea of the hermeneutic of continuity. By declaring war on the old Mass again, Francis makes the common ground of Benedict's position untenable and makes the Lefebvrite position more credible.

In fact, Pope Francis has gone on to compare the permission to say the old Mass along with the new as a form of "bi-ritualism." This has a very precise meaning and does quite a bit to explicitly undermine Benedict's formula of calling the traditional Latin Mass "the Extraordinary Form" of the Roman Rite, and the modern vernacular Mass as "the Ordinary Form" of that same rite. By suggesting priests who say both are bi-ritual — a term used normally to describe a priest who has permission to say both the Roman Rite and (say) the Byzantine Rite liturgy — Francis is implying something that even Archbishop Lefebvre shied away from saying: that after the Second Vatican Council, the Roman Rite had not been reformed, but rather replaced by something else entirely. If Pope Francis can toss away the hermeneutic of continuity, on what basis can defenders of this pontificate oblige me to remain faithful to it?

Amiri and Lewis went on to write that my essay was "the latest and most prominent piece of evidence justifying the necessity" of Francis's suppression of the traditional Latin Mass. A number of others have made similar observations then and since. Any sin in my life — I have many that are evident to friend and foe alike — or any theological statement in my op-ed that could be interpreted as an error (whether by generous or tendentious readings) was taken to demonstrate the fundamental defect in the traditionalist movement itself.

This was an odd argument. Why should scores of thousands — perhaps millions — of Catholics be denied something that was their right on the account of one man's sins? You can throw a stone and hit any number of Catholics who regularly attend the traditional Mass who disagree with my views or did not like the way I stated them. So what?

It never occurs to those making this argument to say, "Joe Biden believes abortion should be legal; this demonstrates the fundamental problem of the modern liturgy." Why not? I go out and say candidly that I think the pope has made an error. This seems normal to me because, being a Catholic, I was taught that in most situations the pope is not protected by a guarantee of infallibility. But Francis's defenders use the criticism itself as evidence in a trial where the punishment is already decided to be meted out collectively, not just to me. Modernist theologians such as Edward Schillebeeckx were absolutely scabrous about the papacies of Paul VI and John Paul II, seeing in them a betrayal of the spirit of Vatican II. Why is my criticism taken as emblematic of the traditional Mass, but those of Schillebeeckx are considered entirely exceptional, emblematic of nothing in particular? My argument that the new Mass informs and produces this dissent is never met and confronted; it is simply waved away.

I would submit that this can be done only when one is committed to papal positivism. If the pope says it, it must be true. Many conservatives unwittingly set the stage for this error themselves when, in the wake of the council, they tended to concentrate on Pope Paul VI's document *Humanae Vitae* and the papal pronouncements of John Paul II as the primary — perhaps sole — manifestation of the dogma of the church's indefectibility. Instead of following the ancient formula of Saint Vincent of Lérins, "We hold that faith which has been believed everywhere, always, by all," modern apologists tended to look around and orient themselves to, well, "Where Peter Is."

When one looks back to Catholic history, it's easier to see how distorted this hyper-papalism is. When you look at the great theological works from the past, like the *Summa Theologica* of Thomas Aquinas, or the *Sentences* of Peter Lombard, they rarely cite a papal statement unless that pope was himself a great theologian. They certainly don't do what we do now. Modern catechisms overflow with quotations from the last four or five papacies, many of them enigmatic and unclear. The papacy itself is increasingly treated as a kind of independent and semi-oracular authority. Thus we have the absolute scandal that in the lifetime of my father-in-law, Catholic catechisms have articulated three different — and contradictory — teachings on the justice of the death penalty. This incoherence comes out in the suppression of the Latin Mass itself by Pope Francis, which plainly misrepresents and distorts the reasoning given by Pope Benedict for the permission, before outright contradicting Benedict's religious reasoning to maintain it. Benedict wrote that the old Mass could not "all of a sudden" be forbidden. That's precisely what Francis did.

In fact, I think this hyper-papalism is itself a consequence of the liturgical reform. The old Mass, a product of many centuries of organic development and slow reform, provided a deep spiritual connection for Catholics to the lives of saints going back ages. The Mass itself was the center of Catholic faith, devotion, and mystery.

Having severed the connection to what the Eastern Church calls "holy tradition," the search for that tie to the divine has brought about a mystification of the papacy. Catholic media and apologists have gotten into the habit of treating the bishop of Rome's thoughts, attitudes, predispositions, and initiatives as if they were the main show of the Catholic faith — the primary theater of God's will for the world today. They point to the curia — which we know from history and current gossip to be a den of the most vicious politicking — and presume that *this is where the magic happens*. Well, not in Catholicism, I'm afraid.

When I look to scripture for *where Peter is*, I see him upbraided by other apostles, outdone by the women who follow Jesus, making solemn vows and breaking them minutes later. That is, I see a man in full, loved by God. I'm grateful for him. I see something else, too. In Matthew 17, I see Peter babbling totally absentmindedly about his grand liturgical vision at the Transfiguration. How lucky we are that even "as he was yet still speaking," God descends on a cloud to interrupt and silence him.

69

Can a Catholic Have "Doubts" about Vatican II?[†]

JEAN-PIERRE MAUGENDRE

Renaissance Catholique

September 20, 2021

"TO DOUBT THE COUNCIL IS TO DOUBT THE INTEN-tions of those very Fathers who exercised their collegial power in a solemn manner *cum Petro et sub Petro* in an ecumenical council, and, in the final analysis, to doubt the Holy Spirit himself who guides the Church." This is the fundamental reason Pope Francis gives in the motu proprio *Traditionis Custodes* for the ultimate abolition of the celebration of the Mass according to the traditional form of the Roman Rite. The supporters of these celebrations supposedly doubt the Council and thus call into question the Holy Spirit's assistance to the Church.

To doubt, according to *Larousse*, is both "to be uncertain about the reality of a fact" and "not to have confidence in." It seems difficult to question the very existence of the Second Vatican Council. The question of trust is more delicate and could be formulated as follows: Is it permissible to question whether it was indeed the Holy Spirit who directed the Council? First of all, it is surprising to note that the Holy Father seems to think that the opponents of the Council are questioning the *intentions* of the Council Fathers. However, it is clear that the objections or reservations about the Council expressed by Archbishop Lefebvre, Bishop Schneider, Msgr. Gherardini, Jean Madiran, Roberto de Mattei, etc., concern texts and facts, not intentions, which, as we know, even if they are good, can pave the way to hell, and remain the secret of consciences.

THE COURSE OF THE COUNCIL

Opened on October 11, 1962 by Pope John XXIII, the Council ended on December 8, 1965 with the famous closing address of Paul VI. Is it reasonable to think that during these three years the 2,500 Council Fathers were

† Translated from the French by Zachary Thomas and Peter Kwasniewski; published at *Rorate Caeli* on September 25.

continuously faithful to the breath of the Holy Spirit? A few facts, among others, allow us to doubt it.

As early as October 13, the date of the first meeting of the Fathers, things did not go as planned. While the participants were supposed to vote to elect the members of the working commissions based on the lists of those who had participated in the elaboration of the preparatory schemas, Cardinal Liénart, President of the Assembly of Cardinals and Archbishops of France, and then Cardinal Frings, President of the German Bishops' Conference, intervened so that the vote would not take place immediately, but at a later date, in order (they argued) to allow the Fathers to get to know each other. The vote took place on October 16, with intense lobbying to promote bishops in the commissions who were largely different from the ones who had prepared the initial plans. The Council opened with a veritable rebellion against the *modus operandi* planned and validated by the pope. Some historians speak of "the October revolution in the Church." Was that day of October 13 really animated by the Holy Spirit?

On October 30, Cardinal Ottaviani, prefect of the Holy Office, already elderly and almost blind, intervened to protest against the radical changes to the Mass that were being proposed. Caught up in his subject, he exceeded his allotted speaking time. Cardinal Alfrink, president of the session, had his microphone cut off. Cardinal Ottaviani noticed this and, humiliated, had to sit down again. The most powerful cardinal in the Curia had been silenced, and many of the Council Fathers applauded with joy. "See how they love one another."

In October 1965, four hundred and fifty Council Fathers sent a petition to the commission in charge of the document on the Church in the world [*Gaudium et Spes*], asking that the question of Communism be addressed, which did not seem to be unrelated to the subject. Mysteriously, this petition disappeared and the question was not addressed. It was later learned that secret negotiations had taken place in 1962 between Cardinal Tisserant, representing the Holy See, and Archbishop Nicodemus, representing the Moscow Patriarchate, ensuring that the question of Communism would not be discussed at the Council in exchange for allowing the presence of Eastern Orthodox observers. This silence on the part of the Council caused astonishment among the bishops, especially those from Eastern Europe and Asia, who were suffering from Communist persecution.

THE TEXTS OF THE COUNCIL

The Acts of the Council represent 789 pages in the text published by Éditions du Cerf in 1966. They consist of four "constitutions" (two of them dogmatic), nine "decrees," three "declarations" (a new category), and various "messages." Many of these texts are long, very long, too long. They all breathe (in Cardinal Ratzinger's expression) a "naïve optimism," which no longer seems to be very relevant.

As for the degree of authority these documents possess, the question is lost in conjecture. Is it possible to entertain doubts about a "pastoral" constitution on the Church in the world "today" (*Gaudium et Spes*) that was written in 1965? Or about a decree on the means of social communication (*Inter Mirifica*) written in 1963, therefore before the appearance of the Internet? For example, it institutes an annual day in each diocese "during which the faithful will be instructed in their duties in this area and invited to pray for this cause and to make financial contributions to it." Is it not pathetic, with the benefit of hindsight, that *Gaudium et Spes* states: "At the same time there is a growing awareness of the eminent dignity of the human person, who is superior to all things and whose rights and duties are universal and inviolable"? At a time when abortion is commonplace and publicly funded, and at a time when the application of Sharia law is becoming more and more widespread, this statement is at least doubtful. And let us not forget the serious doctrinal questions posed by the declaration on religious freedom *Dignitatis Humanae*, or that on relations with non-Christian religions *Nostra Aetate*.

AFTER THE COUNCIL

The words of the Gospel are clearer than the conciliar texts: "Beware of false prophets, who come to you in the clothing of sheep, but inwardly they are ravening wolves. By their fruits you shall know them... A good tree cannot bring forth evil fruit, neither can an evil tree bring forth good fruit. Every tree that bringeth not forth good fruit, shall be cut down, and shall be cast into the fire" (Matt 7 : 15 – 19). We will not be cruel enough to insist on the advanced state of decomposition in which the Church finds itself today: the collapse of vocations and religious practice, the absence of liturgical and doctrinal unity, the virtual schism of the Church in Germany, etc. Not to mention the increasing distance of civil legislation from the teaching of the Church or even from simple respect for the natural law. Faced with this collapse, the most lucid of the innovators justified themselves: "Without the Council, the situation would be worse." Objectively, on the one hand it is difficult to imagine anything worse, and on the other hand there is never a shred of reasoning to support this desperate statement. The massive and inescapable fact is that the communities and priests who have maintained traditional forms of practice and apostolate have not only *not* participated in this general collapse, but have even burgeoned in the midst of a generally very hostile ecclesial environment.

This is perhaps the crux of the difficulty. For Pope Francis, ordained in 1969, as well as for bishops who have just retired (Bishop Minnerath, etc.), the years of the Council were those of their studies and their first steps in the priestly life. They sincerely believed in the "new Pentecost" that was to regenerate the Church. However, at the end of the road the result was not there; quite the contrary. Hence an understandable bitterness. Worse: the methods they had all rejected turned out to be fruitful. They now enliven the youngest and most dynamic part of the Christian people. This is an unbearable affront that should be wiped out because it raises a painful question that many people refuse to ask themselves: Have we not made a mistake?

Courageous men can, like the first apostles after their failure to follow Christ to the Cross, come to sacrifice their lives for God in the end. But ah ... *l'amour-propre!*

Public Statement

70

Letter of the Faithful Attached to the Traditional Mass to the Catholics of the Whole World†

What father, if his son asks him for bread,
will give him a stone? (Mt 7:9)

DEAR BROTHERS AND SISTERS IN CHRIST,

It is with great sadness that we learned of Pope Francis's decision to abrogate the main provisions of the motu proprio *Summorum Pontificum,* promulgated by Pope Benedict XVI on July 7, 2007. After decades of divisions and quarrels, that motu proprio was, for all the Catholic faithful, a work of peace and reconciliation.

Rome violates the word given by Pope Benedict XVI with brutality and intransigence, far from the much vaunted fraternal welcoming.

The explicit will of Pope Francis, stated in the motu proprio *Traditionis Custodes,* of July 16, 2021, is to see the celebration of the Mass of the Tradition of the Church disappear. This decision drives us to great dismay. How can we understand this rupture with the traditional Missal, a "venerable and ancient" actualization of the "law of faith," which has borne fruit through so many nations, so many missionaries, and so many saints? What harm is done by the faithful who simply want to pray as their ancestors had done for centuries? Can we be unaware that the Tridentine Mass converts many souls, that it attracts young and fervent assemblies, that it arouses many vocations, that it has given rise to seminaries, religious communities, monasteries, that it is the backbone of many schools, youth groups, catechism activities, spiritual retreats, and pilgrimages?

Many of you, Catholic brothers and sisters, priests, and bishops, have shared with us your failure to understand this and your deep sorrow: thank you for your many testimonies of support.

To promote peace within the Church, in order to build unity in charity, and also to lead Catholics to reconnect with their own heritage by making

---

† Published in six languages at https://stoptraditioniscustodes.org/.

as many people as possible discover the riches of liturgical tradition, the treasure of the Church: those were the goals pursued by *Summorum Pontificum*. Pope Emeritus Benedict XVI witnesses his work for reconciliation destroyed during his own lifetime.

In a time steeped in materialism and torn by social and cultural divisions, liturgical peace appears to us as an absolute necessity for the Faith and for the spiritual life of Catholics in a world that is dying of thirst. The drastic restriction of the authorization to celebrate Mass in its traditional form will bring back mistrust and doubt, and heralds the return of an agonizing liturgical war for the Christian people.

We solemnly affirm, before God and before men:

We will not let anyone deprive the faithful of this treasure which is first of all that of the Church.

We will not remain inactive in the face of the spiritual suffocation of vocations laid forth in the motu proprio *Traditionis Custodes*.

We will not deprive our children of this privileged means of transmitting the faith which is faithfulness to the traditional liturgy.

As children to their father, we request Pope Francis to reverse his decision, by abrogating *Traditionis Custodes* and restoring full freedom to celebrate the Tridentine Mass, for the glory of God and the good of the faithful.

Bread rather than stones.

September 8, 2021
Nativity of the Blessed Virgin Mary

LIST OF SIGNATORIES
(as of October 7, 2021)

Bernard Antony
Président AGRIF

Xavier Arnaud
Président, Forum catholique

Victor Aubert
Président Academia Christiana

Patrick Banken
Président, Una Voce France

Alex Barbas
Publisher

Heinz-Lothar Barth
Retired professor of classical philology

Monika Gabriela Bartoszewicz
Assistant Professor, Masaryk University

Donna Bethell
Board member Collegium Sanctorum Angelorum & The Paulus Institute

Albert Bikaj
Political scientist

Moh-Christophe Bilek
Fondateur, ND de Kabylie

378

François Billot de Lochner
Président Fondation de Service politique

Benjamin Blanchard
DG de SOS Chrétiens d'Orient

Christoph Blath
*Member of the Board of
Directors, Pro Sancta Ecclesia*

Dominique Boily
Professeur

Thomas Bostock
*Chairman, Australian
Environment Foundation*

Anne Brassié
Journaliste et écrivain

Patrick Buisson
Historien et conseiller politique

Georges Buscemi
Président Québec-Vie

Jason Carabello
Founder, Radio Free Catholic

Humberto Carniero
*Professor da Faculdade
de Direito do Recife*

Jacques Charles-Gaffiot
Historien d'art

Stuart Chessman
President, Society of St. Hugh of Cluny

Pierre Dominique Cochard
Ancien journaliste et chef d'entreprises

Thibaud Collin
Professeur agrégé de philosophie

Edgardo J. Cruz Ramos
President, Una Voce Puerto Rico

Laurent Dandrieu
Journaliste

Yves Daoudal
Journaliste, Directeur de Blog

David Deavel
*Editor, Logos: A Journal of
Catholic Thought and Culture*

Michel De Jaeghere
Journaliste et essayiste

Pierre de Lauzun
Haut fonctionnaire, Ecrivain

Massimo de Leonardis
*President, International
Commission of Military History*

Roberto de Mattei
*Ancien président du CNR
(CNRS italien)*

Jean-Pierre Destrebecq
Professeur

Marie-Pauline Deswarte
Docteur en Droit

Stéphane Deswarte
Docteur en Chimie

Cyrille Dounot
*Docteur en droit, licencié
en droit canonique*

C.J. Doyle
*Executive Director, Catholic Action
League of Massachusetts*

Christian & Fabienne Drouhot
Présidents, Domus Christiani

Alvino-Mario Fantini
*Editor-in-Chief of
The European Conservative*

Timothy Flanders
Editor, OnePeterFive

Rémi Fontaine
Journaliste et écrivain

François Foucart
Journaliste

Matt Gaspers
*Managing Editor of
Catholic Family News*

Jules Gomez
biblical scholar and journalist

Jean Goyard
Chargé de communication

Claude Goyard
Professeur des universités

Giovanni Grimaldi Torelly
*CEO & Co-Founder of
WeThink Solutions*

Max Guazzini
Ancien président de groupe de presse

Michael Hageböck
Summorum Pontificum Freiburg

Gregor Hausmann
*Member of the Board of
Directors, Pro Sancta Ecclesia*

Michael Haynes
Journalist

Joël Hautebert
Professeur de droit, Université d'Angers

Michael Hichborn
President, Lepanto Institute

Maike Hickson
Journalist

Robert Hickson
Writer, Ordodei.net

Jasper Juckel
Journalist

Marek Jurek
Ancien président de la Diète de Pologne

Paul N. King
*President, The Paulus Institute for
the Propagation of Sacred Liturgy*

Peter Kwasniewski
Writer, composer, researcher

John Lamont
D. Phil. (Oxon)

Philippe Lauvaux
*Professeur de droit public
ULB Paris & Assas*

Philip Lawler
Editor, Catholic World News

Leila Lawler
Author, Blog

Anne Le Pape
Journaliste

Maria Madise
Director of Voice of the Family

Christian Marquant
Président de Paix Liturgique

Taylor Marshall
YouTube commentator & writer

Patrick Martin
Historien et théologien

Oleg-Michael Martynov
Una Voce Russia

Martial Mathieu
Docteur en Droit Université de Grenoble

Gertraud Marx
*Initiativkreis kath. Priester u.
Laien, Pro Sancta Ecclesia e.V.*

Michael Matt
Editor, The Remnant

Jean-Pierre Maugendre
Président, Renaissance Catholique

Philippe Maxence
*Rédacteur en Chef de
L'Homme Nouveau*

Jack Maxey
journalist and political analyst

Brian McCall
Chair in Law University of Oklahoma,
Editor-in-Chief *Catholic Family News*

Bronwen McShea
Ph.D., *Historian*

Charles de Meyer
Président de SOS Chrétiens d'Orient

Paweł Milcarek
*Fondateur et Editeur en
chef Christianitas*

Dominique Millet-Girard
Professur à la Sorbonne

Jean-Marie Molitor
Journaliste

Martin Mosebach
Writer

Maureen Mullarkey
Writer

Georges Neumayr
Book *author*

Hugh Owen
*Director, Kolbe Center for
the Study of Creation*

Luc Perrin
Historien

Hugues Petit
Docteur en Droit

Olivier Pichon
*Professeur agrégé de l'université
journaliste TV libertes*

Philippe Pichot-Bravard
Docteur en Droit

Claudio Pierantoni
*PhD History of Christianity
& PhD Philosophy*

Jean-Baptiste Pierchon
Docteur en Droit

Constance Prazel
Présidente de Liberté politique

Enrico Maria Radaelli
Research Director and Professor ICSA

Carlo Regazzoni
Philosopher of Culture

David Reid
President, Una Voce Canada

Christophe Réveillard
Docteur en Histoire, Universitaire

Monika Rheinschmitt
President, Pro Missa Tridentina

Kevin Rowles
Catholic author

Hervé Rolland
Vice-Président de ND de Chrétienté

Eric Sammons
Editor-in-Chief of Crisis Magazine

Edward Schaefer
*President, Collegium
Sanctorum Angelorum*

Wolfram Schrems
Mag. theol., Mag. phil., catechist

Reynald Secher
Historien

Aaron Seng
President of Tradivox, Inc.

Jean Sévillia
Journaliste, Historien, Ecrivain

Pierre-Yves Simonin
*Ambassadeur de Suisse, a. Ambassadeur
de l'Ordre de Malte près l'ONU*

Henry Sire
Historian, writer

Michael Sirilla
PhD, Steubenville, Ohio

John Smeaton
Past CEO of SPUC

Jeanne Smits
Journaliste, Directrice de Blog

Christian Spaemann
MD, psychiatrist and psychotherapist

Peter Stephan
*Professor for Art History and Theory
of Architecture, Postdam Univ.*

Pierre-Edouard Stérin
Entrepreneur

Anthony Stine
Return to Tradition blog

Jean de Tauriers
Président de ND de Chrétienté

Guillaume de Thieulloy
Editeur de presse

Inge M. Thürkauf
katholische Publizistin

Marco Tosatti
Blog Editor, Stilum Curiae

Jérôme Triomphe
Avocat

José Ureta
Book author

Philippe de Villiers
Ancien ministre, écrivain

John-Henry Westen
*Co-Founder and Editor-in-
Chief of LifeSiteNews*

Elizabeth Yore
Attorney, Founder, YoreChilden

Alberto Luiz Zucchi
Presidente, Associação cultural montfort

382

THE CONTRIBUTORS

ARCHBISHOP HÉCTOR AGUER is an Argentine bishop known for his very broad culture, his conduct openly favorable to the natural order, and his struggle against the enemies of the Faith and the Church. After a fruitful ecclesiastical career, he became Archbishop of the City of La Plata, capital of the Province of Buenos Aires. He retired in June 2018.

CHRISTOPHER R. ALTIERI is a journalist, editor, and author of three books. He is contributing editor to *Catholic World Report*.

ABBÉ CLAUDE BARTHE entered the seminary of the Priestly Fraternity of Saint Pius X in Econe, where he was ordained in 1979 by Marcel Lefebvre. Having left the Society, after a period of "canonical limbo" he was incardinated in 2005 into the diocese of Fréjus-Toulon. He has taught for the seminary of the Institute of the Good Shepherd and the Institute of Christ the King Sovereign Priest and has published numerous liturgical studies. He also serves as chaplain of the annual *Summorum Pontificum* Pilgrimage in Rome.

CARDINAL WALTER BRANDMÜLLER earned a doctorate in theology and taught medieval and modern church history at the University of Augsburg until 1997. From 1998 to 2009 he served as President of the Pontifical Commission for Historical Sciences. He is a world-renowned scholar of church history and has published many books and articles on the Crusades, on the Spanish Inquisition, and on the Reformation. In November 2010, he was ordained bishop and created a cardinal by Benedict XVI.

CARDINAL RAYMOND LEO BURKE was ordained a priest by Pope Paul VI in 1975 and a bishop in 1995 by Pope John Paul II. He served for almost nine years as Bishop of La Crosse, where he founded the Shrine of Our Lady of Guadalupe, and for over four years as Archbishop of St. Louis. He was named a cardinal in 2010 by Pope Benedict XVI. A member of the Supreme Tribunal of the Apostolic Signatura, Cardinal Burke is one of the world's foremost canon lawyers.

PHILLIP CAMPBELL holds a BA in European History from Ave Maria University and a certificate in Secondary Education from Madonna University. He is the author of the popular "Story of Civilization" series by TAN

Books, as well as *Heroes and Heretics of the Reformation* and *Power from on High*. Campbell is also the founder of Cruachan Hill Press, which specializes in works of Catholic history and spirituality. He is the creator of the blog and website *Unam Sanctam Catholicam*.

DAVID DEAVEL is senior contributor at *The Imaginative Conservative*, editor of *Logos: A Journal of Catholic Thought and Culture*, co-director of the Terrence J. Murphy Institute for Catholic Thought, Law, and Public Policy, and Visiting Professor at the University of St. Thomas (Minnesota). He holds a PhD in theology from Fordham and is a winner of the Acton Institute's Novak Award.

TOMASZ DEKERT is a religious scholar who received his PhD at the Jagiellonian University in Krakow with a thesis on the concept of apostasy in Irenaeus of Lyons' *Adversus Haereses*. He works as an assistant professor at the Jesuit University Ignatianum in Krakow and is also a member of the editorial board of *Christianitas*, a Polish quarterly journal for Catholic tradition.

CRISTIANA DE MAGISTRIS is the pen name of a traditional religious sister.

PIETRO DE MARCO, former professor of the sociology of religion at the University of Florence and the Theological Faculty of Central Italy, is a recognized expert on liturgy, who published in 2013 a book together with Andrea Grillo as a contradictor: *Ecclesia universa o introversa? Dibattito sul motu proprio Summorum Pontificum* (San Paolo Edizioni).

JUAN MANUEL DE PRADA is a major Spanish novelist, short story writer, literary critic, journalist, and essayist whose work has received many awards and distinctions and has been translated into many languages. He often participates as a commentator on television and as a panelist in radio discussions.

MICHAEL BRENDAN DOUGHERTY, a senior writer at *National Review* and a visiting fellow for the social, cultural, and constitutional studies division at the American Enterprise Institute, is the author of *My Father Left Me Ireland: An American Son's Search for Home*.

ROSS DOUTHAT joined *The New York Times* as an Op-Ed columnist in April 2009. His column appears every Tuesday and Sunday, and he co-hosts the Times Op-Ed podcast, "The Argument." Previously, he was a senior editor at *The Atlantic* and a blogger on its website. He is the author of *The Decadent Society* (2020); *To Change the Church: Pope Francis and the Future of Catholicism* (2018), and *Bad Religion: How We Became a Nation of Heretics* (2012).

DOUGLAS FARROW is professor of Theology and Ethics at McGill University in Montreal, and sometime holder of the Kennedy Smith chair in Catholic Studies.

EDWARD FESER is a writer and philosopher living in Los Angeles. He teaches philosophy at Pasadena City College. His primary academic research interests are in the philosophy of mind, moral and political philosophy, and philosophy of religion; he also writes on politics, from a conservative point of view; and on religion, from a traditional Roman Catholic perspective. His books include *Five Proofs of the Existence of God* and *The Last Superstition: A Refutation of the New Atheism.*

REV. MICHAEL FIEDROWICZ teaches on the Faculty of Theology in Trier as the Chair of Ancient Church History, Patrology and Christian Archaeology. He is a priest of the Archdiocese of Berlin. His best-known work is *The Traditional Mass: History, Form, and Theology of the Classical Roman Rite* (Angelico, 2020).

CHRISTOPHE GEFFROY is the founder of *La Nef*, an independent French monthly that delivers serious intellectual commentary from a Catholic perspective, in total fidelity to the teaching of the Church and in service to the New Evangelization. He is the author of books on liberalism, Islam, and Benedict XVI.

ABBÉ CHRISTIAN GOUYAUD is a doctor of theology and pastor in the diocese of Strasbourg who regularly collaborates with *La Nef*.

REV. MARTIN GRICHTING was the vicar general of the Diocese of Chur, Switzerland and publishes articles on philosophical as well as religious matters.

ARCHBISHOP THOMAS E. GULLICKSON was ambassador (Apostolic Nuncio) of the Holy See before several nations in the Caribbean (2001–2011), in the Ukraine (2011–2015), and in Switzerland and Liechtenstein (2015–2020). He is now retired and lives in Sioux Falls, South Dakota, where he was born and ordained a priest.

REV. JOHN HUNWICKE, a priest of the Personal Ordinariate of Our Lady of Walsingham, was for nearly three decades at Lancing College, where he taught Latin and Greek language and literature, and was Head of Theology, and Assistant Chaplain. He has served three curacies, been a parish priest, and Senior Research Fellow at Pusey House in Oxford. Since 2011, he has been in full communion with the See of St. Peter.

PETER A. KWASNIEWSKI (B. A. in Liberal Arts, Thomas Aquinas College; M. A. and Ph.D. in Philosophy, Catholic University of America) is a former professor of theology, philosophy, music, and art history, a composer of sacred choral music, and an author and speaker on topics concerning Catholic Tradition. He has written or edited fourteen books, including most recently *The Ecstasy of Love in the Thought of Thomas Aquinas* (Emmaus Academic, 2021) and *Are Canonizations Infallible?* (Arouca, 2021).

PHIL LAWLER has been a Catholic journalist for more than thirty years. His books include *Lost Shepherd: How Pope Francis is Misleading His Flock* (Regnery, 2018), *The Smoke of Satan* (TAN, 2018), and *Contagious Faith: Why the Church Must Spread Hope, Not Fear in a Pandemic* (Crisis Publications, 2021). Founder of *Catholic World News*, he is the news director and lead analyst at CatholicCulture.org.

JEAN-PIERRE MAUGENDRE is the founder and executive director of the lay movement *Renaissance Catholique*, which works to promote the establishment of the Social Kingship of Christ. For thirty years, under the patronage of St. Joan of Arc, the association has been engaged in the pressing task of intellectual and moral reform.

DANIEL MCGLONE, who lives to the west of Ballarat, is a barrister specializing in criminal law. His legal work included time with the Victorian Aboriginal Legal Service, the office of former Attorney-General Rob Hulls, and with Victorian Legal Aid.

LEILA MILLER is a Catholic writer on marriage, family, and human sexuality, and how they intersect with culture, society, and politics. She has published four books: *Primal Loss: The Now-Adult Children of Divorce Speak*; *Raising Chaste Catholic Men: Practical Advice, Mom to Mom*; *Made This Way: How to Prepare Kids to Face Today's Tough Moral Issues* (co-authored with Trent Horn of *Catholic Answers*); and *"Impossible" Marriages Redeemed: They Didn't End the Story in the Middle*.

JOHN A. MONACO is a doctoral student in theology at Duquesne University, and is a Visiting Scholar with the Veritas Center for Ethics in Public Life at Franciscan University of Steubenville.

SEBASTIAN MORELLO was trained in philosophy by Sir Roger Scruton, by whom he was supervised for his master's and doctoral degrees. He is a lecturer, public speaker, and columnist, and has published books on philosophy, history, and education.

MARTIN MOSEBACH, an award-winning German novelist, is also the author of the non-fiction works *The Heresy of Formlessness*, *Subversive Catholicism*, and *The 21* about the Coptic martyrs killed by ISIS in February 2015 in Libya.

CARDINAL GERHARD MÜLLER was made Prefect of the Congregation for the Doctrine of the Faith by Pope Benedict XVI and served from 2012 until 2017. Pope Francis named him a member of the Supreme Tribunal of the Apostolic Signatura in June of 2021. He held the chair of dogmatic theology of the Ludwig Maximilian University of Munich and was Bishop of Regensburg from 2002 – 2012. Cardinal Müller has published extensively in dogmatic theology and is editor of Joseph Ratzinger's *Opera Omnia*.

BISHOP ROB MUTSAERTS is auxiliary bishop of the Diocese of 's-Hertogenbosch, in the Netherlands.

GEORGE NEUMAYR is a senior editor at *The American Spectator* and author of *The Political Pope: How Pope Francis Is Delighting the Liberal Left and Abandoning Conservatives*. His most recent book is *The Biden Deception: Moderate, Opportunist, or the Democrats' Crypto-Socialist?*

MICHEL ONFRAY is a French writer and philosopher who propounds an epicurean anarchic individualism and a form of political hedonism. He is the founder of the "Université populaire" in Caen, France, where he teaches, and the author of over a hundred books, including *Atheist Manifesto: The Case Against Christianity, Judaism, and Islam*.

MSGR. CHARLES POPE is currently a dean and pastor in the Archdiocese of Washington, DC, where he has served on the Priest Council, the College of Consultors, and the Priest Personnel Board. Along with publishing a daily blog at the Archdiocese of Washington website, he has written in pastoral journals and conducted numerous retreats for priests and lay faithful, and has also conducted weekly Bible studies in the U. S. Congress and the White House. He was named a Monsignor in 2005.

DOM ALCUIN REID is the founding Prior of the Monastère Saint-Benoît in the Diocese of Fréjus-Toulon, France. He is a liturgical scholar of international renown and the author of *The Organic Development of the Liturgy* among other works.

RUBÉN PERETÓ RIVAS is a member of the Faculty of Philosophy and Literature at the National University of Cuyo in Mendoza, Argentina. He writes at the blog *Caminante Wanderer*.

CARDINAL ROBERT SARAH is prefect emeritus of the Congregation for Divine Worship and the Discipline of the Sacraments and author of several books including *The Power of Silence* and *God or Nothing*.

MATTHEW SCHMITZ is senior editor of *First Things* magazine and a contributing editor at *The American Conservative*.

BISHOP ATHANASIUS SCHNEIDER, born of German parents in the Soviet Union, joined the Canons Regular of the Holy Cross of Coimbra, received a doctorate in patrology at the Augustinianum, and in 2006 was consecrated Bishop at St. Peter's Basilica, assigned to the position of auxiliary bishop in the Archdiocese of Astana, Kazakhstan. He has written several books on proper reverence for the Most Holy Eucharist and on the Holy Sacrifice of the Mass.

JOSEPH SHAW, educated at Ampleforth College and the University of Oxford, is currently a tutorial fellow in philosophy at St. Benet's Hall, Oxford and chairman of the Latin Mass Society of England and Wales. In 2015, he was elected a fellow of the Royal Society of Arts. His publications include *The Case for Liturgical Restoration* (Angelico, 2019) and *How to Attend the Extraordinary Form* (Catholic Truth Society, 2020). His writing may be seen at *LMS Chairman*, *LifeSiteNews*, *Rorate Caeli*, and *OnePeterFive*.

TIM STANLEY is an historian, journalist, and broadcaster, a leader writer at the *Daily Telegraph* and a contributing editor at the *Catholic Herald*, and a regular panelist on radio. He received his PhD at Trinity College, Cambridge, specializing in US history, and has held fellowships at Sussex and Royal Holloway.

JOSÉ ANTONIO URETA, co-founder of Fundación Roma (Chile) and advisor of its pro-life and pro-family project Acción Familia, is a senior researcher at Société Française pour la Défense de la Tradition, Famille et Propriété (Paris) and author of *Pope Francis's Paradigm Shift: Continuity or Rupture in the Mission of the Church?* (Spring Grove, PA, 2018).

ARCHBISHOP CARLO MARIA VIGANÒ, a doctor of both canon and civil law (*utroque iure*), served in the Diplomatic Corps of the Holy See from 1973 to 2016, holding positions in Iraq and Kuwait, Great Britain, the Vatican City, Nigeria, and finally the United States, where he was the Apostolic Nuncio from 2011 to his retirement in 2016. In August 2018 he began to publish revelations concerning the abuse committed by former Cardinal McCarrick and the cover-up that stretched all the way to the pope.

MASSIMO VIGLIONE is an Italian Catholic traditionalist writer who specializes in the history of modern revolution and counter-revolution and regularly holds conferences throughout Italy in defense of the traditional values of Christian, European, and Italian civilization. He was editorial director of the publishing house Il Minotauro and editorial coordinator of the journal *Nova Historica* and the periodical *Radici Cristiane*.

REV. GERO P. WEISHAUPT is a priest and canon lawyer, who was Judicial Vicar/Official of the Diocese of 's-Hertogenbosch (Netherlands) 2008 – 2013, and is Judge of the Interdiocesan Criminal Court of the Dutch Ecclesiastical Province since 2012, Diocesan Judge at the Archdiocesan Office of the Archdiocese of Cologne since 2013, and Lecturer in Canon Law and Ecclesiastical Documents at the Theological Institute of the Diocese of Roermond since 2015.

CARDINAL JOSEPH ZEN is Bishop emeritus of Hong Kong (China). He served as a Salesian Provincial Superior for China for six years and taught philosophy and sacramental theology in various Chinese seminaries. He received episcopal ordination on December 9, 1996, and was created and proclaimed cardinal by Benedict XVI in the consistory of March 24, 2006.

Printed in Great Britain
by Amazon